D0375054

GLENCOE

Grammar
AND
Composition
Handbook

HIGH SCHOOL 2

New York, New York
Columbus, Ohio
Woodland Hills, California
Peoria, Illinois

Printed in the United States of America.

Send all inquiries to:
Glencoe/McGraw-Hill
8787 Orion Place
Columbus, Ohio 43240

ISBN 0-02-817714-2 (Student Edition)
Language Arts Grammar and Composition Handbook, High School 2

4 5 6 7 8 9 10   026   04 03 02 01 00

Table of Contents at a Glance

Table of Contents

Chapter 6   Subject-Verb Agreement   213

• •

Table of Contents   **ix**

CHAPTER 16 Research Paper Writing   478

CHAPTER 17 Business Writing   508

Part 4   **Resources** 530

Table of Contents

Part One

● ● ● ● ● ● ● ● ● ● ● ● ● ●

Ready
Reference

The **Ready Reference** consists of three parts. The **Glossary of Terms** is a quick reference to language arts terms, defined and cross-referenced to relevant lessons. The **Usage Glossary** lists pairs of words that are easily confused and provides explanation for the correct usage of each word. The third part is **Abbreviations,** which consists of lists of many commonly used abbreviations.

GLOSSARY OF TERMS

abbreviation An abbreviation is a shortened form of a word. Abbreviations save space and time and prevent unnecessary wordiness. For instance, *M.D.* is more concise and easier to write than *Medical Doctor*. Most abbreviations have periods. If you are unsure of how to write an abbreviation, consult a dictionary (pages 86, 360).

EXAMPLE   Gerry left at 8:00 **A.M.**

EXAMPLE   Did she really leave at 8:00 **A.M.?**

absolute phrase An absolute phrase, also known as a nominative absolute, consists of a noun or a pronoun that is modified by a participle or a participial phrase. An absolute phrase has no grammatical relation to the rest of the sentence. An absolute phrase belongs neither to the complete subject nor to the complete predicate of a sentence. It stands "absolutely" by itself in relation to the rest of the sentence (page 156).

EXAMPLE   **Their throats parched by the searing heat,** the firefighters battled the blaze.

EXAMPLE   **The fire [being] out,** they coiled their hoses.

abstract noun An abstract noun names an idea, a quality, or a characteristic (page 97). *See concrete noun.*

EXAMPLES   **attitude   dignity   loyalty   sadness   temperature**

action verb An action verb tells what someone or something does. Some action verbs express physical action. Others express mental action (page 109).

EXAMPLE   Ted **waved** the signal flag. **[physical action]**

EXAMPLE   He **hoped** for success. **[mental action]**

active voice An action verb is in the active voice when the subject of the sentence performs the action (page 206). *See passive voice.*

EXAMPLE   The brown bear **caught** a salmon.

adjective An adjective is a word that modifies a noun or a pronoun by limiting its meaning. An adjective tells *what kind, which one, how many,* or *how much* (page 112).

EXAMPLES

red barn   **that** notebook   **cracked** pitcher

adjective clause An adjective clause is a subordinate clause that modifies a noun or a pronoun. An adjective clause may begin with a relative pronoun *(who, whom, whose, that,* or *which)* or the word *where* or *when.* An adjective clause normally follows the word it modifies (page 167).

EXAMPLE   Magazines **that inform** are best. **[The adjective clause tells *what kind* and modifies *Magazines*.]**

adjective phrase An adjective phrase is a prepositional phrase that modifies a noun or a pronoun (page 146).

EXAMPLE   Sally chose the sandwich **with cheese. [adjective phrase modifying a noun]**

adverb An adverb is a word that modifies a verb, an adjective, or another adverb (page 116).

EXAMPLES

modifying verbs   **Never** swim alone.
                                verb

                                He has **seldom** complained.
                                verb   verb

modifying adjectives   The movie was **very** scary and **too** long.
                                adjective   adjective

modifying adverbs   She **almost** always waited **quite** patiently.
                                        adverb   adverb

Adverbs modify by answering these questions:

EXAMPLES

When?	It should arrive **Saturday.**
Where?	Leave your coat **there.**
How?	He stacked the books **quickly** and **neatly.**
To what degree?	We were **very** sorry.

adverb clause   An adverb clause is a subordinate clause that modifies a verb, an adjective, or another adverb in the main clause. It tells *when, where, how, why, to what extent,* or *under what conditions* (page 168).

EXAMPLE   **Before I took the test,** I studied for hours. [**The adverb clause tells *when* and modifies the verb *studied.***]

adverb phrase   An adverb phrase is a prepositional phrase that modifies a verb, an adjective, or another adverb (page 147).

EXAMPLE   Lynne works well **under pressure.** [**adverb phrase modifying the adverb *well.***]

agreement   Agreement is the match between grammatical forms. A verb must agree with its subject (page 215). A pronoun must agree with its antecedent (page 244).

EXAMPLE   The **freshmen** and **sophomores are debating** today. [**subject-verb agreement**]

EXAMPLE   **Lissa** thanked **her** brother for driving **her** to the dance. [**pronoun-antecedent agreement**]

antecedent   An antecedent is the word or group of words to which a pronoun refers or that a pronoun replaces. All pronouns must agree with their antecedents in number, gender, and person (page 244).

EXAMPLE *Octavio Paz* is one of the greatest poets of **his** era. **[singular masculine pronoun]**

EXAMPLE *Emily Dickinson* wrote **her** poems on scrap paper. **[singular feminine pronoun]**

EXAMPLE *Walt Whitman* and *Emily Dickinson* are famous for **their** poetry. **[plural pronoun]**

apostrophe An apostrophe (') is a punctuation mark used in possessive nouns, possessive indefinite pronouns, and contractions. In contractions it shows that one or more letters have been left out (page 353).

EXAMPLE Leon didn't bring Celia's book, so she needs to borrow someone's.

appositive An appositive is a noun or a pronoun that is placed next to another noun or pronoun to identify it or give additional information about it (page 148).

EXAMPLE My friend **Ethan** works at a bookstore after school. **[The appositive *Ethan* identifies the noun *friend*.]**

appositive phrase An appositive phrase is an appositive plus any words that modify the appositive (page 148).

EXAMPLE He is saving money to travel to Bogotá, **the capital of Colombia. [The appositive phrase, in blue type, identifies *Bogotá*.]**

article Articles are the adjectives *a, an,* and *the*. *A* and *an* are called **indefinite articles.** They can refer to any one of a kind of person, place, or thing. *A* is used before consonant sounds, and *an* is used before vowel sounds. *The* is the **definite article.** It refers to a specific person, place, or thing (page 115).

EXAMPLES

indefinite He found **a** ring.   I ate **an** egg.

I have **a** used computer.   It's been almost **an** hour since he left.

definite   He found **the** ring.   I ate **the** egg.

I have **the** used computer.   It's almost **the** hour for lunch.

auxiliary verb The most common auxiliary verbs are forms of *be* and *have*. They help the main verb express time by forming the various tenses (page 111).

EXAMPLE   We **will** weed the vegetable garden this morning.

EXAMPLE   Sandra **has** already weeded the peppers and the tomatoes.

EXAMPLE   We **were** weeding the flower beds when the rain started.

The other auxiliary verbs are not used primarily to express time. They are often used to emphasize meaning.

EXAMPLE   I **should be** leaving.

EXAMPLE   **Could** he **have** forgotten?

EXAMPLE   Marisa **may** already **be** finished.

B

brackets Use brackets ([ ]) to enclose information that you have inserted into a quotation for clarity. Use brackets to enclose a parenthetical phrase that already appears within parentheses (page 343).

EXAMPLE   We cannot be free until they **[all Americans]** are.

—James Baldwin

EXAMPLE   The name *Oregon* comes from the French word *oura-gan* (which means "hurricane" **[referring to the Columbia River]**).

C

case Personal pronouns have three cases, or forms. The three cases are called **nominative, objective,** and **possessive.**

The case of a personal pronoun depends on the pronoun's function in a sentence—that is, whether it's a subject, a complement, an object of a preposition, or a replacement for a possessive noun (page 234).

PERSONAL PRONOUNS

CASE	SINGULAR PRONOUNS	PLURAL PRONOUNS	FUNCTION IN SENTENCE
nominative	I, you, she, he, it	we, you, they	subject or predicate nominative
objective	me, you, her, him, it	us, you, them	direct object, indirect object, or object of preposition
possessive	my, mine, your, yours, her, hers, his, its	our, ours, your, yours, their, theirs	replacement for possessive noun(s)

clause A clause is a group of words that has a subject and a predicate (verb). A clause can function as a sentence by itself or as part of a sentence (page 163).

EXAMPLE   The curtain rose.

closing A closing is a way to end a letter. It begins with a capital letter and is followed by a comma (pages 300, 335).

EXAMPLES   Yours truly,   Sincerely,   Your friend,

collective noun A collective noun is singular in form but names a group (pages 100, 220).

EXAMPLES

family	herd	company	band	team
audience	troop	committee	jury	flock

colon A colon (:) is a punctuation mark. It's used to introduce a list and to separate the hour and the minutes when you write the time of day. It's also used after the salutation of a business letter (page 321).

EXAMPLE   We need these ingredients: milk, eggs, raisins, and chopped pecans.

EXAMPLE   The race will start at exactly 2:15 P.M.

EXAMPLE   Dear Senator Mathers:

comma A comma (,) is a punctuation mark that's used to separate items or to set them off from the rest of a sentence (page 326).

EXAMPLE   You'll find spoons, forks, and knives in that drawer.

EXAMPLE   The clowns, who had crammed themselves into the tiny car, all jumped out at once.

comma splice One type of run-on sentence, a comma splice, occurs when two main clauses are joined by a comma only (page 177).

EXAMPLE

comma splice   It rained the entire time the boys were on vacation, they still enjoyed the trip.

correct   It rained the entire time the boys were on vacation. They still enjoyed the trip.

correct   It rained the entire time the boys were on vacation, **but** they still enjoyed the trip.

correct   It rained the entire time the boys were on vacation; they still enjoyed the trip.

common noun A common noun is the general—not the particular—name of a person, place, thing, or idea (page 99). *See proper noun.*

EXAMPLES

person	artist, uncle, poet
place	country, lake, park
thing	shuttle, vehicle, play
idea	era, religion, movement

comparative degree The comparative degree of an adjective or adverb is the form that shows two things being compared (page 258).

EXAMPLE   Kim's dog is **smaller** than my dog. **[adjective]**

EXAMPLE   My dog ran **more swiftly** than the cat. **[adverb]**

complement A complement is a word or a group of words that completes the meaning of a verb (page 138). *See also direct objects, indirect objects,* and *subject complements (predicate nominatives* and *predicate adjectives).*

EXAMPLE   Carlos served **dinner.**

EXAMPLE   Maria admires **him** deeply.

complete predicate The complete predicate consists of the simple predicate, or verb, and all the words that modify it or complete its meaning (page 133).

EXAMPLE   The team **will be going from Illinois to Rhode Island by way of Cedar Point in Sandusky, Ohio.**

complete subject The complete subject consists of the simple subject and all the words that modify it (page 133).

EXAMPLE   **The small black kitten in the top cage** is the one for me.

complex sentence A complex sentence has one main clause and one or more subordinate clauses (page 174).

Main Clause

EXAMPLE   I like Toni Cade Bambara's stories
          S V

Subordinate Clause   Subordinate Clause

because they have characters I can believe in.
        S   V   S V   V

Glossary of Terms   **11**

EXAMPLE

Subordinate Clause | Main Clause

When I read her stories, I enjoy them
S   V   S   V

Subordinate Clause

because they are realistic.
        S   V

compound-complex sentence A compound-complex sentence has two or more main clauses and at least one subordinate clause (page 174).

EXAMPLE

Main Clause | Subordinate Clause

I read *Frankenstein*, which Mary Shelley wrote,
S   V   S   V

Main Clause

and I reported on it.
    S   V

compound predicate A compound predicate (or compound verb) is made up of two or more verbs or verb phrases that are joined by a conjunction and have the same subject (page 135).

EXAMPLE Maria **opened** her book, **grabbed** a pencil, and **started** her homework.

EXAMPLE Seagulls **will glide** or **swoop** down to the ocean.

compound preposition A compound preposition is a preposition that is made up of more than one word (page 120).

EXAMPLES

according to	because of	next to
ahead of	by means of	instead of
along with	except for	on account of

compound sentence A compound sentence contains two or more main clauses (page 173).

EXAMPLE

Main Clause

Stories about the Old West are entertaining, **and**
S   V

Main Clause

stories set in foreign countries are interesting.
S   V

EXAMPLE

Main Clause

Stories entertain me, **and** riddles amuse me, **but**
S   V   S   V

Main Clause

poems are my favorite.
S   V

Main Clause

EXAMPLE

Comedies delight us;
S   V

Main Clause

tragedies often teach us something.
S   V

compound subject A compound subject is made up of two or more simple subjects that are joined by a conjunction and have the same verb (page 134).

EXAMPLE **Tomatoes** and **carrots** are colorful vegetables.

EXAMPLE **Tomatoes** or **carrots** would add color to the salad.

EXAMPLE **Tomatoes, carrots,** and **peppers** are healthful.

compound verb *See compound predicate.*

concrete noun A concrete noun names an object that occupies space or can be recognized by any of the senses (sight, smell, hearing, taste, and touch) (page 97). *See abstract noun.*

EXAMPLES   air   melody   stone   aroma   heat

conjunction A conjunction is a word that joins single words or groups of words (page 122). *See coordinating conjunction, correlative conjunction, and subordinating conjunction.*

conjunctive adverb A conjunctive adverb is used to clarify the relationship between clauses of equal weight in a sentence. Conjunctive adverbs are preceded by semicolons and followed by commas (page 125).

EXAMPLES

to replace *and*	also, besides, furthermore, moreover
to replace *but*	however, nevertheless, nonetheless, still, though
to state a result	accordingly, consequently, then, therefore, thus
to state equality	equally, indeed, likewise, similarly

EXAMPLE   Janine is not very organized; **accordingly,** she carries a day planner and consults it often.

contraction   A contraction is a single word made up of two words that have been combined by omitting letters. Common contractions combine a subject and a verb or a verb and the word *not* (page 355).

EXAMPLES

you'd	*is formed from*	you had, you would
you're		you are
who's		who is, who has

coordinating conjunction   A coordinating conjunction joins words or groups of words that have equal grammatical weight in a sentence (page 122).

and   but   or   so   nor   yet   for

EXAMPLE   One **and** six are seven. [two nouns]

EXAMPLE   Merlin was smart **but** irresponsible. [two adjectives]

EXAMPLE   Let's put the note on the TV **or** on the refrigerator. [two prepositional phrases]

EXAMPLE   I wanted a new sun hat, **so** I bought one. [two complete thoughts]

EXAMPLE   He did not complain, **nor** did he object to our plan. [two complete thoughts]

EXAMPLE   Lightning struck the barn, **yet** no fire started. **[two complete thoughts]**

EXAMPLE   We didn't explore the summit that night, **for** the climb had exhausted us. **[two complete thoughts]**

correlative conjunction   Correlative conjunctions work in pairs to join words and groups of words of equal grammatical weight in a sentence (page 123).

both . . . and	just as . . . so	not only . . . but (also)
either . . . or	neither . . . nor	whether . . . or

EXAMPLE   **Both** he **and** I were there.

EXAMPLE   **Either** she will sew new curtains, **or** I will put up the old blinds.

EXAMPLE   I **not only** scrubbed **but also** waxed the floor.

dangling modifier   Dangling modifiers seem logically to modify no word at all. To correct a sentence that has a dangling modifier, you must supply a word that the dangling modifier can sensibly modify (page 270).

EXAMPLES

dangling   **Working all night long,** the fire was extinguished. **[participial phrase logically modifying no word in the sentence]**

clear   **Working all night long,** the firefighters extinguished the fire. **[participial phrase modifying *firefighters*]**

dangling   **Sleeping soundly,** my dream was interrupted by the alarm. **[participial phrase logically modifying no word in the sentence]**

clear   **Sleeping soundly,** I had my dream interrupted by the alarm. **[participial phrase modifying *I*]**

dash A dash (—) is a punctuation mark. It's usually used in pairs to set off a sudden break or change in thought or speech (page 339).

EXAMPLE   Lionel Washington—he was my Boy Scout troop leader—is running for city council.

declarative sentence A declarative sentence makes a statement. A declarative sentence usually ends with a period but can end with an exclamation mark. This type of sentence is the most frequently used in speaking and writing (page 170).

EXAMPLE   I have four pets.

EXAMPLE   Two of my pets are dogs.

EXAMPLE   That's the cutest puppy I've ever seen!

demonstrative adjective A demonstrative adjective modifies a noun and points out something by answering the question *which one?* or *which ones? This, that, these,* and *those* are demonstrative adjectives when they modify nouns (page 113).

EXAMPLE   Bring **this** ticket with you.

EXAMPLE   Give **that** ticket to a friend.

EXAMPLE   We'll need **these** props for the show.

EXAMPLE   The director wrote **those** notes.

demonstrative pronoun A demonstrative pronoun points out specific persons, places, things, or ideas (page 105).

DEMONSTRATIVE PRONOUNS

singular	this	that
plural	these	those

EXAMPLE   Bring **this** with you.

EXAMPLE   Give **that** to a friend.

EXAMPLE   We'll need **these** for the show.

EXAMPLE   The director wrote **those.**

dependent clause *See subordinate clause.*

direct address Direct address is a name used in speaking directly to a person. Direct address may also be a word or phrase used in place of a name. Words used in direct address are set off by commas (page 335).

EXAMPLE **Christie,** do you like my haircut?

EXAMPLE You can't park here, **buddy.**

direct object A direct object answers the question *what?* or *whom?* after an action verb (page 138).

EXAMPLE Carlos served **dinner.**

EXAMPLE Paula called **Carlos** on the telephone.

direct quotation A direct quotation gives the speaker's exact words. It is preceded and followed by quotation marks (page 298).

EXAMPLE My little brother asked, **"Why can't I go too?"**

double comparison Don't use both *-er* and *more*. Don't use both *-est* and *most*. To do so would be an error called a double comparison (page 262).

EXAMPLES

incorrect A redwood grows more taller than an oak.

correct A redwood grows **taller** than an oak.

incorrect Aunt Ellie is my most kindest aunt.

correct Aunt Ellie is my **kindest** aunt.

double negative A double negative is two or more negative words used to express the same idea. Use only one negative word to express a negative idea (page 267).

EXAMPLES

incorrect	I don't have no stereo equipment.
correct	I do**n't** have **any** stereo equipment.
correct	I have **no** stereo equipment.

incorrect	We haven't seen no concerts this year.
correct	We have**n't** seen **any** concerts this year.
correct	We have seen **no** concerts this year.

ellipsis points Use a series of three spaced points, called ellipsis points (**...**), to indicate the omission of material from a quotation. Use three spaced points if the omission occurs at the beginning of a sentence. If the omission occurs in the middle or at the end of a sentence, use any necessary punctuation (for instance, a comma, a semicolon, or a period) plus the three spaced points. When it is necessary to use a period, do not leave any space between the last word and the first point, which is the period (page 344).

EXAMPLE   "Listen, my children, and you shall hear**....**"

—Henry Wadsworth Longfellow

emphatic forms of a verb The present tense and the past tense have additional forms, called emphatic forms, that add special force, or emphasis, to the verb. You make the emphatic forms by using *do, does*, or *did* with the base form of the verb (page 204).

EXAMPLES

present emphatic	I **do hope** the train is on time.
	Tom **does have** a plane to catch.
past emphatic	He **did miss** his plane the last time because of a late train.

end mark An end mark is a punctuation mark used at the end of a sentence. Periods, question marks, and exclamation points are end marks (pages 319–320).

EXAMPLE   Here is your clean laundry.

EXAMPLE   Did you forget your jacket?

EXAMPLE   What a gorgeous salad that is!

essential clause Some adjective clauses are necessary to make the meaning of a sentence clear. Such an adjective clause is called an *essential clause,* or a *restrictive clause.* Do not set off an essential clause with commas (page 167).

EXAMPLE   Magazines **that have no substance** bore me.

EXAMPLE   Many writers **whose works have become famous** began their writing careers at the *New Yorker* magazine.

exclamation point An exclamation point (!) is a punctuation mark used to end a sentence that shows strong feeling (exclamatory). It's also used after strong interjections (page 320).

EXAMPLES   Yikes! We'll be late!

exclamatory sentence An exclamatory sentence expresses strong emotion and ends with an exclamation mark. Note that exclamatory sentences can be declarative (first example), imperative (second example), or interrogative (third example) while expressing strong emotion. In writing, exclamatory sentences should be used sparingly so as not to detract from their effectiveness (page 171).

EXAMPLE   She is such a beautiful dog!

EXAMPLE   Don't chew on that!

EXAMPLE   What do you think you are doing!

future perfect tense Use the future perfect tense to express one future action or condition that will begin *and* end before another future event starts.

You form the future perfect tense by using *will have* or *shall have* with the past participle of a verb: *will have practiced, shall have flown* (page 200).

EXAMPLE By September I **will have saved** fifty dollars. [The money will be saved by the time another future event, the arrival of September, occurs.]

future tense Use the future tense to express an action or a condition that will occur in the future (page 196).

EXAMPLE Robby **will order** the supplies.

EXAMPLE I **will pack** the car in the morning.

gender The gender of a noun may be masculine (male), feminine (female), or neuter (referring to things) (page 244).

EXAMPLES **man** (masculine) **aunt** (feminine) **notebook** (neuter)

gender-neutral language Language that does not assume the gender of a noun is called gender-neutral language. Use gender-neutral language when the gender is unknown or could be either masculine or feminine (pages 245, 452–453).

EXAMPLE An *author* must capture **his or her** readers' interest.

EXAMPLE *Authors* must capture **their** readers' interest.

EXAMPLE *Authors* must capture readers' interest.

gerund A gerund is a verb form that ends in *-ing* and is used in the same ways a noun is used (page 152).

EXAMPLE **Cooking** is an enjoyable activity. **[gerund as subject]**

EXAMPLE My younger sister likes **swimming**. **[gerund as direct object]**

gerund phrase A gerund phrase contains a gerund plus any complements and modifiers (page 152).

EXAMPLE **Cross-country skiing** is good exercise.

EXAMPLE **Billie Holiday's soulful singing** delighted many audiences.

helping verb *See auxiliary verb.*

hyphen A hyphen (-) is a punctuation mark that's used in compound words (page 357).

EXAMPLE Luis's great-grandfather hung twenty-one bird feeders.

imperative mood The imperative mood expresses a command or makes a request (page 207).

EXAMPLE **Take** the express train home.

EXAMPLE Please **don't slam** the door.

imperative sentence An imperative sentence gives a command or makes a request. An imperative sentence usually ends with a period but can end with an exclamation mark. In imperative sentences, the subject *you* is understood (page 171).

EXAMPLE Get off the table.

EXAMPLE Duck!

indefinite pronoun An indefinite pronoun refers to persons, places, things, or ideas in a more general way than a noun does (page 107).

INDEFINITE PRONOUNS

always singular			
another	either	neither	other
anybody	everybody	no one	somebody
anyone	everyone	nobody	someone
anything	everything	nothing	something
each	much	one	

always plural				
both	few	many	others	several

singular or plural					
all	any	enough	most	none	some

EXAMPLE **Everybody** needs food. [The indefinite pronoun *everybody* refers to people in general.]

EXAMPLE Did you get **enough** to eat? [The indefinite pronoun *enough* refers to a general, not a specific, amount.]

EXAMPLE After two bowls of chili, I did not want **another**. [The indefinite pronoun *another* has the antecedent *bowls (of chili)*.]

independent clause An independent clause has a subject and a predicate and expresses a complete thought. It is the only type of clause that can stand alone as a sentence. An independent clause is also called a **main clause** (page 163).

EXAMPLE **The curtain rose.**

EXAMPLE **The cast bowed,** and **the audience applauded.**

EXAMPLE **The curtains closed for several minutes,** but **the applause continued.**

indicative mood The indicative mood, the one used far more often than the imperative mood or the subjunctive mood, makes a statement or asks a question (page 207).

EXAMPLE He **takes** the express train home.

EXAMPLE She **does**n't **slam** the door.

indirect object An indirect object answers the question *to whom? for whom? to what?* or *for what?* after an action verb (page 139).

EXAMPLE   Tyrone served his **sisters** dinner.

EXAMPLE   Kim saved **Rosa** and **Manuel** seats.

indirect quotation An indirect quotation paraphrases a speaker's words and should not be capitalized or enclosed in quotation marks (page 298). *See direct quotation.*

EXAMPLE   My brother asked why he couldn't go.

EXAMPLE   She said that she wanted to leave early.

infinitive An infinitive is a verb form that is usually preceded by the word *to* and is used as a noun, an adjective, or an adverb (page 153).

EXAMPLE   His goal is **to graduate. [infinitive as predicate nominative]**

EXAMPLE   They have the desire **to win. [infinitive as adjective]**

infinitive phrase An infinitive phrase contains an infinitive plus any complements and modifiers (page 154).

EXAMPLE   We stopped **to look at the beautiful scenery.**

EXAMPLE   **To be a good friend** is my goal.

intensive pronoun An intensive pronoun ends with *-self* or *-selves* and is used to draw special attention to a noun or a pronoun already named (pages 104–105, 240).

EXAMPLE   He **himself** delivered the flowers.

EXAMPLE   You must sign the application **yourself.**

EXAMPLE   Mariko **herself** made the bridesmaids' dresses.

interjection An interjection is a word or phrase that expresses emotion or exclamation. An interjection has no grammatical connection to other words (page 127).

EXAMPLE **Oh, my!** What is that?

EXAMPLE **Ouch,** it's hot!

EXAMPLE **Yikes,** I'll be late!

EXAMPLE **Ah,** that's better.

interrogative pronoun An interrogative pronoun is used to form questions (page 106).

who	whom	what	which	whose
whoever	whomever	whatever	whichever	

EXAMPLE **Who** is at the door?

EXAMPLE **Whom** would you prefer?

EXAMPLE **Whose** is this plaid coat?

EXAMPLE **Whatever** is that odd noise?

interrogative sentence An interrogative sentence asks a question. It usually ends with a question mark but can end with an exclamation point if it expresses strong emotion (page 171).

EXAMPLE How many pets do you have**?**

EXAMPLE What in the world were you thinking**!**

intransitive verb An intransitive verb is *not* followed by a word that answers the question *what?* or *whom?* (page 109). *See transitive verb.*

EXAMPLE The batter **swung** wildly. [The verb is followed by a word that tells *how*.]

inverted order A sentence written in inverted order, in which the predicate comes before the subject, serves to add emphasis to the subject (pages 137, 226).

PREDICATE	SUBJECT
Across the field **galloped**	the three **horses.**
In the distance **flowed**	a **river.**

irregular verb An irregular verb forms its past and past participle in some way other than by adding -*ed* or -*d* to the base form (page 187).

EXAMPLES

BASE FORM	PAST FORM	PAST PARTICIPLE
be, am, are, is	was, were	been
swim	swam	swum
put	put	put
write	wrote	written
lie	lay	lain

italics Italics are printed letters that slant to the right. *This sentence is printed in italic type.* Italics are used for the titles of certain kinds of published works, works of art, foreign terms, and other situations. In handwriting, underlining is a substitute for italics (page 350).

EXAMPLE This *Newsweek* magazine has an article about Picasso's painting *Guernica.*

EXAMPLE Cicero's saying *Omnia praeclara rara* can be translated as "All excellent things are scarce."

linking verb A linking verb links, or joins, the subject of a sentence (often a noun or a pronoun) with a noun, a pronoun, or an adjective that identifies or describes the subject. A linking verb does not show action. *Be* in all its forms—

am, is, are, was, were—is the most commonly used linking verb (page 110).

EXAMPLE   The person behind the mask **was** you.

EXAMPLE   The players **are** ready.

EXAMPLE   Archery **is** an outdoor sport.

EXAMPLE   They **were** sports fans.

Several other verbs besides *be* can act as linking verbs.

OTHER VERBS THAT CAN BE LINKING VERBS

appear	grow	seem	stay
become	look	sound	taste
feel	remain	smell	turn

EXAMPLE   This salad **tastes** good.

EXAMPLE   The sun **feels** warm on my shoulders.

EXAMPLE   You **look** comfortable.

EXAMPLE   The leaves **turned** brown.

main clause   A main clause has a subject and a predicate and expresses a complete thought. It is the only type of clause that can stand alone as a sentence. A main clause is also called an **independent clause** (page 163).

EXAMPLE   **The curtain rose.**

EXAMPLE   **The cast bowed,** and **the audience applauded.**

EXAMPLE   **The curtains closed for several minutes,** but **the applause continued.**

main verb   A main verb is the last word in a verb phrase. If a verb stands alone, it's a main verb (page 111).

EXAMPLE   The band members have been **selling** light bulbs for a month.

EXAMPLE   One band member **sold** two cases of light bulbs.

misplaced modifier Misplaced modifiers modify the wrong word, or they seem to modify more than one word in a sentence. To correct a sentence that has a misplaced modifier, move the modifier as close as possible to the word it modifies (page 269).

EXAMPLE

misplaced **Soaring over the edge of the cliff,** the photographer captured an image of the eagle. **[participial phrase incorrectly modifying *photographer*]**

clear The photographer captured an image of the eagle **soaring over the edge of the cliff.** **[participial phrase correctly modifying *eagle*]**

mood of verbs Along with expressing tense and voice, verbs also express mood. A verb expresses one of three moods: the indicative mood, the imperative mood, or the subjunctive mood (page 207). *See indicative mood, imperative mood, and subjunctive mood.*

nominative case Use the nominative case for a pronoun that is a subject or a predicate nominative (page 234).

EXAMPLE **We** have raised enough money.

EXAMPLE The lead soprano will be **she.**

nonessential clause An adjective clause that adds information to a sentence but is not necessary to make the meaning of the sentence clear is called a *nonessential clause* or a *nonrestrictive clause.* Always use commas to set off a nonessential clause (pages 167–168, 329).

EXAMPLE James Thurber, **who was a famous humorist,** wrote for the *New Yorker.*

EXAMPLE His stories, **which include humorous incidents from his childhood in Ohio,** make funny and interesting reading.

nonrestrictive clause *See nonessential clause.*

noun A noun is a word that names a person, a place, a thing, or an idea (page 97).

EXAMPLES

person	uncle, doctor, baby, Luisa, son-in-law
place	kitchen, mountain, Web site, West Virginia
thing	apple, tulip, continent, seagull, amplifier
idea	respect, pride, love, appreciation, century

noun clause A noun clause is a subordinate clause that is used as a noun within the main clause of a sentence. You can use a noun clause as a subject, a direct object, an indirect object, an object of a preposition, or a predicate nominative (page 169).

EXAMPLE **Whoever wins the election** will speak. **[noun clause as subject]**

number Number refers to the form of a word that indicates whether it is singular or plural. A verb must agree with its subject in number (page 215).

EXAMPLES

SINGULAR
The **athlete exercises.**
The **cat scratches.**

PLURAL
The **athletes exercise.**
The **cats scratch.**

object complement An object complement answers the question *what?* after a direct object. That is, it *completes* the meaning of the direct object by identifying or describing it (page 139).

EXAMPLE   Residents find the park **peaceful. [adjective]**

EXAMPLE   Maya appointed me **spokesperson** and **treasurer. [nouns]**

EXAMPLE   My grandmother considers the property **hers. [pronoun]**

object of a preposition An object of a preposition is the noun or pronoun that ends a prepositional phrase (page 121).

EXAMPLE   The diamonds in the **vault** are priceless. [***In* shows the relationship between the diamonds and the object of the preposition, *vault.*]**

objective case Use the objective case for a pronoun that is a direct object, an indirect object, or an object of a preposition (page 234).

EXAMPLE   The coach trained **her. [direct object]**

EXAMPLE   The prompter gave **me** my cues. **[indirect object]**

EXAMPLE   Third prize was split between **me** and **him. [object of preposition]**

parentheses Parentheses ( ) are punctuation marks used to set off words that define or explain another word (page 341).

EXAMPLE   Myanmar **(**formerly Burma**)** is on the Bay of Bengal.

parenthetical expression Parenthetical expressions are side thoughts that add information. Parenthetical expressions should be set off by commas, dashes, or parentheses (pages 331, 339, 341).

EXAMPLES in fact   on the other hand   on the contrary

EXAMPLES by the way   to be exact   after all

EXAMPLE   **By the way,** did Mom call today?

EXAMPLE   I'm responsible for about a hundred tickets—**to be exact,** 106.

participial phrase A participial phrase contains a participle plus any complements and modifiers (page 151).

EXAMPLE   The dog saw many ducks **swimming in the lake.**

EXAMPLE   **Barking loudly,** the dog approached the water.

participle A participle is a verb form that can function as an adjective (pages 113, 150).

EXAMPLE   A **moving** van is parked on our street. **[present participle]**

EXAMPLE   The dogs watched the **striped** cat. **[past participle]**

passive voice An action verb is in the passive voice when its action is performed on the subject (page 206). *See active voice.*

EXAMPLE   A salmon **was caught** by the brown bear.

past perfect tense Use the past perfect tense to indicate that one past action or condition began *and* ended before another past action or condition started. You form the past perfect tense by using the auxiliary verb *had* with the past participle of a verb: *had praised, had written* (page 199).

EXAMPLE

      PAST   **PAST PERFECT**

Pat **dedicated** her play to the drama teacher who **had encouraged** her long ago. **[First the drama teacher encouraged Pat; then years later Patricia acknowledged her teacher's support.]**

past tense Use the past tense to express an action or a condition that was started and completed in the past (page 196).

EXAMPLE   The track meet **went** well.

EXAMPLE   Nan **set** a new school record for the shot put.

period A period (.) is a punctuation mark used to end a sentence that makes a statement (declarative) or gives a command (imperative). It's also used at the end of many abbreviations (pages 319, 360).

EXAMPLE   I can't tell whether this recipe specifies "1 tsp." or "1 tbsp." of cinnamon. **[declarative]**

EXAMPLE   Please mail a check to Dr. Benson. **[imperative]**

personal pronoun   A personal pronoun refers to a specific person, place, thing, or idea by indicating the person speaking (the first person), the person being spoken to (the second person), or any other person, place, thing, or idea being discussed (the third person). Like a noun, a personal pronoun expresses number; that is, it can be singular or plural (pages 102, 234).

	PERSONAL PRONOUNS	
	SINGULAR	**PLURAL**
first person	I, me	we, us
second person	you	you
third person	he, him, she, her, it	they, them

EXAMPLES

first person	The song was dedicated to **me**. [*Me* **refers to the person speaking.**]
second person	Sam will copy the document for **you**. [*You* **refers to the person being spoken to.**]
third person	**She** gave **him** the good news. [*She* **and** *him* **refer to the people being talked about.**]

phrase   A phrase is a group of words that acts in a sentence as a single part of speech (page 146).

positive degree   The positive degree of an adjective or adverb is the form that cannot be used to make a comparison. This form appears as the entry word in a dictionary (page 258).

EXAMPLE   My dog is **small**.

EXAMPLE   The cat ran **swiftly**.

possessive pronoun A possessive pronoun takes the place of the possessive form of a noun (page 103).

POSSESSIVE PRONOUNS

	SINGULAR	PLURAL
first person	my, mine	our, ours
second person	your, yours	your, yours
third person	his, her, hers, its	their, theirs

predicate The predicate is the part of the sentence that says something about the subject (page 131).

EXAMPLE   Garth Brooks **will perform.**

predicate adjective A predicate adjective follows a linking verb and points back to the subject and further describes it (page 141).

EXAMPLE   Firefighters are **brave.**

EXAMPLE   Firefighters must be extremely **careful.**

predicate nominative A predicate nominative is a noun or a pronoun that follows a linking verb and points back to the subject to rename it or to identify it further (page 140).

EXAMPLE   Sopranos are **singers.**

EXAMPLE   Many current opera stars are **Italians** or **Spaniards.**

EXAMPLE   Fiona became both a **musician** and an **architect.**

preposition A preposition is a word that shows the relationship of a noun or a pronoun to another word in a sentence (page 119).

aboard	beneath	in	regarding
about	beside	inside	respecting

EXAMPLE   I read **to** Carlito **from** the new book.

prepositional phrase A prepositional phrase is a group of words that begins with a preposition and ends with a noun or a pronoun that is called the object of the preposition (page 146).

EXAMPLE   The diamonds **in the vault** are priceless. [*In* **shows the relationship between the diamonds and the object of the preposition,** *vault*.]

EXAMPLE   The telephone rang four times **during dinner.** [*During* **shows the relationship between** *rang* **and the object of the preposition,** *dinner*.]

EXAMPLE   Here is a gift **for you.** [*For* **relates** *gift* **to the object of the preposition,** *you*.]

present perfect tense Use the present perfect tense to express an action or a condition that occurred at some *indefinite time* in the past. You form the present perfect tense by using *has* or *have* with the past participle of a verb: *has permitted, have cut* (page 198).

EXAMPLE   The living-room clock **has stopped.**

EXAMPLE   They **have brought** the new couch a day early.

present tense The present tense expresses a constant, repeated, or habitual action or condition. It can also express a general truth or an action or a condition that exists only now. It is sometimes used in historical writing to express past events and, more often, in poetry, fiction, and journalism (especially in sports writing) to convey to the reader a sense of being there. This usage is sometimes called the *historical present tense* (page 193).

EXAMPLE   Isaac **likes** the taste of tea with honey in it. [**not just this cup of tea but every cup of tea; a repeated action**]

EXAMPLE   Emily **bakes** wonderful spice cookies. [**always; a habitual action**]

EXAMPLE   Gold **is** valuable. [**a general truth**]

EXAMPLE   I **see** a hummingbird at the feeder. **[at this very moment]**

EXAMPLE   The goalie **throws** her body across the opening and **blocks** the shot in the final seconds of the game. **[historical present]**

principal parts of verbs   All verbs have four principal parts: a *base form*, a *present participle*, a *simple past form*, and a *past participle*. All the verb tenses are formed from these principal parts (page 185).

EXAMPLES

PRINCIPAL PARTS OF VERBS

BASE FORM	PRESENT PARTICIPLE	PAST FORM	PAST PARTICIPLE
play	playing	played	played
carry	carrying	carried	carried
sing	singing	sang	sung

progressive forms of a verb   Each of the six tenses has a progressive form that expresses a continuing action. You make the progressive forms by using the appropriate tense of the verb *be* with the present participle of the main verb (page 204).

EXAMPLE

present progressive	They *are traveling.*
past progressive	They *were traveling.*
future progressive	They *will be traveling.*
present perfect progressive	They *have been traveling.*
past perfect progressive	They *had been traveling.*
future perfect progressive	They *will have been traveling.*

pronoun   A pronoun is a word that takes the place of a noun, a group of words acting as a noun, or another pronoun. The word or group of words to which a pronoun refers is called its antecedent (page 101).

EXAMPLE   Though Georgia O'Keeffe was born in Wisconsin, **she** grew to love the landscape of the American Southwest. **[The pronoun *she* takes the place of its proper noun antecedent, *Georgia O'Keeffe*.]**

EXAMPLE   When Georgia O'Keeffe and Alfred Stieglitz were married in 1924, **both** were famous artists. **[The pronoun *both* takes the place of the nouns *Georgia O'Keeffe* and *Alfred Stieglitz*.]**

EXAMPLE   Though O'Keeffe **herself** was a painter, **her** husband was a photographer. **[The pronouns *herself* and *her* take the place of the nouns *O'Keeffe* and *O'Keeffe's*.]**

proper adjective   A proper adjective is formed from a proper noun. It begins with a capital letter (page 115).

EXAMPLE   Vancouver is a **Canadian** city.

EXAMPLE   We visited the **London** Zoo.

proper noun   A proper noun is the name of a particular person, place, thing, or idea (page 99). *See common noun.*

EXAMPLES

PROPER NOUNS	
person	Michelangelo, Uncle Louis, Maya Angelou
place	Mexico, Lake Superior, Yellowstone National Park
thing	*Challenger,* Jeep, *Romeo and Juliet*
idea	Industrial Age, Judaism, Romanticism

question mark   A question mark (**?**) is a punctuation mark used to end a sentence that asks a question (interrogative) (page 320).

EXAMPLE   Can you imagine what life would be like without television**?**

quotation marks Quotation marks (" ") are punctuation marks used to enclose the exact words of a speaker. They're also used for titles of certain published works (page 345).

EXAMPLE "Let's record ourselves reading aloud," said Lou, "and give the tape to the children's hospital."

EXAMPLE They decided on something a bit more cheerful than "The Pit and the Pendulum."

reflexive pronoun A reflexive pronoun always ends with *-self* or *-selves* and refers, or reflects back, to the subject of the sentence or a clause, indicating that the same person or thing is involved. A reflexive pronoun always adds information to a sentence (pages 104–105, 240).

EXAMPLE Jim uses a stopwatch to time **himself** on the track.

EXAMPLE She taught **herself** to play the piano.

EXAMPLE We imagined **ourselves** dancing in a forest glade.

regular verb A regular verb forms its past and past participle by adding *-ed* or *-d* to the base form (page 187).

EXAMPLES

REGULAR VERBS

BASE FORM	PAST FORM	PAST PARTICIPLE
climb	climbed	climbed
skate	skated	skated
trot	trotted	trotted

relative pronoun A relative pronoun is used to begin a subordinate clause (page 107).

RELATIVE PRONOUNS

who	whoever	which	that
whom	whomever	whichever	what
	whose	whatever	

EXAMPLE The driver **who** arrived last parked over there. [**The relative pronoun *who* begins the subordinate clause *who arrived last.*]**

EXAMPLE The meal **that** you prepared was delicious. [**The relative pronoun *that* begins the subordinate clause *that you prepared.*]**

restrictive clause *See essential clause.*

run-on sentence A run-on sentence is two or more complete sentences written as though they were one sentence (page 177). *See comma splice.*

EXAMPLE

run-on It rained the entire time the boys were on vacation they still enjoyed the trip.

run-on It rained the entire time the boys were on vacation but they still enjoyed the trip.

run-on It rained the entire time the boys were on vacation, they still enjoyed the trip.

correct It rained the entire time the boys were on vacation. They still enjoyed the trip.

correct It rained the entire time the boys were on vacation, but they still enjoyed the trip.

correct It rained the entire time the boys were on vacation; they still enjoyed the trip.

salutation A salutation is the greeting in a letter. The first word and any proper nouns in a salutation should be capitalized. In a friendly letter, the salutation ends with a comma; in a business letter, the salutation ends with a colon (pages 300, 323, 335).

EXAMPLE   **My** dear cousin **Nancy,**   **Dear Councilwoman Ramos:**

semicolon A semicolon (;) is a punctuation mark used to join the main clauses of a compound sentence (page 324).

EXAMPLE   Juliana will sing the melody; Maurice and Lee will harmonize.

sentence A sentence is a group of words that expresses a complete thought (page 131).

EXAMPLE   Hector Hugh Munro wrote stories using the pseudonym Saki.

sentence fragment A sentence fragment is an error that occurs when an incomplete sentence is punctuated as though it were complete (page 176).

EXAMPLE

fragment   **The two weary hikers walking for hours.**
                    [lacks complete predicate]

complete sentence   The two weary hikers had been walking for hours.

simple predicate The simple predicate is the verb or verb phrase that expresses an action or a state of being about the subject of the sentence (page 132).

EXAMPLE   The team **will be going** from Illinois to Rhode Island by way of Cedar Point in Sandusky, Ohio.

simple sentence A simple sentence contains only one main clause and no subordinate clauses (page 172).

EXAMPLE   Stories entertain.

EXAMPLE   Long, complicated, fantastic stories with aliens, space travelers, and happy endings entertain and educate men, women, and children all over the world.

simple subject The simple subject is the key noun or pronoun (or word or word group acting as a noun) that tells what the sentence is about (page 132).

EXAMPLE   The small black **kitten** in the top cage is the one I want.

subject The subject is the part of the sentence that names whom or what the sentence is about (page 131).

EXAMPLE   **Dogs** were barking.

EXAMPLE   Last in line was **he.**

subject complement A subject complement follows a subject and a linking verb and identifies or describes the subject (page 140). *See predicate nominative and predicate adjective.*

EXAMPLE   Sopranos are **singers.**

EXAMPLE   The star of the opera was **she.**

EXAMPLE   The singer grew **hoarse.**

subjunctive mood The subjunctive mood is often replaced by the indicative mood in informal English. The subjunctive mood does, however, have two important uses in modern formal English (page 208). First, the subjunctive mood expresses, although indirectly, a demand, recommendation, suggestion, or statement of necessity.

EXAMPLE   We demand [*or* recommend *or* suggest] that she **set** her alarm clock for 6:30 A.M. **[To form the subjunctive mood, drop the –s from the third-person singular.]**

EXAMPLE   It is necessary that she **be** on time for school. [**The sub-junctive mood uses** *be* **instead of** *am, is,* **or** *are.*]

Second, the subjunctive mood is used to state a condition or a wish that is contrary to fact. Notice that this use of the subjunctive always requires the past tense.

EXAMPLE   If she **were** to oversleep, she would miss her ride to school. [**The subjunctive mood uses** *were,* **not** *was.*]

EXAMPLE   I wish (that) I **were** in San Antonio.

EXAMPLE   You are speaking to me as if I **were** a child.

PEANUTS reprinted by permission of United
Feature Syndicate, Inc.

subordinate clause A subordinate clause, also called a dependent clause, has a subject and a predicate but does not express a complete thought, so it cannot stand alone as a sentence (page 164).

EXAMPLE   **When I was young,** dolls **that spoke** were my favorites.

EXAMPLE   **Whoever joins the circus** will travel across the country.

subordinating conjunction A subordinating conjunction joins two clauses, or ideas, in such a way as to make one grammatically dependent on the other. The idea, or clause, that a subordinating conjunction introduces is said to be "subordinate," or dependent, because it cannot stand by itself as a complete sentence (page 124).

after	as though	since	until
although	because	so long as	when
as	before	so (that)	whenever

EXAMPLE We can skate on the pond **when** the ice is thicker.

EXAMPLE We can't skate **until** the ice is thicker.

EXAMPLE **Because** the ice is still too thin, we must wait for a hard freeze.

superlative degree The superlative degree of an adjective or adverb is the form that shows three or more things being compared (page 258).

EXAMPLE Of the three dogs, Ray's dog is the **smallest** one.

EXAMPLE The squirrel ran **most swiftly** of all.

syllable When a word must be divided at the end of a line, it is generally divided between syllables or pronounceable parts. Because it is often difficult to decide where a word should be divided, consult a dictionary. In general, if a word contains two consonants occurring between two vowels or if it contains double consonants, divide the word between the two consonants (page 359).

EXAMPLES foun-tain struc-ture lin-ger

tense Tenses are the forms of a verb that help to show time. There are six tenses in English: *present, past, future, present perfect, past perfect*, and *future perfect* (page 193).

EXAMPLE

present tense	I **sing.**
past tense	I **sang.**
future tense	I **shall** (*or* will) **sing.**
present perfect tense	I **have sung.**
past perfect tense	I **had sung.**
future perfect tense	I **shall** (*or* will) **have sung.**

transitive verb A transitive verb is an action verb followed by a word or words that answer the question *what?* or *whom?* (page 109). *See intransitive verb.*

EXAMPLE   The batter **swung** the bat confidently. **[The action verb *swung* is followed by the noun *bat*, which answers the question *swung what?*]**

verb A verb is a word that expresses action or a state of being and is necessary to make a statement (page 108).

EXAMPLE   The bicyclist **grinned.**

EXAMPLE   The riders **seem** enthusiastic.

verbal A verbal is a verb form that functions in a sentence as a noun, an adjective, or an adverb. Verbals are *participles, gerunds,* and *infinitives.* Each of these can be expanded into phrases (page 150).

EXAMPLE   **Exhausted,** the team headed for the locker room. **[past participle]**

EXAMPLE   **Swimming** is my sport. **[gerund]**

EXAMPLE   I want **to win. [infinitive]**

verb phrase A verb phrase consists of a main verb and all its auxiliary, or helping, verbs (page 111). The most common auxiliary verbs are forms of *be* and *have*. They help the main verb express time by forming the various tenses.

EXAMPLE   We **will weed** the vegetable garden this morning.

EXAMPLE   Sandra **has** already **weeded** the peppers and the tomatoes.

EXAMPLE   We **were weeding** the flowerbeds when the rain started.

The other auxiliary verbs are not used primarily to express time. They are often used to emphasize meaning.

EXAMPLE I **should be leaving.**

EXAMPLE **Could** he **have forgotten?**

EXAMPLE Marisa **may** already **be finished.**

verbal phrase A verbal phrase is a verbal plus any complements and modifiers (page 150).

EXAMPLE **Frightened by the barking dogs,** the kittens ran to their mother. **[participial phrase]**

EXAMPLE **Swimming twenty laps a day** is my goal. **[gerund phrase]**

EXAMPLE I like **to sing the fight song. [infinitive phrase]**

voice Voice is the form a verb takes to explain whether the subject performs the action or the action is performed upon the subject. An action verb is in the active voice when the subject of the sentence performs the action. An action verb is in the passive voice when its action is performed on the subject (page 206).

EXAMPLE The brown bear **caught** a salmon. **[active voice]**

EXAMPLE A salmon **was caught** by the brown bear. **[passive voice]**

USAGE GLOSSARY

This glossary presents some particularly troublesome matters of usage. The glossary will guide you in choosing between words that are often confused. It will also alert you to certain words and expressions you should avoid when you speak or write for school or business.

a, an Use *a* before words that begin with a consonant sound. Use *an* before words that begin with a vowel sound.

EXAMPLES **a** poem, **a** house, **a** yacht, **a** union, **a** one-track mind

EXAMPLES **an** apple, **an** icicle, **an** honor, **an** umbrella, **an** only child

accede, exceed *Accede* means "to agree." *Exceed* means "to go beyond."

EXAMPLE I **acceded** to Mom's wishes.

EXAMPLE Don't **exceed** the speed limit.

accept, except *Accept* is a verb that means "to receive" or "to agree to." *Except* is usually a preposition meaning "but." *Except* may also be a verb that means "to leave out or exclude."

EXAMPLE Will you **accept** our thanks?

EXAMPLE The president **accepted** the terms of the treaty.

EXAMPLE Everyone will be there **except** you. **[preposition]**

EXAMPLE The government **excepts** people with very low incomes from paying taxes. **[verb]**

access, excess *Access* means "admittance." An *excess* is a surplus.

EXAMPLE The thief gained **access** to the building with a stolen key.

EXAMPLE We have an **excess** of musical talent in our class.

adapt, adopt *Adapt* means "to change to meet new requirements" or "to adjust." *Adopt* means "to accept and take as one's own."

EXAMPLE I can **adapt** to new surroundings easily.

EXAMPLE We can **adapt** this old bathrobe for a Roman senator's costume.

EXAMPLE I think that dog has **adopted** you.

advice, advise *Advice*, a noun, means "an opinion offered as guidance." *Advise*, a verb, means "to give advice" or "to counsel."

EXAMPLE Why should I **advise** you when you never accept my **advice**?

affect, effect *Affect* is a verb that means "to cause a change in" or "to influence the emotions of." *Effect* may be a noun or a verb. As a noun, it means "result." As a verb, it means "to bring about or accomplish."

EXAMPLE The mayor's policies have **affected** every city agency.

EXAMPLE The mayor's policies have had a positive **effect** on every city agency. **[noun]**

EXAMPLE The mayor has **effected** positive changes in every city agency. **[verb]**

aggravate, annoy To aggravate something is to make it graver or more serious. Things that can be aggravated are, for example, illnesses and crimes. In informal speaking and writing, *aggravate* has another meaning: "to annoy, to irritate." When you are writing or speaking formally, don't use *aggravate* when *annoy* or *irritate* would be correct.

EXAMPLE Donna's asthma was **aggravated** by the wind-blown pollen.

EXAMPLE Now here's another letter from that same company; I think they want to **annoy [*not* aggravate]** me to death!

ain't *Ain't* is unacceptable in speaking and writing unless you're quoting someone's exact words or writing dialogue. Use *I'm not; you, we,* or *they aren't; he, she,* or *it isn't.*

all ready, already *All ready* means "completely ready." *Already* is an adverb that means "before" or "by this time."

EXAMPLE The band was **all ready** to play its last number, but the fans were **already** leaving the stadium.

all right, alright The spelling *alright* is not acceptable in formal writing. Use *all right.*

EXAMPLE Don't worry; everything will be **all right**.

all the farther, all the faster These expressions are not acceptable in formal speech and writing. Use *as far as* and *as fast as.*

EXAMPLE Five hundred miles was **as far as** [*not* **all the farther**] we could drive in a single day.

EXAMPLE This is **as fast as** [*not* **all the faster**] I can pedal.

all together, altogether Use *all together* to mean "in a group." Use *altogether* to mean "completely" or "in all."

EXAMPLE Let's cheer **all together**.

EXAMPLE You are being **altogether** silly.

EXAMPLE I have three dollars in quarters and two dollars in dimes; that's five dollars **altogether**.

allusion, illusion An *allusion* is an indirect reference. An *illusion* is a false idea or appearance.

EXAMPLE Her speech included an **allusion** to one of Robert Frost's poems.

EXAMPLE The shimmering heat produced an **illusion** of water on the road.

almost, most Don't use *most* in place of *almost*.

EXAMPLE   Marty **almost** [*not* most] always makes the honor roll.

a lot, alot, allot *A lot* should always be written as two words. It means "a large number or amount." Avoid using *a lot* in formal writing; be specific. The verb *allot* means "to assign or set aside" or "to distribute."

EXAMPLE   **A lot** [*not* Alot] of snow fell last night.

[*Better:* A great deal of snow fell last night.]

EXAMPLE   The legislature will **allot** funds for a new capitol.

altar, alter An *altar* is a raised structure at which religious ceremonies are performed. *Alter* means "to change."

EXAMPLE   The bride and groom approached the **altar**.

EXAMPLE   The wardrobe manager **altered** some of the costumes to fit the new cast members.

among, between In general use *among* to show a relationship in which more than two persons or things are considered as a group.

EXAMPLE   The committee will distribute the used clothing **among** the poor families in the community.

EXAMPLE   There was confusion **among** the players on the field.

In general, use *between* to show a relationship involving two persons or things, to compare one person or thing with an entire group, or to compare more than two items within a group.

EXAMPLE   Mr. and Mrs. Ito live halfway **between** Seattle and Portland. **[relationship involving two places]**

EXAMPLE   What was the difference **between** Frank Sinatra and other vocalists of the twentieth century? **[one person compared with a group]**

EXAMPLE   Emilio could not decide **between** the collie, the cocker spaniel, and the beagle. **[items within a group]**

amount, number *Amount* and *number* both refer to quantity. Use *amount* for things that can't be counted. Use *number* for things that can be counted.

EXAMPLE   Fort Knox contains a vast **amount** of gold.

EXAMPLE   Fort Knox contains a large **number** of gold bars.

and/or This expression, once common in legal language, should be avoided in general writing. Change *and/or* to "this *or* that *or both*."

EXAMPLE   We'll go hiking **or** skiing **or both**. [*not* We'll go hiking and/or skiing.]

anxious, eager *Anxious* comes from *anxiety;* therefore, it implies uneasiness or apprehension. It is not a synonym for *eager,* which means "filled with enthusiasm."

EXAMPLE   Jean was **anxious** about her test results.

EXAMPLE   She was **eager** [*not* anxious] to begin college.

anyways, anywheres, everywheres, nowheres, somewheres Write and speak these words without the final *s: anyway, anywhere, everywhere, nowhere, somewhere.*

ascent, assent An *ascent* is a rise or an act of climbing. *Assent* as a verb means "to agree or consent"; as a noun, it means "agreement" or "consent."

EXAMPLE   We watched the **ascent** of the balloon.

EXAMPLE   Will your parents **assent** to our plans? [verb]

EXAMPLE   They were happy to give their **assent** to the plans. [noun]

a while, awhile Use *a while* after a preposition. Use *awhile* as an adverb.

EXAMPLE   She read for **a while**.

EXAMPLE   She read **awhile**.

bad, badly *Bad* is an adjective; use it before nouns and after linking verbs to modify the subject. *Badly* is an adverb; use it to modify action verbs.

EXAMPLE   Clara felt **bad** about the broken vase.

EXAMPLE   The team performed **badly** in the first half.

bare, bear *Bare* means "naked." A *bear* is an animal.

EXAMPLE   Don't expose your **bare** skin to the sun.

EXAMPLE   There are many **bears** in Yellowstone National Park.

base, bass One meaning of *base* is "a part on which something rests or stands." *Bass* pronounced to rhyme with *face* is a type of voice. When *bass* is pronounced to rhyme with *glass*, it's a kind of fish.

EXAMPLE   Who is playing first **base**?

EXAMPLE   We need a **bass** singer for the part.

EXAMPLE   We caught several **bass** on our fishing trip.

because of, due to Use *because of* with action verbs. Use *due to* with linking verbs.

EXAMPLE   The game was canceled **because of** rain.

EXAMPLE   The cancellation was **due to** rain.

being as, being that Some people use these expressions instead of *because* in informal conversation. In formal speaking and writing, use *because*.

EXAMPLE   **Because** [*not* **Being as**] their car broke down, they were late.

EXAMPLE   They were late **because** [*not* **being that**] their car broke down.

beside, besides *Beside* means "at the side of" or "next to." *Besides* means "in addition to."

EXAMPLE   Katrina sat **beside** her brother at the table.

EXAMPLE   **Besides** yogurt and fruit, the lunchroom serves muffins and bagels.

blew, blue *Blue* is the color of a clear sky. *Blew* is the past tense of *blow*.

EXAMPLE   She wore a **blue** shirt.

EXAMPLE   The dead leaves **blew** along the driveway.

boar, bore A *boar* is a male pig. *Bore* means "to tire out with dullness"; it can also mean "a dull person."

EXAMPLE   Wild **boars** are common in parts of Africa.

EXAMPLE   Please don't **bore** me with your silly jokes.

born, borne *Born* means "given life." *Borne* means "carried" or "endured."

EXAMPLE   The baby was **born** at three o'clock in the morning.

EXAMPLE   Migrant workers have **borne** many hardships over the years.

borrow, lend, loan *Borrow* means "to take something with the understanding that it will be returned." *Lend* means "to give something with the understanding it will be returned." *Borrow* and *lend* are verbs. *Loan* is a noun. Some people use *loan* as a verb, but most authorities prefer *lend*.

EXAMPLE   May I **borrow** your bicycle for an hour?

EXAMPLE   Will you **lend** me five dollars? **[verb]**

EXAMPLE   I'll repay the **loan** on Friday. **[noun]**

bow When *bow* is pronounced to rhyme with *low*, it means "a knot with two loops." When *bow* rhymes with *how*, it means "to bend at the waist."

EXAMPLE   Can you tie a good **bow**?

EXAMPLE   Actors **bow** at the end of a play.

brake, break As a noun, a *brake* is a device for stopping something or slowing it down. As a verb, *brake* means "to stop or slow down"; its principal parts are *brake, braking, braked,* and *braked.* The noun *break* has several meanings: "the result of breaking," "a fortunate chance," or "a short rest." The verb *break* also has many meanings. A few are "to smash or shatter," "to destroy or disrupt," "to force a way through or into," or "to surpass or excel." Its principal parts are *break, breaking, broke,* and *broken.*

EXAMPLE   Rachel, please put a **brake** on your enthusiasm. **[noun]**

EXAMPLE   He couldn't **brake** the car in time to avoid the accident. **[verb]**

EXAMPLE   To fix the **break** in the drainpipe will cost a great deal of money. **[noun]**

EXAMPLE   Don't **break** my concentration while I'm studying. **[verb]**

bring, take *Bring* means "to carry from a distant place to a closer one." *Take* means "to carry from a nearby place to a more distant one."

EXAMPLE   Will you **bring** me some perfume when you return from Paris?

EXAMPLE   Remember to **take** your passport when you go to Europe.

bust, busted Don't use these words in place of *break, broke, broken,* or *burst.*

EXAMPLE   Don't **break** [*not* bust] that vase!

EXAMPLE   Who **broke** [*not* busted] this vase?

EXAMPLE   Someone has **broken** [*not* busted] this vase.

Usage Glossary   **51**

EXAMPLE   The balloon **burst** [*not* busted] with a loud pop.

EXAMPLE   The child **burst** [*not* busted] into tears.

buy, by   *Buy* is a verb. *By* is a preposition.

EXAMPLE   I'll **buy** the gift tomorrow.

EXAMPLE   Stand **by** me.

·can, may   *Can* indicates ability. *May* expresses permission or possibility.

EXAMPLE   I **can** tie six kinds of knots.

EXAMPLE   "You **may** be excused," said Dad. [**permission**]

EXAMPLE   Luanna **may** take some college classes during her senior year. [**possibility**]

can't hardly, can't scarcely   These phrases are considered double negatives. Don't use *hardly* or *scarcely* with *not* or the contraction *n't*.

EXAMPLE   I **can** [*not* can't] **hardly** lift this box.

EXAMPLE   The driver **can** [*not* can't] **scarcely** see through the thick fog.

capital, capitol   A *capital* is a city that is the seat of a government. *Capital* can also mean "money or property." As an adjective, capital can mean "involving execution" or "referring to an uppercase letter." *Capitol*, on the other hand, refers only to a building in which a legislature meets.

EXAMPLE   What is the **capital** of Vermont?

EXAMPLE   Anyone starting a business needs **capital**.

EXAMPLE   **Capital** punishment is not used in this state.

EXAMPLE   Hester Prynne embroidered a **capital** *A* on her dress.

EXAMPLE   The **capitol** has a gold dome.

carat, caret, carrot, karat A *carat* is a unit of weight for measuring gems. (A similar word, *karat,* is a measure for expressing the fineness of gold.) A *caret* is a proofreader's mark indicating an insertion. A *carrot* is a vegetable.

EXAMPLE   She was wearing a one-**carat** diamond set in a ring of eighteen-**karat** gold.

EXAMPLE   Draw a **caret** at the point where you want to insert a word.

EXAMPLE   Lottie fed her horse a **carrot**.

cent, scent, sent A *cent* is a penny. A *scent* is an odor. *Sent* is the past and past participle of *send*.

EXAMPLE   I haven't got one **cent** in my pocket.

EXAMPLE   The **scent** of a skunk is unpleasant.

EXAMPLE   I **sent** my grandma a birthday card.

choose, chose *Choose* is the base form; *chose* is the past tense. The principal parts are *choose, choosing, chose,* and *chosen.*

EXAMPLE   Please **choose** a poem to recite in class.

EXAMPLE   Brian **chose** to recite "The Charge of the Light Brigade."

cite, sight, site To *cite* is to quote or refer to. *Cite* can also mean "to summon to appear in a court of law." As a noun, *sight* means "vision." As a verb, *sight* means "to see." As a noun, a *site* is a place or a location; as a verb, *site* means "to place or locate."

EXAMPLE   Consuela **cited** three sources of information in her report.

EXAMPLE   The officer **cited** the driver for speeding.

EXAMPLE   My **sight** is perfect. **[noun]**

EXAMPLE   We **sighted** a scarlet tanager on our hike. **[verb]**

EXAMPLE   The board of education has chosen a **site** for the new high school. [noun]

EXAMPLE   The school will be **sited** on Meadow Boulevard. [verb]

clothes, cloths   *Clothes* are what you wear. *Cloths* are pieces of fabric.

EXAMPLE   Please hang all your **clothes** in your closet.

EXAMPLE   Use these **cloths** to wash the car.

coarse, course   *Coarse* means "rough," "crude," "not fine," "of poor quality." *Course* can mean "a school subject," "a path or way," "order or development," or "part of a meal." *Course* is also used in the phrase *of course*.

EXAMPLE   To begin, I will need some **coarse** sandpaper.

EXAMPLE   Mrs. Baldwin won't tolerate **coarse** language.

EXAMPLE   Are you taking any math **courses** this year?

EXAMPLE   The hikers chose a difficult **course** through the mountains.

complement, complementary; compliment, complimentary   As a noun, *complement* means "something that completes"; as a verb, it means "to complete." As a noun, *compliment* means "a flattering remark"; as a verb, it means "to praise." *Complementary* and *complimentary* are the adjective forms of the words.

EXAMPLE   This flowered scarf will be the perfect **complement** for your outfit. [noun]

EXAMPLE   This flowered scarf **complements** your outfit perfectly. [verb]

EXAMPLE   Phyllis received many **compliments** on her speech. [noun]

EXAMPLE   Many people **complimented** Phyllis on her speech. [verb]

EXAMPLE Either hat would be **complementary** to that outfit.
[adjective]

EXAMPLE The hostess was especially **complimentary** to Phyllis.
[adjective]

compose, comprise *Compose* means "to make up." *Comprise* means "to include."

EXAMPLE The mayor, the superintendent of schools, and the police chief **compose** the committee.

EXAMPLE The committee **comprises** the mayor, the superintendent of schools, and the police chief.

consul; council, councilor; counsel, counselor A *consul* is a government official living in a foreign city to protect his or her country's interests and citizens. A *council* is a group of people gathered for the purpose of giving advice. A *councilor* is one who serves on a council. As a noun, *counsel* means "advice" or "an attorney." As a verb, *counsel* means "to give advice." A *counselor* is one who gives counsel.

EXAMPLE The **consul** protested to the foreign government about the treatment of her fellow citizens.

EXAMPLE The city **council** met to discuss the lack of parking facilities at the sports field.

EXAMPLE The defendant received **counsel** from his **counsel**.
[nouns]

EXAMPLE The attorney **counseled** his client to plead innocent.
[verb]

continual, continually; continuous, continuously *Continual* describes action that occurs over and over but with pauses between occurrences. *Continuous* describes an action that continues with no interruption. *Continually* and *continuously* are the adverb forms of the adjectives.

EXAMPLE   I could not concentrate because of the **continual** banging of the screen door and the **continuous** blare of the radio.

EXAMPLE   This television ad is aired **continually**; I've seen it six times tonight.

EXAMPLE   The rain fell **continuously**.

could of, might of, must of, should of, would of   After the words *could, might, must, should,* and *would,* use the helping verb *have* or its contraction, *'ve,* not the word *of.*

EXAMPLE   **Could** you **have** prevented the accident?

EXAMPLE   You **might have** swerved to avoid the other car.

EXAMPLE   You **must have** seen it coming.

EXAMPLE   I **should've** warned you.

dear, deer   *Dear* is a word of affection and is used to begin a letter. It can also mean "expensive." A *deer* is an animal.

EXAMPLE   Talia is my **dear** friend.

EXAMPLE   We saw a **deer** at the edge of the woods.

desert, dessert   *Desert* has two meanings. As a noun, it means "dry, arid land" and is accented on the first syllable. As a verb, it means "to leave" or "to abandon" and is accented on the second syllable. A *dessert* is something sweet eaten after a meal.

EXAMPLE   This photograph shows a sandstorm in the **desert**. **[noun]**

EXAMPLE   I won't **desert** you in your time of need. **[verb]**

EXAMPLE   Strawberry shortcake was served for **dessert**.

different from, different than   In most cases, *different from* is the correct choice. Use *different than* only if *than* introduces a subordinate clause.

EXAMPLE Square dancing is **different from** ballroom dancing.

EXAMPLE I felt **different than** I had felt before.

diner, dinner A *diner* is someone who dines or a place to eat. A *dinner* is a meal.

EXAMPLE The **diners** at the corner **diner** enjoy the corned beef hash.

EXAMPLE **Dinner** will be served at eight.

discover, invent *Discover* means "to come upon something for the first time." *Invent* means "to produce something original."

EXAMPLE Marie Curie **discovered** radium.

EXAMPLE Eli Whitney **invented** the cotton gin.

discreet, discrete These two adjectives have identical pronunciations but very different meanings. *Discreet* means "having good judgment," "prudent," or "unobtrusive." *Discrete* means "disconnected," "separate," or "individual."

EXAMPLE The actor's agent read the reporters a brief, **discreet** statement that did not satisfy their curiosity.

EXAMPLE The detective followed his subject at a **discreet** distance.

EXAMPLE This floor, which looks like one piece of stone, is actually made of thousands of tiny **discrete** pieces glued together.

doe, dough A *doe* is a female deer. *Dough* is a mixture of flour and a liquid.

EXAMPLE A **doe** and a stag were visible among the trees.

EXAMPLE Knead the **dough** for three minutes.

doesn't, don't *Doesn't* is a contraction of *does not*. It is used with *he, she, it,* and all singular nouns. *Don't* is a contraction of *do not*. It is used with *I, you, we, they,* and all plural nouns.

EXAMPLE   She **doesn't** know the answer to your question.

EXAMPLE   The twins **don't** like broccoli.

emigrate, immigrate Use *emigrate* to mean "to leave one country and go to another to live." Use *immigrate* to mean "to come to a country to settle there." Use the preposition *from* with *emigrate*. Use *to* or *into* with *immigrate*.

EXAMPLE   Karl **emigrated** from Germany.

EXAMPLE   He **immigrated** to the United States.

eye, I An *eye* is what you see with; it's also a small opening in a needle. *I* is a personal pronoun.

EXAMPLE   **I** have something in my **eye**.

farther, further Use *farther* in referring to physical distance. Use *further* in all other situations.

EXAMPLE   San Antonio is **farther** south than Dallas.

EXAMPLE   We have nothing **further** to discuss.

fewer, less Use *fewer* with nouns that can be counted. Use *less* with nouns that can't be counted. *Less* may also be used with numbers that are considered as single amounts or single quantities.

EXAMPLE   There are **fewer** students in my math class than in my physics class.

EXAMPLE   I used **less** sugar than the recipe recommended.

EXAMPLE David had **less** than two dollars in his pocket.
[*Two dollars* is treated as a single sum, not as individual dollars.]

EXAMPLE I can be there in **less** than thirty minutes. **[*Thirty minutes* is treated as a single period of time, not as individual minutes.]**

figuratively, literally *Figuratively* means "not truly or actually but in a symbolic way." *Literally* means "truly" or "actually."

EXAMPLE Dad hit the ceiling, **figuratively** speaking.

EXAMPLE You can't take him **literally** when he talks about the fish he's caught.

flaunt, flout *Flaunt* means "to make a showy display." *Flout* means "to defy."

EXAMPLE Enrique **flaunted** his knowledge of computer science at every opportunity.

EXAMPLE Darla **flouted** the law by jaywalking.

flour, flower *Flour* is used to bake bread. A *flower* grows in a garden.

EXAMPLE Sift two cups of **flour** into a bowl.

EXAMPLE A daisy is a **flower**.

for, four *For* is a preposition. *Four* is a number.

EXAMPLE Wait **for** me.

EXAMPLE I have **four** grandparents.

formally, formerly *Formally* is the adverb form of *formal*, which has several meanings: "according to custom, rule, or etiquette"; "requiring special ceremony or fancy clothing"; or "official." *Formerly* means "previously."

EXAMPLE The class officers will be **formally** installed on Thursday.

EXAMPLE Ed was **formerly** employed by Kwik Kar Kleen.

go, say Don't use forms of *go* in place of forms of *say*.

EXAMPLE I tell her the answer, and she **says** [*not* goes], "I don't believe you."

EXAMPLE I told her the news, and she **said** [*not* went], "Are you serious?"

good, well *Good* is an adjective; use it before nouns and after linking verbs to modify the subject. *Well* is an adverb; use it to modify action verbs. *Well* may also be an adjective meaning "in good health."

EXAMPLE You look **good** in that costume.

EXAMPLE Joby plays the piano **well**.

EXAMPLE You're looking **well** in spite of your cold.

grate, great A *grate* is a framework of bars set over an opening. *Grate* also means "to shred by rubbing against a rough surface." *Great* means "wonderful" or "large."

EXAMPLE The little girl dropped her lollipop through the **grate**.

EXAMPLE Will you **grate** this cheese for me?

EXAMPLE You did a **great** job!

had of Don't use *of* between *had* and a past participle.

EXAMPLE I wish I **had known** [*not* had of known] about this sooner.

had ought, hadn't ought, shouldn't ought *Ought* never needs a helping verb. Use *ought* by itself.

EXAMPLE   You **ought** to win the match easily.

EXAMPLE   You **ought** not to blame yourself. *or* You **shouldn't** blame yourself.

hanged, hung   Use *hanged* when you mean "put to death by hanging." Use *hung* in all other instances.

EXAMPLE   This state **hanged** three convicts between 1900 and 1950.

EXAMPLE   We **hung** Yoko's painting over the fireplace.

healthful, healthy   *Healthful* means "favorable to one's health," or "wholesome." *Healthy* means "in good health."

EXAMPLE   We chose **healthful** picnic foods: whole-grain breads, juices, cheese, and fresh fruits.

EXAMPLE   A **healthy** person is likely to live longer than an unhealthy one.

hear, here   *Hear* is a verb meaning "to be aware of sound by means of the ear." *Here* is an adverb meaning "in or at this place."

EXAMPLE   I can **hear** you perfectly well.

EXAMPLE   Please put your books **here**.

he, she, it, they   Don't use a pronoun subject immediately after a noun subject, as in *The **girls they** baked the cookies.* Omit the unnecessary pronoun: *The **girls** baked the cookies.*

holey, holy, wholly   *Holey* means "having holes." *Holy* means "sacred." *Wholly* means "completely."

EXAMPLE   I hate wearing **holey** socks.

EXAMPLE   Religious travelers make pilgrimages to **holy** places.

EXAMPLE   That dog is **wholly** devoted to you.

how come   In formal speech and writing, use *why* instead of *how come.*

EXAMPLE **Why** weren't you at the meeting? [*not* **How come you weren't at the meeting?**]

imply, infer *Imply* means "to suggest." *Infer* means "to draw a conclusion from something."

EXAMPLE The baby's crying **implied** that he was hungry.

EXAMPLE I **inferred** from the baby's crying that he was hungry.

in, into, in to Use *in* to mean "inside" or "within." Use *into* to show movement from the outside to a point within. Don't write *into* when you mean *in to*.

EXAMPLE Jeanine was sitting outdoors **in** a lawn chair.

EXAMPLE When it got too hot, she went **into** the house.

EXAMPLE She went **in to** get out of the heat.

ingenious, ingenuous *Ingenious* means "clever," "inventive," "imaginative." *Ingenuous* means "innocent," "childlike," "sincere."

EXAMPLE What an **ingenious** plan you have dreamed up!

EXAMPLE Her **ingenuous** enthusiasm for the cafeteria food made us smile.

inside of Don't use *of* after the preposition *inside*.

EXAMPLE **Inside** [*not* **inside of**] the cupboard were several old photograph albums.

irregardless, regardless Use *regardless*. Both the prefix *ir-* and the suffix *-less* have negative meanings; therefore, *irregardless* is a double negative, which is incorrect.

EXAMPLE **Regardless** [*not* **Irregardless**] of what the critics said, I liked that movie.

its, it's *Its* is the possessive form of *it*. *It's* is a contraction of *it is* or *it has*.

EXAMPLE The dishwasher has finished **its** cycle.

EXAMPLE **It's [It is]** raining again.

EXAMPLE **It's [It has]** been a pleasure to meet you, Ms. Donatello.

kind of, sort of Don't use these expressions as adverbs. Use *somewhat* or *rather* instead.

EXAMPLE We were **rather** sorry to see him go. [*not* **We were kind of sorry to see him go.**]

kind of a, sort of a, type of a Omit the word *a*.

EXAMPLE What **kind of** dog is that? [*not* **What kind of a dog is that?**]

knead, need *Knead* means "to mix or work into a uniform mass." As a noun, a *need* is a requirement. As a verb, *need* means "to require."

EXAMPLE **Knead** the clay to make it soft.

EXAMPLE I **need** a new jacket.

knight, night A *knight* was a warrior of the Middle Ages. *Night* is the time of day during which it is dark.

EXAMPLE A handsome **knight** rescued the fair maiden.

EXAMPLE **Night** fell, and the moon rose.

last, latest When you are speaking or writing of an author and say, "This is her latest book," you're understood to mean that she has written some books and that this is the most recent one. If, however, you had said, "This is her last book," then two meanings are possible. One is the same as in the first sentence; the other is that this is the last book that author will ever write. To be clear, get into the habit of saying *last* only when you mean "last" and saying *latest* instead when it's appropriate.

EXAMPLE In her **last** poem, my sister explained why she is giving up writing poetry forever.

EXAMPLE In her **latest** poem, my sister explained a family incident that happened only last weekend.

later, latter *Later* is the comparative form of *late*. *Latter* means "the second of two."

EXAMPLE They will arrive on a **later** flight.

EXAMPLE He arrived **later** than usual.

EXAMPLE Both Scott and Sabrina are running for class president; I'm voting for the **latter**.

lay, lie *Lay* means "to put" or "to place." Its principal parts are *lay, laying, laid,* and *laid.* Forms of *lay* are usually followed by a direct object. *Lie* means "to rest or recline" or "to be positioned." Its principal parts are *lie, lying, lay,* and *lain.* Forms of *lie* are never followed by a direct object.

EXAMPLE **Lay** your coat on the bed.

EXAMPLE The children are **laying** their beach towels in the sun to dry.

EXAMPLE Dad **laid** the baby in her crib.

EXAMPLE Myrna had **laid** the book beside her purse.

EXAMPLE **Lie** down for a few minutes.

EXAMPLE The lake **lies** to the north.

EXAMPLE The dog is **lying** on the back porch.

EXAMPLE This morning I **lay** in bed listening to the birds.

EXAMPLE You have **lain** on the couch for an hour.

lead, led As a noun, *lead* has two pronunciations and several meanings. When it's pronounced to rhyme with *head,* it means "a metallic element." When it's pronounced to rhyme with *bead,* it can mean "position of being in first place in a race or contest," "example," "clue," "leash," or "the main role in a play."

EXAMPLE **Lead** is no longer allowed as an ingredient in paint.

EXAMPLE Jason took the **lead** as the runners entered the stadium.

EXAMPLE Follow my **lead**.

EXAMPLE The detective had no **leads** in the case.

EXAMPLE Only dogs on **leads** are permitted in the park.

EXAMPLE Who will win the **lead** in this year's musical production?

As a verb, *lead* means "to show the way," "to guide or conduct," "to be first." Its principal parts are *lead, leading, led,* and *led.*

EXAMPLE Ms. Bachman **leads** the orchestra.

EXAMPLE The trainer was **leading** the horse around the track.

EXAMPLE An usher **led** us to our seats.

EXAMPLE Gray has **led** the league in hitting for two years.

learn, teach *Learn* means "to receive knowledge." *Teach* means "to give knowledge."

EXAMPLE Manny began to **learn** to play the piano at the age of six.

EXAMPLE Ms. Guerrero **teaches** American history.

leave, let *Leave* means "to go away." *Let* means "to allow to."

EXAMPLE I'll miss you when you **leave**.

EXAMPLE **Let** me help you with those heavy bags.

like, as, as if, as though *Like* can be a verb or a preposition. It should not be used as a subordinating conjunction. Use *as, as if,* or *as though* to introduce a subordinate clause.

EXAMPLE I **like** piano music. [verb]

EXAMPLE Teresa plays the piano **like** a professional. [preposition]

EXAMPLE Moira plays **as** [*not* like] her teacher taught her to play.

EXAMPLE He looked at me **as if** [*not* like] he'd never seen me before.

EXAMPLE You sound **as though** [*not* like] you disagree.

like, say Don't use the word *like* in place of forms of *say*.

EXAMPLE I tell him to scroll down, and **he says** [*not* he's like], "What's scrolling down?"

EXAMPLE I told her to turn left, and **she said** [*not* she was like], "Left!"

loath, loathe *Loath* means "reluctant or unwilling." *Loathe* means "to hate."

EXAMPLE Jeanine was **loath** to accept the responsibility.

EXAMPLE Leonardo **loathes** sports.

loose, lose The adjective *loose* means "free," "not firmly attached," or "not fitting tightly." The verb *lose* means "to misplace" or "to fail to win."

EXAMPLE Don't **lose** that **loose** button on your shirt.

EXAMPLE If we **lose** this game, we'll be out of the tournament.

mail, male *Mail* is what turns up in your mailbox. A *male* is a man.

EXAMPLE We received four pieces of **mail** today.

EXAMPLE The **males** in the chorus wore red ties.

main, mane *Main* means "most important." A *mane* is the long hair on a horse's neck.

EXAMPLE   What is your **main** job around the house?

EXAMPLE   The horse's **mane** was braided with colorful ribbons.

marshal, Marshall, martial, marital The first three words are pronounced the same. A *marshal* is a military official or a law officer. *Marshall* refers to the Marshall Islands in the Pacific Ocean. The adjective *martial* means "pertaining to war" or "pertaining to military life." The adjective *marital*, however, is pronounced with three syllables and means "pertaining to marriage."

EXAMPLE   The actor playing the town **marshal** walked onto the set carrying his Stetson.

EXAMPLE   Carol and her parents often spend the summer in the **Marshalls**, where they have relatives.

EXAMPLE   Roberto is a **martial** arts student.

EXAMPLE   The bride and groom wrote their own **marital** vows.

masterful, masterly *Masterful* means "strong," "bossy," or "domineering." *Masterly* means "like a master" or "showing great skill."

EXAMPLE   The overlord made a **masterful** gesture, and all the people bowed.

EXAMPLE   My violin teacher played a **masterly** solo at the end of our recital.

mean, medium, average The *mean* of a set of numbers is a middle point. To get the arithmetic mean, you add up all the items in the set and divide by the number of items. The *medium* is the middle number when the items are arranged in order of size. The *average*, a noun, is the same as the arithmetic mean; as an adjective, *average* is "usual" or "typical."

EXAMPLE   The **mean** value of houses in a neighborhood is found by adding together all their selling prices and dividing the sum by the number of houses.

EXAMPLE   We lined up all the ponies from smallest to biggest, and Taminka chose the **medium** one, the one in the center of the row.

EXAMPLE   Let's figure out the **average** of all our test scores; then we can tell whether as a class we've improved.

EXAMPLE   This crop of tomatoes is nothing unusual; it's pretty **average**.

meat, meet *Meat* is food from an animal. Some meanings of *meet* are "to come face to face with," "to make the acquaintance of," and "to keep an appointment."

EXAMPLE   Some people don't eat **meat**.

EXAMPLE   **Meet** me at the library at three o'clock.

miner, minor *Miner* is a noun that means "one who works in a mine." *Minor* can be a noun or an adjective. As a noun, it means "a person under legal age." As an adjective, it means "small in importance."

EXAMPLE   Coal **miners** often suffer from a disease known as black lung.

EXAMPLE   **Minors** are restricted by law from certain activities.

EXAMPLE   Several well-known actors had **minor** roles in the film.

minute When *minute* is pronounced min'it, it means "sixty seconds" or "a short period of time." When *minute* is pronounced mī nōot', it means "very small."

EXAMPLE   I'll be with you in a **minute**.

EXAMPLE   Don't bother me with **minute** details.

moral, morale As a noun, a *moral* is a lesson taught by a fable or a story. As an adjective, *moral* means "decent," "right," "proper." *Morale* means "mental attitude."

EXAMPLE Did you understand the **moral** of that story?

EXAMPLE Jackson has strong **moral** principles.

EXAMPLE The team's **morale** would be improved by a win.

nauseated, nauseous *Nauseated* means "feeling nausea" or "experiencing nausea, as in sea-sickness." *Nauseous,* on the other hand, means "causing nausea" or "sickening."

EXAMPLE My **nauseated** family could not stand to look any longer at the **nauseous** dish of scrambled eggs and left-overs I had placed in front of them.

object *Object* is stressed on the first syllable when it means "a thing." *Object* is stressed on the second syllable when it means "oppose."

EXAMPLE Have you ever seen an unidentified flying **object**?

EXAMPLE Mom **objected** to the proposal.

off Don't use *off* in place of *from.*

EXAMPLE I'll borrow some money **from** [*not* **off**] my brother.

off of Don't use *of* after the preposition *off.*

EXAMPLE He fell **off** [*not* **off of**] the ladder, but he didn't hurt himself.

ordinance, ordnance An *ordinance* is a law. *Ordnance* is a word for military weapons and equipment.

EXAMPLE Our town has an **ordinance** against lying on the sidewalk.

EXAMPLE Private Malloy was assigned to guard the **ordnance**.

ought to of Don't use *of* in place of *have* after *ought to*.

EXAMPLE   You **ought to have** [*not* ought to of] known better.

outside of Don't use *of* after the preposition *outside*.

EXAMPLE   I'll meet you **outside** [*not* outside of] the library.

overlook, oversee Overlook can mean "to look past or miss" and "to look down at from above." *Oversee* means "to supervise workers or work."

EXAMPLE   Lynn calculated the net profit we made from the car wash, but she had **overlooked** the cost of the lemonade and snacks provided for the workers.

EXAMPLE   The ridgetop cabin **overlooks** the whole valley.

EXAMPLE   Part of the caretaker's job is to **oversee** the garden staff, the groundskeeping staff, and the security staff.

pair, pare, pear A *pair* is two. *Pare* means "to peel." A *pear* is a fruit.

EXAMPLE   I bought a new **pair** of socks.

EXAMPLE   **Pare** the potatoes and cut them in quarters.

EXAMPLE   Would you like a **pear** or a banana?

passed, past *Passed* is the past form and the past participle of the verb *pass*. *Past* can be an adjective, a preposition, an adverb, or a noun.

EXAMPLE   We **passed** your house on the way to school. [verb]

EXAMPLE   The **past** week has been a busy one for me. [adjective]

EXAMPLE   We drove **past** your house. [preposition]

EXAMPLE   At what time did you drive **past**? [adverb]

EXAMPLE   I love Great-grandma's stories about the **past**. [noun]

pause, paws A *pause* is a short space of time. *Pause* also means "to wait for a short time." *Paws* are animal feet.

EXAMPLE   We **pause** now for station identification.

EXAMPLE   I wiped the dog's muddy **paws**.

peace, piece *Peace* means "calmness" or "the absence of conflict." A *piece* is a part of something.

EXAMPLE   We enjoy the **peace** of the countryside.

EXAMPLE   The two nations have finally made **peace**.

EXAMPLE   May I have another **piece** of pie?

persecute, prosecute *Persecute* means "to torment." *Prosecute* means "to bring legal action against."

EXAMPLE   Bullies sometimes **persecute** younger, weaker children.

EXAMPLE   The government **prosecuted** Al Capone for tax evasion.

personal, personnel *Personal* means "private" or "individual." *Personnel* are employees.

EXAMPLE   Employees should not make **personal** telephone calls during working hours.

EXAMPLE   All **personnel** will receive a bonus in July.

plain, plane *Plain* means "not fancy," "clear," or "a large area of flat land." A *plane* is an airplane or a device for smoothing wood; it can also mean "a flat surface."

EXAMPLE   He wore a **plain** blue tie.

EXAMPLE   The solution is perfectly **plain** to me.

EXAMPLE   Buffalo once roamed the **plains**.

EXAMPLE   We took a **plane** to Chicago.

EXAMPLE   Jeff used a **plane** to smooth the rough wood.

EXAMPLE   The two metal surfaces of this machine must be perfect **planes**.

precede, proceed *Precede* means "to go before" or "to come before." *Proceed* means "to continue" or "to move along."

EXAMPLE   Our band **preceded** the homecoming floats as the parade **proceeded** through town.

precedence, precedents *Precedence* means "superiority of rank or position." *Precedents* are previous events that serve as examples for future actions or decisions.

EXAMPLE   Doing your schoolwork has **precedence** over playing computer games.

EXAMPLE   The legal **precedents** for the decision were clear and numerous.

principal, principle As a noun, *principal* means "head of a school"; it can also mean "a sum of money borrowed or invested." As an adjective, *principal* means "main" or "chief." *Principle* is a noun meaning "basic truth or belief" or "rule of conduct."

EXAMPLE   Mr. Washington, our **principal**, will speak at the morning assembly. **[noun]**

EXAMPLE   What was your **principal** reason for joining the club? **[adjective]**

EXAMPLE   The **principle** of fair play is important in sports.

quiet, quit, quite The adjective *quiet* means "silent" or "motionless." The verb *quit* means "to stop" or "to give up or resign." The adverb *quite* means "very" or "completely."

EXAMPLE   Please be **quiet** so I can think.

EXAMPLE   Shirelle has **quit** the swim team.

EXAMPLE   We were **quite** sorry to lose her.

raise, rise *Raise* means "to cause to move upward." It can also mean "to breed or grow" and "to bring up or rear." Its principal parts are *raise, raising, raised,* and *raised.* Forms of *raise* are usually followed by a direct object. *Rise* means "to move upward." Its principal parts are *rise, rising, rose,* and *risen.* Forms of *rise* are never followed by a direct object.

EXAMPLE **Raise** your hand if you know the answer.

EXAMPLE My uncle is **raising** chickens.

EXAMPLE Grandma and Grandpa Schwartz **raised** nine children.

EXAMPLE Steam **rises** from boiling water.

EXAMPLE The sun is **rising**.

EXAMPLE The children **rose** from their seats when the principal entered the room.

EXAMPLE In a short time, Loretta **had risen** to the rank of captain.

rap, wrap *Rap* means "to knock." *Wrap* means "to cover."

EXAMPLE **Rap** on the door.

EXAMPLE **Wrap** the presents.

rational, rationale *Rational,* an adjective, means "sensible," "sane." A *rationale* is a reason for doing something. *Rationale* is a noun.

EXAMPLE Melody always behaves in a **rational** manner.

EXAMPLE I didn't understand Clive's **rationale** for quitting his job.

read, reed *Read* means "to understand the meaning of something written." A *reed* is a stalk of tall grass.

EXAMPLE Will you **read** Jimmy a story?

EXAMPLE We found a frog in the **reeds** beside the lake.

real, really *Real* is an adjective; use it before nouns and after linking verbs to modify the subject. *Really* is an adverb; use it to modify action verbs, adjectives, and other adverbs.

EXAMPLE   Winona has **real** musical talent.

EXAMPLE   She is **really** talented.

real, reel *Real* means "actual." A *reel* is a spool to wind something on, such as a fishing line.

EXAMPLE   I have a **real** four-leaf clover.

EXAMPLE   My dad bought me a new fishing **reel**.

reason is because Don't use *because* after *reason is.* Use *that* after *reason is,* or use *because* alone.

EXAMPLE   The **reason** I'm tired **is that** I didn't sleep well last night.

EXAMPLE   I'm tired **because** I didn't sleep well last night.

respectfully, respectively *Respectfully* means "with respect." *Respectively* means "in the order named."

EXAMPLE   The audience listened **respectfully** as the poet read his latest work.

EXAMPLE   Sue, Jerry, and Chad will be president, secretary, and treasurer, **respectively**.

root, rout, route, en route A *root* is a part of a plant. As a verb, *rout* means "to defeat"; as a noun, it means "a defeat." A *route* is a road or way for travel. *En route* means "on the way."

EXAMPLE   A carrot is a **root**.

EXAMPLE   The Tigers **routed** the Bears in last week's game. **[verb]**

EXAMPLE   The game ended in a **rout** for the Bears. **[noun]**

EXAMPLE   Let's take the **route** that runs along the river.

EXAMPLE   We stopped for lunch **en route**.

row When *row* is pronounced to rhyme with *low,* it means "a series of things arranged in a line" or "to move a boat by using oars." When *row* is pronounced to rhyme with *how,* it means "a noisy quarrel."

EXAMPLE   We sat in the last **row** of the theater.

EXAMPLE   Let's **row** across the lake.

EXAMPLE   My sister and I had a serious **row** yesterday, but today we've forgotten about it.

said, says *Said* is the past form and the past participle of *say. Says* is used in the present tense with *he, she, it,* and all singular nouns. Don't use *says* when you should use *said.*

EXAMPLE   At dinner last night, Neil **said** he wasn't hungry.

EXAMPLE   He always **says** that, but he eats everything anyway.

sail, sale A *sail* is part of a boat. It also means "to travel in a boat." A *sale* is a transfer of ownership in exchange for money.

EXAMPLE   As the boat **sails** away, the crew raise the **sail**.

EXAMPLE   The **sale** of the house was completed on Friday.

sea, see A *sea* is a body of water. *See* means "to be aware of with the eyes."

EXAMPLE   The **sea** is rough today.

EXAMPLE   I can **see** you.

set, sit *Set* means "to place" or "to put." Its principal parts are *set, setting, set,* and *set.* Forms of *set* are usually followed by a direct object. *Sit* means "to place oneself in a seated position" or "to be in a seated position." Its principal parts are *sit, sitting, sat,* and *sat.* Forms of *sit* are not followed by a direct object.

Set is an intransitive verb when it's used with *sun* to mean "the sun is going down" or "the sun is sinking below the horizon." When *set* is used in this way, it is not followed by a direct object.

EXAMPLE   Lani **sets** the pots on the stove after the sun **sets**.

EXAMPLE   The children **sit** quietly at the table.

sew, sow *Sew* means "to work with needle and thread." When *sow* is pronounced to rhyme with *how*, it means "a female pig." When *sow* is pronounced to rhyme with *low*, it means "to plant."

EXAMPLE   Can you **sew** a button on a shirt?

EXAMPLE   The **sow** has five piglets.

EXAMPLE   Some farmers **sow** corn in their fields.

shear, sheer *Shear* has to do with cutting or breaking off. *Sheer* can mean "thin and fine," "utter or complete," or "steep."

EXAMPLE   It's time to **shear** the sheep.

EXAMPLE   He decided to **shear** off his beard.

EXAMPLE   The bride's veil was made of a **sheer** fabric.

EXAMPLE   You are talking **sheer** nonsense.

EXAMPLE   It was a **sheer** drop from the top of the cliff.

shined, shone, shown Both *shined* and *shone* are past tense forms and past participles of *shine.* Use *shined* when you mean "polished"; use *shone* in all other instances.

EXAMPLE   Clete **shined** his shoes.

EXAMPLE   The sun **shone** brightly.

EXAMPLE   Her face **shone** with happiness.

Shown is the past participle of *show;* its principal parts are *show, showing, showed,* and *shown.*

EXAMPLE You **showed** me these photographs yesterday.

EXAMPLE You have **shown** me these photographs before.

slow, slowly *Slow* may be used as an adverb only in such expressions as *Go slow* or *Drive slow*. In other instances where an adverb is needed, *slowly* should be used. You can't go wrong if you always use *slow* as an adjective and *slowly* as an adverb.

EXAMPLE We took a **slow** ferry to the island.

EXAMPLE The ferry moved **slowly** through the water.

some, somewhat Don't use *some* as an adverb in place of *somewhat*.

EXAMPLE The team has improved **somewhat** [*not* some] since last season.

son, sun A *son* is a male child. A *sun* is a star.

EXAMPLE Kino is Mr. and Mrs. Akawa's **son**.

EXAMPLE We watched as the **sun** rose over the horizon.

stationary, stationery *Stationary* means "fixed" or "unmoving." *Stationery* is writing paper.

EXAMPLE This classroom has **stationary** desks.

EXAMPLE Rhonda likes to write letters on pretty **stationery**.

straight, strait *Straight* means "not crooked or curved"; it can also mean "direct" or "directly." A *strait* is a narrow waterway connecting two larger bodies of water. In the plural, it can also mean "difficulties" or "distress."

EXAMPLE Can you draw a **straight** line without a ruler?

EXAMPLE We drove **straight** to the airport.

EXAMPLE The **Strait** of Gibraltar connects the Mediterranean Sea and the Atlantic Ocean.

Usage Glossary **77**

EXAMPLE   People who don't control their spending often find themselves in financial **straits**.

suit, suite To distinguish these similar-looking nouns, focus on what constitutes them. For instance, *suit* is usually used in the phrases "a suit of clothes" and "a suit of cards." *Suite*, on the other hand, is usually used in the phrases "a suite of furniture" and "a suite of rooms." To further distinguish them, *suit* rhymes with *boot*, and *suite* is pronounced *sweet*.

EXAMPLE   David bought himself a new **suit** for his interview.

EXAMPLE   After the cards were dealt, I saw that I held in my hand cards from every **suit** except diamonds.

EXAMPLE   The Pattersons bought a **suite** of maple living-room furniture.

EXAMPLE   The hotel offered the large family a **suite** of interconnecting rooms.

sure, surely *Sure* is an adjective; use it before nouns and after linking verbs to modify the subject. *Surely* is an adverb; use it to modify action verbs, adjectives, and other adverbs.

EXAMPLE   Are you **sure** about that answer?

EXAMPLE   You are **surely** smart.

tail, tale A *tail* is what a dog wags. A *tale* is a story.

EXAMPLE   The dog's **tail** curled over its back.

EXAMPLE   Everyone knows the **tale** of Goldilocks and the three bears.

tear When *tear* is pronounced to rhyme with *ear*, it's a drop of fluid from the eye. When *tear* is pronounced to rhyme with *bear*, it means "a rip" or "to rip."

EXAMPLE   A **tear** fell from the child's eye.

EXAMPLE   **Tear** this rag in half.

than, then   *Than* is a conjunction used to introduce the second part of a comparison.

EXAMPLE   LaTrisha is taller **than** LaToya.

EXAMPLE   Ted ordered more food **than** he could eat.

Then has several related meanings that have to do with time: "at that time," "soon afterward," "the time mentioned," "at another time." *Then* can also mean "for that reason" or "in that case."

EXAMPLE   My grandmother was a young girl **then**.

EXAMPLE   We ate lunch and **then** washed the dishes.

EXAMPLE   I look forward to seeing you **then**.

EXAMPLE   Sometimes I feel completely confident; **then** I feel totally incompetent.

EXAMPLE   "It's raining," said Joy.
"**Then** we can't go," wailed her brother.

that there, this here   Don't use *there* or *here* after *that, this, those,* or *these.*

EXAMPLE   I can't decide whether to read **this** [*not* **this here**] magazine or **that** [*not* **that there**] book.

EXAMPLE   Fold **these** [*not* **these here**] towels and hang **those** [*not* **those there**] shirts in the closet.

that, which, who   *That* may refer to people or things. *Which* refers only to things. *Who* refers only to people.

EXAMPLE   The poet **that** wrote *Leaves of Grass* is Walt Whitman.

EXAMPLE   I have already seen the movie **that** is playing at the Bijou.

EXAMPLE   The new play, **which** closed after a week, received poor reviews.

EXAMPLE   Students **who** do well on the test will receive scholarships.

their, there, they're   *Their* is a possessive form of *they;* it's used to modify nouns. *There* means "in or at that place." *They're* is a contraction of *they are.*

EXAMPLE   A hurricane damaged **their** house.

EXAMPLE   Put your books **there**.

EXAMPLE   **They're** our next-door neighbors.

theirs, there's   *Theirs* is a possessive form of *they* used as a pronoun. *There's* is a contraction of *there is.*

EXAMPLE   **Theirs** is the white house with the green shutters.

EXAMPLE   **There's** your friend Chad.

them   Don't use *them* as an adjective in place of *those.*

EXAMPLE   I'll take one of **those** [*not* them] hamburgers.

this kind, these kinds   Use the singular forms *this* and *that* with the singular nouns *kind, sort,* and *type.* Use the plural forms *these* and *those* with the plural nouns *kinds, sorts,* and *types.*

EXAMPLE   Use **this kind** of lightbulb in your lamp.

EXAMPLE   Do you like **these kinds** of lamps?

EXAMPLE   Many Pakistani restaurants serve **that sort** of food.

EXAMPLE   **Those sorts** of foods are nutritious.

EXAMPLE   **This type** of dog makes a good pet.

EXAMPLE   **These types** of dogs are good with children.

thorough, through, threw *Thorough* means "complete." *Through* is a preposition meaning "into at one side and out at another." *Through* can also mean "finished." *Threw* is the past tense of *throw.*

EXAMPLE   We gave the bedrooms a **thorough** cleaning.

EXAMPLE   A breeze blew **through** the house.

EXAMPLE   At last I'm **through** with my homework.

EXAMPLE   Lacey **threw** the ball.

to, too, two *To* means "in the direction of"; it is also part of the infinitive form of a verb. *Too* means "very" or "also." *Two* is the number after *one.*

EXAMPLE   Jaleela walks **to** school.

EXAMPLE   She likes **to** study.

EXAMPLE   The soup is **too** salty.

EXAMPLE   May I go **too**?

EXAMPLE   We have **two** kittens.

toward, towards People in Great Britain use *towards*, but the preferred form in the United States is *toward.*

EXAMPLE   Smiling, she walked **toward** me.

try and Use *try to.*

EXAMPLE   Please **try to** [*not* try and] be on time.

type, type of Don't use *type* as an adjective.

EXAMPLE   What **type of** music [*not* what type music] do you like?

uninterested, disinterested *Uninterested* means "not interested," "unenthusiastic," and "indifferent." *Disinterested* means "impartial," "unbiased, not favoring either side in a dispute."

EXAMPLE   I threw the collie a biscuit, but, supremely **uninterested**, he let it lie where it fell.

EXAMPLE   The judge listened carefully to all the witnesses in that tangled case before handing down her **disinterested** and even-handed decision.

unless, without Don't use *without* in place of *unless*.

EXAMPLE   **Unless** [*not* **Without**] I earn some money, I can't go to camp.

used to, use to The correct form is *used to*.

EXAMPLE   We **used to** [*not* **use to**] live in Cleveland, Ohio.

waist, waste Your *waist* is where you wear your belt. As a noun, *waste* means "careless or unnecessary spending" or "trash." As a verb, it means "to spend or use carelessly or unnecessarily."

EXAMPLE   She tied a colorful scarf around her **waist**.

EXAMPLE   Buying those skis was a **waste** of money.

EXAMPLE   Put your **waste** in the dumpster.

EXAMPLE   Don't **waste** time worrying.

wait, weight *Wait* means "to stay or remain." *Weight* is a measurement.

EXAMPLE **Wait** right here.

EXAMPLE Her **weight** is 110 pounds.

wait for, wait on *Wait for* means "to remain in a place in anticipation of something expected." *Wait on* means "to act as a server."

EXAMPLE **Wait for** me at the bus stop.

EXAMPLE Nat and Tammy **wait on** diners at The Golden Griddle.

way, ways Use *way*, not *ways*, in referring to distance.

EXAMPLE It's a long **way** [*not* **ways**] to Tipperary.

weak, week *Weak* means "feeble" or "not strong." A *week* is seven days.

EXAMPLE She felt **weak** for a **week** after the operation.

weather, whether *Weather* is the condition of the atmosphere. *Whether* means "if"; it is also used to introduce the first of two choices.

EXAMPLE The **weather** in Portland is mild and rainy.

EXAMPLE Tell me **whether** you can go.

EXAMPLE I can't decide **whether** to fly or drive.

when, where Don't use *when* or *where* incorrectly in writing a definition.

EXAMPLE A simile is a comparison using *like* or *as*. [*not* **A simile is when you compare two things using** *like* **or** *as*.]

EXAMPLE A watercolor wash is a thin coat of paint applied to paper that has been dampened with water. [*not* **A watercolor wash is where you dampen the paper before applying paint.**]

where Don't use *where* in place of *that*.

EXAMPLE I see **that** [*not* **where**] the Cubs are in the basement again.

where . . . at Don't use *at* after *where*.

EXAMPLE **Where** is your mother? [*not* **Where is your mother at?**]

who, whom *Who* is the nominative case. Use it for subjects and predicate nominatives. *Whom* is the objective case. Use it for direct objects, indirect objects, and objects of prepositions.

EXAMPLE **Who** is that woman with the red umbrella?

EXAMPLE **Whom** did you see at the mall?

who's, whose *Who's* is a contraction of *who is* or *who has*. *Whose* is the possessive form of *who*.

EXAMPLE **Who's** [**Who is**] conducting the orchestra?

EXAMPLE **Who's** [**Who has**] read this book?

EXAMPLE **Whose** umbrella is this?

wind When *wind* rhymes with *finned*, it means "moving air." When *wind* rhymes with *fined*, it means "to wrap around."

EXAMPLE The **wind** is strong today.

EXAMPLE **Wind** the bandage around your ankle.

wood, would *Wood* comes from trees. *Would* is a helping verb.

EXAMPLE **Would** you prefer a **wood** bookcase or a metal one?

wound When *wound* is pronounced to rhyme with *sound*, it is the past tense of *wind*. When *wound* is pronounced wo͞ond, it means "an injury in which the skin is broken."

EXAMPLE   I **wound** the bandage around my ankle to cover the **wound**.

your, you're *Your* is the possessive form of *you*. *You're* is a contraction of *you are*.

EXAMPLE   **Your** arguments are convincing.

EXAMPLE   **You're** doing a fine job.

ABBREVIATIONS

An abbreviation is a short way to write a word or a group of words. Abbreviations should be used sparingly in formal writing except for a few that are actually more appropriate than their longer forms. These are *Mr., Mrs.,* and *Dr. (doctor)* before names, A.M. and P.M., and B.C. and A.D.

Some abbreviations are written with capital letters and periods, and some with capital letters and no periods; some are written with lowercase letters and periods, and some with lowercase letters and no periods. A few may be written in any one of these four ways and still be acceptable. For example, to abbreviate *miles per hour,* you may write *MPH, M.P.H., mph,* or *m.p.h.*

Some abbreviations may be spelled in more than one way. For example, *Tuesday* may be abbreviated *Tues.* or *Tue. Thursday* may be written *Thurs.* or *Thu.* In the following lists, only the most common way of writing each abbreviation is given.

When you need information about an abbreviation, consult a dictionary. Some dictionaries list abbreviations in a special section in the back. Others list them in the main part of the book.

MONTHS

Jan.	January	none	July
Feb.	February	Aug.	August
Mar.	March	Sept.	September
Apr.	April	Oct.	October
none	May	Nov.	November
none	June	Dec.	December

DAYS

Sun.	Sunday	Thurs.	Thursday
Mon.	Monday	Fri.	Friday
Tues.	Tuesday	Sat.	Saturday
Wed.	Wednesday		

TIME AND DIRECTION

CDT	central daylight time	MST	mountain standard time
CST	central standard time	PDT	Pacific daylight time
DST	daylight saving time	PST	Pacific standard time
EDT	eastern daylight time	ST	standard time
		NE	northeast
EST	eastern standard time	NW	northwest
		SE	southeast
MDT	mountain daylight time	SW	southwest

A.D.	in the year of the Lord (Latin *anno Domini*)
B.C.	before Christ
B.C.E.	before the common era
C.E.	common era
A.M.	before noon (Latin *ante meridiem*)
P.M.	after noon (Latin *post meridiem*)

MEASUREMENT

The same abbreviation is used for both the singular and the plural meaning of measurements. Therefore, *ft.* stands for both *foot* and *feet*, and *in.* stands for both *inch* and *inches.* Note that abbreviations of metric measurements are commonly written without periods. U.S. measurements, on the other hand, are usually written with periods.

Metric System

Mass and Weight

t	metric ton
kg	kilogram
g	gram
cg	centigram
mg	milligram

Capacity

kl	kiloliter
l	liter
cl	centiliter
ml	milliliter

Length

km	kilometer
m	meter
cm	centimeter
mm	millimeter

U.S. Weights and Measures

Weight

wt.	weight
lb.	pound
oz.	ounce

Capacity

gal.	gallon
qt.	quart
pt.	pint
c.	cup
tbsp.	tablespoon
tsp.	teaspoon
fl. oz.	fluid ounce

Length

mi.	mile
rd.	rod
yd.	yard
ft.	foot
in.	inch

MISCELLANEOUS MEASUREMENTS

p.s.i.	pounds per square inch
MPH	miles per hour
MPG	miles per gallon
d.p.i.	dots per inch
rpm	revolutions per minute
C	Celsius, centigrade
F	Fahrenheit
K	kelvin
kn	knot
kW	kilowatt

COMPUTER AND INTERNET

CPU	central processing unit
CRT	cathode ray tube
DOS	disk operating system
e-mail	electronic mail
K	kilobyte
URL	uniform resource locator
DVD	digital video disc
d.p.i	dots per inch
WWW	World Wide Web
ISP	internet service provider
DNS	domain name system

UNITED STATES (U.S.)

In most cases, state names and street addresses should be spelled out. The postal abbreviations in the following lists should be used with ZIP codes in addressing envelopes. They may also be used with ZIP codes for return addresses and inside addresses in business letters. The traditional state abbreviations are seldom used nowadays, but occasionally it's helpful to know them.

State	Traditional	Postal
Alabama	Ala.	AL
Alaska	none	AK
Arizona	Ariz.	AZ
Arkansas	Ark.	AR
California	Calif.	CA
Colorado	Colo.	CO
Connecticut	Conn.	CT
Delaware	Del.	DE
District of Columbia	D.C.	DC
Florida	Fla.	FL
Georgia	Ga.	GA
Hawaii	none	HI
Idaho	none	ID
Illinois	Ill.	IL
Indiana	Ind.	IN
Iowa	none	IA
Kansas	Kans.	KS
Kentucky	Ky.	KY
Louisiana	La.	LA
Maine	none	ME
Maryland	Md.	MD
Massachusetts	Mass.	MA
Michigan	Mich.	MI
Minnesota	Minn.	MN
Mississippi	Miss.	MS

Missouri	Mo.	MO
Montana	Mont.	MT
Nebraska	Nebr.	NE
Nevada	Nev.	NV
New Hampshire	N.H.	NH
New Jersey	N.J.	NJ
New Mexico	N. Mex.	NM
New York	N.Y.	NY
North Carolina	N.C.	NC
North Dakota	N. Dak.	ND
Ohio	none	OH
Oklahoma	Okla.	OK
Oregon	Oreg.	OR
Pennsylvania	Pa.	PA
Rhode Island	R.I.	RI
South Carolina	S.C.	SC
South Dakota	S. Dak.	SD
Tennessee	Tenn.	TN
Texas	Tex.	TX
Utah	none	UT
Vermont	Vt.	VT
Virginia	Va.	VA
Washington	Wash.	WA
West Virginia	W. Va.	WV
Wisconsin	Wis.	WI
Wyoming	Wyo.	WY

PEANUTS reprinted by permission of United
Feature Syndicate, Inc.

POSTAL ADDRESS ABBREVIATIONS

The following address abbreviations are recommended by the U.S. Postal Service to speed mailing. In most writing, these words should be spelled out.

Alley	ALY	North	N
Annex	ANX	Parkway	PKY
Avenue	AVE	Place	PL
Boulevard	BLVD	Plaza	PLZ
Center	CTR	River	RIV
Circle	CIR	Road	RD
Court	CT	South	S
Drive	DR	Square	SQ
East	E	Station	STA
Estates	EST	Street	ST
Expressway	EXPY	Terrace	TER
Heights	HTS	Trace	TRCE
Highway	HWY	Trail	TRL
Island	IS	Turnpike	TPKE
Lake	LK	Viaduct	VIA
Lane	LN	Village	VLG
Lodge	LDG	West	W
Mount	MT		

ADDITIONAL ABBREVIATIONS

ac	alternating current
dc	direct current
AM	amplitude modulation
FM	frequency modulation
RF	radio frequency
ASAP	as soon as possible
e.g.	for example (Latin *exempli gratia*)
etc.	and others, and so forth (Latin *et cetera*)
i.e.	that is (Latin *id est*)
Inc.	incorporated
ISBN	International Standard Book Number
lc	lowercase
misc.	miscellaneous
p.	page
pp.	pages
re	with regard to
R.S.V.P.	please reply (French *répondez s'il vous plaît*)
SOS	international distress signal
TM	trademark
uc	uppercase
vs.	versus
w/o	without

Part Two

• • • • • • • • • • • • •

Grammar, Usage, and Mechanics

Chapter 1

Parts of Speech

● ● ● ● ● ● ● ● ● ● ● ● ● ● ●

PRETEST **Identifying Parts of Speech**

For each numbered word in the paragraph below, write one of these words to identify its part of speech: noun, pronoun, verb, adjective, adverb, preposition, conjunction, interjection.

The end[1] of[2] each[3] school[4] year[5] is[6] a joyous[7] time[8] for[9] most[10] students. They[11] feel a sense of completion,[12] and[13] closure is[14] coupled[15] with[16] anticipation[17] of freedom[18] from rigid[19] schedules[20] and the opportunity[21] for relaxation. Vacation[22] usually[23] promises fun. The next[24] year seems[25] far away. For just a short[26] time,[27] the future looks rosy[28] and all[29] pressures are lifted. Alas,[30] a new school year is just three short months away.

1.1 NOUNS

A **noun** is a word that names a person, a place, a thing, or an idea.

EXAMPLES	**PERSON**	aunt, ecologist, Rodrigo, father-in-law, child
EXAMPLES	**PLACE**	playground, city, living room, Arizona
EXAMPLES	**THING**	moon, whale, chipmunk, Empire State Building
EXAMPLES	**IDEA**	democracy, hope, century, impatience

CONCRETE AND ABSTRACT NOUNS

A **concrete noun** names an object that occupies space or can be recognized by any of the senses.

| EXAMPLES | salt | whisper | thunder | sand | scent |

An **abstract noun** names an idea, a quality, or a characteristic.

| EXAMPLES | confusion | grief | patience | clarity | friendship |

SINGULAR AND PLURAL NOUNS

Most **nouns** are singular or plural. A singular noun names one person, place, thing, or idea. A plural noun names more than one.

| EXAMPLES | **SINGULAR** | boy, branch, story, hoof, woman |
| EXAMPLES | **PLURAL** | boys, branches, stories, hooves, women |

Write the plural form of each noun. Consult a dictionary if you need help.

1. reason
2. picture
3. melon
4. person
5. glass
6. keyboard
7. jury
8. democracy
9. ratio
10. child

PATIENCE IS A VIRTUE, YOUNG MAN

I THOUGHT IT WAS A NOUN

Used with permission. 1998 Vince McKeon.
Originally appeared in The Saturday Evening Post.

POSSESSIVE NOUNS

The possessive form of a noun can show possession, ownership, or the general relationship between two nouns. For instance, if we want to say "the chair of Lynn," we can say "**Lynn's** chair."

To form the possessive of a singular noun, even one that ends in *s*, add an apostrophe and an *s*.

EXAMPLES **Susie's** calculator   **Morris's** strobe light

To form the possessive of a plural noun that ends in *s*, add just an apostrophe.

EXAMPLES the **Wilsons'** newspaper   the **boys'** headaches

To form the possessive of a plural noun that doesn't end in *s*, add an apostrophe and an *s*.

EXAMPLES the **women's** meeting

the **sheep's** noses

PRACTICE **Possessive Form of Nouns**

Rewrite each phrase below, using the possessive form of the noun in parentheses.

1. the (tomato) color
2. the (restaurant) prices
3. the (professor) lecture
4. the (post office) location
5. the (sun) temperature
6. the (men) business cards
7. the (books) covers
8. the (secretaries) computers
9. the (trees) leaves
10. the (meetings) agendas

COMPOUND NOUNS

A **compound noun** is a noun made up of two or more words. Compound nouns may be open, hyphenated, or closed.

EXAMPLES **OPEN**	music box, press secretary, public defender	
EXAMPLES **HYPHENATED**	great-grandfather, good-bye, sister-in-law	
EXAMPLES **CLOSED**	bedroom, headache, mailbox	

COMMON AND PROPER NOUNS

A **common noun** is the general—not the particular—name of a person, place, thing, or idea.

A **proper noun** is the name of a particular person, place, thing, or idea.

Proper nouns are capitalized. Common nouns are usually not capitalized.

PROPER NOUNS

EXAMPLES	**PERSON**	James Baldwin, Toni Morrison, Sandra Cisneros
EXAMPLES	**PLACE**	Chicago, Great Britain, Antarctica, Madison Square Garden
EXAMPLES	**THING**	Ford Motor Company, World Trade Center, *Tom Sawyer*
EXAMPLES	**IDEA**	Jazz Age, Buddhism, Industrial Revolution, Romanticism

PRACTICE Common and Proper Nouns

Identify each noun by writing common *or* proper. *If a noun is common, also write* concrete *or* abstract *to further identify it.*

1. The Rocky Mountains in Colorado are majestic.
2. Cats are frequently accused of mischief.
3. A spirit of goodwill pervades the Special Olympics.
4. John eats tomatoes in the summer.
5. Henry met my aunts in Paris.

COLLECTIVE NOUNS

A **collective noun** is singular in form but names a group.

EXAMPLES	family	class	crew	band	committee
	troop	jury	flock	swarm	audience

A collective noun is sometimes considered singular and sometimes considered plural. If you're talking about a group as a whole acting together, consider the collective noun singular. If you're talking about the individual members of a group, consider the collective noun plural.

EXAMPLE **SINGULAR** The band *travels* in an old bus.

EXAMPLE **PLURAL** The band *are going* to assemble here at noon.

PRACTICE **Collective Nouns**

Write each collective noun. Label it S *if it's singular and* P *if it's plural.*

1. The committee is concluding its report.
2. The jury sit to the left of the judge.
3. During periods of heavy rain, the traffic police wear their rain gear.
4. The orchestra is opening the concert with an overture.
5. The herd grazes on government grassland.
6. The audience show their appreciation with applause.
7. Each winter the family goes skiing in Utah.
8. The band are wearing their uniforms.
9. The volleyball team received medallions last week.
10. The crowd cheers when the team enters the field.

1.2 PRONOUNS

A **pronoun** is a word that takes the place of a noun, a group of words acting as a noun, or another pronoun. The word or group of words to which a pronoun refers is called its **antecedent**.

EXAMPLE When N. Scott Momaday wrote *The Way to Rainy Mountain*, **he** was retelling Kiowa legends. [**The pronoun *he* takes the place of the noun *N. Scott Momaday*.**]

EXAMPLE Langston Hughes and Arna Bontemps were major figures of the Harlem Renaissance. **Both** edited *The Book of Negro Folklore*. [**The pronoun *both* takes the place of the nouns *Langston Hughes* and *Arna Bontemps*.**]

EXAMPLE Very **few** can still remember poems **they** memorized for class. [**The pronoun *they* takes the place of the pronoun *few*.**]

There are about seventy-five pronouns in English. Each pronoun belongs in one or more of these categories: personal and possessive pronouns, reflexive and intensive pronouns, demonstrative pronouns, interrogative pronouns, relative pronouns, and indefinite pronouns.

PERSONAL AND POSSESSIVE PRONOUNS

A **personal pronoun** refers to a specific person, place, thing, or idea by indicating the person speaking (the first person), the person or people being spoken to (the second person), or any other person, place, thing, or idea being talked about (the third person).

Personal pronouns express number—that is, they are either singular or plural.

PERSONAL PRONOUNS		
	SINGULAR	**PLURAL**
FIRST PERSON	I, me	we, us
SECOND PERSON	you	you
THIRD PERSON	he, him, she, her, it	they, them

EXAMPLE FIRST PERSON **We** will keep the pup with **us**. [***We*** and ***us*** refer to the people speaking.]

EXAMPLE SECOND PERSON **You** may use the spell-checking program. [***You*** refers to the person or people being addressed.]

EXAMPLE **THIRD PERSON** **They** accomplished all the tasks assigned to **them**. [*They* and *them* refer to persons being discussed.]

Third-person singular pronouns also express **gender**. *He* and *him* are masculine; *she* and *her* are feminine; *it* is neuter—that is, neither masculine nor feminine.

Among the personal pronouns are forms that show possession or ownership. These are called **possessive pronouns**, and they take the place of the possessive forms of nouns.

GRAMMAR/USAGE/MECHANICS

POSSESSIVE PRONOUNS

	SINGULAR	PLURAL
FIRST PERSON	my, mine	our, ours
SECOND PERSON	your, yours	your, yours
THIRD PERSON	his her, hers its	their, theirs

Some of the pronouns in the chart above are paired. In the pairs, the first form can be used before a noun. The second form in each pair can stand alone as a noun does. *His* and *its* can be used in both ways.

EXAMPLE **USED BEFORE A NOUN** Is that **her** journal?

EXAMPLE **USED ALONE** That journal is **hers**.

Notice that possessive pronouns do not contain apostrophes. Take particular note that the possessive pronoun *its* has no apostrophe. It is a common error to mistake *its* and the contraction *it's*.

EXAMPLE The cat was eating **its** food. [possessive pronoun]

EXAMPLE **It's** my mother's cat. [contraction for *It is*]

PRACTICE Personal Pronouns

Write each pronoun. Identify it by writing first person, second person, *or* third person. *Then write* singular *or* plural. *If the pronoun is possessive, write* possessive.

1. Workers must pay income tax if their earnings are in excess of a specified limit.
2. When the accused was confronted with the evidence, he confessed.
3. Deciduous trees lose their leaves in autumn.
4. Despite her heavy practice schedule, Jeanette maintained a B+ average.
5. Ours is the first house on the right.
6. We moved from Wyoming three years ago.
7. The dog wagged its tail.
8. Please fasten your seatbelts.
9. Dogs pant because they do not perspire as humans do.
10. I am amazed by the forces of nature.

REFLEXIVE AND INTENSIVE PRONOUNS

To form the reflexive and intensive pronouns, add *–self* or *–selves* to certain personal and possessive pronouns.

REFLEXIVE AND INTENSIVE PRONOUNS

	SINGULAR	PLURAL
FIRST PERSON	myself	ourselves
SECOND PERSON	yourself	yourselves
THIRD PERSON	himself, herself, itself	themselves

Notice that there are no such words as *hisself, theirself,* or *theirselves.*

A **reflexive pronoun** refers back to the subject of the sentence or clause and indicates that the same person or thing is involved. A reflexive pronoun adds information to a sentence.

EXAMPLE   We considered **ourselves** lucky to have avoided the tornado.

EXAMPLE   In stage makeup, I don't even look like **myself**.

An **intensive pronoun** adds emphasis to another noun or pronoun. It does not add information to a sentence. If the intensive pronoun is omitted, the meaning of the sentence will still be the same.

EXAMPLE   You **yourself** decided not to rename the file.

An **intensive pronoun** is often placed directly after its antecedent. However, an intensive pronoun may appear anywhere in a sentence.

EXAMPLE   I **myself** balanced the checkbook.

EXAMPLE   I balanced the checkbook **myself**.

DEMONSTRATIVE PRONOUNS

A **demonstrative pronoun** points out specific persons, places, things, or ideas.

DEMONSTRATIVE PRONOUNS		
SINGULAR	this	that
PLURAL	these	those

EXAMPLE   **This** is your new toothbrush.

EXAMPLE   Let me do **that** for you.

EXAMPLE   Are **these** the cookies you liked so well?

EXAMPLE   I think I'll take **those**.

INTERROGATIVE AND RELATIVE PRONOUNS

An **interrogative pronoun** is used to form questions.

INTERROGATIVE PRONOUNS		
who?	whom?	whose?
whoever?	whomever?	whatever?
which?	whichever?	what?

EXAMPLE   **Who** made this delicious salad dressing?

EXAMPLE   **Whom** are you expecting?

EXAMPLE   **Whose** are these cute earrings?

EXAMPLE   **What** did she say?

EXAMPLE   **Which** of the flavors is your favorite?

EXAMPLE   **Whatever** were you thinking?

EXAMPLE   **Whomever** are you calling at this time of night?

A **relative pronoun** is used to begin a special subject-verb word group called a subordinate clause. (See Chapter 4.)

RELATIVE PRONOUNS			
who	whoever	which	that
whom	whomever	whose	what
	whichever	whatever	

EXAMPLE Rhonda held out paper cups of water to the marathon runners, **who** grabbed them eagerly. [The relative pronoun *who* begins the subordinate clause *who grabbed them eagerly*.]

EXAMPLE The novel **that** she wrote is on the best-seller list. [The relative pronoun *that* begins the subordinate clause *that she wrote*.]

INDEFINITE PRONOUNS

An **indefinite pronoun** refers to a person, a place, a thing, or an idea in a more general way than a noun does.

EXAMPLE Do you know **anyone** in your class? [The indefinite pronoun *anyone* does not refer to a specific person.]

EXAMPLE **Several** have submitted applications for college. [The indefinite pronoun *several* does not refer to a specific group of people.]

EXAMPLE The group responsible for posters reported that **none** were ready. [The indefinite pronoun *none* has the specific antecedent *posters*.]

SOME INDEFINITE PRONOUNS

all	both	everything	nobody	others
another	each	few	none	several
any	either	many	no one	some
anybody	enough	most	nothing	somebody
anyone	everybody	much	one	someone
anything	everyone	neither	other	something

PRACTICE Pronouns

Write each pronoun. Identify it by writing reflexive,
intensive, demonstrative, interrogative, relative, *or*
indefinite.

1. The kitten saw itself in the mirror and scampered away.
2. Has anybody seen the car keys?
3. This is number one on the best-seller list of books.
4. For whom is the phone call?
5. Maria herself prepared every dessert on the menu.
6. The person whom the director appointed had ten years
of experience.
7. Deliver the memo to someone in the attendance office.
8. Steve and John need transportation to the game;
neither has a driver's license.
9. Which is the better choice?
10. Why is that so difficult a task?

1.3 VERBS

A **verb** is a word that expresses an action or a state
of being and is necessary to make a statement.

EXAMPLES   The author **summarized** his story.

The artist **cleaned** her brushes.

The actor **winked** at the audience.

This banner **appears** dusty.

Verbs express time—present, past, and future—by means of various *tense* forms.

EXAMPLE   **PRESENT TENSE**   I **smell** the roses.

EXAMPLE   **PAST TENSE**   I **smelled** the roses.

EXAMPLE   **FUTURE TENSE**   I **will smell** the roses.

ACTION VERBS

An **action verb** tells what someone or something does.

Action verbs can express action that is either physical or mental.

EXAMPLE   **PHYSICAL ACTION**   The chorus **sang** the new song.

EXAMPLE   **MENTAL ACTION**   The chorus **liked** the new song.

A **transitive verb** is followed by a word or words that answer the question *what?* or *whom?*

The word or words that answer the question *what?* or *whom?* after a transitive verb are called the **direct object.** (See Chapter 2.)

EXAMPLE   She **spoke** the words of the challenge. [**The verb *spoke* is followed by the noun *words*, which answers the question *spoke what?***]

An **intransitive verb** is *not* followed by a word that answers the question *what?* or *whom?*

EXAMPLE   She **spoke** clearly. [**The verb is followed by a word that tells *how*.**]

Write each verb. Identify it by writing transitive *or* intransitive. *If it is transitive, write the word or words that answer the questions* what? *or* whom?

1. Luis takes criticism very well.
2. Butterflies and hummingbirds prefer certain plants.
3. Tran worked diligently on his term paper.
4. A person gains respect more by actions than by words.
5. Everyone doubts himself or herself from time to time.
6. The sun sets early in the winter.
7. The water table rises after a drenching rain.
8. We finally settled on a price for the computer.
9. Sherry speaks four languages fluently.
10. History repeats itself.

LINKING VERBS

A **linking verb** links, or joins, the subject of a sentence (often a noun or a pronoun) with a noun, a pronoun, or an adjective that identifies or describes the subject. A linking verb does not show action.

Be in all its forms is the most commonly used linking verb. Forms of *be* include *am, is, are, was, were, will be, has been,* and *was being.*

EXAMPLES That tailor **is** an expert.

This spring **has been** rainy.

These rosebushes **are** rare.

Tomorrow **will be** a sunny day.

Several other verbs besides *be* can act as linking verbs.

OTHER VERBS THAT CAN BE LINKING VERBS

look	remain	seem	become
stay	grow	appear	sound
taste	smell	feel	turn

EXAMPLE   This lemonade **tastes** sour.

VERB PHRASES

The verb in a sentence may consist of more than one word. The words that accompany the main verb are called **auxiliary**, or helping, **verbs**.

A **verb phrase** consists of a main verb and all its auxiliary, or helping, verbs.

AUXILIARY VERBS			
FORMS OF BE	am, is, are, was, were, being, been		
FORMS OF HAVE	has, have, had, having		
OTHER AUXILIARIES	can, could do, does, did	may, might shall, should	must will, would

The most common auxiliary verbs are forms of *be* and *have*. They help the main verb express time by forming the various tenses.

EXAMPLE   We **had expected** the letter for days.

The other auxiliary verbs are not used primarily to express time. They are often used to emphasize meaning.

EXAMPLE   You **should exercise** daily.

PRACTICE Verbs and Verb Phrases

Write each verb and verb phrase. Identify it by writing transitive, intransitive, *or* linking.

1. Should I make another appointment?
2. On Sunday we will be going on a picnic.
3. Allie, see me after the third-period bell.
4. Could I be wrong about this?
5. The birds seem strangely quiet this morning.
6. Redeem these coupons for valuable merchandise.
7. This has been a special day!
8. The screenwriter has been making many script changes.
9. When will you be leaving?
10. They charted the plane's course to Detroit.

1.4 ADJECTIVES

An **adjective** is a word that modifies a noun or a pronoun by limiting its meaning.

EXAMPLES **three** dollars   **any** objections   **baby** ducks

Chinese teacup   **purple** balloon   **no** parking

An adjective may describe a noun or pronoun by answering one of these questions: *What kind? Which one? How many? How much?*

EXAMPLES **WHAT KIND?** **blue** scarf   **artistic** license

EXAMPLES **WHICH ONE?** **that** attitude   **second** try

EXAMPLES **HOW MANY?** **thirty** pages   **several** improvements

EXAMPLES **HOW MUCH?** **any** trouble   **no** mayonnaise

Two verb forms can also act as adjectives: the present participle, which ends in *–ing,* and the past participle, which ends in *–ed* or is irregularly formed.

EXAMPLES a **dancing** hen   the **crumpled** paper   a **broken** dish

Pronouns can also serve as adjectives. For example, possessive pronouns (*my, our, your, his, her, its,* and *their*) act as adjectives when they modify nouns. Demonstrative pronouns (*this, that, these,* and *those*) can also be considered demonstrative adjectives when they modify nouns. Similarly, nouns can serve as adjectives. Possessive nouns, like possessive pronouns, can be used as adjectives. In fact, any noun that modifies another noun can be considered an adjective.

EXAMPLES   **my** kitten **[possessive adjective]**

           those bicycles **[demonstrative adjective]**

           Lucy's report **[possessive noun acting as adjective]**

           leather shoes **[noun acting as adjective]**

An adjective's position in relation to the word it modifies may vary.

EXAMPLES   How **spicy** the *chili* is!

          The **spicy** *chili* steamed in its kettle.

          The *chili* is **spicy**.

          Peppers make the *chili* **spicy**.

          The *chili*, **spicy** as tamales, steamed in its kettle.

          Spicy as tamales, the *chili* steamed in its kettle.

PRACTICE **Adjectives**

Write each adjective and the word it modifies.

  1. The apple pie is delicious.
  2. Several large trees fell in the storm.

3. Strong winds radiate from the eye of a hurricane.
4. His left arm is in a soft cast.
5. Recycling makes good use of throwaway items.
6. The devastating poliovirus has been nearly eradicated in the United States.
7. I seldom wear my dress shoes.
8. Quiet music is soothing to babies.
9. A good stylist could hide that stubborn cowlick.
10. Fifty years is a short time in history.

FoxTrot

by Bill Amend

FOXTROT © Bill Amend. Reprinted with permission of UNIVERSAL PRESS SYNDICATE. All rights reserved.

ADJECTIVES THAT COMPARE

Many adjectives have different forms to indicate their degree of comparison. The **positive form** indicates no comparison. The **comparative form** compares two nouns or pronouns. The **superlative form** compares more than two nouns or pronouns.

EXAMPLES

POSITIVE	COMPARATIVE	SUPERLATIVE
slow	slower	slowest
lucky	luckier	luckiest
strenuous	more strenuous	most strenuous
good, well	better	best
bad	worse	worst

Adjectives That Compare

Write the correct comparative or superlative form of the adjective in parentheses. Consult a dictionary if necessary.

1. This is the (good) choice of the two.
2. I am (tall) than my brother.
3. Of the three athletes, Hal is (good).
4. That is the (complicated) math problem I have ever tackled.
5. The seniors voted Manuel (likely) to succeed.
6. This work is (difficult) than I had originally thought it was.
7. Let's go to the (sandy) beach we can find.
8. Mangoes are among the (sweet) fruits.
9. Your contribution will provide (good) programming than we now have.
10. Flu is usually (bad) than a cold.

ARTICLES

Articles are the adjectives *a, an,* and *the. A* and *an* are called **indefinite articles.** *A* is used before consonant sounds, and *an* is used before vowel sounds. *The* is called the **definite article.**

EXAMPLES

INDEFINITE	I wrote **a** play.	Ernesto wrote **an** article.
DEFINITE	I wrote **the** play.	Ernesto wrote **the** article.

PROPER ADJECTIVES

A **proper adjective** is formed from a proper noun and begins with a capital letter.

EXAMPLE   We attended the **Shakespearean** Drama Festival.

EXAMPLE   The **Texan** barbecue was a success.

EXAMPLE   The **Victorian** Era in England lasted from 1837 to 1901.

The following suffixes, along with others, are often used to form proper adjectives: *-an, -ian, -n, -ese,* and *-ish.* Sometimes there are other changes as well. Check the spelling in a dictionary.

EXAMPLES

PROPER NOUNS	PROPER ADJECTIVES
America	American
China	Chinese
England	English
Brazil	Brazilian
Africa	African

PRACTICE Proper Adjectives

Rewrite each phrase, changing the noun in blue type into a proper adjective. Consult a dictionary if necessary.

1. the soil of **Mexico**
2. the eruption of **Vesuvius**
3. the people of the **Netherlands**
4. the language of **Spain**
5. the coastline of the **Atlantic**
6. the islands of **Greece**
7. a citizen of **China**
8. the largest lake of **Russia**
9. the legislature of **Britain**
10. the food of **France**

1.5 ADVERBS

An **adverb** is a word that modifies a verb, an adjective, or another adverb by making its meaning more specific.

The following sentences illustrate the use of adverbs to modify verbs, adjectives, and adverbs.

EXAMPLES	**MODIFYING VERBS**	She ran **quickly**.
		She has **often** won.
EXAMPLE	**MODIFYING ADJECTIVES**	She is **very** talented and **extremely** diligent.
EXAMPLE	**MODIFYING ADVERBS**	She **almost** always runs **quite** fast.

Adverbs tell *when, where, how,* and *to what degree.*

EXAMPLE	**WHEN**	I got your letter **yesterday**.
EXAMPLE	**WHERE**	The wagon train headed **west**.
EXAMPLE	**HOW**	Play this section **softly** and **sweetly**.
EXAMPLE	**TO WHAT DEGREE**	This railing is **dangerously** rickety.

POSITION OF ADVERBS

An adverb that is modifying a verb can sometimes be placed in different positions in relation to the verb. An adverb that modifies an adjective or another adverb, however, must immediately precede the word it modifies.

EXAMPLES

MODIFYING A VERB	**Generally** we *eat* at six.
	We **generally** *eat* at six.
	We *eat* at six **generally**.
MODIFYING AN ADJECTIVE	The soup was **definitely** *lukewarm*.
MODIFYING AN ADVERB	We **almost** *never* have dessert.

NEGATIVE WORDS AS ADVERBS

The word *not* and the contraction *n't* are adverbs. Certain adverbs of time, place, and degree also have negative meanings.

EXAMPLES   The color did**n't** fade.

The dye **hardly ever** fades.

EXAMPLES   If correctly set, this dye **never** fades.

The tints can **barely** be distinguished.

EXAMPLES   There are **no** undyed patches.

We can**not** complain about the color.

PRACTICE Adverbs

Write each adverb and what it modifies. Then tell whether what is modified is a verb, *an* adjective, *or another* adverb.

1. Soraya often shops at outlet stores.
2. I am thoroughly disgusted!
3. Seldom can I select a good watermelon.
4. Please set the table properly.
5. A rather brisk wind is blowing.
6. The air conditioner is barely working.
7. In the spring, the grass grows too fast.
8. Lately, our math tests have been challenging.
9. My coach is somewhat dismayed by this year's schedule.
10. Dan is an unusually good driver.

ADVERBS THAT COMPARE

Some adverbs, like adjectives, have different forms to indicate the degree of comparison.

EXAMPLES

POSITIVE	COMPARATIVE	SUPERLATIVE
sat **near**	sat **nearer**	sat **nearest**
talks **slowly**	talks **more slowly**	talks **most slowly**
dances **well**	dances **better**	dances **best**
writes **badly**	writes **worse**	writes **worst**
draws **beautifully**	draws **more beautifully**	draws **most beautifully**
looks **far**	looks **farther**	looks **farthest**
left **early**	left **earlier**	left **earliest**

PRACTICE Adverbs That Compare

Write the comparative and superlative forms of each adverb. Consult a dictionary if necessary.

1. fast
2. carelessly
3. early
4. frequently
5. high

6. deeply
7. recently
8. delicately
9. poorly
10. low

1.6 PREPOSITIONS

A **preposition** is a word that shows the relationship of a noun or a pronoun to another word in a sentence.

EXAMPLE   The mother **of** the kittens lives here. [*Of* **shows the relationship of** *the mother* **to** *the kittens*.]

EXAMPLE   I will see you **after** lunch. [*After* **expresses the time relationship between** *lunch* **and when I** *will see* **you.**]

EXAMPLE   She sang her song **for** them. [*For* **relates the verb** *sang* **to the pronoun** *them*.]

COMMONLY USED PREPOSITIONS

aboard	beneath	in	regarding
about	beside	inside	respecting
above	besides	into	since
across	between	like	through
after	beyond	near	throughout
against	but (meaning *except*)	of	to
along	by	off	toward
amid	concerning	on	under
among	despite	onto	underneath
around	down	opposite	until
as	during	out	up
at	except	outside	upon
before	excepting	over	with
behind	for	past	within
below	from	pending	without

A **compound preposition** is a preposition that is made up of more than one word.

COMPOUND PREPOSITIONS

according to	because of	instead of
ahead of	by means of	next to
along with	except for	on account of
apart from	in addition to	on top of
aside from	in front of	out of
as to	in spite of	owing to

A **prepositional phrase** is a group of words that begins with a preposition and ends with a noun or a pronoun called the **object of the preposition**.

EXAMPLE Jorge and Mei Ling went **to the fair**.

EXAMPLE César rode **along with them**.

EXAMPLE I met them **at the candied-apples stand**.

EXAMPLE Everyone **but César** had a candied apple.

EXAMPLE César satisfied his sweet tooth **with saltwater taffy**.

Some words may be used as either prepositions or adverbs. A word is used as a preposition if it has a noun or a pronoun as its object. A word is used as an adverb if it does not have an object.

WORD USED AS PREPOSITION	**WORD USED AS ADVERB**
EXAMPLE I left my boots **outside** the back door.	I left my boots **outside**.
EXAMPLE The bird flew **over** the fence.	The bird flew **over**.
EXAMPLE Everyone came **aboard** the boat.	Everyone came **aboard**.

PRACTICE Prepositional Phrases

Write each prepositional phrase. Underline the preposition and draw a circle around the object of the preposition.

1. The diameter of a circle extends from one side to the other.
2. Because of the power outage, we could not videotape the game.
3. During my study period, I consulted the adviser about my schedule.
4. On the outskirts of town are several parks.
5. In spite of the heat, band practice continued through the afternoon and into the evening.

6. In the fifties, people danced to the music of the big bands.
7. The blue of the sea stretched to the horizon.
8. Without a guide, white-water rafting can be dangerous.
9. Snorkeling is good in the shallow waters around coral reefs.
10. In the beginning of summer, builders added a porch to the rear of our house.

1.7 CONJUNCTIONS

A **conjunction** is a word that joins single words or groups of words.

COORDINATING CONJUNCTIONS

A **coordinating conjunction** joins words or groups of words that have equal grammatical weight in a sentence.

COORDINATING CONJUNCTIONS						
and	but	or	so	nor	for	yet

EXAMPLE   Their skit includes a rabbit **and** a bird.

EXAMPLE   Ms. Fernandez dresses fashionably **but** tastefully.

EXAMPLE   Hang the snowshoes in the mudroom **or** in the garage.

EXAMPLE   Winter days are short, **so** houseplants may need extra light.

EXAMPLE   We didn't stop to ask directions, **nor** did we even consult a map.

EXAMPLE   I'm glad Andrea won first prize, **for** she deserves it.

EXAMPLE   Joe claims Italian descent, **yet** he doesn't like pasta.

CORRELATIVE CONJUNCTIONS

Correlative conjunctions work in pairs to join words and groups of words of equal grammatical weight in a sentence.

CORRELATIVE CONJUNCTIONS		
both . . . and	just as . . . so	not only . . . but (also)
either . . . or	neither . . . nor	whether . . . or

Correlative conjunctions make the relationship between words or groups of words a little clearer than do coordinating conjunctions.

EXAMPLES

COORDINATING CONJUNCTIONS	CORRELATIVE CONJUNCTIONS
Kim **and** I must test the software.	**Both** Kim **and** I must test the software.
You **or** José can make the call.	**Either** you **or** José can make the call.
He spray painted the security camera **and** robbed the bank.	He **not only** spray painted the security camera **but also** robbed the bank.

PRACTICE | Coordinating and Correlative Conjunctions

Write all conjunctions. Then identify them as either coordinating *or* correlative.

1. Do you want the apple or the pear?
2. I'll serve your eggs either scrambled or poached.
3. Neither the attorney nor the client wanted to appeal the case.
4. Was your trip to Hawaii in the spring or in the fall?

5. The bride's family hired a caterer to prepare the food and serve it.

6. Both Ricardo and Jessica won prizes for their writing.

7. She is allergic not only to cats but also to dogs.

8. Rain was forecast for today, but the skies are perfectly clear.

9. Whether a person is six or sixty, she can enjoy the beach.

10. I do not like the taste of squid, nor do I like the appearance of it.

SUBORDINATING CONJUNCTIONS

A **subordinating conjunction** joins two clauses, or thoughts, in such a way as to make one grammatically dependent on the other.

The thought, or clause, that a subordinating conjunction introduces is said to be subordinate, or dependent, because it cannot stand by itself as a complete sentence.

EXAMPLE **Since** you learned to dance, you have become more graceful.

EXAMPLE **Whenever** I skate, I wear elbow and knee pads.

EXAMPLE The children may come along **provided that** they stay with us.

EXAMPLE We sat by the lake **while** the sun set.

COMMON SUBORDINATING CONJUNCTIONS

after	as though	provided (that)	unless
although	because	since	until
as	before	so long as	when
as far as	considering (that)	so (that)	whenever

as if	if	than	where
as long as	inasmuch as	though	whereas
as soon as	in order that	till	wherever
			while

PRACTICE Subordinating Conjunctions

Write each subordinating conjunction.

1. Here is the spot where I usually fish for spotted trout.
2. If Sue calls, give her my message.
3. No one could explain how the trick was done.
4. Unless I am mistaken, the bell will ring in one minute.
5. You look as if you had seen a ghost.
6. Where you stand for the picture is not important.
7. Because there has been no rain, I am watering the lawn.
8. We cannot pay the landscapers inasmuch as they have not completed their work.
9. Provided that your plane is on time, we'll meet at the restaurant at eight.
10. When you are finished, please hand your paper to the proctor.

CONJUNCTIVE ADVERBS

A **conjunctive adverb** is used to clarify the relationship between clauses of equal grammatical weight in a sentence.

Conjunctive adverbs are usually stronger, more precise, and more formal than coordinating conjunctions. Notice that when a coordinating conjunction is used between clauses, a comma precedes the coordinating conjunction. When a conjunctive adverb is used between clauses, a semicolon precedes the conjunctive adverb, and a comma follows it.

EXAMPLES

COORDINATING CONJUNCTION	I don't mind bright green kitchen walls myself**, but** shouldn't we ask your mother?
CONJUNCTIVE ADVERB	I don't mind bright green kitchen walls myself**; still,** shouldn't we ask your mother?

Conjunctive adverbs have many uses, as the following examples show.

EXAMPLES	**TO REPLACE *AND***	also, besides, furthermore, moreover
EXAMPLES	**TO REPLACE *BUT***	however, nevertheless, nonetheless, still
EXAMPLES	**TO STATE A RESULT**	accordingly, consequently, then, therefore, thus
EXAMPLES	**TO STATE EQUALITY**	equally, likewise, similarly

PRACTICE Conjunctive Adverbs

Rewrite each sentence, changing coordinating conjunctions to conjunctive adverbs.

1. My older sister lives in Germany, but she visits us every spring.
2. Hillary is a sports enthusiast, so she often attends football games.
3. Joseph is a talented musician: He plays the piano, and he composes music for school plays.
4. Our French teacher is strict, but he is always fair.
5. Charles enjoys swimming, but his favorite pastime is reading.

6. I love the Pre-Raphaelites, so my friend Manuel gave me a book about Dante Gabriel Rossetti.
7. Tom Hanks starred in *Splash,* and he starred in *Sleepless in Seattle.*
8. My brother went away to school, but I decided to attend the local community college.
9. Danielle volunteers at the library, and she organizes fundraisers at the elementary school.
10. I tidy my desk every night, yet I often misplace my pencils.

1.8 INTERJECTIONS

An **interjection** is a word or a phrase that expresses emotion or exclamation. An interjection has no grammatical connection to other words in the sentence and is set off from the other words by an exclamation point or a comma.

Different emotions are expressed by different interjections.

EXAMPLE	**SURPRISE**	**Oh, my!** I had no idea.
EXAMPLE	**DELIGHT**	**Ah**, that's good.
EXAMPLE	**CONFUSION**	**Good grief!** Is that true?
EXAMPLE	**PAIN**	**Ouch!** That hurts.
EXAMPLE	**JOY**	**Wow!** This is super!

Interjections are mainly used in speaking. Use them sparingly when you write.

PRACTICE Interjections

Identify each interjection.

1. Oh, no! I've lost my keys again.
2. Thank goodness, I found them.

3. Whew, that test was hard!

4. Ha, I caught you.

5. Yippee! We both aced the exam.

6. Your diamond ring is beautiful. Wow!

7. Alas, it's started to rain.

8. Ah, that lotion feels good on my sunburn.

9. You can come to the party? Fantastic!

10. Hey, what are you doing?

PRACTICE | Parts of Speech

Use each word below in two sentences as two different parts of speech. You will write a total of twenty sentences. In each sentence, circle the word. After each sentence, give the word's part of speech.

EXAMPLE   bow

She wore a (bow) in her hair. noun.

The dancers (bow) after each performance. verb

1. this

2. fast

3. outside

4. those

5. picture

6. well

7. color

8. over

9. but

10. star

PRACTICE | Proofreading

Rewrite the following passage, correcting errors in spelling, capitalization, grammar, and usage. Add any missing punctuation. There are ten errors. Some sentences are correct.

Colonial Literature

[1]The subjects of american colonial literature were as diverse as the people who settled America. [2]Some colonial literature had religious themes. [3]*The New England Primer,* for example, was a childrens'

textbook that used religious instruction to teach reading, writing, and arithmetic. [4]Among the most famous literature from this period was a sermon called *Sinners in the Hands of an Angry God* by Jonathan edwards. [5]Edwards wrote his' sermon to convince colonialists to adopt the religious commitment of the first Puritan settlers. [6]His congregation was very moved when they heard this passionate sermon.

[7]Some writers was moved by the injustice of slavery. [8]Samuel Sewall wrote *The Selling of Joseph,* which became a early anti-slavery tract. [9]Abolitionists read this tract one hundred years after it's publication in 1700. [10]It is one of the most good arguments against slavery ever written.

[11]Colonial literature was based on the beliefs and experiences of the writers. [12]Students who read colonial literature today can imagine theirselves living in these interesting times.

POSTTEST **Identifying Parts of Speech**

For each numbered word in the paragraph below, write one of these words to identify its part of speech: noun, pronoun, verb, adjective, adverb, preposition, conjunction, interjection.

When I[1] was a little[2] kid,[3] my toys were[4] my friends.[5] We played[6] together.[7] I talked[8] to them.[9] My very[10] favorite[11] toy was my Big Wheel, a snazzy[12] black and blue tricycle[13] with[14] big, black plastic[15] wheels.[16] Up[17] and down[18] the driveway[19] I clacked,[20] feeling so very grown up and powerful.[21] I would whisper,[22] "Go faster! [23] Go faster!" as[24] my beauty[25] sped downhill.[26] Alas,[27] all[28] of my pride was shattered when[29] my plastic friend and I collided[30] with the garbage can!

Chapter 2

Parts of the
Sentence

• • • • • • • • • • • • • • • • •

PRETEST   **Identifying Subjects and Predicates**

Identify each underlined word or group of words in the paragraph by writing one of these labels: simple subject, complete subject, simple predicate, complete predicate.

Public <u>parks</u>[1] <u>are assets to any town or city</u>.[2] They <u>are</u>[3] pleasant places for people of all ages. <u>Young children</u>[4] <u>use the playground equipment</u>.[5] There are often <u>ballparks</u>[6] for softball and baseball. <u>Some parks</u>[7] <u>have picnic tables and shelter houses</u>.[8] <u>In large parks may be found</u>[9] <u>restroom facilities</u>.[10] <u>Trees, grass, and colorful flowers</u>[11] <u>beautify a park and make an oasis in a city</u>.[12] The attractive green <u>space</u>[13] <u>is a welcome break from buildings and pavement</u>.[14] Are there <u>adequate parks</u>[15] near you?

Identify each underlined word or group of words by writing one of these labels: direct object, indirect object, object complement, predicate nominative, predicate adjective.

The Great Smoky Mountains of North Carolina and Tennessee are a North American <u>treasure</u>.[16] They challenge the <u>hiker</u>[17] and offer <u>him</u>[18] or her panoramic <u>vistas</u>[19] of surrounding states. The mountain streams are cold and <u>clear</u>.[20] Wildlife abounds. Visitors can frequently photograph <u>bears</u>[21] during the summer season. Some consider <u>them</u>[22] a <u>nuisance</u>[23] because they scavenge for food, but the sight of a mother and her cubs is almost always a <u>cause</u>[24] for excitement. The mountain flora is <u>beautiful</u>,[25] especially in spring and fall. Laurels and rhododendrons provide soft <u>color</u>[26] in the spring; in autumn the forests look <u>beautiful</u>[27] with brilliant red, yellow, and orange leaves. Gatlinburg, at the foot of the mountains, is the main tourist <u>center</u>[28] for the area. It offers <u>visitors</u>[29] <u>entertainment</u>[30] as well as food and lodging.

2.1 SIMPLE SUBJECTS AND SIMPLE PREDICATES

A **sentence** is a group of words that expresses a complete thought.

Every sentence has two basic parts, a *subject* and a *predicate*.

The **subject** is the part of the sentence that names whom or what the sentence is about.

The **predicate** is the part of the sentence that says something about the subject.

Both the subject and the predicate can consist of more than one word.

The **simple subject** is the key noun or pronoun that tells whom or what the sentence is about.

The **simple predicate** is the verb or verb phrase that expresses the action or state of being of the subject of the sentence.

Remember, a simple predicate that is a verb phrase consists of a verb and any auxiliary, or helping, verbs.

EXAMPLES

SIMPLE SUBJECT	SIMPLE PREDICATE
Nikki Giovanni	writes.
Everyone	will attend.
Cookies	were baking.
Traffic	slowed.

You find the simple subject by asking *who?* or *what?* about the verb. For example, in the first sentence above, the proper noun *Nikki Giovanni* answers the question *Who writes?*

"GOT IDEA. TALK BETTER. COMBINE WORDS. MAKE SENTENCES."

Reprinted by permission of Sidney Harris

Write each simple subject and simple predicate. Underline the simple predicate.

1. The members of the track team have been striving for perfection.
2. An assortment of rare books is on the shelf.
3. In preparation for the bar examination, Elena has been studying around the clock.
4. The woodchuck slept soundly in its winter quarters underground.
5. Grains of salt clung to the hot, buttered corn.
6. The family had agreed on their course of action.
7. The sandpipers in single file hopped along the shore at the water's edge.
8. Our friends from Nebraska will be visiting here in May.
9. Not a sound could be heard that night.
10. The road through the woods suddenly came to an end.

2.2 COMPLETE SUBJECTS AND COMPLETE PREDICATES

In most sentences, the addition of other words and phrases to the simple subject and the simple predicate expands or modifies the meaning of the sentence.

The **complete subject** consists of the simple subject and all the words that modify it.

The **complete predicate** consists of the simple predicate (the verb or verb phrase) and all the words that modify it or complete its meaning.

COMPLETE SUBJECT	COMPLETE PREDICATE
The celebrated Nikki Giovanni	writes fantastic poetry.
Everyone in the French club	will attend the meeting.
Chocolate chip cookies	were baking in the oven.
The rush-hour traffic	slowed to a snail's pace.

PRACTICE Complete Subjects and Complete Predicates

Identify each underlined complete subject or complete predicate by writing CS *(complete subject) or* CP *(complete predicate).*

1. Several prize-winning posters <u>are being displayed this week</u>.
2. <u>The Aztecs of Mexico</u> played a game similar to basketball.
3. A disturbing haze <u>appeared in the distance</u>.
4. The country of France <u>presented the Statue of Liberty to the United States</u>.
5. One of my friends <u>gave me a recipe for making bread</u>.
6. <u>My friend Harold</u> has been waiting twenty minutes for the bus.
7. Our trip <u>was organized yesterday</u>.
8. <u>Julio and his team members</u> outlined their ideas for the debate.
9. <u>The Mississippi River</u> flows south through the center of the United States.
10. <u>Our refrigerator door</u> is covered with photographs.

2.3 COMPOUND SUBJECTS AND COMPOUND PREDICATES

A **compound subject** is made up of two or more simple subjects that are joined by a conjunction and have the same verb.

Coordinating and correlative conjunctions are commonly used to join the subjects in a compound subject.

EXAMPLE **Books** and **magazines** are sold at the new store.

EXAMPLE **Water** or **soda** will be served with dinner.

EXAMPLE Neither the **bus** nor the **subway** goes there.

EXAMPLE Both **experience** and adequate **training** are necessary.

When there are more than two subjects in the compound subject, the conjunction is usually used only between the last two words, and the words are separated by commas.

EXAMPLE **Crimson, cerise,** and **vermilion** are shades of red.

Some sentences have more than one simple predicate.

A **compound predicate** (or **compound verb**) is made up of two or more verbs or verb phrases that are joined by a conjunction and have the same subject.

EXAMPLE Artists **draw** and **paint**.

EXAMPLE Yvette **sat** on a bench, **opened** her lunch box, and **ate** a sandwich.

In compound verbs that contain verb phrases, the auxiliary verb may or may not be repeated before the second verb.

EXAMPLE Cats **will hiss** and **will scratch** when frightened.

EXAMPLE Cats **will hiss** and **scratch** when frightened.

A sentence may have both a compound subject and a compound predicate.

EXAMPLE **Comedians** and **musicians delight** and **entertain** audiences.

Compound Subjects and Compound Predicates

Write CS if a sentence has a compound subject. Write CP if a sentence has a compound predicate. Then write each simple subject and simple predicate.

1. The bird flew out the window and disappeared.
2. Cheese and walnuts are delicious additions to a salad.
3. Richie and his sister learned French.
4. For my birthday, my brother washed and waxed my car and also filled the gas tank.
5. Fresh flowers and sunshine make a room cheerful.
6. Your teacher or your principal will give you your schedule and direct you to your locker.
7. Sima and her friend jog together every morning.
8. Peanuts, Linus, and Peppermint Patty are my favorite cartoon characters.
9. Neither sunrise nor sunset was visible today through the gloom.
10. Blue, white, and red are the colors of the French flag.

2.4 ORDER OF SUBJECT AND PREDICATE

In English the subject comes before the verb in most sentences. Some exceptions to this normal word order are discussed below.

In **commands** and **requests**, the subject is usually not stated. The predicate is the entire sentence. The pronoun *you* is understood to be the subject.

EXAMPLES [You] Listen!   [You] Please see me.   [You] Be careful.

Questions frequently begin with a verb or a helping verb or the words *who, whom, what, when, where, why,* or *how.*

EXAMPLE **Did** he reply?

EXAMPLE **Have** you **read** Nikki Giovanni's poetry?

EXAMPLE **What** do they sing?

In these cases, the subject generally follows the verb or helping verb. To find the subject of a question, rearrange the words to form a statement.

	SUBJECT	PREDICATE
EXAMPLE	He	did reply.
EXAMPLE	You	have read Nikki Giovanni's poetry.
EXAMPLE	They	do sing what.

A sentence written in **inverted order**, in which the predicate comes before the subject, serves to add emphasis to the subject.

	PREDICATE	SUBJECT
EXAMPLE	Under the moonlight **sat**	the old cypress **tree.**
EXAMPLE	Above the forest **circled**	three **hawks.**

Remember, a word in a prepositional phrase is never the subject.

When the word *there* or *here* begins a sentence and is followed by a form of the verb *to be*, the subject follows the verb. The word *there* or *here* is almost never the subject of a sentence.

	PREDICATE	SUBJECT
EXAMPLE	Here **are**	the **quilts** from my grandma.
EXAMPLE	There **is**	the **book** on the table.

PRACTICE Simple Subjects and Simple Predicates

Write each simple subject and simple predicate. If a subject is understood, write (You).

1. At the edge of the forest stood a watchful deer.

2. Please pass the salt.

3. Here is your first-period classroom.
4. Devastating were the effects of the tornado!
5. Why was the siren blaring?
6. Dip the fish in the batter and lower it into the fryer.
7. From the west came a driving rain.
8. Did you see the meteor shower last night?
9. Not a scrap of food remained after the picnic.
10. Print your full name on the first line.

2.5 COMPLEMENTS

A **complement** is a word or a group of words that completes the meaning of a verb.

There are four kinds of complements: *direct objects, indirect objects, object complements,* and *subject complements.*

DIRECT OBJECTS

A **direct object** answers the question *what?* or *whom?* after an action verb.

The subject of a sentence usually performs the action indicated by the verb. That action may be directed toward or received by someone or something—the direct object. Direct objects are nouns, pronouns, or words acting as nouns; and they may be compound. Only transitive verbs have direct objects.

EXAMPLE Estella sold her **computer**. [Estella sold *what?*]

EXAMPLE Tamara watched the **professor**. [Tamara watched *whom?*]

EXAMPLE Estella sold her **computer** and **radio**. [Estella sold *what?*]

INDIRECT OBJECTS

> An **indirect object** answers the question *to whom? for whom? to what?* or *for what?* after an action verb.

A sentence can have an indirect object only if it has a direct object. Two clues can help you identify indirect objects. First, an indirect object always comes between the verb and the direct object.

EXAMPLE   The owner gave **us** a discount. [**The owner gave a discount *to whom?***]

EXAMPLE   Ahmad bought **Jeremy** and **Sean** candy. [**Ahmad bought candy *for whom?***]

Second, if you add the word *to* or *for* in front of an indirect object, the sentence will still make sense.

EXAMPLE   Rami left Jennifer a message.

Rami left a message for Jennifer.

Notice that in the second sentence, the proper noun *Jennifer* is no longer an indirect object. It has become the object of a preposition. (See Chapter 1.)

OBJECT COMPLEMENTS

> An **object complement** answers the question *what?* after a direct object. That is, it *completes* the meaning of the direct object by identifying or describing it.

Object complements occur only in sentences with direct objects and only in those sentences with the following action verbs or with similar verbs that have the general meaning of "make" or "consider":

appoint	consider	make	render
call	elect	name	think
choose	find	prove	vote

An object complement usually follows a direct object. It may be an adjective, a noun, or a pronoun.

EXAMPLE   The bonus made Susan **happy**. [adjective]

EXAMPLE   I named my dog **Sadie**. [proper noun]

EXAMPLE   Our cat considers that pillow **hers**. [pronoun]

SUBJECT COMPLEMENTS (PREDICATE NOMINATIVES, PREDICATE ADJECTIVES)

A **subject complement** follows a subject and a linking verb and identifies or describes the subject.

There are two kinds of subject complements: *predicate nominatives* and *predicate adjectives*.

A **predicate nominative** is a noun or a pronoun that follows a linking verb and points back to the subject to rename it or to identify it further.

EXAMPLE   Cellists are **musicians**.

EXAMPLE   The soloist for this concert is **someone** from Dallas.

EXAMPLE   My favorite singer is **he**.

Predicate nominatives are usually found in sentences that contain forms of the linking verb *be*. A few other linking verbs as well (for example, *become* and *remain*) can be followed by a predicate nominative.

EXAMPLE   Alexis remains an **admirer** and a **friend**.

EXAMPLE   That class became a **challenge** for me.

A **predicate adjective** is an adjective that follows a linking verb and points back to the subject and further describes it.

EXAMPLE   My sister is **generous**.

EXAMPLE   Some doctors are **compassionate**.

Predicate adjectives may follow any linking verb.

EXAMPLE   I feel very **insecure**.

EXAMPLE   The coffee shop looked **busy**.

EXAMPLE   The author seemed **intelligent** and **thoughtful**.

EXAMPLE   Lori's tale sounded **preposterous** to me.

EXAMPLE   The boy appeared **happy**.

EXAMPLE   Dinner smells **delicious**.

EXAMPLE   The milk tastes **sour**.

PRACTICE Complements

Write each complement and identify it by writing DO *for a direct object,* IO *for an indirect object,* OC *for an object complement,* PN *for a predicate nominative, or* PA *for a predicate adjective.*

1. My favorite playwright is William Shakespeare.
2. Not one person considered Claude our leader.
3. George became the head lifeguard at the city pool.
4. The team voted Li and Nancy co-captains.
5. The volcano eruption was terrifying.
6. The lull in the storm gave the tourists a false sense of security.
7. Try the hard-boiled eggs.

8. Julia Child demonstrated the technique for kneading bread.
9. The young couple named their baby Vincenzo.
10. My mediocre grades were predictable.

PRACTICE Proofreading

Rewrite the following passage, correcting errors in spelling, capitalization, grammar, and usage. Add any missing punctuation. There are ten errors. Some sentences are correct.

Phillis Wheatley

[1]Phillis Wheatley was only seventeen when her first collection of poems, *Poems on Various Subjects, Religious and Moral,* was published [2]Wheatleys collection recieved much public attention because Wheatley was so young and because she was an enslaved woman.

[3]Phillis Wheatley was born in Africa and was kidnapped and sent to boston in 1761 at the age of eight. [4]She became a enslaved person in the home of John and Susannah Wheatley. [5]The Wheatleys recognized Phillis's talent, and they taught her to read English and Latin. [6]At age thirteen, Phillis wrote her first poem, and she became a celebrity in Boston and around the world.

[7]Two important events occured in Wheatley's life when she turned twenty. [8]She was formally granted her freedom she traveled to England. [9]When she returned to Boston, she continued to write poetry. [10]In 1778 Wheatley married John Peters, a free african american man.

[11]by the end of her short life, Wheatley was working as a servant because her husband had been imprisoned for debt. [12]In spite of her literary genius, she died poor and alone. [13]At age thirty-one. [14]However, in the 1830s, over fifty years after her death, abolitionists reprinted her poems, and her literary talents were once again celebrated.

Identify each underlined word or group of words in the paragraph by writing one of these labels: simple subject, complete subject, simple predicate, complete predicate.

A well-equipped kitchen[1] is a necessity for a gourmet cook.[2] Mixers and blenders[3] are considered standard equipment.[4] A fully-stocked spice rack[5] makes available to the cook a selection of seasonings.[6] There must be[7] a good collection[8] of utensils as well. In the cupboards should be[9] all sizes of baking pans and dishes.[10] Various pots, pans, and kettles[11] are[12] necessary too. How would a cook[13] manage without a good stove? It[14] is the most important appliance in the work area.[15]

Identify each underlined word or group of words by writing one of these labels: direct object, indirect object, object complement, predicate nominative, predicate adjective.

Bird feeders can provide us[16] yearlong enjoyment.[17] Finches, bluebirds, and cardinals are colorful.[18] The songs of many birds are delightful[19] to hear. We can place the feeders[20] right outside a window for close-up viewing. The experience of bird-watching is an education.[21] We can also consider it[22] quiet entertainment.[23] Ornithologists give us[24] one important piece[25] of advice, though. Birds need this food supply[26] all year, so we must be faithful[27] in our feeding and replenish the feeder[28] regularly. We must consider ourselves[29] the birds' caretakers.[30]

GRAMMAR/USAGE/MECHANICS

Chapter 3

Phrases

● ● ● ● ● ● ● ● ● ● ● ● ● ● ● ●

PRETEST **Identifying Prepositional Phrases**

There are ten prepositional phrases in the paragraph below. Write the prepositional phrases. For each, write the word or words modified by the phrase. Then write ADJ (adjective) or ADV (adverb) to identify the type of phrase.

The bride came down the steps of the circular stairway and threw her bouquet toward the crowd of young girls. Her junior bridesmaid, who caught it, jumped for joy. At home, she dried the flowers in a dark closet as a memento of a perfect day in her young life.

PRETEST **Identifying Verbals and Appositives**

Identify each italicized word by writing one of these labels: participle, gerund, infinitive, appositive.

11. I was beginning to sound like a *broken* record.

12. *Working* as quickly as he could, Pedro secured the boat.

13. My brother bought an antique car, an MG *convertible.*

14. *To win* fairly is the goal.

15. The old house, a Tudor *mansion,* could be a beautiful residence.

16. I am not good at *typing.*

17. The parade is about *to start.*

18. A captain is not to leave a *sinking* ship until all the passengers have safely disembarked.

19. *Sewn* into the hem of the draperies, small weights keep the fabric hanging correctly.

20. You will enjoy *swimming* in that pool.

Identify each italicized group of words by writing one of these labels: prepositional phrase, appositive phrase, participial phrase, infinitive phrase, gerund phrase, absolute phrase.

21. On a farm, one gets accustomed to *working in the heat.*

22. We arrived safely, *the roads being dry and virtually free of traffic.*

23. *By midsummer* the corn was in tassel.

24. *Learning a new language* is difficult for many people.

25. *Waiting impatiently for the rain to stop,* my grandmother paced at the door of the grocery.

26. The storm raged *along the southern coastline.*

27. I have always wanted *to learn woodworking.*

28. *Struck by lightning,* the tree bears a six-inch scar from top to bottom.

29. Fruits and vegetables, *the vitamin-rich foods,* are also the colorful ones.

30. Many cities encourage residents *to separate recyclable items.*

3.1 PREPOSITIONAL PHRASES

A **phrase** is a group of words that acts in a sentence as a single part of speech.

A **prepositional phrase** is a group of words that begins with a preposition and ends with a noun or a pronoun, which is called the **object of the preposition.**

EXAMPLE   The new picture hangs **on the wall.**
[*Wall* is the object of the preposition *on.*]

EXAMPLE   The room **beside the kitchen** is empty.
[*Kitchen* is the object of the preposition *beside.*]

EXAMPLE   That puzzle is too difficult **for me.**
[*Me* is the object of the preposition *for.*]

For a list of common prepositions, see page 120.

Be careful to distinguish between the preposition *to* (**to** *the house,* **to** *Tucson*) and the *to* that marks an infinitive (**to** *read,* **to** *jog*). See pages 153–154 for more about infinitives.

Adjectives and other modifiers may be placed between a preposition and its object. Also, a preposition may have more than one object.

EXAMPLE   He looked **across the broad, serene river.**
[adjectives added]

EXAMPLE   The view was **to the east and the south.** [two objects]

Prepositional phrases may also occur in a sequence of two or more.

EXAMPLE   The bird **at the top of that tree** is chirping.

A prepositional phrase usually functions as an adjective or an adverb. When it is used as an adjective, it modifies a noun or a pronoun and is called an *adjective phrase.* An adjective phrase always follows the word it modifies.

EXAMPLE   I pressed the button **on the right.**
[adjective phrase modifying the noun *button*]

EXAMPLE   Which **of the buttons** starts the engine?
[adjective phrase modifying the pronoun *which*]

When a prepositional phrase is used as an adverb, it modifies a verb, an adjective, or an adverb and is called an *adverb phrase*.

EXAMPLE   **After work** I returned the shirt **to the store.**
[adverb phrases modifying the verb *returned*]

EXAMPLE   This bus will be convenient **for you.**
[adverb phrase modifying the adjective *convenient*]

EXAMPLE   This lawnmower works well **for its age.**
[adverb phrase modifying the adverb *well*]

An adverb phrase that modifies a verb may appear in different positions in a sentence.

EXAMPLE   She wore a beautiful diamond ring **on her finger.**
[adverb phrase modifying *wore*]

EXAMPLE   She wore **on her finger** a beautiful diamond ring.
[adverb phrase modifying *wore*]

EXAMPLE   **On her finger,** she wore a beautiful diamond ring.
[adverb phrase modifying *wore*]

Writing Tip

Place adjective and adverb phrases exactly where they belong.
A misplaced phrase can be confusing. See page 269 for more about misplaced modifiers.

Write the prepositional phrases. For each, write the word or words modified by the phrase. Then write ADJ *(adjective) or* ADV *(adverb) to identify the type of phrase.*

1. In the morning, please water the garden.
2. Everyone should drink eight glasses of water a day.
3. The nightly news is a summary of the day's events.
4. Please keep this information to yourself.
5. The primary colors can be seen in a rainbow.
6. I am carrying a pocketful of change.
7. For my family, I would do almost anything.
8. The ground under the front porch remains damp all year.
9. Because we were late, we stopped at a fast food restaurant.
10. Across the street lives my best friend.

3.2 APPOSITIVES AND APPOSITIVE PHRASES

An **appositive** is a noun or a pronoun that is placed next to another noun or pronoun to identify it or give additional information about it.

EXAMPLE   My sister **Jodi** works at the hospital. [**The appositive Jodi identifies the noun *sister*.**]

An **appositive phrase** is an appositive plus any words that modify the appositive.

EXAMPLE   She works with Dr. Martin, **an award-winning pediatrician.** [**The appositive phrase, in blue type, identifies *Dr. Martin*.**]

Use commas to set off any appositive or appositive phrase that is not essential to the meaning of the sentence.

EXAMPLE Jodi's coworker **Emma** has five children. [**The appositive** *Emma* **is essential because Jodi has more than one coworker.**]

EXAMPLE Emma's husband, **Phil,** is a carpenter. [**The appositive** *Phil* **is not essential because Emma has only one husband.**]

Usually an appositive or an appositive phrase follows the noun or pronoun it identifies or explains. Occasionally an appositive phrase precedes the noun or pronoun.

EXAMPLE **A compassionate person,** Jodi helps many patients.

PRACTICE **Appositives and Appositive Phrases**

Write each appositive or appositive phrase and the noun or pronoun that is identified or explained by the appositive.

1. My friend Liam has applied to four law schools.
2. Those trees, an elm and a maple, are giants.
3. The boxing match, a championship bout, is on television tonight.
4. Our best mechanic, Don has worked here for many years.
5. Mail your story to Mr. Arcaro, the contest director.
6. The potato, a good source of Vitamin C, is a member of the nightshade family.
7. An oil refinery, this plant is important to the town's economy.
8. The novel *To Kill a Mockingbird* remains a favorite.
9. A valuable player, Rocco will be missed in tonight's playoff game.
10. The finale, five minutes of spectacular fireworks, delighted the Fourth of July crowd.

3.3 VERBALS AND VERBAL PHRASES

A **verbal** is a verb form that functions in a sentence as a noun, an adjective, or an adverb.

A **verbal phrase** is a verbal plus any complements and modifiers.

Verbals are *participles, gerunds,* and *infinitives.* Each of these can be expanded into phrases.

PARTICIPLES AND PARTICIPIAL PHRASES

A **participle** is a verb form that can function as an adjective.

Present participles always end in *-ing (losing).* Past participles often end in *-ed (winded),* but some are irregularly formed *(broken).* Many commonly used adjectives are actually participles.

EXAMPLE   The baseball team is on a **losing** streak.
[present participle as an adjective]

EXAMPLE   The **winded** runner stopped to rest.
[past participle as an adjective]

EXAMPLE   The **fallen** trees were remnants of a **devastating** storm. **[irregular past participle and present participle as adjectives]**

When a participle is part of a verb phrase, the participle is not functioning as an adjective.

EXAMPLES

PARTICIPLE AS AN ADJECTIVE   The **lost** package was never recovered.

PARTICIPLE IN A VERB PHRASE   The warehouse **had lost** my shipment

A **participial phrase** contains a participle plus any complements and modifiers.

Participial phrases can be placed in various positions in a sentence. They always act as adjectives.

EXAMPLE **Preparing for the lunar eclipse,** we set our alarm clocks.

EXAMPLE The full moon, **suspended in the sky,** was brilliant.

EXAMPLE **Badly needing sleep** but **delighted by the spectacle,** we maintained our vigil.

A participial phrase at the beginning of a sentence is usually followed by a comma.

A past participle may be used with the present participle of the auxiliary verb *have* or *be.*

EXAMPLE **Having read about the eclipse,** we were anxious to see it.

EXAMPLE We watched the moon **being consumed by shadow.**

PRACTICE **Participles and Participial Phrases**

Write the participles and participial phrases. Then write the word or words each participle or participial phrase modifies.

1. The gathering clouds foretold a storm.
2. Born in Italy, Dino moved first to France and then to the United States.
3. Having learned German as a child, I could understand Florian.
4. These shoes, made of cork, are very comfortable.
5. Refreshed after a long night's sleep, the golfer shot an amazing second round.
6. Newly clipped and groomed, the poodle hid under the bed in embarrassment.

7. The fallen apples littered the ground.
8. Dreaming of sun and surf, the three women booked passage on a cruise ship to the tropics.
9. After the fire, nothing was left but some charred furniture.
10. Maria, being a realist, spoke openly about the problem.

GERUNDS AND GERUND PHRASES

A **gerund** is a verb form that ends in *-ing* and is used in the same way a noun is used.

EXAMPLE **Training** is essential. [gerund as subject]

EXAMPLE My aunt enjoys **golfing**. [gerund as direct object]

EXAMPLE We should give **communicating** more attention. [gerund as indirect object]

EXAMPLE Do we get credit for **trying?** [gerund as object of preposition]

EXAMPLE His passion was **sailing**. [gerund as predicate nominative]

EXAMPLE My favorite sports, **boxing** and **wrestling**, require strength and agility. [gerunds as appositives]

A **gerund phrase** contains a gerund plus any complements and modifiers.

EXAMPLE **Climbing the mountain** was a challenging activity.

EXAMPLE I enjoy my grandma's **down-home cooking.**

Although both a gerund and a present participle end in *-ing*, they function as different parts of speech. A gerund is used as a noun, whereas a present participle is used as part of a verb phrase or as an adjective.

EXAMPLES

PARTICIPLE IN A VERB PHRASE **I am sewing** this hem. [present participle functioning as main verb]

PARTICIPLE AS AN ADJECTIVE	**Sewing a button on her shirt,** Beth pricked her finger. **[present participle in participial phrase modifying *Beth*]**
GERUND	**Sewing** is Beth's favorite pastime. **[gerund functioning as subject]**

PRACTICE Gerunds and Gerund Phrases

Write the gerunds and gerund phrases. Identify the way each is used by writing one of these labels: subject, direct object, indirect object, object of a preposition, predicate nominative, appositive.

1. Seeing all her grandchildren gave Nana great pleasure.
2. The boys enjoy fishing.
3. Constant complaining is an annoyance.
4. The teacher gave his singing high praise.
5. We can save money by conserving energy.
6. After the rain, the child looked forward to his favorite pastime, jumping in mud puddles.
7. The band improved greatly by practicing every day.
8. My least favorite chore is mowing the lawn.
9. Greta loves reading the morning paper.
10. My parents' regimen, exercising for an hour every morning, keeps them physically fit.

INFINITIVES AND INFINITIVE PHRASES

An **infinitive** is a verb form that is usually preceded by the word *to* and is used as a noun, an adjective, or an adverb.

When you use the word *to* before the base form of a verb, *to* is not a preposition but part of the infinitive form of the verb.

EXAMPLE   **To volunteer** is rewarding. [infinitive as subject]

EXAMPLE   No one wants **to leave.** [infinitive as direct object]

EXAMPLE   Their decision was **to merge.** [infinitive as predicate nominative]

EXAMPLE   I felt the need **to call.** [infinitive as adjective]

EXAMPLE   Everyone was prepared **to sacrifice.** [infinitive as adverb]

An **infinitive phrase** contains an infinitive plus any complements and modifiers.

EXAMPLE   Would you prefer **to sleep until noon?**

EXAMPLE   **To speak slowly and clearly** is important.

EXAMPLE   We plan **to work safely and effectively.**

Occasionally, an infinitive phrase may have its own subject.

EXAMPLE   Our neighbor encourages **the dog to bark.** [*Dog* is the subject of the infinitive *to bark.* The entire infinitive phrase *the dog to bark* acts as the direct object of the sentence.]

EXAMPLE   The teacher asked **Maria to give a speech.** [*Maria* is the subject of the infinitive *to give.* The entire infinitive phrase *Maria to give a speech* acts as the direct object of the sentence.]

Note that the subject of the infinitive phrase comes between the main verb and the infinitive. The subject of an infinitive phrase always follows an action verb.

Sometimes the word *to* is dropped before an infinitive.

EXAMPLE   Let me [to] do the dishes.

EXAMPLE   We could have heard **a pin [to] drop.**

Infinitives and Infinitive Phrases

Write the infinitives and infinitive phrases. For each, write noun, adjective, *or* adverb *to tell how the infinitive or infinitive phrase is being used.*

1. I don't like to wash dishes.
2. The counselors will explain the way to make out your schedule.
3. To eat properly is imperative.
4. Our plan is to build in the spring.
5. Will you help plan the program?
6. I use a calculator to help me with difficult math problems.
7. I was unable to hear in the auditorium.
8. Let me help you.
9. Alisa wants to go home.
10. The team asked Bob to get the pizza.

Verbals and Appositives

Identify each italicized word by writing one of these labels: participle, gerund, infinitive, appositive.

1. Jill practiced *tumbling* yesterday.
2. The goldfinch, a *songbird,* perches on our tall flowers.
3. *Bothered* by the mosquitoes, we moved the activities indoors.
4. I enjoyed *visiting* Alaska.
5. Julie calmed herself by *whistling.*
6. *Traveling* along a country road, we spotted deer in the fields.
7. The defendant refused *to answer* the prosecutor's question.

8. The cabin doesn't have *running* water.
9. *Hidden* away in the attic, the love letters had yellowed and become brittle.
10. Jake plays the dulcimer, a stringed *instrument.*

3.4 ABSOLUTE PHRASES

An **absolute phrase,** also known as a nominative absolute, consists of a noun or a pronoun that is modified by a participle or a participial phrase. An absolute phrase has no grammatical relation to the rest of the sentence.

An absolute phrase belongs neither to the complete subject nor to the complete predicate of a sentence. It stands "absolutely" by itself in relation to the rest of the sentence.

EXAMPLE **Its wings badly damaged in the storm,** the aircraft crashed.

EXAMPLE We departed on schedule, **the weather [being] perfect.**

PRACTICE Absolute Phrases

Write each absolute phrase.

1. Their chores completed, the children played until bedtime.
2. We pulled the car into the garage, its engine still smoking.
3. Their wings singed by the fire, the butterflies were barely able to fly.

4. The two boys, their hopes dashed, dropped out of the competition.
5. The construction completed, the family moved into their new cottage by the lake.
6. We wore jackets, the air being cold.
7. The sun having set, lights dotted the mountainside.
8. His plane approaching the airport, the pilot lowered the wheels.
9. Their mouths burning from the jalapeño peppers, our friends gulped cold water.
10. The students, their eyes glazed and tired, slowly filed from the testing room.

PRACTICE Phrases

Identify each italicized group of words by writing one of these labels: participial phrase, infinitive phrase, gerund phrase, appositive phrase, absolute phrase, prepositional phrase.

1. Every Wednesday, Letitia goes *to the store.*
2. *Exhausted after the race,* the athlete rested for an hour.
3. *His pants spattered with mud,* the banker returned home to change his clothes.
4. Children like *working with clay.*
5. *Standing under a beech tree,* I stayed dry during the shower.
6. Carlos, *a diligent worker,* excels at his job.
7. *Sitting in the third row of the theater,* we could hear every word the actors uttered.
8. I am determined *to learn more about geography.*
9. That book, *a guide for tourists,* costs very little.
10. Don't try *to do everything at once.*

Rewrite the paragraph, correcting errors in spelling, capitalization, grammar, and usage. Add any missing punctuation. There are ten errors. Some sentences are correct.

William Shakespeare

[1]William Shakespeare is among the most famous of all writers. [2]The details of his life, however, are few [3]There is some debate about his birthday, but most scholars believe he was born on April 23 1564. [4]Shakespeare, one of eight children in his family attended King's New School in Stratford-upon-Avon. [5]Since he did not excel at his elementary schooling, he did not attend college.

[6]Shakespeare married anne Hathaway in 1582. [7]Anne and William had three children, Susannah Hamnet, and Judith.

[8]In 1592 Shakespeare left his hometown of Stratford to work in London as an actor and playwrite. [9]Shakespeare acted and wrote for Lord Chamberlain's Men a successful acting troupe. [10]This acting troupe performed in the Globe theater near the thames River. [11]Many of Shakespeare's thirty-seven plays was performed in the Globe.

[12]In 1612 Shakespeare retired to Stratford, where he continued to write plays and sonnets. [13]He died on April 23, 1616. [14]Buried at Holy Trinity Church in Stratford.

Write the prepositional phrases. For each, write the word or words modified by the phrase. Then write ADJ (adjective) or ADV (adverb) to identify the type of phrase.

1. For her birthday, Adrienne requested yellow cake with chocolate icing.

2. Turn left at the fourth traffic light.

3. The next time I buy a car, I want to get one with a

sunroof.

4. A group of coworkers had bought the winning lottery ticket.

5. Chapter seven of the book deals with sound waves.

6. The announcer on the sports channel graduated from this high school.

7. With a little luck, he will get a scholarship to an art school.

8. This package came for you.

9. The farmers' market springs to life before dawn.

10. I'll make some pasta with pesto sauce.

POSTTEST Identifying Verbals and Appositives

Identify each italicized word by writing one of these labels: participle, gerund, infinitive, appositive.

11. Students in *writing* class enjoy *reading* their own stories.

12. *To putt* accurately takes years of practice.

13. Lightning caused me *to run* for cover.

14. *Sliding* mud covered the highway.

15. The first scene of the movie, a *flashback* to World War II, captured the audience's attention.

16. *Bent* with age, the old Greek sailor still hobbled to the sea every day.

17. *Spoken* language is somewhat more casual than written language.

18. We invited our neighbors, the *McCorkles,* to dinner.

19. *Grown* in California, this fruit was shipped east in one day.

20. *Typing* my research paper took me five hours.

Identify each italicized group of words by writing one of these labels: participial phrase, infinitive phrase, gerund phrase, appositive phrase, absolute phrase, prepositional phrase.

21. The law prohibits *picking the wildflowers.*

22. *To be given a difficult assignment* is a challenge.

23. *Having promised my little niece a treat,* I spun homemade cotton candy for her.

24. Our team took the field, *the storm having passed.*

25. *Drilling for oil* requires financial risk.

26. Here and there on the rocky shoreline, fishermen hunched over their lines *waiting for some luck.*

27. The restaurant, *a replica of an old railroad dining car,* serves only Italian food.

28. *Written by a teenager,* this article expresses perfectly a young person's views on education.

29. Manuel decided *to visit his old neighborhood.*

30. I had toast, eggs, and orange juice *for breakfast.*

Chapter 4

Clauses and Sentence Structure

• • • • • • • • • • • • • • •

PRETEST **Identifying Main Clauses and Subordinate Clauses**

Copy each sentence. Underline each main clause once and each subordinate clause twice.

1. When the bell rings, the school day will end.
2. I can't remember what your e-mail address is.
3. The dish that I brought is the macaroni salad.
4. Let me know when you are ready to leave.

5. Before they left for vacation, Earl and Rob borrowed the movie camera that is used by the theater department.
6. Whenever he goes to Saint Louis, Dominick visits his favorite bookstore.
7. The operator with whom I spoke gave me your address.
8. I wonder when the next space shuttle launch is scheduled.
9. It was amazing that I managed to stay dry in the storm.
10. I am sorry for whatever my brother said to you.

PRETEST Identifying Simple, Compound, Complex, and Compound-Complex Sentences

Identify each sentence by writing S *for simple,* C *for compound,* CX *for complex, or* CC *for compound-complex.*

11. When is the concert, and how much are the tickets?
12. Listening to the lesson are interested students who love grammar.
13. Before the pilot lands the plane, she will instruct the flight attendants to fasten their seatbelts.
14. Ask many questions; learn as much as possible before you graduate.
15. Lynne will attend the meeting provided that it is not canceled.
16. There were many excited fans at the basketball game.
17. Juan is nervous; his palms are sweaty, and his heart is pounding.
18. What you have won is a trip to Hawaii.
19. What you said was impolite; you should apologize.
20. Charles and Maria ate breakfast and put the dishes in the sink.

Identify each of the following groups of words by writing F for fragment, R for run-on sentence, or S for sentence.

21. Running around not knowing what she was doing.

22. The clock struck three, and we were on our way.

23. Roger pitched in the game, but he gave up three runs.

24. What we have known all along.

25. Caught in a web of lies and misunderstandings.

26. I prefer eating fruits at room temperature.

27. The audience was on their feet I couldn't see a thing.

28. As far as I know.

29. Many diseases are as yet incurable, more research is needed.

30. Take these flowers home with you.

4.1 MAIN CLAUSES

A **clause** is a group of words that has a subject and a predicate and functions as part of a sentence or as a whole sentence.

Clauses fall into two categories: *main clauses,* which are also called *independent clauses,* and *subordinate clauses,* which are also called *dependent clauses.*

A **main clause** has a subject and a predicate and expresses a complete thought. It is the only type of clause that can stand alone as a sentence.

Every sentence must have at least one main clause. A coordinating conjunction is not part of a main clause.

Main Clause

EXAMPLE Lori walked the dog.
            S   V

Main Clause   Main Clause

EXAMPLE Lori took her dog to the store, and she bought him treats.
     S   V   S   V

Both the subject and the predicate of a main clause
may be compound.

Main Clause   Main Clause

EXAMPLE Lori and Zeke walk to the park, and Zeke runs and plays.
     S   S   V   S   V   V

FRANK & ERNEST® by Bob Thaves

FRANK AND ERNEST reprinted by permission
of Newspaper Enterprise Association, Inc.

4.2 SUBORDINATE CLAUSES

A **subordinate clause** has a subject and a predicate but
does not express a complete thought, so it cannot
stand alone as a sentence.

There are three types of subordinate clauses:
adjective clauses, which modify nouns or pronouns;
adverb clauses, which modify verbs, adjectives, or
adverbs; and **noun clauses,** which function as nouns.

A subordinate clause is dependent on the rest of the
sentence because a subordinate clause does not make
sense by itself. A subordinating conjunction or a relative
pronoun usually introduces a subordinate clause.

(See page 124 for a list of common subordinating conjunctions and page 107 for a list of relative pronouns.) Note that unlike a coordinating conjunction connecting two main clauses, a subordinating conjunction or a relative pronoun is part of the subordinate clause.

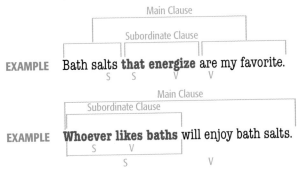

EXAMPLE   I enjoy a hot bath **after I work a full day.**

In some cases, the relative pronoun can also function as the subject of a subordinate clause.

EXAMPLE   Bath salts **that energize** are my favorite.

EXAMPLE   **Whoever likes baths** will enjoy bath salts.

In the first example, the subordinating conjunction *after* placed before *I work a full day* creates a word group—*after I work a full day*—that cannot stand alone as a main clause. Although the clause has a subject and a predicate, it does not express a complete thought.

In the second example, the relative pronoun *that* begins a subordinate clause that comes between the subject and the verb of the main clause. *That* also serves as the subject of the subordinate clause, and *energize* is its verb. *That energize* cannot, however, stand alone.

In the third example, the subordinate clause functions as the subject of the sentence. *Whoever* functions as the subject of the subordinate clause, *whoever likes baths. Likes* is the verb, and *baths* is the direct object. *Whoever likes baths* cannot, however, stand alone.

PRACTICE Subordinate Clauses

Write the subordinate clause or clauses from each sentence.

1. Television is a medium that is now universal.
2. A chimney sweep is a person who cleans chimneys.
3. I am thankful for everything that I have.
4. How a mother of triplets manages I will never know.
5. An automobile can easily hydroplane when the pavement is wet.
6. Would you please explain again to me how shortwave radios work?
7. The teachers whom the students admire are the ones who are always fair.
8. Because I like music, I often listen to the radio.
9. Before you take the test, read your notes.
10. Grocery managers try to stock everything that the customers want.

PRACTICE Main Clauses and Subordinate Clauses

Copy the sentences. Underline the main clauses once and the subordinate clauses twice.

1. We wondered when the speech would end.
2. Raisa's predicament was that she didn't have enough money.
3. How a reporter interviews is important.
4. While you are at the market, buy some fresh tomatoes.
5. Because we are moving, our house is not a pleasant sight.
6. Disneyland is a park that has been tremendously successful.
7. When the phone rang, I was on the front porch and didn't hear it.

8. This concert ticket will go to whoever knows the answer.

9. The leaves that cover our lawn are all from the huge sycamore tree.

10. Call me in the evening if you can.

4.3 ADJECTIVE CLAUSES

An **adjective clause** is a subordinate clause that modifies a noun or a pronoun.

An adjective clause may begin with a relative pronoun (*who, whom, whose, that,* and *which*) or *where* or *when.* An adjective clause normally follows the word it modifies.

EXAMPLE   Athletes **who perform in the Olympics** must spend years in training.

EXAMPLE   Cities **that host the Olympics** need many athletic facilities.

EXAMPLE   The city **where the 1996 Summer Olympics took place** was Atlanta.

Sometimes the relative pronoun is dropped from the beginning of an adjective clause.

EXAMPLE   The mug **I use most often** came from those Olympics. **[The relative pronoun *that* has been omitted.]**

Some adjective clauses are needed to make the meaning of a sentence clear. Such an adjective clause is called an *essential clause,* or a *restrictive clause.* It must not be set off with commas.

EXAMPLE   Tourists **who travel to the games** stay in hotels.

EXAMPLE   The living area **that is designated for the athletes** is called the Olympic Village.

An adjective clause that adds information to a sentence but is not necessary to make the meaning of the sentence clear is called a *nonessential clause,* or a *nonrestrictive clause.* Always use commas to set off a nonessential clause.

EXAMPLE   The Columbia Broadcasting System, **which televised the 1998 Winter Olympics,** set up a Web site for the athletes.

EXAMPLE   The athletes, **who received thousands of messages,** appreciated this service.

When choosing between *that* and *which* to introduce an adjective clause, use *that* to begin an essential clause and *which* to begin a nonessential clause.

EXAMPLE   Millions watched the 1998 Winter Olympics, **which took place in Nagano.**

EXAMPLE   Other competitions **that include similar events** are less publicized.

4.4 ADVERB CLAUSES

An **adverb clause** is a subordinate clause that modifies a verb, an adjective, or an adverb. It tells *when, where, how, why, to what extent,* or *under what conditions.*

Adverb clauses begin with subordinating conjunctions. An adverb clause can come either before or after the main clause. When the adverb clause comes first, separate it from the main clause with a comma. (See Lesson 11.6.)

EXAMPLE   **Before winter began,** I planted bulbs. [The adverb clause tells *when* and modifies the verb *planted.*]

EXAMPLE   Bulbs usually do well **if you use fertilizer.** [The adverb clause tells *under what conditions* and modifies the adverb *well.*]

EXAMPLE   The flowers are beautiful **because the winter was mild.** [The adverb clause tells *why* and modifies the adjective *beautiful.*]

Elliptical adverb clauses have words left out of them. You can easily supply the omitted words because they are understood or implied.

EXAMPLE The hyacinths are more fragrant **than the tulips [are fragrant].**

EXAMPLE **While [I am] gardening,** I always take time to enjoy the flowers.

4.5 NOUN CLAUSES

A **noun clause** is a subordinate clause that is used as a noun within the main clause of a sentence.

You can use a noun clause as a subject, a direct object, an indirect object, an object of a preposition, or a predicate nominative.

EXAMPLE **Whatever you can learn about computers** will prove useful in the workplace. **[noun clause as subject]**

EXAMPLE You should take **whichever computer classes are offered. [noun clause as direct object]**

EXAMPLE The instructor gave **whoever was available** word-processing lessons. **[noun clause as indirect object]**

EXAMPLE You can get by on **what you learn in this class. [noun clause as object of the preposition]**

EXAMPLE The basics of computers is **what you must learn. [noun clause as predicate nominative]**

The following are some words that can be used to introduce noun clauses.

how	whatever	which	whose
however	when	whichever	why
if	where	who, whom	
that	wherever	whoever	
what	whether	whomever	

Sometimes the introductory word is dropped from a noun clause.

EXAMPLE   I think **computers will be even more important in the future.** [*That* has been omitted from the beginning of the clause.]

PRACTICE **Subordinate Clauses**

Write the subordinate clause from each sentence. Then write ADJ if it's an adjective clause, ADV if it's an adverb clause, or N if it's a noun clause.

1. That is not what I told the investigator.
2. The outcome was fairly certain before the game ever started.
3. If you have any doubts, don't take the job.
4. I have no idea of what I am supposed to say during the interview.
5. The old chair that Sean refinished looks beautiful now.
6. You may sit wherever you wish.
7. I can't remember how those pieces fit together.
8. The nearest street, which runs north and south, is Wilson Street.
9. For his birthday, four-year-old Jamie got a bike that has training wheels.
10. Why that light blinks constantly is a mystery.

4.6 FOUR KINDS OF SENTENCES

Sentences are often classified according to their purpose. There are four purposes that sentences may have: to make a statement, to give an order or make a request, to ask a question, and to express strong emotion.

A **declarative sentence** makes a statement.

EXAMPLE   Andrew moved to Miami.

EXAMPLE   He has lived there since January.

A declarative sentence usually ends with a period but can end with an exclamation mark. This type of sentence is the most frequently used in speaking and writing.

An **imperative sentence** gives a command or makes a request.

EXAMPLE   Write me a letter.

EXAMPLE   Andrew, please send your address.

An imperative sentence usually ends with a period but can end with an exclamation mark. In imperative sentences, the subject *you* is understood.

An **interrogative sentence** asks a question.

EXAMPLE   Do you like the weather?

EXAMPLE   What do you do after work?

An interrogative sentence usually ends with a question mark but can end with an exclamation mark if it expresses strong emotion.

An **exclamatory sentence** expresses strong emotion.

EXAMPLE   I can't believe you moved!

EXAMPLE   Call me soon!

EXAMPLE   What were you thinking!

An exclamatory sentence ends with an exclamation mark. Note that sentences are not exclusively exclamatory but can be declarative (first example), imperative (second example), or interrogative (third example) while expressing strong emotion. In writing, exclamatory sentences should be used sparingly so as not to detract from their effectiveness.

Identify each sentence by writing D *for declarative,* IT *for interrogative,* IM *for imperative, or* E *for exclamatory.*

1. How fast that meteorite is moving!
2. Why were you late?
3. Please leave your shoes at the door.
4. You need some help.
5. That cat is going to fall out of the tree.
6. Seventeen is an exciting age.
7. Isn't there a clock anywhere in this room?
8. First, convert the whole numbers to fractions.
9. A funnel cloud is forming right over there!
10. Buy your tickets before next Thursday.

4.7 SIMPLE AND COMPOUND SENTENCES

Sentences are sometimes classified by their structure. Sentence structures are *simple, compound, complex,* and *compound-complex.*

A **simple sentence** contains only one main clause and no subordinate clauses.

A simple sentence may contain a compound subject or a compound predicate or both. The subject and the predicate can be expanded with adjectives, adverbs, prepositional phrases, appositives, and verbal phrases.

EXAMPLE Musicians perform. **[simple sentence]**

EXAMPLE Musicians and singers travel and perform. **[simple sentence with compound subject and compound predicate]**

EXAMPLE Musicians in popular bands give performances frequently. **[simple sentence including a prepositional phrase, a direct object, and an adverb]**

A **compound sentence** contains two or more main clauses.

The main clauses in a compound sentence are usually joined by a comma and a coordinating conjunction (*and, but, or, nor, yet, for, so*).

EXAMPLE   Many popular bands play rock and roll, but others play rhythm and blues.

EXAMPLE   Sting sings rock and roll, and Puff Daddy raps, but they performed together at the MTV Video Music Awards.

Main clauses in a compound sentence may be joined by a semicolon used alone or by a semicolon and a conjunctive adverb (such as *however, therefore, nevertheless*) or by a semicolon and an expression such as *for example*.

EXAMPLE   Different types of music can be fused together; ska combines rock and reggae.

EXAMPLE   People often have set opinions about music; **nevertheless,** one should keep an open mind.

EXAMPLE   Different styles of music influence one another; **for example,** rock and roll developed from jazz.

PRACTICE   **Simple and Compound Sentences**

Identify each sentence by writing S *for a simple sentence or* C *for a compound sentence.*

1. Dark, threatening clouds rolled overhead, yet there was no rain.
2. In the morning, the bus arrives at nine o'clock.
3. Please listen carefully, and the instructions will be clear.
4. Our team was clearly superior, but they lost the game.
5. Somewhere in this area is a wildlife refuge with deer and buffalo.

6. California is a huge state and is also populous.
7. Band members must remember both the music and their positions in formations.
8. Alicia baked the birthday cake, but Susanna iced and decorated it.
9. Many people want to attend the exhibit; however, tickets are no longer available.
10. Clothing styles move in cycles; today's fashions will reappear at some time in the future.

4.8 COMPLEX AND COMPOUND-COMPLEX SENTENCES

A **complex sentence** has one main clause and one or more subordinate clauses.

EXAMPLE

Subordinate Clause | Main Clause
If you study the development of music, you will learn

Subordinate Clause
that music has been heavily influenced by society.

EXAMPLE

Subordinate Clause
When you listen to a song,

Main Clause | Subordinate Clause
you should think about the culture that influenced it.

A **compound-complex sentence** has two or more main clauses and at least one subordinate clause.

EXAMPLE

Main Clause
Subordinate Clause
Billie Holiday, who lived from 1915 to 1959, grew up in

Main Clause
a poor family, and she became a famous jazz singer.

Complex and Compound-Complex Sentences

Identify each sentence by writing CX *for complex sentence or* CC *for compound-complex sentence. Then write the subordinate clause from each sentence.*

1. When he was in the third grade, Billy was energetic and friendly.
2. While you were in the shower, your mother called, and the letter carrier brought you a package.
3. No one knows what the future will bring.
4. Jennifer promised again and again that she would be here on time.
5. When a person hurries too much, mistakes are made, and accidents happen.
6. I scheduled a physics class; Joe chose biology because he prefers the natural sciences.
7. Because they are both warm and comfortable, sweatshirts are great in cool weather.
8. Because bananas are so rich in potassium, they are staples in the American diet; they are relatively inexpensive, too.
9. Today's topic is the Civil War; however, we'll talk about your research papers before we begin the lesson.
10. Apple pie is best when it is served with ice cream.

PRACTICE **Simple, Compound, Complex, and Compound-Complex Sentences**

Copy the following sentences. Identify each sentence by writing S *for simple,* C *for compound,* CX *for complex, and* CC *for compound-complex. Underline each main clause once and each subordinate clause twice.*

1. A soda fountain was standard equipment in a drug store when my dad was a boy.
2. In some countries, students attend school on Saturdays.

Chapter 4 Clauses and Sentence Structure **175**

GRAMMAR/USAGE/MECHANICS

3. Eat well today; tomorrow, on the backpacking trip, we will have very little to eat.

4. Whichever tie you choose, you will have a good time at the dance.

5. I wanted to go to the movies on Friday; however, my aunt asked me to baby-sit my nephew.

6. If he were wise, he would get a job, and he would save all his money.

7. The car should be repainted before you sell it.

8. My friends and I enjoy sports; consequently, we attend a sporting event every week.

9. Between the two of us, we can get this wood chopped into fireplace logs before the snowstorm.

10. Ricardo and his band members played dance music all evening at Carlotta's wedding reception.

4.9 SENTENCE FRAGMENTS

A **sentence fragment** is an error that occurs when an incomplete sentence is punctuated as though it were complete.

There are three things you should look for when you review your work for sentence fragments. First, look for a group of words without a subject. Then, look for a group of words without a complete predicate, especially a group that contains a verbal or a verbal phrase. Finally, be sure you haven't punctuated a subordinate clause as if it were a complete sentence.

Many times, you can correct a sentence fragment by attaching it to a main clause. Other times, you may need to add words to make the sentence complete.

FRAGMENT	COMPLETE SENTENCE
Danielle is on the basketball team. **Played for fun as a child.** [lacks subject]	Danielle is on the basketball team. She played for fun as a child.
Danielle scoring more points than any other player. [lacks complete predicate]	Danielle was scoring more points than any other player.
The injured Danielle. [lacks complete predicate and contains verbal]	The injured Danielle was taken to the emergency room.
Because she was taken out of the game. The opposing team won. [subordinate clause]	Because she was taken out of the game, the opposing team won.

Sentence fragments can be used to produce special effects, such as adding emphasis or conveying realistic dialogue. Remember that professional writers use sentence fragments carefully and intentionally. In most of the writing you do, including your writing for school, you should avoid sentence fragments.

4.10 RUN-ON SENTENCES

A **run-on sentence** is two or more complete sentences written as though they were one sentence.

There are two types of run-on sentences. The first occurs when two main clauses are joined by a comma only. This is called a *comma splice.*

EXAMPLE   RUN-ON   Meteorology is fascinating to me, I watch the Weather Channel every day.

GRAMMAR/USAGE/MECHANICS

The second type of run-on sentence occurs when two main clauses have no punctuation separating them. This can occur with or without a conjunction.

EXAMPLE   **RUN-ON**   Meteorology is fascinating to me I watch the Weather Channel every day.

EXAMPLE   **RUN-ON**   Meteorology is fascinating to me and I watch the Weather Channel every day.

You can correct a run-on sentence in several ways. The method you choose in correcting your writing will depend on the relationship you want to convey between the two clauses.

METHOD OF CORRECTING RUN-ON	COMPLETE SENTENCE
Add end punctuation between the clauses and make two sentences.	Meteorology is fascinating to me. **I** watch the Weather Channel every day.
Separate the clauses with both a comma and a coordinating conjunction.	Meteorology is fascinating to me**, and** I watch the Weather Channel every day.
Separate the clauses with a semicolon.	Meteorology is fascinating to me**;** I watch the Weather Channel every day.
Add a semicolon and a conjunctive adverb between the clauses.	Meteorology is fascinating to me**; therefore,** I watch the Weather Channel every day.
Change one of the main clauses to a subordinate clause. Separate the two clauses with a comma if appropriate.	**Because** meteorology is fascinating to me, I watch the Weather Channel every day. I watch the Weather Channel every day **because** meteorology is fascinating to me.

PRACTICE   Fragments and Run-on Sentences

Identify each numbered item by writing F for fragment or R for run-on sentence. Then rewrite each item, correcting the error.

1. I picked some violets I like a spot of color in the house.
2. There goes my next-door neighbor, Eduardo Munoz, do you know him?

3. While we were waiting for the bus.

4. He could not answer the question, he was not discouraged.

5. If you are free tomorrow night.

6. Before you complete the assigned term paper.

7. Reading and basic addition in the first grade.

8. Lee Ann repaired the sink she was pleased with herself.

9. A tornado is approaching take cover immediately.

10. When a person is sound asleep.

PRACTICE Proofreading

Rewrite the following passage, correcting errors in spelling, capitalization, grammar, and usage. Add any missing punctuation. There are ten errors. Some sentences are correct.

John Milton

[1]As a young man, John Milton read any book he could find, he also learned Latin, Greek, Italian, and Hebrew. [2]Even wrote poems in Latin and Italian. [3]After graduating from Cambridge University, he decided to travel through Europe for a year. [4]Because he wanted to learn more about the world.

[5]Milton married Mary Powell in 1642 she was seventeen, nearly half her husband's age. [6]After only six weeks of marriage, Mary left Milton and returned to her parents house. [7]Milton was convinced there marriage would fail. [8]He wrote a series of articles about divorce which were very controversial. [9]Mary returned to him in 1645, and they eventually had three daughters.

[10]Milton went blind around 1652 and he had to rely on assistants to help him write. [11]His political writing continued to get attention and even landed him in prison. [12]He was saved by his freinds, who helped him obtain his freedom with a fine and loss of property. [13]Poor and defeated in his final years, milton still managed to compose his famous epic poem, *Paradise Lost.*

Identify each boldface, numbered clause as M *for main or* S *for subordinate. Then identify each subordinate clause as adjective* (ADJ), *adverb* (ADV), *or noun* (N).

Whatever you decide to do[1] is all right with us.

I refused to climb the mountain path[2] **because I do not like heights.**[3]

When the movie is over,[4] we can go back to my house for pizza.

Please give me some idea of[5] **where you would like to go for vacation.**[6]

If you need help, **call me.**[7]

The information **that was presented yesterday**[8] was entirely new to me.

When you are doubtful,[9] consult the dictionary; **do not guess.**[10]

POSTTEST Identifying Simple, Compound, Complex, and Compound-Complex Sentences

Identify each sentence by writing S *for simple,* C *for compound,* CX *for complex, or* CC *for compound-complex.*

11. Jim finished his project and handed it in early.

12. Help to keep your home safe; take precautions against the dangers that lurk in your medicine cabinet.

13. That time is precious is true; don't waste it.

14. What you have purchased was expensive.

15. Janice is better; her breathing is normal, and her pulse is regular.

16. There was a drowsy buzz of insects in the hot sunshine.

17. On the map, the route looks as if it crosses the mountains.

18. When you walk into the capitol building, you will see a kiosk that serves as an information center.

19. Meandering through the wheat field is a narrow but deep creek that irrigates the area.

20. When is the next flight to Cheyenne, and how long will it take?

POSTTEST **Identifying Fragments, Run-on Sentences, and Sentences**

Identify each numbered item by writing F *for fragment,* R *for run-on sentence, or* S *for sentence.*

21. We have played ball there before no one has objected.
22. Then walked out of the room.
23. Due to the fact that the temperature is so high.
24. The class picnic will be held next Friday, I cannot attend because of a conflict.
25. Drifting across the parched land.
26. When a droning noise became audible overhead.
27. I put bubble bath in the water for my little sister's bath.
28. Make the necessary corrections, then rewrite your paper.
29. Let the fun begin.
30. The newspaper remained on the front doorstep I knew they hadn't been home.

Chapter 5

Verb Tenses and Voice

● ● ● ● ● ● ● ● ● ● ● ● ● ●

PRETEST **Identifying the Correct Verb Form**

Read each sentence. Then write the correct form of the verb in parentheses.

1. I have (write) some literature about our national parks.

2. The test scores are not yet (know).

3. The boy (keep) all of his baseball cards until he moved abroad.

4. Last year the principal of our school (throw) out the first pitch of the season.

5. Our best debater has (win) a full scholarship to a state university in California.

6. I have (swear) that I will not tell anyone how the movie ends.

7. Somehow the mouse had (spring) the trap before it took the cheese.

8. The dog (steal) into the bedroom and stretched out on the bed.

9. Felicia has (grow) three inches since this time last year.

10. By the time he reaches the other bank of the river, Lester will have (swim) almost three miles.

11. The prize-winning apples were (grow) by a local 4-H club.

12. I have never (ride) in an antique roadster, but I would like to.

13. After the air turned cool last night, I (sleep) more soundly than I had been sleeping.

14. I was (choose) to represent our school at a local fund-raiser.

15. Kiri (draw) an amusing sketch of her brother in art class last week.

16. Outlaws were often (hang) during America's pioneer days.

17. I had (drink) a sip of that water before I realized that it was yours.

18. This same candy wrapper has (lie) in the corner for a week now.

19. It turned out to be Sam, not Darren, who (break) the record in the high jump.

20. At the zoo the monkeys (swing) from trapezes that hung from tree limbs.

PRETEST **Identifying the Verb Tense 1**

Identify the italicized verb tense by writing one of these labels: present, past, future, present perfect, past perfect, future perfect.

21. Julieta *will begin* her experiment in a few minutes.

22. The legislative committee *has appointed* a new chairperson.

23. The shipment of office supplies *arrived* Friday.
24. Someone always *misplaces* the tools so that I can never find them.
25. I *had seen* the movie twice before my friends asked me to see it with them.
26. Pedro *will have graduated* by next May.
27. I trust my counselor and *tell* her all my troubles.
28. I *have notified* the post office of my new address.
29. No one *had been* in the room all day.
30. You *will see* her picture in tomorrow's edition of the newspaper.

PRETEST Identifying the Verb Tense 2

Identify the italicized verb form by writing one of these labels: present progressive, past progressive, future progressive, present perfect progressive, past perfect progressive, future perfect progressive, present emphatic, past emphatic.

31. We *are looking* forward to the celebration.
32. He *does bother* me with his pranks.
33. Two persons *were seeking* the same job.
34. Only one of us *will be taking* the early flight tomorrow.
35. The twins certainly *do stick* together.
36. Someone *has been opening* my mail.
37. I *had been thinking* about seeing that movie.
38. By tomorrow they *will have been driving* for six days.
39. The meeting *is going* very smoothly.
40. Le *did explain* that we weren't leaving until six o'clock.

Rewrite each sentence. Correct verbs in the wrong tense, or change verbs in passive voice to active voice.

41. The songs were heard over a loudspeaker by the audience.

42. When the wind blows, the leaves fell.

43. I am taught good values by my parents.

44. The videotape of the game will be seen by the team.

45. We were listening to the radio yesterday while we are working.

46. Send your photograph if you wanted to.

47. By the time I got home, my father cooked dinner.

48. This new kind of cereal was eaten by me.

49. The alphabet is known by all the five-year-olds in the class.

50. When the senator spoke at the bake sale last month, everyone listen.

5.1 PRINCIPAL PARTS OF VERBS

All verbs have four **principal parts: a base form**, a **present participle**, a **simple past form**, and a **past participle.** All the verb tenses are formed from these principal parts.

Principal Parts of Verbs

Base Form	Present Participle	Past Form	Past Participle
open	opening	opened	opened
fall	falling	fell	fallen
cry	crying	cried	cried
speak	speaking	spoke	spoken
be	being	was, were	been

You can use the base form (except the base form of *be*) and the past form by themselves as main verbs. To function as the simple predicate in a sentence, the present participle and the past participle must always be preceded by one or more auxiliary verbs.

EXAMPLE   Doors **open.** [base or present form]

EXAMPLE   Doors **opened.** [past form]

EXAMPLE   Doors **are opening.** [present participle with the auxiliary verb *are*]

EXAMPLE   Doors **have opened.** [past participle with the auxiliary verb *have*]

PRACTICE **Principal Parts of Verbs**

Write the correct form of the principal part of the verb in parentheses.

1. We (past form of *spend*) a lot of time reviewing last year's math.

2. By the time I am finished, I (past participle of *write* preceded by the auxiliary verbs *will have*) fourteen thank-you notes.

3. Some construction workers (present participle of *replace* preceded by the auxiliary verb *are*) the brick in our front walkway.

4. They (base form of *seem*) rather tired.

5. Not one question (past participle of *ask* preceded by the auxiliary verb *was*) at the town meeting.

6. My family (present participle of *put* preceded by the auxiliary verb *are*) pressure on me to succeed.

7. The awards (past participle of *present* preceded by the auxiliary verbs *will be*) at Saturday's banquet.

8. We (past form of *fly*) over the Grand Canyon.

9. Noelle (past form of *try*) to do her homework in her study period.

10. I (past form of *go*) with Ramón to visit his family in Venezuela.

5.2 REGULAR AND IRREGULAR VERBS

A **regular verb** forms its past and past participle by adding *–ed* or *–d* to the base form.

REGULAR VERBS		
BASE FORM	**PAST FORM**	**PAST PARTICIPLE**
laugh	laughed	laughed
talk	talked	talked
like	liked	liked

Some regular verbs undergo spelling changes when a suffix that begins with a vowel is added.

EXAMPLE   fry + **-ed** = fri**ed**

EXAMPLE   stop + **-ed** = stop**ped**

An **irregular verb** forms its past and past participle in some way other than by adding *–ed* or *–d* to the base form.

COMMON IRREGULAR VERBS		
BASE FORM	**PAST FORM**	**PAST PARTICIPLE**
be, am, are, is	was, were	been
bear	bore	borne
beat	beat	beaten *or* beat
become	became	become

GRAMMAR/USAGE/MECHANICS

BASE FORM	PAST FORM	PAST PARTICIPLE
begin	began	begun
bite	bit	bitten *or* bit
blow	blew	blown
break	broke	broken
bring	brought	brought
burst	burst	burst
buy	bought	bought
cast	cast	cast
catch	caught	caught
choose	chose	chosen
come	came	come
creep	crept	crept
cut	cut	cut
dive	dived *or* dove	dived
do	did	done
draw	drew	drawn
drink	drank	drunk
drive	drove	driven
eat	ate	eaten
fall	fell	fallen
feel	felt	felt
find	found	found
fling	flung	flung
fly	flew	flown

Common Irregular Verbs, continued

BASE FORM	PAST FORM	PAST PARTICIPLE
freeze	froze	frozen
get	got	got *or* gotten
give	gave	given
go	went	gone
grow	grew	grown
hang	hung *or* hanged**	hung *or* hanged**
have	had	had
hit	hit	hit
hold	held	held
keep	kept	kept
know	knew	known
lay*	laid	laid
lead	led	led
leave	left	left
lend	lent	lent
let	let	let
lie*	lay	lain
lose	lost	lost
make	made	made
pay	paid	paid
put	put	put
read	read	read
ride	rode	ridden
ring	rang	rung

Common Irregular Verbs, continued

BASE FORM	PAST FORM	PAST PARTICIPLE
rise*	rose	risen
run	ran	run
say	said	said
see	saw	seen
seek	sought	sought
sell	sold	sold
set*	set	set
shake	shook	shaken
shine	shone *or* shined***	shone *or* shined***
shrink	shrank *or* shrunk	shrunk *or* shrunken
sing	sang	sung
sink	sank	sunk
sit*	sat	sat
sleep	slept	slept
speak	spoke	spoken
spend	spent	spent
spring	sprang *or* sprung	sprung
steal	stole	stolen
sting	stung	stung
swear	swore	sworn
swim	swam	swum
swing	swung	swung
take	took	taken
teach	taught	taught

Common Irregular Verbs, *continued*

BASE FORM	PAST FORM	PAST PARTICIPLE
tear	tore	torn
tell	told	told
think	thought	thought
throw	threw	thrown
wear	wore	worn
weave	wove	woven
win	won	won
write	wrote	written

*For more detailed instruction on *lay* versus *lie* and *rise* versus *raise*, see Usage Glossary pages 64 and 73.

*For more detailed instruction on *sit* versus *set*, see Usage Glossary page 75.

**Use *hanged* only when referring to death by hanging.

***Shone* is intransitive. (The sun *shone*.) *Shined* is transitive. (I *shined* my shoes.)

PRACTICE   Past and Past Participle Forms of Verbs

Copy and complete the chart. Make sure that you have spelled each form correctly.

BASE FORM	PAST FORM	PAST PARTICIPLE
1. drive		
2. do		
3. think		

Practice, Past and Past Participle Forms of Verbs, continued

BASE FORM	PAST FORM	PAST PARTICIPLE
4. steal		
5. choose		
6. begin		
7. love		
8. say		
9. put		
10. leave		
11. grow		
12. let		
13. hold		
14. find		
15. wear		
16. dive		
17. shake		
18. break		
19. learn		
20. serve		
21. draw		
22. tell		
23. rise		
24. pay		
25. read		

Write the correct form of the verb in parentheses.

1. The sun (shine) so brightly that I had to wear sunglasses.
2. Three children were (sting) by bees during recess.
3. Last month, a huge banner (hang) from a bar suspended over the street.
4. Your dog has (tear) a hole in my shirt.
5. The man and his wife have (sit) in the same seats in the ballpark for five years.
6. Bed linens are (weave) very tightly.
7. That uniform number has been (wear) by some of the best players.
8. The children (draw) sketches in class yesterday.
9. It has (take) seven years for their business to make a profit.
10. Horse thieves were (hang) in public squares in the 1800s.

5.3 TENSE OF VERBS

The **tenses** of a verb are the forms that help to show time.

There are six tenses in English: **present, past, future, present perfect, past perfect,** and **future perfect.**

PRESENT TENSE

The present-tense form of a verb is the same as the verb's base form, except for the third-person singular, which adds *–s* or *–es*. Exceptions are the verbs *be* and *have*.

PRESENT TENSE OF THE VERB *PAINT*

	SINGULAR	PLURAL
FIRST PERSON	I **paint**.	We **paint**.
SECOND PERSON	You **paint**.	You **paint**.
THIRD PERSON	She, he, or it **paints**.	They **paint**.
	Kris **paints**.	The artists **paint**.

PRESENT TENSE OF THE VERB *BE*

	SINGULAR	PLURAL
FIRST PERSON	I **am** honest.	We **are** honest.
SECOND PERSON	You **are** honest.	You **are** honest.
THIRD PERSON	She, he, or it **is** honest.	They **are** honest.
	Tomás **is** honest.	The girls **are** honest.

PRESENT TENSE OF THE VERB *HAS*

	SINGULAR	PLURAL
FIRST PERSON	I **have** a dog.	We **have** a dog.
SECOND PERSON	You **have** a dog.	You **have** a dog.
THIRD PERSON	She, he, or it **has** a dog.	They **have** a dog.
	Danny **has** a dog.	The Smiths **have** a dog.

The **present tense** expresses a constant, repeated, or habitual action or condition. It can also express a general truth.

EXAMPLE   Molly **puts** horseradish on ham sandwiches. [not just *this* ham sandwich but every ham sandwich; a repeated action]

EXAMPLE   The Yazoo River **flows** into the Mississippi River. [always; a habitual action]

EXAMPLE   Ice **melts** at thirty-two degrees Fahrenheit. [a general truth]

The **present tense** can also express an action or a condition that exists only now.

EXAMPLE   Mindy **has** a headache. [not always but just now]

EXAMPLE   The fireplace wall **feels** dangerously hot. [at this very moment]

The **present tense** is sometimes used in historical writing to express past events and, more often, in poetry, fiction, and journalism (especially in sports writing) to convey to the reader a sense of "being there." This usage is sometimes called the *historical present tense.*

EXAMPLE   Though he **is** aware of the danger, Benjamin Franklin **decides** to risk electrocution to verify his theory.

EXAMPLE   The runner on first base **inches** toward second.

PRACTICE   Present Tense

Write a sentence using each of the following verb forms. The content of your sentence should express the kind of present tense indicated in parentheses.

1. spends (generally true)
2. thinks (at this very moment)

3. revolves (a habitual action)
4. has (not always, but just now)
5. swims (an event in history)
6. drives (a constant action)
7. burst (generally true)
8. wear (a repeated action)
9. seems (at this very moment)
10. takes (a repeated action)

PAST TENSE

Use the **past tense** to express an action or a condition that was started and completed in the past.

EXAMPLE   General Lee **shook** General Grant's hand.

EXAMPLE   The Confederate troops **unloaded** their supplies.

Nearly all regular and irregular verbs (except *be*) have just one past-tense form, such as *climbed* or *ran*. The verb *be* has two past-tense forms, *was* and *were*.

PAST TENSE OF THE VERB *BE*		
	SINGULAR	**PLURAL**
FIRST PERSON	I **was** glad.	We **were** glad.
SECOND PERSON	You **were** glad.	You **were** glad.
THIRD PERSON	She, he, or it **was** glad.	They **were** glad.
	Bob **was** glad.	The girls **were** glad.

FUTURE TENSE

Use the **future tense** to express an action or a condition that will occur in the future.

You form the future tense of any verb by using the auxiliary verb *shall* or *will* with the base form: *I shall wait; you will telephone.* Note: In modern American English, *shall* is very seldom used except for questions in which *I* or *we* is the subject: *Shall I meet you there? Shall we have lunch now?*

EXAMPLE Ignacio **will mask** the woodwork.

EXAMPLE Elaine **will paint** the room.

There are three other ways to express future time besides using the future tense. They are as follows:

1. Use *going to* with the present tense of *be* and the base form of a verb.

EXAMPLE Ignacio **is *going to* mask** the woodwork.

2. Use *about to* with the present tense of *be* and the base form of a verb.

EXAMPLE Ignacio **is *about to* mask** the woodwork.

3. Use the present tense with an adverb or an adverb phrase that shows future time.

EXAMPLE Elaine **paints** the room *tomorrow.*

EXAMPLE Elaine **paints** the room *next Tuesday morning.*

FRANK & ERNEST® by Bob Thaves

FRANK AND ERNEST reprinted by permission of
Newspaper Enterprise Association, Inc.

Chapter 5 Verb Tenses and Voice **197**

Rewrite each sentence so that the verb expresses the future tense in the four ways taught in this lesson.

1. Donna painted her bedroom.
2. Those trees lost their leaves.
3. The streets were repaved.
4. They drank their milkshakes.
5. The flight landed at Washington National Airport.

PRACTICE Present, Past, and Future Tense

Identify the italicized verb tense by writing one of these labels: present, past, future.

1. I *worried* all night long about my history test.
2. *Shall* I *leave* the videotape here with you?
3. My dad *makes* more money in an hour than I make all day.
4. The sky *turned* a very strange shade of purple.
5. The directions *will* not *make* any sense to you until you see the video.
6. The volunteers *planned* the July Fourth celebration.
7. According to the weather report, it *will rain* tomorrow.
8. Some students *were* not able to hear the announcements.
9. Good manners *make* life more pleasant.
10. A black Corvette *raced* around the corner.

5.4 PERFECT TENSES

PRESENT PERFECT TENSE

Use the **present perfect tense** to express an action or a condition that occurred at some *indefinite time* in the past.

Do not be confused by the word *present* in the name of the present perfect tense. This tense expresses past time. The word *present* refers to the tense of the auxiliary verb *has* or *have*.

You form the present perfect tense by using *has* or *have* with the past participle of a verb: *has studied, have known.*

EXAMPLE   The cake **has fallen** in the oven.

EXAMPLE   I **have promised** to bring cakes for the bake sale.

The present perfect tense can refer to completed action in past time only in an indefinite way. Adverbs such as *yesterday* cannot be added to make the time more specific.

EXAMPLE   We **have seen** this movie.

EXAMPLE   The beans **have grown** taller.

To be specific about completed past time, you would normally use the simple past tense.

EXAMPLE   We **saw** this movie during spring break.

EXAMPLE   The beans **grew** a foot taller over the weekend.

The present perfect tense can also be used to express the idea that an action or a condition *began in the past and is still happening*. To communicate this idea, you would normally add adverbs (or adverb phrases or clauses) of time.

EXAMPLE   Lionel **has studied** ballet **for two years.**

EXAMPLE   Beth Ann **has hit** three home runs **in a row.**

PAST PERFECT TENSE

Use the **past perfect tense** to indicate that one past action or condition began *and* ended before another past action or condition started.

You form the past perfect tense by using the auxiliary verb *had* with the past participle of a verb: *had painted, had sung*.

EXAMPLE   Past

Frank **won** the race in the car whose carburetor

Past Perfect

he **had rebuilt**. [First Frank rebuilt the carburetor; the rebuilding was complete; then he won the race.]

Past Perfect

EXAMPLE   LaVerne **had perfected** her dance routine before she

Past

entered the contest. [She practiced until her routine was perfect; the perfecting was complete; then she entered the dance contest.]

FUTURE PERFECT TENSE

Use the **future perfect tense** to express one future action or condition that will begin *and* end before another future event starts.

You form the future perfect tense by using *will have* or *shall have* with the past participle of a verb: *will have rested, shall have won*.

EXAMPLE   By August you **will have learned** how to swim. [Learning how to swim will be complete by the time another future event, the arrival of August, happens.]

EXAMPLE   Before she has paid all her debts, she **will have paid** hundreds of dollars in interest. [The interest will already have been paid by the time another future event, the paying of all her debts, is reached.]

Read the verb in parentheses. Then write the tense indicated in brackets.

EXAMPLE   When the president resigned, he (hold) office for three years. **[past perfect]**

Answer: had held

1. She (drive) in a car pool for each of the last seven years. **[present perfect]**

2. As of tomorrow Jeremy (work) for twenty years without missing one day. **[future perfect]**

3. Speaking in front of large groups (give) me self-confidence. **[present perfect]**

4. Raul (be) in this country for over a year when his family arrives. **[future perfect]**

5. Lumberjacks (cut) at least half of the trees in the forest south of here. **[present perfect]**

6. By the time she reached her house, her reason (give) way to anger. **[past perfect]**

7. Carlene (read) every book on the book list. **[present perfect]**

8. This (be) a very good year for baseball. **[present perfect]**

9. I (speak) with the principal before I talked with the counselor. **[past perfect]**

10. By the time we arrive home from our trip, the builders (rebuild) the damaged front of the house. **[future perfect]**

PRACTICE Tense of Verbs

Identify the italicized verb tense by writing one of these labels: present, past, future, present perfect, past perfect, future perfect.

1. By the time the heat wave broke, our air conditioner *had run* for twenty-three straight days.

2. At the rate we're going, the plane *will have left* before we get to the airport.

3. Please *send* me a picture of the baby.
4. After the rain the fishing *was* good.
5. If I *had written* faster, I could have sent this letter today.
6. This restaurant *offers* lobster in season.
7. Your test score *will determine* your placement in the program.
8. A crowd ten thousand strong *has congregated* in the city streets.
9. *Will* you *be* home for supper?
10. How many chapters *have* we *covered* now?

PRACTICE The Six Tenses

Write two paragraphs in which you use each of the six tenses. Try to use at least three of the irregular verbs from the chart that begins on page 187. Be sure that each verb agrees with its subject in number. (See page 215 for more information about subject-verb agreement.)

FRANK & ERNEST® by Bob Thaves

FRANK AND ERNEST reprinted by permission of Newspaper Enterprise Association, Inc.

VERB TENSE TIME LINE

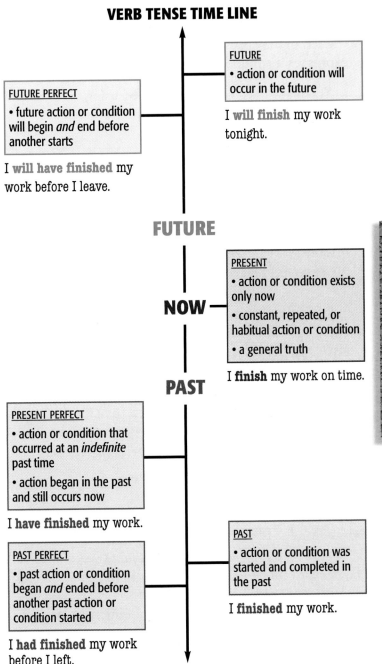

FUTURE PERFECT
• future action or condition will begin *and* end before another starts

I **will have finished** my work before I leave.

FUTURE
• action or condition will occur in the future

I **will finish** my work tonight.

FUTURE

PRESENT
• action or condition exists only now
• constant, repeated, or habitual action or condition
• a general truth

I **finish** my work on time.

NOW

PAST

PRESENT PERFECT
• action or condition that occurred at an *indefinite* past time
• action began in the past and still occurs now

I **have finished** my work.

PAST PERFECT
• past action or condition began *and* ended before another past action or condition started

I **had finished** my work before I left.

PAST
• action or condition was started and completed in the past

I **finished** my work.

5.5 PROGRESSIVE AND EMPHATIC FORMS

Each of the six tenses has a **progressive** form that expresses a continuing action.

You make the progressive forms by using the appropriate tense of the verb *be* with the present participle of the main verb.

PRESENT PROGRESSIVE	They *are* studying.
PAST PROGRESSIVE	They *were* studying.
FUTURE PROGRESSIVE	They *will be* studying.
PRESENT PERFECT PROGRESSIVE	They *have been* studying.
PAST PERFECT PROGRESSIVE	They *had been* studying.
FUTURE PERFECT PROGRESSIVE	They *will have been* studying.

The present tense and the past tense have additional forms, called **emphatic forms,** that add special force, or emphasis, to the verb.

You make the emphatic forms by using *do, does,* or *did* with the base form of the verb.

PRESENT EMPHATIC	We **do have** enough money for lunch.
	Cindy **does have** her umbrella with her.
PAST EMPHATIC	We **did leave** a large tip.

PRACTICE Progressive and Emphatic Forms

Identify the italicized verb form by writing one of these labels: present progressive, past progressive, future progressive, present perfect progressive, past perfect progressive, future perfect progressive, present emphatic, past emphatic.

1. What color you choose for the background *does matter*.
2. *Have* you *been listening* to the news today?

3. Researchers *are working* every day to find a cure for cancer.

4. All students *will be getting* letters in the mail about changes for the coming year.

5. I *did love* my birthday gifts.

6. What *were* those boys *doing* in the creek?

7. Planted after the turn of the century, this tree soon *will have been growing* for over one hundred years.

8. The city planners *had been making* changes in traffic patterns long before the citizens called for them.

9. You *did say* that, even though you don't remember doing so.

10. Last night we *were trying* to place a call to Egypt, but we couldn't get through.

5.6 CONSISTENCY OF TENSES

Don't shift, or change, tenses when two or more events occur at the same time.

EXAMPLE **INCORRECT** The dogs **caught** sight of the cat, and at once they **chase** it. [**The tense needlessly shifts from the past to the present.**]

EXAMPLE **CORRECT** The dogs **caught** sight of the cat, and at once they **chased** it. [**Now it is clear that both events happened at nearly the same time.**]

Do shift tenses to show that one event precedes or follows another.

EXAMPLE **INCORRECT** By the time the omelet **was** ready, I **set** the table. [**The two past-tense verbs give the mistaken impression that both events—the omelet's cooking and the setting of the table— happened at the same time.**]

EXAMPLE **CORRECT** By the time the omelet **was** ready, I **had set** the table. **[The shift from the past tense *(was)* to the past perfect tense *(had set)* clearly shows that the setting of the table happened before the omelet was cooked.]**

Keep a statement about a general truth in the present tense even if other verbs are in the past tense.

We **learned** that water **expands** when it **freezes.**

5.7 VOICE OF VERBS

An action verb is in the **active voice** when the subject of the sentence performs the action.

EXAMPLE The new student **threw** a wicked fastball.

An action verb is in the **passive voice** when its action is performed on the subject.

EXAMPLE A wicked fastball **was thrown** by the new student.

Generally the active voice is stronger, but at times the passive voice is preferable or even necessary. If you don't want to call attention to the performer of the action or don't know who the performer is, use the passive voice.

EXAMPLE Doorbells up and down the street **were rung.** **[You may not want to identify the culprit.]**

EXAMPLE The tires **were slit.** **[You may not know who the culprit is.]**

You form the passive voice by using a form of the auxiliary verb *be* with the past participle of the verb. The tense of a passive verb is determined by the tense of the auxiliary verb.

EXAMPLE The gift **is wrapped** in pretty paper. **[present tense, passive voice]**

EXAMPLE The gift **was wrapped** in pretty paper. **[past tense, passive voice]**

EXAMPLE   The gift **will be wrapped** in pretty paper. **[future tense, passive voice]**

PRACTICE   Voice of Verbs

Rewrite each sentence, changing active verbs to passive and passive verbs to active.

EXAMPLE   The queen planned a party for the princess.

Answer: A party for the princess was planned by the queen.

1. Ten points were scored by the home team.
2. The accident was reported by a witness.
3. Manuela will give the committee's report.
4. The dinner dishes were done by me.
5. The candidate is known by almost everyone in the city.
6. The vote will be determined by a show of hands.
7. A commercial photographer took these pictures.
8. Someone holds the winning ticket.
9. The book was read by the students.
10. The issue was discussed by members of the House of Representatives.

5.8 MOOD OF VERBS

Along with expressing tense and voice, verbs also express mood.

A verb expresses one of three **moods:** the **indicative mood,** the **imperative mood,** or the **subjunctive mood.**

The indicative mood—the one most frequently used—makes a statement or asks a question. The imperative mood expresses a command or makes a request.

EXAMPLE   **INDICATIVE MOOD**   She **sets** her alarm clock for 6:30 A.M.

EXAMPLE   **IMPERATIVE MOOD**   **Set** your alarm clock for 6:30 A.M.

The subjunctive mood is often replaced by the indicative mood in informal English. The subjunctive mood does, however, have two important uses in modern formal English.

1. The subjunctive mood expresses, although indirectly, a demand, recommendation, suggestion, or statement of necessity.

EXAMPLE   We demand [*or* recommend *or* suggest] that she **set** her alarm clock for 6:30 A.M. [**To form the subjunctive mood, drop the –*s* from the third-person singular.**]

EXAMPLE   It is necessary that she **be** on time for school. [**The subjunctive mood uses *be* instead of *am, is,* or *are.***]

2. The subjunctive mood is used to state a condition or a wish that is contrary to fact. Notice that this use of the subjunctive always requires the past tense.

EXAMPLE   If she **were** to oversleep, she would miss her ride to school. [**The subjunctive mood uses *were*, not *was*.**]

EXAMPLE   I wish (that) I **were** a genius.

EXAMPLE   You are speaking to me as if I **were** a child.

PRACTICE   Mood of Verbs

Identify the mood of each italicized verb by writing indicative, imperative, *or* subjunctive.

1. If I *were* in charge, I would eliminate all dues.
2. It is recommended that Juan *learn* Japanese before living in Japan.
3. Both moles and voles *tunnel* in the ground.
4. Set clear goals and *remain* dedicated to them.
5. Some colors *clash* with each other.
6. *Be* sure before you enter marriage.
7. I recommend that this job *be given* to a student.

8. She dressed for the concert as though she *were going* to a fashion show.

9. We usually *get* what we deserve.

10. Please *speak* softly when you enter the baby's room.

PRACTICE Proofreading

Rewrite the passage, correcting the errors in spelling, grammar, and usage. There are ten errors. Some sentences are correct. (For this exercise, no sentences should be in the historical present.)

Henry David Thoreau

[1]Henry David Thoreau was born in Concord, Massachusetts, in 1817. [2]As a young boy he loved the outdoors; he hunted, fishes, and played sports. [3]Later, when he attended Harvard, Thoreau keeped a journal; he continued to do so all his life. [4]By the end of his life, he had wrote more than two million words in his journals. [5]He often wrote about transcendentalism, a philosophy about nature and spirit that was popular in nineteenth-century New England.

[6]After college, Thoreau teached at a school in Concord. [7]Then he lived with and works for Ralph Waldo Emerson, another follower of transcendentalism. [8]Thoreau has become a member of the Transcendental Club in the early 1840s. [9]To fully concentrate on his writing, Thoreau builded a hut at Walden Pond, where he lived for two years, two months, and two days.

[10]Thoreau was adamantly against slavery, and he was the first to speak in support of John Brown, an abolitionist who was arrested for raiding Harpers Ferry. [11]Brown had hope to make Harpers Ferry the base for his antislavery operations, but instead he was arrested and charged with treason. [12]Despite the support of Thoreau and others, Brown was later hung.

[13]During his last years, Thoreau became weakened by tuberculosis. [14]He died in 1862 at the age of forty-four.

Write the correct form of the verb in parentheses.

1. Instructions for assemblage are (give) on page one.
2. I (call) home when I arrived.
3. Bones have been (break) by a simple misstep.
4. I have (pay) all my bills.
5. As more people talked, the rumors (grow).
6. I think you (do) the best thing when you helped her.
7. Rosanna (sing) in the alto section when she was in the choir.
8. The conductor (lead) the band in a rousing march before the rally last week.
9. All the details of the new law are not yet (know).
10. This problem can be (break) down into three separate parts.
11. By the time they got up, the sun had (rise) and the beach was crowded.
12. After his walk yesterday, the dog (drink) an entire bowl of water.
13. I (catch) a cold last week.
14. Before my sister awakens in the morning, I will have (creep) into her room to decorate it for her birthday.
15. Don't worry. Jimmy has (dive) off the high board many times before.
16. Your front right tire has (spring) a leak.
17. When I (bite) into the apple, I realized that it wasn't yet ripe.
18. There were so many phone calls that I (become) annoyed.
19. The evening at the folk festival (be) the highlight of our trip to Ohio last summer.
20. Years ago, a family's water supply was (draw) from a well.

Identify the italicized verb tense by writing one of these labels: present, past, future, present perfect, past perfect, future perfect.

21. By next week we *will have put* our boat away for the winter.

22. Pasteurized cream *remains* fresh for quite a long time.

23. The snake in our creek *was* not a poisonous one.

24. He *has announced* that he will not be the chairperson again.

25. *Will* the freshmen *make* a float for the parade?

26. I *had* not *thought* about the appointment until you mentioned it.

27. *Will* you *be* at home tonight?

28. Today *has seemed* exceptionally dreary.

29. Cedar *protects* woolen clothing from damage by moths.

30. A golf ball *shattered* the plate glass window.

Identify the italicized verb form by writing one of these labels: present progressive, past progressive, future progressive, present perfect progressive, past perfect progressive, future perfect progressive, present emphatic, past emphatic.

31. The studio *does have* my photographs ready after all.

32. *Will* you *be sending* this letter overseas?

33. JoAnn *had been working* for hours before any help arrived.

34. Our gymnastics team *is collecting* newspapers and soda cans to raise money.

35. I *did write* the story just as you told it to me.

36. *Are* you *planning* a trip to South America anytime soon?

GRAMMAR/USAGE/MECHANICS

37. Stella's mother *has been working* all day.

38. Some people *do enjoy* skiing, despite what you say!

39. Our recycling efforts *are making* a difference in the amount of waste taken to landfills.

40. You *will be hearing* from us within a week in regard to your application.

POSTTEST **Correcting Verb Tense and Changing Voice**

Rewrite each sentence. Correct verbs in the wrong tense, or change verbs in passive voice to active voice.

41. Used cars are sold by the Jensen dealership.

42. A novel called *A Portrait of the Artist as a Young Man* was written by James Joyce.

43. By the time I remembered to call Matthew, he went.

44. Good wages were earned by Bill.

45. We have been eating pizza yesterday evening.

46. The computer was used by a graphic artist to produce advertisements.

47. The ground is very wet this morning because it rains last night.

48. By next year, there were drastic changes in the tax laws.

49. She sat down at the piano, opened her music book, and begins to play.

50. The charming scene was photographed by me.

Chapter 6

Subject-Verb Agreement

• • • • • • • • • • • • • • •

PRETEST **Identifying the Simple Subject and the Correct Verb Form**

Write the simple subject of each sentence. Then write the correct verb from the choice in parentheses.

1. There (was, were) two alligators at the edge of the swamp.
2. Neither the windows nor the door (was, were) locked.

3. A grove of oak trees (protect, protects) the house from the wind.

4. Neither the hammer nor the nails (was, were) in the toolbox.

5. Maria, one of the star skaters in the ice revue, (teaches, teach) ice-skating in her free time.

6. Eighty percent of this test in mathematics (deals, deal) with fractions.

7. Here (is, are) the statistics from the Bureau of the Census.

8. Toast with peanut butter and bananas (is, are) Olga's favorite breakfast.

9. The center of attraction (was, were) the three clowns.

10. Everyone in the organization (participates, participate) in the fund-raiser.

11. To raise horses (takes, take) patience.

12. All of the bicycles in the parade (was, were) decorated.

13. (Has, Have) the contest winners been announced yet?

14. The pedestrians who crossed in the middle of the street (was, were) given traffic tickets.

15. News of events in foreign countries (reaches, reach) this country in minutes.

16. Ninety-nine cents (is, are) the price of the bottle of vitamins.

17. Every boy and girl in school (has, have) purchased a ticket for the field trip.

18. The United States (is, are) bordered by Canada and Mexico.

19. The chorus (joins, join) the orchestra in the opening number of the concert.

20. The class of '90 (is, are) coming from many parts of the country for the reunion.

6.1 AGREEMENT OF SUBJECTS AND VERBS

Number refers to the form of a word that indicates whether it is singular or plural. A verb must agree with its subject in number.

Singular subjects indicate one and require a singular verb. Plural subjects indicate more than one and require a plural verb. With most regular verbs, add *–s* or *–es* to form the singular.

EXAMPLES **SINGULAR** The **author writes.** The **champion boxes.**

EXAMPLES **PLURAL** The **authors write.** The **champions box.**

An exception to the rule occurs with the pronouns *I* and *you*. Both take the plural form of a verb, even when *you* refers to one person. The only exception is *be;* when *I* is the subject, the verb form is *am.*

EXAMPLE **I eat** breakfast.

EXAMPLE **You prepare** dinner.

Whether functioning as main verbs or auxiliary verbs, *be, have,* and *do* change in form to show agreement. In fact, the number of a verb phrase is indicated by these auxiliary verbs. Notice in the verb phrases the main verbs do not change form.

EXAMPLES **SINGULAR** I **am** late.

He **is laughing.**

The applicant **has** experience.

She **has listened** intently.

Does he **need** help?

EXAMPLES **PLURAL** We **are** late.

We **are laughing.**

The applicants **have** experience.

They **have listened** intently.

Do they **need** help?

Write the correct verb from the choice in parentheses.

1. (Has, Have) the invitations been sent?
2. She (sits, sit) in the second row from the left.
3. The new shopping mall (opens, open) in two weeks.
4. I (is, am) going to the mall when it opens.
5. (Does, Do) she always check her arithmetic?
6. The cars (is, are) covered with dust.
7. That story (is, are) one of the saddest I've ever heard.
8. Mile markers (was, were) placed along the interstate highway.
9. The last few days (has, have) been perfect.
10. The wheat (is, are) turning gold all across the Midwest.

6.2 INTERVENING PHRASES AND CLAUSES

Don't mistake a word in an intervening phrase or clause for the subject of a sentence. The simple subject is never in a prepositional phrase. Make sure the verb agrees with the actual subject and not with the object of the preposition.

EXAMPLE The **paper** in those boxes **is** for the copy machine. [**The singular verb _is_ agrees with the singular subject _paper,_ not with the plural object of the preposition, _boxes._**]

EXAMPLE The **dogs** in that class **are** well behaved. [**The plural verb _are_ agrees with the plural subject _dogs,_ not with the object of the preposition, _class._**]

If a singular subject is linked to another noun by a phrase, the subject is still considered singular. Expressions such as _accompanied by, as well as, in addition to, plus,_ and _together with_ introduce phrases that modify the subject without changing its number. Although their meaning is similar to that of _and,_ these expressions don't form compound subjects.

EXAMPLE **Fried rice,** along with wonton soup, **makes** a delicious meal.

EXAMPLE **Isaac,** accompanied by Jerome, **goes** to the movies on Saturday.

Appositives and adjective clauses give information about the subject but don't change its number. Make sure you don't mistake a word in an appositive or an adjective clause for the subject of the sentence.

APPOSITIVES

EXAMPLE **Emma,** one of my good friends, **visits** Australia every year.

EXAMPLE Four well-known **writers,** all very skilled at their craft, **lecture** at the seminar.

ADJECTIVE CLAUSES

EXAMPLE **Virginia Woolf,** who was one of the Bloomsbury Group members, **expresses** emotion in her writing.

EXAMPLE The **rivers** that bordered Mesopotamia **are** the Tigris and the Euphrates.

Most of the following sentences contain an error in subject-verb agreement. For each sentence, write the subject and the corrected verb. If a sentence is already correct, write C.

1. Her computer plus her suitcase were checked through to New York.

2. Gasoline, one of the many existing fuels, is most efficient for powering automobiles.

3. A new menu, in addition to the existing one, are offered in the cafeteria today.

4. That vase of roses are about to topple.

5. The arms of the chair are soiled.

6. Birds that prey on small animals are called raptors.

7. The maple, as well as the oak and pine trees, grow all across the country.

8. The peaks of the mountain range is covered with snow.

9. The loose change in the pocket of my pants are for laundry.

10. *Gone with the Wind*, one of my favorite books, takes place during the Civil War.

6.3 AGREEMENT WITH COMPOUND SUBJECTS

A compound subject that is joined by *and* or *both . . . and* is plural unless its parts belong to one unit or they both refer to the same person or thing.

EXAMPLES   **PLURAL**   The **Tigris** and the **Euphrates flow** through southwestern Asia.

Both **rivers** and **streams provide** irrigation for farmland.

EXAMPLES **SINGULAR** **Toast** and **tea is** my favorite breakfast.
[one unit]

Her **friend** and **companion is** George.
[one person]

With compound subjects joined by *or* or *nor* (or by *either . . . or* or *neither . . . nor*), the verb agrees with the subject closer to it.

EXAMPLES **SINGULAR** Either the **tortoise** or the **hare wins** the race.

Raisins or an **apple makes** a good snack.

EXAMPLES **PLURAL** Neither **Kara** nor her **friends like** winter.

Neither **foxes** nor **dogs eat** only meat.

PRACTICE **Agreement with Compound Subjects**

Write the complete subject of each sentence. Then write the correct verb form from the choice in parentheses.

1. Both trucks and buses (is, are) hard on road surfaces.
2. Neither the equipment nor the uniforms (has, have) arrived yet.
3. Her attorney and confidant (is, are) Rosa.
4. Bread and butter (is, are) an American staple.
5. Neither a letter of recommendation nor good grades (guarantees, guarantee) a scholarship.
6. Either an orange or prunes (is, are) healthful for breakfast.
7. Both Florida and California (thrives, thrive) on tourism.
8. Peanuts and popcorn (is, are) common party snacks.
9. Ham and cheese (is, are) my regular sandwich.
10. Neither falling rocks nor icy pavement (keeps, keep) automobiles off the road.

6.4 AGREEMENT WITH SPECIAL SUBJECTS

COLLECTIVE NOUNS

A **collective noun** names a group of persons, things, or animals.

When a collective noun refers to a group as a whole, it requires a singular verb. When a collective noun refers to each member of a group individually, it requires a plural verb.

EXAMPLE   SINGULAR   The **chorus sings** beautifully.

EXAMPLE   PLURAL   The **chorus have** separate parts to learn.

When deciding the number of the verb needed for a collective noun, it is helpful to look for the pronouns *its* and *their.* When a collective noun is referred to by *its,* the collective noun requires a singular verb. When a collective noun is referred to by *their,* the collective noun needs a plural verb.

EXAMPLE   SINGULAR   The **litter** of kittens **stays** in *its* cage.

EXAMPLE   PLURAL   The **litter follow** *their* mother in a single-file line.

SPECIAL NOUNS

Certain nouns that end in *s*, such as *mathematics, molasses,* and *news*, require singular verbs.

EXAMPLE   **Molasses is** the key ingredient in my pecan pie.

EXAMPLE   The **news arrives** later here.

Certain other nouns that end in *s*, such as *scissors, pants, binoculars,* and *eyeglasses*, require plural verbs.

EXAMPLE   The **scissors are** in the drawer.

EXAMPLE   **Binoculars are** handy for bird-watching.

Many other nouns that end in *s*, such as *mumps, measles, ethics, statistics,* and *politics,* depending on the meaning, may require either a singular or a plural verb. In general, if the noun refers to a whole, such as a disease or a science, it requires a singular verb. If it is referring to qualities, activities, or individual items, it requires a plural verb.

EXAMPLE   **SINGULAR**   **Mumps is** contagious.

EXAMPLE   **PLURAL**   **Mumps are** itchy.

EXAMPLE   **SINGULAR**   **Statistics is** one of my favorite courses.

EXAMPLE   **PLURAL**   **Statistics are** the basis for many reports.

MANY A, EVERY, AND *EACH*

When *many a, every,* or *each* precedes a subject, whether simple or compound, the subject is considered singular.

EXAMPLE   *Many a* **decision was made.**

EXAMPLE   *Many a* **joke** and **cartoon was included.**

EXAMPLE   *Every* **dog has** a distinct personality.

EXAMPLE   *Every* **restaurant** and **diner serves** sandwiches.

EXAMPLE   *Each* **author writes** differently.

EXAMPLE   *Each* **penny** and **dime was counted.**

NOUNS OF AMOUNT

When a plural noun of amount refers to one unit, it acts as a singular subject. When it refers to individual units, it acts as a plural subject.

EXAMPLE   **SINGULAR**   Eight **dollars is** the cost of the ticket.

EXAMPLE   **PLURAL**   Eight **dollars lie** on the table.

When a fraction or a percentage refers to a singular word, it requires a singular verb. When it refers to a plural word, it requires a plural verb.

EXAMPLE   **SINGULAR**   Sixty **percent** of the *money* **was spent** on food.

EXAMPLE   **PLURAL**   Sixty **percent** of our *resources* **were used.**

Units of measurement usually require singular verbs.

EXAMPLE   **Sixteen by twenty inches is** a standard size for a picture frame.

EXAMPLE   **Ten millimeters equals** one centimeter.

TITLES

A title of a creative work always acts as a singular subject, even if a noun within the title is plural.

EXAMPLE   ***All the King's Men* was** the 1947 Pulitzer Prize winner.

EXAMPLE   **"Giant Steps" is** one of John Coltrane's masterworks.

COUNTRIES AND CITIES

Names of countries and cities require singular verbs.

EXAMPLE   The **United States has** a democratic government.

EXAMPLE   **Los Angeles is** in California.

PRACTICE   **Agreement with Special Subjects**

Write the correct verb form from the choice in parentheses.

1. Fourteen by twenty feet (is, are) the size of the room.
2. Many a day (passes, pass) without significance, or so it seems.

3. On its way south, the flock (feeds, feed) in lakes and ponds.

4. One half of the amount called for in the recipe (is, are) usually enough.

5. Economics (is, are) a popular college course.

6. Seven percent of our salaries (goes, go) toward retirement.

7. Three dollars (is, are) in my coat pocket.

8. Every entrant (receive, receives) a prize.

9. The Union of Soviet Socialist Republics (was, were) a former political unit.

10. "The Bean Eaters" (is, are) a poem by Gwendolyn Brooks.

6.5 INDEFINITE PRONOUNS AS SUBJECTS

Some indefinite pronouns are always singular, some are always plural, and others may be singular or plural, depending on their use.

INDEFINITE PRONOUNS	
SINGULAR	another, anyone, anybody, anything, each, either, everybody, everyone, everything, neither, nobody, no one, nothing, one, other, somebody, someone, something
PLURAL	both, few, many, others, several
SINGULAR OR PLURAL	all, any, enough, most, much, none, some

Singular indefinite pronouns require singular verbs. Plural indefinite pronouns require plural verbs.

EXAMPLES   **SINGULAR**   **Everyone is** welcome.

Someone gives me the number.

EXAMPLES   **PLURAL**   **Both are** able to play.

Few are coming to the party.

Chapter 6 Subject-Verb Agreement   **223**

The number of the pronouns in the last row of the chart depends on the words to which they refer. If the pronoun refers to a singular word, then it requires a singular verb. If the pronoun refers to a plural word, then it requires a plural verb.

EXAMPLE   **SINGULAR**   **None** of the candy **was left.** [*none* refers to *candy,* a singular noun]

EXAMPLE   **PLURAL**   **None** of the sweets **were left.** [*none* refers to *sweets,* a plural noun]

PRACTICE   **Indefinite Pronouns as Subjects 1**

Write the correct verb from the choice in parentheses for each sentence.

1. Everything (tastes, taste) better when camping outside.
2. The seniors have a group picture taken, and most (buys, buy) it.
3. Most of the jam (is, are) gone.
4. A state trooper stopped the driver of a truck and the driver of a car; both (was, were) traveling too fast.
5. Students read poems in school, but few (memorizes, memorize) them.
6. Everybody (hopes, hope) for good health.
7. Vacation for students begins soon; many (is, are) leaving town.
8. Bill and his classmate work at a grocery store; neither (likes, like) the job.
9. All of the notebook paper (is, are) lined.
10. Do any of the sweaters (has, have) short sleeves?

PRACTICE   **Indefinite Pronouns as Subjects 2**

From the chart in this lesson, choose five indefinite pronouns that are always singular and write sentences using each as a subject. Then do the same for five that are always plural and five that can be either singular or plural. Underline the verb in each sentence and be ready to explain why you used that verb form.

6.6 PHRASES AND CLAUSES AS SUBJECTS

Whenever a phrase or a clause acts as a subject, the verb must be singular.

EXAMPLE **Swimming laps is** good exercise. [**The gerund phrase** *swimming laps* **functions as the subject and agrees with the singular verb** *is.*]

EXAMPLE **To eat three pies is** gluttonous. [**The infinitive phrase** *to eat three pies* **functions as the subject and agrees with the singular verb** *is.*]

EXAMPLE **Whoever receives the most votes wins** the election. [**The noun clause** *whoever receives the most votes* **functions as the subject and agrees with the singular verb** *wins.*]

PRACTICE **Phrases and Clauses as Subjects**

Write the correct verb from the choice in parentheses for each sentence.

1. Which careers appeal to you (depends, depend) on your interests.
2. Digging ditches (is, are) hard work.
3. How defendants answer questions (makes, make) a big difference.
4. Climbing mountains (is, are) a challenge many enjoy.
5. Whoever wins the game (receives, receive) the award.
6. To drive all day (tires, tire) the eyes.

7. Cleaning up debris along the highways (has, have) become a volunteer effort.

8. Freezing tomatoes (is, are) my mother's summer activity.

9. To design bridges (requires, require) an engineering background.

10. To start a fire using sticks or flints for friction (is, are) rather difficult.

6.7 AGREEMENT IN INVERTED SENTENCES

In an **inverted sentence** the subject follows the verb.

Inverted sentences often begin with prepositional phrases. Don't mistake the object of the preposition for the subject.

EXAMPLE   **SINGULAR**   By the tables **sits** the **student.**

EXAMPLE   **PLURAL**   At the table **sit** the **students.**

In sentences beginning with *there* or *here*, the subject follows the verb. The words *there* and *here* almost never function as the subject of a sentence.

EXAMPLE   **SINGULAR**   Here **is** the **map.**

         There **is no one** available.

EXAMPLE   **PLURAL**   Here **are** the **maps.**

         There **are** no **volunteers** available.

In a question, an auxiliary verb usually comes before the subject. Look for the subject between the auxiliary verb and the main verb.

EXAMPLE   **SINGULAR**   **Does Katy like** pizza?

EXAMPLE   **PLURAL**   **Do they like** pizza?

Most of the following sentences contain an error in subject-verb agreement. For each sentence, write the incorrect verb and the correct verb. If a sentence is correct, write C.

1. There are no reason for this delay.
2. Does the television sound loud to you?
3. Along country roads grows flowers.
4. Here live the oldest man in the village.
5. Down the steps of the courthouse stride the sheriff.
6. There is the document you wanted.
7. In this campground are bathing facilities.
8. There is the bananas and the grapes.
9. Over these roads travel everyone on his or her way to La Paz.
10. On the floor is your homework assignments.

PRACTICE Subject-Verb Agreement

Write the subject of each sentence. Then write the correct verb from the choice in parentheses.

1. News (travels, travel) fast in a small community.
2. Shingles, a sometimes painful infection, (attacks, attack) certain nerves.
3. Even fifty thousand dollars (does, do) not buy what it did twenty years ago.
4. There (is, are) the missing pieces of the puzzle.
5. Everyone (knows, know) that Earth is round.
6. Only 3 percent of the homeowners in our area (has, have) swimming pools.
7. Managing restaurants (is, are) very demanding work.
8. The United States (has, have) many different climates.
9. Many a person (wishes, wish) to live a life of leisure.
10. All of the information (has, have) now been released.

6.8 AGREEMENT WITH SUBJECT, NOT PREDICATE NOMINATIVE

Don't be confused by a predicate nominative that is different in number from the subject. Only the subject affects the number of the linking verb.

EXAMPLE   Her great **joy was** Japanese gardens. [The singular verb *was* agrees with the singular subject *joy,* not with the plural predicate nominative *gardens.*]

EXAMPLE   Japanese **gardens were** her great joy. [The plural verb *were* agrees with the plural subject *gardens,* not with the singular predicate nominative *joy.*]

PRACTICE Agreement with Subject, Not Predicate Nominative

Write the subject of each sentence. Then write the correct verb from the choice in parentheses.

1. Bushels of donated wheat (was, were) the salvation of the starving populace during the famine.
2. Traffic jams (is, are) a problem during construction.
3. My favorite photographic subject (is, are) waterfalls.
4. Beans (is, are) the mainstay of a vegetarian diet.
5. Virginia's greatest culinary accomplishment (is, are) cream puffs.
6. Ocean sunsets (is, are) her passion.
7. The Greek islands (is, are) a treat for history lovers.
8. The shoe factory's greatest asset (is, are) its employees.
9. Tonight's special (is, are) mixed greens and rice.
10. Long fingers (is, are) an advantage for a pianist.

6.9 AGREEMENT IN ADJECTIVE CLAUSES

When the subject of an adjective clause is a relative pronoun, the verb in the clause must agree with the word to which the relative pronoun refers.

If the relative pronoun is the subject of the clause and it refers to a singular word, the verb in the adjective clause must be singular.

The **man who teaches** my yoga class dresses in white.

If the relative pronoun is the subject of the clause and it refers to a plural word, then the verb in the adjective clause must be plural.

Classrooms that have computers are convenient.

If an adjective clause is preceded by *one of (plural word)*, then the relative pronoun will refer to the plural word, and the verb in the clause must be plural.

Sanctuary is one of my favorite **books that were** written by Faulkner. **[The relative clause refers to *books* because all of the books are written by Faulkner.]**

If an adjective clause is preceded by *the only one of (plural word)*, the relative pronoun will refer to the word *one*, and the verb in the clause must be singular.

Pedro is the only **one** of the Fernandez children **who owns** a car. **[The relative clause refers to *one* because only one person owns a car.]**

PRACTICE **Agreement with Relative Pronouns**

Write the relative pronoun and the word to which it refers. Then write the correct verb from the choice in parentheses.

1. Don't enter that yard. There is a dog that (bites, bite).

2. Mathematics is the only one of his classes that (challenges, challenge) him.

3. The motel rooms that (has, have) an ocean view are more expensive.

4. In the city, the streets that (is, are) named for states run east and west.

5. Bing Crosby's "White Christmas" is one of the most popular recordings that (was, were) ever made.

6. Hercules is the only one of the dogs that (catches, catch) a Frisbee.

7. The broker who (sells, sell) stocks and bonds left you a phone message.

8. The only one of the students who (reads, read) every day is Roberto.

9. Antiques that (is, are) sold in antique stores are usually quite expensive.

10. The music that (entertains, entertain) us most is rock music.

PRACTICE Proofreading

Rewrite the following passage, correcting the errors in capitalization, grammar, and usage. Add any missing punctuation. There are ten errors. Some sentences are correct.

Richard Wright

¹Richard Wright was born in Mississippi in 1908, and he grew up in poverty. ²His work as a teenager were a series of menial jobs. ³Wright moved to Chicago when he was nineteen, he later began writing for the Federal Writers' Project. ⁴He wrote a series of stories, called *Uncle Tom's Children,* about the african american experience in the United States. ⁵*Uncle Tom's Children* were so impressive that it won a prize from *Story* magazine. ⁶In 1940 Wright published *Native Son* a novel set in Chicago. ⁷Wright played it's hero, Bigger Thomas, in the movie version of his book. ⁸*Native Son* is one of the most famous books that was written by Wright.

⁹Wright and his wife later moved to Paris. ¹⁰Some of Wright's friends there was famous; for example, he knew the writers Gertrude Stein and Jean-Paul Sartre.

¹¹There is two books by Wright about his life. ¹²Both *Black Boy* and *American Hunger* is autobiographical.

Write the simple subject of each sentence. Then write the correct verb from the choice in parentheses.

1. A steak or the scallops (is, are) the best choice tonight.
2. The paper clips on the desk (is, are) for everyone's use.
3. *Short Stories for Young Americans* (contains, contain) many tales of courage.
4. Sylvia's interest (is, are) lamps.
5. Many of these plants (has, have) lost their leaves.
6. The hat, as well as the jewels, (adds, add) interest to the costume.
7. Both mother and child (is, are) to receive the immunization.
8. Some of the audience members (leaves, leave) the performance early.
9. (Has, Have) any of the cards been printed yet?
10. My best friend and my chess partner (is, are) Miguel.
11. To take risks (is, are) sometimes costly.
12. None of my friends (is, are) going to attend the local university.
13. My favorite pants (needs, need) to be ironed.
14. Ten cents (is, are) on the table.
15. Writing stories (is, are) not as easy as it might seem.
16. Either the moon or the planets (shines, shine) brightly at certain times.
17. A large percent of the soccer team (is, are) graduating this year.
18. Rhonda, along with the other cheerleaders, (rides, ride) the team bus.
19. This one page of expenditures (indicates, indicate) a shortage of company funds.
20. The candidate, along with her assistant and her speechwriter, (is, are) taking the flight.

Chapter 7

Using Pronouns Correctly

● ● ● ● ● ● ● ● ● ● ● ● ● ● ●

PRETEST   **Identifying the Correct Pronoun**

*For each sentence, write the correct pronoun from the
choice in parentheses.*

1. The charging bull frightened Marty and (I, me).
2. Mother and (they, them) went to the political rally.
3. (Who, Whom) do you think threw the cake in the trash
   by mistake?
4. Few of the men leave town for (his, their) vacations.
5. (Who's, Whose) skis did you borrow?
6. I was disappointed at (you, your) not sharing your idea
   with me.

7. (We, Us) people whose names begin with *B* usually end up in the front of the room.

8. The last two students to finish the test, Benny and (I, me), got the best grades on it.

9. Everyone should keep (his or her, their) locker clean.

10. The coach knows that she can depend on (we, us) players to be at practice.

11. She swims better than (he, him).

12. (We, Us) Americans believe in freedom of speech for every person.

13. Class rings will be delivered to (whoever, whomever) ordered them.

14. (Them, Their) laughing disturbed those who were asleep.

15. Between you and (I, me), I think Juan is going to be class president.

16. You may have as your best man (whoever, whomever) you choose.

17. My sister participates in more outdoor activities than (I, me).

18. Who did he say had won the tennis championship— (her, she) or Angela?

19. The person whom you are thinking of is probably (she, her).

20. Miss Brown seems to think that you are more capable than (I, me).

21. I am more studious than (he, him).

22. That is (he, him) in the phone booth. Do you know him?

23. I dished (me, myself) a huge bowl of chocolate ice cream.

24. His dad gets upset over (him, his) playing his stereo so loudly.

25. The English class give (its, their) speeches to the student body today.

7.1 CASE OF PERSONAL PRONOUNS

Pronouns that refer to persons or things are called **personal** pronouns.

Personal pronouns have three **cases,** or forms. The three cases are called **nominative, objective,** and **possessive.** The case of a personal pronoun depends on the pronoun's function in a sentence—that is, whether it is a subject, a complement, an object of a preposition, or a replacement for a possessive noun.

PERSONAL PRONOUNS			
CASE	**SINGULAR PRONOUNS**	**PLURAL PRONOUNS**	**FUNCTION IN SENTENCE**
NOMINATIVE	I, you, she, he, it	we, you, they	subject or predicate nominative
OBJECTIVE	me, you, her, him, it	us, you, them	direct object, indirect object, or object of preposition
POSSESSIVE	my, mine, your, yours, her, hers, his, its	our, ours, your, yours, their, theirs	replacement for possessive noun(s)

Use these rules to avoid errors with the case of personal pronouns:

1. Use the nominative case for a personal pronoun in a compound subject.

EXAMPLE   Dorothy and **I** planted the perennials.

EXAMPLE   **She** and Luke planted the annuals.

EXAMPLE   **He** and **I** designed the drip irrigation system.

2. Use the objective case for a personal pronoun in a compound object.

EXAMPLE   Lana brought Dorothy and **them** some lemonade.

EXAMPLE   For Luke and **me,** there was iced tea.

Hint: When you are choosing a pronoun for a sentence that has a compound subject or a compound object, try saying the sentence to yourself without the conjunction and the other subject or object.

EXAMPLE   The sprinkler sprayed [Dorothy and] **me.**

Note: It is considered courteous to place the pronoun *I* or *me* last in a series.

EXAMPLE   **Kris, Rick,** and **I** transplanted this rosebush.
           [nominative case]

EXAMPLE   The tiller was rented by **Edmund** and **me.**
           [objective case]

3. Use the nominative case for a personal pronoun after a linking verb.

EXAMPLE   The best garden designer was **he.**

EXAMPLE   The most careful weeders are **we.**

EXAMPLE   The creakiest in the knees am **I!**

This rule is changing. In informal speech, people often use the objective case after a linking verb; they say, *It's me, It was him.* Some authorities even recommend using the objective case in informal writing to avoid sounding pretentious. To be strictly correct, however, use the nominative case after a linking verb, especially in formal writing.

4. Never spell possessive personal pronouns with apostrophes.

EXAMPLE   This shovel is **hers.**
           The pitchforks are **theirs.**
           This is **yours.**

It's is a contraction for *it is* or *it has.* Don't confuse *it's* with the possessive pronoun *its.*

EXAMPLE   **It's** time to thin the carrots. Please bring me the kneeler and **its** cushion.

5. Use possessive pronouns before gerunds (-*ing* forms used as nouns).

EXAMPLE   **Your** mowing the lawn was a big help.

EXAMPLE   **His** eating all the ripe berries was to be expected.

EXAMPLE   We are glad of **their** lending us the wheelbarrow.

PRACTICE **Personal Pronouns**

Write the correct personal pronoun from the choice in parentheses.

1. It was David and (I, me) who sent the flowers.
2. The dog loves to chase (it's, its) tail.
3. She and (I, me) will take care of the arrangements.
4. The person who called was (she, her).
5. I always enjoy (you, your) singing.
6. This application was sent to both you and (I, me).
7. (Theirs, Their's) is the convertible with the white top.
8. (We, Us) and (they, them) decided on the campsite.
9. This old television loses (its, it's) picture from time to time.
10. Winter gives Raul and (they, them) a chance to take a break from work at the harbor.

7.2 PRONOUNS WITH AND AS APPOSITIVES

Use the nominative case for a pronoun that is an appositive to a subject or a predicate nominative.

EXAMPLE   The ringmasters, **Keri** and **she,** had a difficult task. **[*Ringmasters* is the subject of the sentence.]**

EXAMPLE The stars of the show were two brothers, **Ananda** and **he.**
[*Brothers* is a predicate nominative.]

Use the objective case for a pronoun that is an appositive to a direct object, an indirect object, or an object of a preposition.

EXAMPLE The crowd applauded the jugglers, **Reed** and **him.**
[*Jugglers* is a direct object.]

EXAMPLE The strongest acrobats gave the climbers, **Kate** and **her,** boosts to help them climb. [*Climbers* is an indirect object.]

EXAMPLE The best costumes were worn by the tightrope

walkers, **Leeza** and **him.** [*Walkers* is the object of the preposition *by.*]

It is considered courteous to place the pronoun *I* or *me* last in a pair or series of appositives.

EXAMPLE The jugglers, **William, Abeni,** and **I,** performed our routines perfectly. [nominative case]

EXAMPLE The audience gave the unicycle riders, **Cai** and **me,** a special prize. [objective case]

When a pronoun is followed by an appositive, choose the case of the pronoun that would be correct if the appositive were omitted.

EXAMPLE **We performers** were pleased with the circus we had organized. [*We*, which is in the nominative case, is correct because *we* is the subject of the sentence.]

The circus earned money for the local hospital and for **us students. [*Us*, which is in the objective case, is correct because *us* is the object of the preposition *for*.]**

Hint: When you are choosing the correct pronoun, it is often helpful to say the sentence to yourself leaving out the appositive.

EXAMPLE **We** were pleased with the circus we had organized.

EXAMPLE The circus earned money for the local hospital and for **us.**

PRACTICE Pronouns as Appositives

Write the correct pronoun from the choice in parentheses. Then write the word to which the pronoun is an appositive, and tell how this word is used in the sentence.

EXAMPLE The audience applauded the winners, Kenny and (I, me).

Answer: me; winners; direct object

1. His assistants, Jack and (she, her), were there.

2. The troop leaders, Rosanna and (I, me), planned some pool activities.

3. Next week's schedule was given to the only people at the meeting, (we, us).

4. We are all indebted to the people who made this celebration possible, (they, them).

5. The legal department sent the officers, Rocky and (I, me), an explanation of the law.

6. The first persons there were the triplets, Larry, James, and (he, him).

7. Mr. Willis gave his best student, (I, me), an award for excellence.

8. The first violinist, (her, she), is playing a solo tonight.

9. The chauffeur drove our group, my six neighborhood friends and (I, me), to the door of the auditorium.

10. The firefighter showed the equipment to everyone there, (they, them) and (we, us).

"So, then . . . Would that be 'us the people' or 'we the people?'"

7.3 PRONOUNS AFTER THAN AND AS

When words are left out of an adverb clause that begins with *than* or *as,* choose the case of the pronoun that you would use if the missing words were fully expressed.

EXAMPLE   You skate more skillfully than **I.** [That is, . . . *than I skate.* **The nominative pronoun *I* is the subject of the adverb clause *than I skate.***]

EXAMPLE   The crash startled Becca as much as **me.** [That is, . . . *as much as it startled me.* **The objective pronoun *me* is the direct object in the adverb clause *as much as it startled me.***]

Some sentences can be completed with either a nominative or an objective pronoun, depending on the meaning intended by the speaker or writer.

EXAMPLE The manager respects the director more than **I [respect the director]**.

EXAMPLE The manager respects the director more than **[the manager respects] me.**

PRACTICE **Pronouns After *Than* and *As***

Rewrite each sentence, choosing the correct pronoun from the choice in parentheses and adding the necessary words to complete the incomplete comparison.

EXAMPLE The alarm's buzzer startled Rafe as much as (I, me).

Answer: The alarm's buzzer startled Rafe as much as it startled me.

1. José is a better worker than (I, me).
2. He should do better on the test than (I, me).
3. Our employer doesn't pay Roger as much as (I, me).
4. Les goes to movies more often than (I, me).
5. The weight lifter is no stronger than (I, me).
6. The family next door hasn't planted as many trees as (we, us).
7. My sister has saved more money than (I, me).
8. I cannot swim as well as (she, her).
9. I was not as late as (she, her).
10. Mr. Andrews told me more than (she, her).

7.4 REFLEXIVE AND INTENSIVE PRONOUNS

Observe the following rules when you use reflexive and intensive pronouns.

Don't use *hisself, theirself,* or *theirselves.* All three are incorrect forms. Use *himself* and *themselves.*

EXAMPLE   Billy pruned the apple tree **himself.**

EXAMPLE   My sisters **themselves** put the family budget on the computer.

Use a reflexive pronoun when a pronoun refers to the subject of the sentence.

EXAMPLE   **INCORRECT**   I made me a tuna sandwich.

          CORRECT   I made **myself** a tuna sandwich.

EXAMPLE   **INCORRECT**   We found us a new house.

          CORRECT   We found **ourselves** a new house.

Don't use a reflexive pronoun unnecessarily. Remember that a reflexive pronoun must refer to the subject, but it must not take the place of the subject.

EXAMPLE   **INCORRECT**   Deliver the papers to Mr. Morton or myself, please.

          CORRECT   Deliver the papers to Mr. Morton or **me,** please.

EXAMPLE   **INCORRECT**   Tam and yourself have done good work.

          CORRECT   Tam and **you** have done good work.

GRAMMAR/USAGE/MECHANICS

PRACTICE Reflexive and Intensive Pronouns

Most of the sentences below contain errors in pronoun use. Rewrite the incorrect sentences, correcting the errors by replacing the incorrect pronouns. If a sentence is already correct, write C.

EXAMPLE   Caitlin and myself will be ready at nine o'clock.
           Answer: Caitlin and I will be ready at nine o'clock.

1. I fried me some eggs and potatoes.
2. He wrote hisself a note about the bill.

3. The girls treated themselves to banana splits.
4. Simon Hudson built the patio hisself.
5. Give yourself a little more time.
6. I sometimes find that I am talking to myself.
7. Please send Lois and myself a postcard when you go to Italy.
8. We did ourself a favor by staying away from the crowd in the street.
9. We bought us hot dogs and chips at the baseball game.
10. At the spa, the women pampered theirselves with mud baths and facials.

7.5 *WHO* AND *WHOM* IN QUESTIONS AND SUBORDINATE CLAUSES

In questions use the nominative pronoun *who* for subjects and the objective pronoun *whom* for direct and indirect objects and for objects of a preposition.

EXAMPLE **Who** needs a ride home? [***Who* is the subject of the verb *needs.***]

EXAMPLE **Whom** did you call? [***Whom* is the direct object of the verb *did call.***]

EXAMPLE **Whom** did they send a telegram? [***Whom* is the indirect object of the verb *did send.***]

EXAMPLE **For whom** is this bouquet of roses? [***Whom* is the object of the preposition *for.***]

In questions that have an interrupting expression (such as *did you say* or *do you think*), it often helps to drop the interrupting phrase to make it easier to decide whether to use *who* or *whom*.

EXAMPLE **Who** do you think broke the window? [**Think, "*Who* broke the window?" *Who* is the subject of the verb *broke*.**]

In subordinate clauses, use the nominative pronouns *who* and *whoever* for subjects and predicate nominatives.

EXAMPLE	Ask them **who** will be home for dinner. [***Who** is the subject of the noun clause **who will be home for dinner**.*]
EXAMPLE	They know **who** her supervisor is. [***Who** is the predicate nominative of the noun clause **who her supervisor is**.*]
EXAMPLE	The winner of the Miss Congeniality Award will be **whoever** deserves it. [***Whoever** is the subject of the noun clause **whoever deserves it**.*]

In subordinate clauses, use the objective pronouns *whom* and *whomever* for direct and indirect objects and for the objects of prepositions.

EXAMPLE	They told her **whom** she could call. [***Whom** is the direct object of the verb **could call** in the noun clause **whom she could call**.*]
EXAMPLE	Rembrandt is a painter about **whom** I have read quite a bit. [***Whom** is the object of the preposition **about** in the adjective clause **about whom I have read quite a bit**.*]
EXAMPLE	The new president will be **whomever** the voters elect. [***Whomever** is the direct object of the verb **elect** in the noun clause **whomever the voters elect**.*]

In informal speech, many people generally use *who* in place of *whom* in sentences such as *Who did you vote for?* In writing and in formal speaking situations, however, make the distinctions between *who* and *whom*.

When the pronouns *who* and *whom* are used in questions, they are called **interrogative pronouns;** when *who/whoever* and *whom/whomever* are used to introduce subordinate clauses, they are called **relative pronouns.**

For each sentence, write the correct pronoun from the choice in parentheses.

1. Listen to the person (who, whom) you trust most.
2. (Who, Whom) is your favorite actor?
3. (Who, Whom) are they paging?
4. The rules state that the winner is (whoever, whomever) comes closest to guessing the number of peanuts in the jar.
5. For (who, whom) is this gift?
6. I'm sure that (whoever, whomever) leaves the concert early will be disappointed.
7. A person (who, whom) is fair and honest is usually respected.
8. The boy (who, whom) I met last night only recently enrolled in our school.
9. (Whoever, Whomever) wants to go to the amusement park should be on the bus by eight in the morning.
10. (Who, Whom) cuts your hair?

7.6 PRONOUN-ANTECEDENT AGREEMENT

An **antecedent** is the noun or pronoun to which a pronoun refers or that a pronoun replaces. All pronouns must agree with their antecedents in **number** (singular or plural), **gender** (masculine, feminine, or neuter), and **person** (first, second, or third).

A pronoun's antecedent may be a noun, another pronoun, or a phrase or a clause acting as a noun. In the following examples, the pronouns appear in blue type and their antecedents appear in blue italic type. Notice that they agree in both number and gender.

EXAMPLE ***Samuel Clemens*** used Mark Twain as **his** pseudonym. **[singular masculine pronoun]**

EXAMPLE ***Mary Anne Evans*** used George Eliot as **her** pseudonym. **[singular feminine pronoun]**

EXAMPLE Dogwood ***blossoms*** are admired for **their** beauty. **[plural pronoun]**

EXAMPLE I subscribe to this ***magazine*** for **its** monthly column on writing. **[singular neuter pronoun]**

Traditionally, a masculine pronoun was used when the gender of an antecedent was not known or might be either masculine or feminine. When you are reading literature written before the 1970s, remember that *his* may mean *his,* it may mean *her,* or it may mean *his or her.*

EXAMPLE A careful ***diver*** checks **his** equipment before each dive.

This usage has changed, however. Many people now feel that the use of masculine pronouns excludes half of humanity.

Use gender-neutral language when the gender is unknown or could be either masculine or feminine. Here are three ways to avoid using a masculine pronoun when the antecedent may be feminine:

1. Use *his or her, he or she,* and so on.
2. Make the antecedent plural and use a plural pronoun.
3. Eliminate the pronoun.

EXAMPLE A careful ***diver*** checks **his or her** equipment before each dive.

EXAMPLE Careful ***divers*** check **their** equipment before each dive.

EXAMPLE A careful ***diver*** checks **the** equipment before each dive. **[no pronoun]**

PRACTICE Gender-Neutral Pronoun-Antecedent Agreement

Rewrite each sentence in three different ways, using gender-neutral language.

EXAMPLE   A pilot must run his checklist before every flight.
        Answer: A pilot must run his or her checklist before every flight.
                Pilots must run their checklists before every flight.
                A pilot must run checklists before every flight.

1. A student must buy himself school supplies.
2. A schoolteacher often volunteers his time to help students.
3. A student should do his homework before class.
4. An employee must get himself to work on time.
5. Every day, a doctor must make his rounds at the hospital.

When the antecedent of a pronoun is a **collective noun,** the number of the pronoun depends on whether the collective noun is meant to be singular or plural.

EXAMPLE   The ***team*** plays **its** last game of the season. [The collective noun *team* conveys the singular sense of one unit. Therefore, the singular pronoun *its* is used.]

EXAMPLE   The ***team*** argue among **themselves** about **their** batting order. [The collective noun *team* conveys the plural sense of several people with different opinions. Therefore, the plural reflexive pronoun *themselves* and the plural personal pronoun *their* are used.]

EXAMPLE   The ***orchestra*** play **their** instruments with passion. [The collective noun *orchestra* is being used in the plural sense of several people performing separate actions. Therefore, the plural pronoun *their* is used.]

EXAMPLE The ***orchestra*** gives **its** best performance of the year.
[The collective noun *orchestra* is being used in the singular sense of one single group working together. Therefore, the singular pronoun *its* is used.]

PRACTICE **Agreement with Collective Nouns**

Write the correct pronoun from the choice in parentheses. Then write the collective noun that is the subject of each sentence and tell whether it is singular or plural in the sentence.

EXAMPLE The jury is always accompanied by a bailiff on (its, their) way to the courtroom.

Answer: its, jury, singular

1. The jury renders (its, their) verdict after deliberations.
2. The panel take turns giving (its, their) opinions.
3. The board of directors of the zoo speak to various organizations about (its, their) needs.
4. The band always plays a lively polka for (its, their) last number.
5. Each class chooses (its, their) gift to the school prior to commencement.

A pronoun must agree in **person** (first, second, or third person) with its antecedent.

Don't use *you*, a second-person pronoun, to refer to an antecedent in the third person. Either change *you* to an appropriate third-person pronoun or replace it with a suitable noun.

EXAMPLE **POOR** Linda and Soo will visit Spain, where **you** can see Arabic architecture.

BETTER Linda and Soo will visit Spain, where **they** can see Arabic architecture.

| BETTER | Linda and Soo will visit Spain, where **visitors** can see Arabic architecture. |

When the antecedent of a pronoun is another pronoun, be sure that the two pronouns agree in person. Avoid unnecessary shifts from *they* to *you*, *I* to *you*, or *one* to *you*.

EXAMPLE	POOR	**They** love to walk the forest trails, where **you** can hear the birds singing.
	BETTER	**They** love to walk the forest trails, where **they** can hear the birds singing.
EXAMPLE	POOR	**I** visited the coast of Maine, where **you** can go on a whale watch.
	BETTER	**I** visited the coast of Maine, where **I** was able to go on a whale watch.
EXAMPLE	POOR	When **one** teaches something to a child, **you** can learn a lot.
	BETTER	When **one** teaches something to a child, **one** can learn a lot.
	BETTER	When **you** teach something to a child, **you** can learn a lot.

PRACTICE   Agreement in Person

Rewrite each item, correcting the inappropriate use of you *by substituting a third-person pronoun or a suitable noun.*

EXAMPLE   Amateur chefs can take cooking classes, where you can learn professional techniques.

Answer: Amateur chefs can take cooking classes, where they can learn professional techniques.

1. When one keeps an open mind, you can appreciate many points of view.

2. I bought a new encyclopedia set, which you can read to learn about many subjects.

3. Some students take the woodworking class where you learn how to make furniture.

4. When a person goes to work, you should be on time.

5. He watches the kinds of movies that make you weep.

An **indefinite pronoun** must agree with its antecedent in **number.** Use a singular personal pronoun when the antecedent is a singular indefinite pronoun. Use a plural personal pronoun when the antecedent is a plural indefinite pronoun.

INDEFINITE PRONOUNS					
ALWAYS SINGULAR	another	either	neither	other	
	anybody	everybody	no one	somebody	
	anyone	everyone	nobody	someone	
	anything	everything	nothing	something	
	each	much	one		
ALWAYS PLURAL	both	few	many	others	several
SINGULAR OR PLURAL	all	any	enough	most	none	some

EXAMPLE   *Each* of the women had to put **her** suitcase in storage.

EXAMPLE   *One* of the men brought **his** antique abacus.

EXAMPLE   *Many* of the dentists have **their** own X-ray equipment.

Note that the plural nouns in the prepositional phrases—*of the women, of the men*—don't affect the number of the personal pronouns. *Her* and *his* are singular because *each* and *one,* their antecedents, are singular.

When no gender is specified, use gender-neutral wording.

EXAMPLE   **Everyone** must bring **his or her** own lunch.

If you find the preceding sentence a bit awkward, the best solution may be to reword the sentence. You might use a plural indefinite pronoun or a suitable noun (such as *people*) to replace the singular indefinite pronoun. You might even eliminate the personal pronoun entirely.

EXAMPLE   *All* must bring **their** own lunches.

EXAMPLE   *People* must bring **their** own lunches.

EXAMPLE   *Everyone* must bring **a** lunch. **[no pronoun]**

PRACTICE   **Gender-Neutral Agreement with Indefinite Pronoun Antecedents**

Rewrite each sentence in three ways, using gender-neutral language.

EXAMPLE   Each of the performers makes his costume.

        Answer: Each of the performers makes his or her costume.
                All of the performers make their costumes.
                Each of the performers makes a costume.

1. Each of the seniors will receive his diploma.
2. Everyone must bake his own cake.
3. Everybody is entitled to his opinion.
4. Anyone who does not do his homework will not pass the class.
5. Everyone must pay his taxes.

7.7 CLEAR PRONOUN REFERENCE

Make sure that the antecedent of a pronoun is clearly stated. Make sure that a pronoun cannot possibly refer to more than one antecedent.

VAGUE PRONOUN REFERENCE

To avoid a **vague pronoun reference,** don't use the pronoun *this, that, which, it, any,* or *one* without a clearly stated antecedent.

EXAMPLE **VAGUE** Gwendolyn Brooks is a creative and gifted writer, and **this** is apparent from her poetry. **[What is apparent from Brooks's poetry? Her talent is apparent, but *talent* is not specifically mentioned in the sentence.]**

CLEAR Gwendolyn Brooks is a creative and gifted writer, and **her talent** is apparent from her poetry.

EXAMPLE **VAGUE** In 1906 many buildings in San Francisco burned, **which** was caused by the great earthquake of April 18. **[What was caused by the earthquake? A fire was caused, but the word *fire* does not appear in the sentence.]**

CLEAR In 1906 a fire, **which** was caused by the great earthquake of April 18, burned many buildings in San Francisco.

GRAMMAR/USAGE/MECHANICS

PRACTICE Clear Pronoun Reference

Rewrite each item, replacing vague pronouns with specific words.

1. Harry phoned Sally every night for a week, but it was always busy.
2. I hear that Pierre paints beautifully, but he'll never show me any.
3. The streets in my neighborhood were flooded, which was caused by a hurricane.

4. I saw the local ballet company perform *Swan Lake* last night; it was great!

5. My friend Jean is a fantastic baker, and she often brings one for a snack.

UNCLEAR AND INDEFINITE PRONOUN REFERENCE

If a pronoun seems to refer to more than one antecedent, either reword the sentence to make the antecedent clear or eliminate the pronoun.

EXAMPLE	**UNCLEAR ANTECEDENT**	When Mrs. Baines told Lisa not to drive to school again, **she** was upset. [**Which word is the antecedent of *she*? Is Mrs. Baines upset or is Lisa?**]
	CLEAR ANTECEDENT	Mrs. Baines was upset when **she** told Lisa not to drive to school again.
	NO PRONOUN	When Mrs. Baines told Lisa not to drive to school again, **Mrs. Baines** was upset.

The pronouns *it, you,* and *they* should not be used as if they were indefinite pronouns. Instead, you should name the performer of the action. In some cases, you may be able to reword the sentence in such a way that you do not name the performer of the action and you do not use a pronoun.

EXAMPLE	**INDEFINITE**	In college **you** learn to be independent.
	CLEAR	In college **students** learn to be independent.
EXAMPLE	**INDEFINITE**	In some neighborhoods, **they** pick up the garbage twice a week.
	CLEAR	In some neighborhoods, the garbage **is picked up** twice a week.

EXAMPLE **INDEFINITE** In *Healthy Teen* magazine, **it** suggests eating more than four servings of vegetables each day.

CLEAR *Healthy Teen* magazine suggests eating more than four servings of vegetables each day.

PRACTICE **Correcting Unclear and Indefinite Pronoun Reference**

Rewrite each sentence, correcting any unclear or indefinite pronoun references.

EXAMPLE In some parts of Mexico, you retire to your room for a siesta, or a short rest.

Answer: In some parts of Mexico, people retire to their rooms for a siesta, or a short rest.

1. As Susan was talking to Sarah, she got another phone call.
2. They say the temperature will reach ninety degrees today.
3. My dad snapped at Rick; he was just goofing around.
4. In preschool you learn to play nicely with others.
5. Both the president and his aide agreed that he would attend the meeting of world leaders.

PRACTICE **Proofreading**

Rewrite the paragraph, correcting the errors in capitalization, grammar, and usage. Add any missing punctuation. There are ten errors. One sentence is correct.

William Wordsworth

[1]In twelfth grade, they often assign the poems of William Wordsworth. [2]Wordsworth was born in England in 1770 his mother died when he was

only eight years old. ³His father sent he and his brothers to a boarding school in Hawkshead. ⁴Many of the beautiful scenes in Wordsworth's poetry come from his memories of this. ⁵A great lover of nature was him!

⁶After graduating from Cambridge a famous university, Wordsworth developed a friendship with Samuel Taylor Coleridge. ⁷Coleridge was the poet with who Wordsworth would spent a great deal of time discussing and writing poetry. ⁸During this time, few poets published and wrote as much as them. ⁹This good friendship, however, was not to last. ¹⁰In 1810, Wordsworth and Coleridge argued; it was never completely settled.

¹¹Wordsworth died in 1850, but the poems that him and Coleridge wrote will be read and loved for many years to come.

POSTTEST   Identifying the Correct Pronoun

For each sentence, write the correct pronoun from the choice in parentheses.

1. It was (she, her) who addressed the group.
2. People should use (his or her, their) time creatively.
3. Marta and Jerry speak Spanish much better than (I, me).
4. (He, Him) and I were expected to make up a list of projects.
5. Neither she nor I was annoyed by (him, his) taking up our time.
6. (Who, Whom) do you think was at the party yesterday?
7. Everyone forgot to bring (their, his or her) swimming trunks.
8. Each of the women had (her, their) own opinion about the political candidate.
9. The Dallas Symphony Orchestra gives (its, their) last performance of the year tonight.
10. People must listen carefully if (you, they) hope to fol-

low instructions.

11. Our group chose three new members, Carlos, Ramon and (he, him), because their interests were similar to ours.

12. Here is (someones, someone's) textbook. Is it yours?

13. The school board vote tomorrow on (its, their) new president.

14. People are talking about the island where (you, they) can buy beachfront property inexpensively.

15. The boy (who, whom) delivers the paper is always on time.

16. He doesn't know (who, whom) to trust.

17. Both of the politicians expressed (his, their) ideas well.

18. Carmen dances better than (I, me).

19. We set (us, ourselves) some pretty high goals.

20. The salesperson (who, whom) sold me this computer no longer works for the store.

21. A party was given for the two retiring employees, (he and she, him and her).

22. A man can keep (hisself, himself) in good physical shape through exercise.

23. Both of us were unhappy about (their, them) leaving.

24. It was (I, me) who called around midnight last night.

25. When writing a letter to the editor of a newspaper, a person should always sign (their, his or her) name.

Chapter 8

Using Modifiers Correctly

• • • • • • • • • • • • • •

PRETEST   **Using Modifiers Correctly**

Write each sentence, choosing the correct word or words in parentheses.

1. This is the (satisfying, more satisfying, most satisfying) work that I have ever done.
2. The last hour of class went (faster, more fast) than any I have ever experienced.
3. The first pitch was thrown (bad, badly).
4. The new student did (good, well) on the geometry test.
5. A small food chopper is (handier, more handier) than a food processor.
6. The mountains in Colorado are (more majestic, most majestic) than the mountains in Tennessee.

7. This traffic circle is (rounder, more nearly round) than the one on Third Street.

8. As a supervisor, Ricardo is (demanding, less demanding, least demanding) than his brother.

9. Of all the candy I have tasted, this is (sweetest, more sweet, most sweet).

10. He is (more perfect, most perfect, more nearly perfect) in his calculations than most people.

11. Jody is the (happier, most happy, happiest) person I know.

12. Of the three alternatives, I consider the first the (less, least) attractive.

13. Our secretary and our bookkeeper are both ill; the former is (worse, more ill) than the latter.

14. Michael writes very little for the newspaper, but Don writes even (littler, less, least).

15. I eat breakfast (more often, most often) than not.

PRETEST Correcting Incomplete Comparisons, Double Negatives, and Misplaced and Dangling Modifiers

Rewrite each sentence, correcting any errors.

16. He deserves the award more than anyone.

17. I don't have hardly any homework tonight.

18. She hasn't seen no new movies this year.

19. I only made two mistakes on my typing test this week.

20. Rewriting his paper, the words seemed to come easily to Ramon.

21. The wording in the letter is clearer than the office memo.

22. The grocery store chain supports local causes, serving customers in the Southeast.

23. Practicing daily for hours, her piano playing is improving.

24. The siren only blares when there is a tornado warning.

25. The chairperson spoke about the new communications system by telephone.
26. The laundry dried fast on the clothesline, whipped by a strong wind.
27. Please only ask questions after the videotape is finished.
28. The captain told us when we enlisted to obey orders.
29. The newest employees don't make hardly any sales.
30. To understand our foreign policy, history books were read.

8.1 THE THREE DEGREES OF COMPARISON

Most adjectives and adverbs have three degrees: the positive, or base, form; the comparative form; and the superlative form.

The **positive** form of a modifier cannot be used to make a comparison. (This form appears as the entry word in a dictionary.)

The **comparative** form of a modifier shows two things being compared.

The **superlative** form of a modifier shows three or more things being compared.

EXAMPLES	POSITIVE	This computer is **fast.**
		I ran **slowly.**
EXAMPLES	COMPARATIVE	This computer is **faster** than that one.
		I ran **more slowly** than my friend.
EXAMPLES	SUPERLATIVE	Of these three computers, this one is the **fastest** machine.
		I ran **most slowly** of all.

In general, for one-syllable modifiers, add -er to form the comparative and -est to form the superlative.

EXAMPLE	small, small**er,** small**est**
	My cousin's room is **smaller** than mine.
	That is the **smallest** dog I have ever seen.

For some words, adding -er and -est requires spelling changes.

EXAMPLE   late, later, latest

EXAMPLE   flat, flatter, flattest

EXAMPLE   merry, merrier, merriest

With some one-syllable modifiers, it may sound more natural to use *more* and *most* instead of -er and -est.

EXAMPLE   apt, **more** apt, **most** apt

EXAMPLE   I am **more apt** to drink diet soda than you are.

For most two-syllable adjectives, add -er to form the comparative and -est to form the superlative.

EXAMPLE   friendly, friendlier, friendliest

That parrot is **friendlier** than this one.

This cockatoo is the **friendliest** bird here.

If -er and -est sound awkward with a two-syllable adjective, use *more* and *most* instead.

EXAMPLE   prudent, **more** prudent, **most** prudent

My father's new business plan is **more prudent** than his old plan.

In general, for adverbs ending in -ly, use *more* and *most* to form the comparative and superlative degrees.

EXAMPLE   sweetly, **more** sweetly, **most** sweetly

Of my three friends, I think Jane sings **most sweetly.**

For modifiers of three or more syllables, always use *more* and *most* to form the comparative and superlative degrees.

EXAMPLE   significant, **more** significant, **most** significant

These data are the **most significant** ones for our future research.

Less and *least,* the opposite of *more* and *most,* can also be used with most modifiers to show comparison.

EXAMPLE   You used to be **less thoughtful** than you are now.

EXAMPLE   This salad is the **least fattening** thing on the menu.

Less and *least* are used before modifiers that have any number of syllables.

Some adjectives, such as *unique, perfect, final, dead,* and *square,* cannot logically be compared because they describe an absolute condition. For instance, something is or is not perfect, so it would be impossible for a thing to be more perfect than another thing. However, you can sometimes use *more nearly* and *most nearly* with absolute modifiers.

EXAMPLE   Clara's rug is **more nearly square** than Paula's.

EXAMPLE   The form of that sonnet is the **most nearly perfect** one I have ever seen.

PRACTICE   The Three Degrees of Comparison

Rewrite each sentence to correct the error in comparison. If the sentence is already correct, write C.

1. Of the two track stars, Althea runs fastest.
2. Of all the ornaments in the living room, this ornament is most shiny.
3. Little Danny played calmlier than the other children.
4. Of all the movies I've seen, *Gone with the Wind* is longest.
5. Of all the students in art class, Danielle is more artistic.

6. This is the best job of the two.
7. Her second idea was even worser than her first one.
8. Maria is the smartest person in our class.
9. We live farthest from school than anyone else.
10. All of us tried making square knots; mine was the squarest.

8.2 IRREGULAR COMPARISONS

A few modifiers form their comparative and superlative degrees irregularly. It is most helpful simply to memorize their forms.

MODIFIERS WITH IRREGULAR FORMS OF COMPARISON

POSITIVE	COMPARATIVE	SUPERLATIVE
good	better	best
well	better	best
bad	worse	worst
badly	worse	worst
ill	worse	worst
far (distance)	farther	farthest
far (degree, time)	further	furthest
little (amount)	less	least
many	more	most
much	more	most

Write the correct comparison from the choice in parentheses.

1. I have (more, most) homework than my young brothers.
2. I play the piano badly, but my sister plays (more badly, worse).
3. Saturn is (farther, further) from Earth than Mars.
4. The damage from the hurricane was (badder, worse) than originally reported.
5. I have little free time, but you have (less, littler).
6. Her dedication makes her the (better, best) employee of the group.
7. Although I am not well, I feel (better, best) than he.
8. Jim has written only the introduction to his required paper, Sal is halfway finished, and Ryan is (farthest, furthest) along.
9. She speaks (best, better) in public than her brother does.
10. Of all the pups, the black one is (less, least) aggressive.

8.3 CORRECTING DOUBLE COMPARISONS

Don't use both *-er* and *more.* Don't use both *-est* and *most.* To do so would be an error called a **double comparison.**

EXAMPLE	**INCORRECT**	Chimpanzees are more smaller than gorillas.
	CORRECT	Chimpanzees are **smaller** than gorillas.
EXAMPLE	**INCORRECT**	That is the most saddest song on the album.
	CORRECT	That is the **saddest** song on the album.
EXAMPLE	**INCORRECT**	She is the most attractivest girl in school.
	CORRECT	She is the **most attractive** girl in school.

Rewrite each sentence to correct the error in comparison. If the sentence is already correct, write C.

1. Today is the most hottest day of the summer.

2. The gargoyle over the doorway is most ugliest.

3. Washing dishes is the most boringest work in the house.

4. Today's job search proved to be less fruitful than yesterday's.

5. That is the most astounding news of the year!

6. Fish used to be more abundanter in the ocean than they are now.

7. I actually feel more worse than I did yesterday.

8. Some days are more better than others.

9. I drove more farther yesterday than I did today.

10. Algebra is Andrew's most difficult class.

8.4 CORRECTING INCOMPLETE COMPARISONS

Do not make an incomplete or unclear comparison by omitting the word *other* or the word *else* when you compare a person or thing with its group.

EXAMPLE	UNCLEAR	New York City has more skyscrapers than any city in the United States. [*Any city includes New York City.*]
	CLEAR	New York City has more skyscrapers than any **other** city in the United States.
EXAMPLE	UNCLEAR	Juanita received more gifts than anyone. [*Anyone includes Juanita.*]
	CLEAR	Juanita received more gifts than anyone **else.**

Be sure your comparisons are between like things—that is, similar things.

EXAMPLE	UNCLEAR	The salary of a teacher is lower than a lawyer. [The salary of a teacher is being compared illogically with a person, namely, a lawyer.]
	CLEAR	The salary of a teacher is lower than **that of a lawyer.**
	CLEAR	The salary of a teacher is lower than **the salary of a lawyer.**
	CLEAR	A teacher's salary is lower than **a lawyer's.** [The word *salary* is understood after *lawyer's.*]

GRAMMAR/USAGE/MECHANICS

PRACTICE Correcting Incomplete Comparisons

Rewrite each sentence, correcting the error in comparison. If a sentence is already correct, write C.

1. Jacques got better grades than anyone in his class.
2. My handwriting is worse than the other boy.
3. The seeds of some peppers are hotter than the seeds of others.
4. I think I learned more than anyone at band camp.
5. In my opinion, biology is more interesting than any subject.
6. That river has flooded more often than any other river in the state.
7. Darkness in the country is more nearly black than darkness in the city, except, perhaps, on a moonlit night.
8. Your designs are more creative than mine.
9. The bedrooms in this house are smaller than the first house we saw.
10. The skin of a child is usually softer than an adult.

Rewrite each sentence, correcting the error in comparison. If a sentence is already correct, write C. Consult a dictionary if necessary.

1. I am readier for this test than I was for the last.
2. This pine tree is taller than any other tree in the lot.
3. José ran better in today's race than he ran in last week's.
4. The pattern of a snowflake is even more intricate than a spider web.
5. The Smiths have traveled more farther than the Wilsons.
6. There is no question that this watermelon is more better than that one.
7. I feel more well today than I did yesterday.
8. Saul polishes and cleans his car most often than anyone else.
9. Of the two weight lifters, he is definitely most muscular.
10. Of the three nurses, Michael was thoughtfullest.

8.5 *GOOD* OR *WELL; BAD* OR *BADLY*

Always use *good* as an adjective. *Well* may be used as an adverb of manner telling how ably or how adequately something is done. *Well* may also be used as an adjective meaning "in good health."

EXAMPLE   Jaleel is a **good** guitarist. [adjective]

EXAMPLE   Your new perfume smells **good.** [adjective after a linking verb]

EXAMPLE   I feel **good** when I hear our song. [adjective after a linking verb]

EXAMPLE   Aziza plays the violin **well. [adverb of manner]**

EXAMPLE   She isn't feeling **well. [adjective meaning "in good health"]**

Always use *bad* as an adjective. Use *badly* as an adverb.

EXAMPLE   The quarterback made a **bad** throw. **[adjective]**

EXAMPLE   That meat tastes **bad. [adjective after a linking verb]**

EXAMPLE   I feel **bad** about my mistake. **[adjective after a linking verb]**

EXAMPLE   This pitcher is leaking **badly. [adverb after an action verb]**

PRACTICE *Good or Well; Bad or Badly*

Rewrite each sentence, correcting all errors in comparison. If a sentence is already correct, write C.

1. The team's quarterback runs so good that no one can stop him.
2. I feel badly about the damage to your house.
3. Although she is generally in good health, she isn't feeling good today.
4. This soup tastes badly; I think I added too much salt.
5. It is looking badly for our outing because dark clouds are rolling in.
6. I know well what constitutes a hard day's work.
7. Choosing to stay in bed until noon was a bad decision.
8. I write badly when I am overtired.
9. The financial situation for the newly independent country looks badly.
10. The pitcher was throwing so bad last night that he was replaced in the second inning.

Give the comparative and superlative forms of each modifier. Consult a dictionary if necessary.

1. perfect
2. good
3. satisfactory
4. pleasant
5. lazy

6. unique
7. bad
8. well
9. fattening
10. fast

FoxTrot
by Bill Amend

8.6 CORRECTING DOUBLE NEGATIVES

Don't use two or more negative words to express the same idea. To do so is an error called a **double negative.** Use only one negative word to express a negative idea.

EXAMPLE **INCORRECT** I didn't hear no thunder.

  CORRECT I did**n't** hear **any** thunder.

  CORRECT I heard **no** thunder.

EXAMPLE **INCORRECT** She hasn't had no visitors.

  CORRECT She has**n't** had **any** visitors.

  CORRECT She has had **no** visitors.

EXAMPLE	INCORRECT	He never eats no ice cream.
	CORRECT	He **never** eats **any** ice cream.
	CORRECT	He eats **no** ice cream.

The words *hardly* and *scarcely* are negative words. Don't use them with other negative words, such as *not.*

EXAMPLES	INCORRECT	I didn't hardly look at the map.
		There isn't scarcely enough time for lunch.
	CORRECT	I **hardly** looked at the map.
		There is **scarcely** enough time for lunch.

PRACTICE Correcting Double Negatives

Revise each sentence that has a double negative. When possible, show two or more correct revisions. If a sentence is already correct, write C.

1. These situations don't never seem to correct themselves.
2. We never have no fun on the weekend.
3. I don't have scarcely any money left to buy clothes.
4. There isn't hardly any food in the refrigerator.
5. If you don't attend classes, you won't get no diploma.
6. One should never do nothing that would cause harm to others.
7. I read nothing in the paper about the infestation of mosquitoes.
8. There weren't no signs of a tornado.
9. Don't make no sound because the baby is sleeping.
10. There isn't scarcely enough time in the day to get everything done.

8.7 CORRECTING MISPLACED AND DANGLING MODIFIERS

Misplaced modifiers modify the wrong word, or they seem to modify more than one word in a sentence.

Place modifiers as close as possible to the words they modify in order to make the meaning of the sentence clear.

EXAMPLES

MISPLACED   At the last meeting, the mayor discussed the enormous cost of filling in the Westfields Gorge **with city council members.** [prepositional phrase incorrectly modifying *filling in*]

CLEAR   At the last meeting, the mayor discussed **with city council members** the enormous cost of filling in the Westfields Gorge. [prepositional phrase correctly modifying *discussed*]

MISPLACED   **Running smoothly and easily,** the crowd watched the marathoners. [participial phrase incorrectly modifying *crowd*]

CORRECT   The crowd watched the marathoners **running smoothly and easily.** [participial phrase correctly modifying *marathoners*]

Sometimes a misplaced modifier can be corrected by revising the sentence, for example, rephrasing the main clause or adding a subordinate clause.

EXAMPLE

MISPLACED   **Blowing from the north,** the pines were tossed by the wind. [participial phrase incorrectly modifying *pines*]

CLEAR   The pines were tossed by the wind, **which blew from the north.** [participial phrase recast as a subordinate clause correctly modifying *wind*]

CLEAR   **Blowing from the north,** the wind tossed the pines. [After the main clause has been recast, the participial phrase correctly modifies *wind*.]

Place the adverb *only* immediately before the word or group of words that it modifies.

If *only* is not positioned correctly in a sentence, the meaning of the sentence may be unclear.

EXAMPLE   UNCLEAR   Ainsley **only** has music class on Tuesday. [Does Ainsley have only one class on Tuesday, or does he have music class on no other day than Tuesday, or is Ainsley the only person (in a group) who has one class on Tuesday?]

CLEAR   Ainsley has **only** music class on Tuesday. [He has no other class that day.]

CLEAR   Ainsley has music class **only** on Tuesday. [He does not have music class on any other day.]

CLEAR   **Only** Ainsley has music class on Tuesday. [No one else has music class on Tuesday.]

Dangling modifiers seem logically to modify no word at all. To correct a sentence that has a dangling modifier, you must supply a word that the dangling modifier can sensibly modify.

EXAMPLES   DANGLING   **Using high-powered binoculars,** the lost child was found. [participial phrase logically modifying no word in the sentence]

CLEAR	Using high-powered binoculars, the rescuers found the lost child. [participial phrase correctly modifying *rescuers*]
CLEAR	The rescuers found the lost child because they used high-powered binoculars. [subordinate clause modifying *found*]
DANGLING	Celebrating my victory, a dinner with my friends lasted till midnight. [participial phrase logically modifying no word in the sentence]
CLEAR	Celebrating my victory, my friends and I stayed at the dinner table till midnight. [participial phrase modifying *my friends and I*]

PRACTICE Correcting Misplaced and Dangling Modifiers

Rewrite each sentence, correcting the misplaced and dangling modifiers.

1. The marathoner stubbed his toe on a stone running a victory lap in his bare feet.
2. The written test only has two parts.
3. Steering the ship to the north, the storm was avoided.
4. Reaching California, the search for gold began.
5. The proud father announced the birth of his twins with pink and blue balloons.
6. His kite was caught in a tree with a long tail.
7. Discouraged by criticism, his bid for office was given up by the candidate.
8. The teacher only gave us two assignments.

9. The car crossed the finish line with a badly damaged engine.

10. My dad couldn't hear the phone singing in the shower.

Rewrite the following passage, correcting errors in grammar and usage. Add any missing punctuation. There are ten errors.

Elizabeth Barrett Browning

[1]During her lifetime, Elizabeth Barrett Browning was one of England's more famous poets. [2]She received a completer education than most women of her time, studying Latin, Greek, history, philosophy, and literature with her brother's tutor. [3]Her first book of poetry was published when she was just thirteen

[4]At an early age, Elizabeth Barrett's health began to fail. [5]To make matters more worse, her overprotective father refused to let any of his eleven children marry. [6]Barrett did receive some visitors living in her father's house. [7]One of these visitors was Robert Browning, who was also a poet Browning and Barrett secretly married and went to Italy in 1846. [8]Barrett Browning's father didn't never forgive her for eloping.

[9]Once settled in Italy, Barrett Browning felt more well and regained much of her strength. [10]She continued to write throughout her marriage, and many believed that she expressed Victorian values better than any other Victorian poetry.

Write each sentence, choosing the correct word or words in parentheses.

1. Kino became the (more, most) envied man in La Paz.

2. Of the two animals, a collie and a cheetah, the latter is (faster, fastest).

3. The (better, best) of the six cakes was the chocolate one with peanut butter icing.

4. Walking is (less, least) rigorous than running.

5. She is the (most unique, most nearly unique) artist whose work I have seen.

6. With a choice between climbing one mountain or the other, I chose to climb the (higher, highest) one.

7. Louisa is the (more, most) determined girl of the two.

8. I did (bad, badly) on my practical driving test.

9. I think that my dad was always a little (lenienter, more lenient) than yours.

10. The film footage of houses disintegrating in a mud slide was one of the (saddest, most sad) sights I have ever seen.

11. Our coach was ill with appendicitis, but now he is (good, well).

12. Don't feel so (bad, badly) about your mistakes.

13. This is the (roundest, most nearly round) tomato I've seen.

14. This is a (deeper, more deep) well than our old one.

15. I think that Maria was the (more, most) appreciative of all the girls because she had never won anything before.

GRAMMAR/USAGE/MECHANICS

POSTTEST Correcting Incomplete Comparisons, Double Negatives, and Misplaced and Dangling Modifiers

Rewrite each sentence, correcting any errors.

16. The management doesn't serve no alcohol here.

17. Gazing out the window, the view of the ocean was breathtaking to the visitors.

18. Using radar, planes were detected in the area.

19. A teacher's job requires more public speaking than a librarian.
20. Escaping from its cage, the little boy was bitten by the dog.
21. The diver photographed rare, colorful fish breathing through scuba gear.
22. The other members of my book club enjoy the novels of Stephen Crane more than they enjoy Jack London.
23. Painting with assurance, the canvas was quickly covered with figures.
24. I enjoy visiting San Diego more than any city.
25. Remembering what my mother had taught me, the thank-you notes were promptly written.
26. I don't never get any mail.
27. Donetta has more stuffed animals than anyone.
28. Quietly sipping their tea, a loud knock on the door surprised the ladies.
29. I discussed the high cost of attending university with my family.
30. Exhausted after a long day at work, my dog greeted me at the door.

Chapter 9

Diagraming Sentences

• • • • • • • • • • • • • • •

PRETEST Diagraming Sentences

Diagram each sentence.

1. The teacher gave me a reading list.
2. Inspecting the automobile parts requires close attention.
3. Your prom dress is beautiful.
4. Gentlemen, start your engines.
5. The conclusion of the movie was a complete surprise.
6. That day Donetta will never forget.
7. Our assignment for tomorrow is the poem "Birches."
8. Winning is not the only point of competition.
9. There are few foods that I do not like.
10. Beans and lentils are sources of protein.
11. The waves crashed as the squall crossed the inlet.
12. Some birds migrate, but many do not.
13. Carefully move that picture to the right.
14. Its shelves fully stocked, the new store opened for business.

15. They left early because the concert was a disappointment.
16. An air freshener removes cooking odors that are offensive.
17. The Griffins enjoyed building their new house.
18. My mother does not like to drive.
19. Living in Spain, I discovered new foods and new recipes.
20. If you can, get me a ticket, and I will pay you for it.

9.1 DIAGRAMING SIMPLE AND COMPOUND SENTENCES

A **sentence diagram** shows how the various words and parts of a sentence function in the sentence and relate to the sentence as a whole.

It is vital to know the parts of a sentence before you begin diagraming. Diagraming just gives you a visual picture of how these parts relate to one another.

When writing a sentence in a diagram, retain the capitalization but leave out the punctuation.

SUBJECTS AND VERBS

Start your diagram with a horizontal line, called a baseline, bisected by a vertical line. Find the simple subject of the sentence and place it on the left of the vertical line; then place the simple predicate to the right of the vertical line.

EXAMPLE   Trees grow.

| Trees | grow |

A sentence with an understood subject is diagramed in the same way; however, the understood subject is placed in parentheses.

EXAMPLE   Hurry!

| (you) | Hurry |

Diagram each sentence.

1. Bees sting.
2. Stop!
3. Bells were ringing.
4. Snakes slither.
5. Remember.

COMPOUND SUBJECTS AND COMPOUND VERBS

To diagram compound subjects and compound verbs, follow the example diagram. If a correlative conjunction, such as *both . . . and,* is used, place the introductory conjunction to the left of the dotted line and the second part to the right.

EXAMPLE   Both juries and judges evaluate and decide.

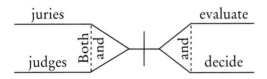

NOUNS OF DIRECT ADDRESS

To diagram nouns of direct address, follow the example diagram.

EXAMPLE   Felix, stay.

<u>Felix</u>

| (you) | stay |

Diagram each sentence.

1. Listen, students.
2. Blue and yellow blend.
3. He sings and dances.
4. Mei, stop and think.
5. Both television and radio enlighten and entertain.

ADJECTIVES AND ADVERBS

Both adjectives and adverbs are placed on slanted lines leading from the modified words. If an adverb modifies an adjective or another adverb, the adverb is placed on a slanted line parallel to the adjective or adverb and is connected with a straight line.

EXAMPLE   Young pine trees grow quite fast.

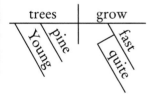

SENTENCES BEGINNING WITH *HERE* OR *THERE*

Here and *there* often function as adverbs when they begin a sentence.

EXAMPLE   Here comes the bus.

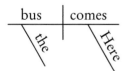

If *there* begins a sentence and does not modify the verb, then it functions as an expletive.

EXAMPLE   There is a new plan.

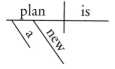

PRACTICE   **Diagraming Adjectives and Adverbs**

Diagram each sentence.

1. Here stood the old log cabin.
2. Their new sailboat skims along quite fast.
3. This wiry weed grows rampantly.
4. There is no way out.
5. Northward flows the murky river.

DIRECT OBJECTS AND INDIRECT OBJECTS

A direct object appears on the baseline to the right of the verb. The verb and the direct object are separated by a vertical line that does not cross the baseline. Indirect objects are placed on a horizontal line parallel to the baseline and are linked to the verb by a slanted line.

EXAMPLE   Jone gave her mother a gift.

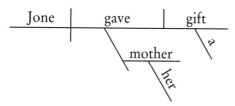

Diagram compound direct and indirect objects in the same way you diagram compound subjects.

EXAMPLE Kris gave her dog and cat food and attention.

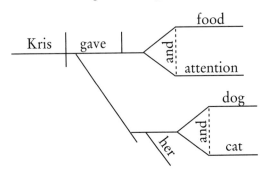

Diagraming Direct Objects and Indirect Objects

Diagram each sentence.

1. I gave her my answer.
2. The bank will send you a statement.
3. Homework and tests determine your grades and your placement.
4. I can lend you my class notes and my textbook.
5. The florist gave the flowers and the foliage a new cut and some floral preservative.

SUBJECT COMPLEMENTS AND OBJECT COMPLEMENTS

Subject complements are placed on the baseline to the right of the verb. They are separated from the verb by a slanted line that does not cross the baseline.

EXAMPLE Whales are mammals.

Whales | are \ mammals

Diagram compound subject complements in the same way you diagram compound subjects.

EXAMPLE Whales are both friendly and intelligent.

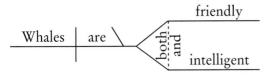

Object complements are diagramed the same way subject complements are, but a direct object comes between the verb and the object complement.

EXAMPLE Critics consider Woolf's books influential.

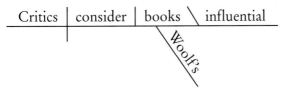

Diagram compound object complements the same way you diagram compound subjects.

EXAMPLE Biographers consider Woolf's life rich but tragic.

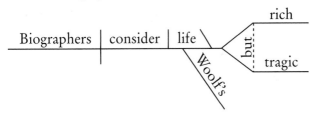

PRACTICE **Diagraming Subject Complements and Object Complements**

Diagram each sentence.

1. I consider you my mentor and friend.
2. Concert tickets were scarce and expensive.
3. She seems somewhat sad and nervous.
4. Frank Sinatra was both a singer and an actor.
5. The veterinarian pronounced my dog fit and healthy.

APPOSITIVES AND APPOSITIVE PHRASES

To diagram an appositive, simply place the word in parentheses beside the noun or pronoun it identifies. To diagram an appositive phrase, place the appositive in parentheses and place any modifying words on slanted lines directly beneath the appositive.

EXAMPLE   William Shakespeare, the English playwright, was a commoner.

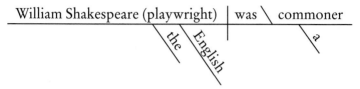

PRACTICE   **Diagraming Appositives and Appositive Phrases**

Diagram each sentence.

1. Gerard Manley Hopkins, a Jesuit priest, was a poet.
2. My grandfather drives a shiny Model-T Ford, his favorite toy.
3. The distance, a mere mile, consumed an hour.
4. Class, this plant is a parasite, an unwelcome guest.
5. His second dive, a full twist, was executed perfectly.

PREPOSITIONAL PHRASES

To diagram prepositional phrases, follow the example diagram.

EXAMPLE   Students of history study cultures of the past.

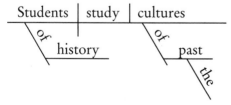

PRACTICE **Diagraming Prepositional Phrases**

Diagram each sentence.

1. Boxes of fruit were stacked on the table.
2. I walk through the park in the morning.
3. Different shades of the same color often clash.
4. Flakes of snow accumulated into drifts.
5. Dirty snow and chunks of ice covered the streets after a bad storm.

PARTICIPLES AND PARTICIPIAL PHRASES

To diagram participles and participial phrases, follow the example diagram.

EXAMPLE   Perplexed astronomers continue their work research-ing the origin of our galaxy.

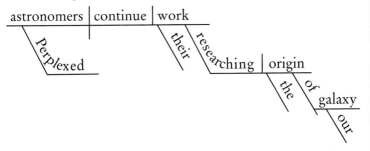

PRACTICE **Diagraming Participles and Participial Phrases**

Diagram each sentence.

1. Driven by hunger, the buffalo expanded their range.
2. Loosened from their moorings by the hurricane, the yachts crashed into the pier.
3. The aroma of the recently mown hay filled the air.
4. The ink sketch signed by the artist costs ninety-nine dollars.
5. Tasting the stew, Nathan requested more pepper.

GERUNDS AND GERUND PHRASES

To diagram gerunds and gerund phrases, follow the example diagram.

EXAMPLE   Establishing an alibi is one way of proving your innocence.

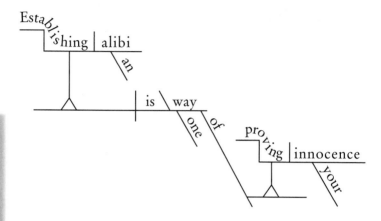

PRACTICE   **Diagraming Gerunds and Gerund Phrases**

Diagram each sentence.

1. Forgetting was his excuse.
2. Keeping bees is the work of an apiarist.
3. In the summer, he earns money by judging cattle.
4. Their grandmother tried reasoning with the children.
5. The job of the president is guiding the nation.

INFINITIVES AND INFINITIVE PHRASES

If an infinitive or an infinitive phrase functions as an adverb or an adjective, diagram it as you would diagram a prepositional phrase. Infinitives and infinitive phrases functioning as nouns are also diagramed as prepositional phrases are; however, these are placed on stilts.

EXAMPLE To restore a historical home is a worthwhile goal.

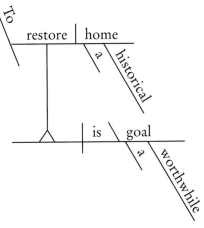

To diagram an infinitive phrase that has a subject, follow the example diagram.

EXAMPLE My father helped me restore my house.

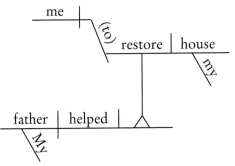

Even though *to* was omitted in the sentence, it is implied and, therefore, is included in the diagram. The parentheses signify the omission in the sentence.

PRACTICE **Diagraming Infinitives and Infinitive Phrases**

Diagram each sentence.

1. This moped is too light to carry us.
2. Ma'am, at this time, the store is unable to fill your order.

3. After Thanksgiving dinner, my brothers helped Mom wash the dishes.
4. Help Carmen do the painting more professionally.
5. To balance the budget is the government's goal.

ABSOLUTE PHRASES

An absolute phrase is placed above the rest of the sentence and is not connected to it in any way. Place the subject of the phrase on a horizontal line, and connect the participle and any modifiers to the subject of the phrase.

EXAMPLE   Its exterior freshly painted, the house looked almost new.

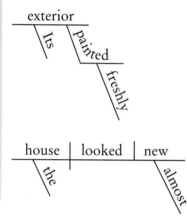

PRACTICE   **Diagraming Absolute Phrases**

Diagram each sentence.

1. Its left hind leg broken, the dog maneuvered on three feet.
2. The bathroom gleamed, its fixtures recently replaced with shiny new ones.
3. Its antenna damaged, the television's reception was poor.

4. The north side of the house was green, its surface completely covered with ivy.

5. The new mother was radiant, her dream fulfilled by the birth of her daughter.

PRACTICE **Diagraming Phrases**

Diagram each sentence.

1. At noon an important announcement was made.
2. There was a joyous moment of congratulation.
3. Judge O'Connor became the first female member of the Supreme Court.
4. The boys soon reached the creek, a narrow stream.
5. André, your cleaning is ready for you to collect.
6. This subscription, a year of *Sports Illustrated,* is a gift from your dad.
7. The fishers did not want to wait for daylight.
8. The dreaded chore, cutting wood, demanded everyone's help.
9. The club elected Bill vice president for the second time.
10. Exhausted, the runner fell across the finish line.

COMPOUND SENTENCES

A **compound sentence** is two or more simple sentences joined by either a semicolon, a colon, or a comma and a conjunction.

Diagram each main clause of a compound sentence separately. If the clauses are connected by a semicolon or a colon, use a dotted line to connect the verbs of each main clause. If the main clauses are connected by a conjunction, place the conjunction on a solid horizontal line, and connect it to the verbs of each main clause by dotted lines.

Reading is my favorite pastime, for it is educational and enjoyable.

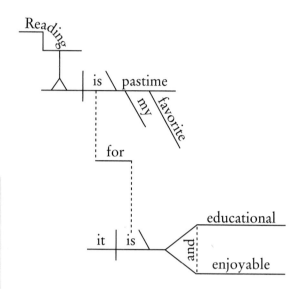

PRACTICE Diagraming Compound Sentences

Diagram each sentence.

1. School will be dismissed early; everyone must leave the building by noon.
2. My summer clothes have shrunk, or maybe I have gained weight.
3. I enjoyed the movie, but I would not see it again.
4. Pumpkin pie is delicious, but I prefer chocolate pie with whipped cream.
5. All of us have hopes and dreams, and we pursue them throughout our lives.

9.2 DIAGRAMING COMPLEX AND COMPOUND-COMPLEX SENTENCES

A **complex sentence** has one main clause and one or more subordinate clauses.

ADJECTIVE CLAUSES

To diagram a complex sentence containing an adjective clause, place the main clause in one diagram and the adjective clause in another diagram beneath it. Use a dotted line to connect the introductory word of the clause to the modified noun or pronoun in the main clause.

EXAMPLE   The author whom you like wrote a novel that is a best-seller.

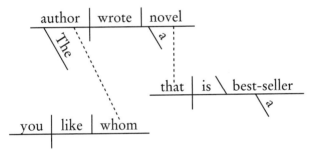

PRACTICE **Diagraming Complex Sentences: Adjective Clauses**

Diagram each sentence.

1. Lynn Davis is the woman whose store was burglarized.
2. Four of us have entered the race that will be run tomorrow.
3. My friend who lives in Oregon occasionally sends fruit.

4. These are the fish that we caught on our trip.

5. The Merchandise Mart is the building where Norma works.

ADVERB CLAUSES

To diagram a complex sentence containing an adverb clause, place the adverb clause in a separate diagram beneath the main clause. Connect the two clauses with a diagonal dotted line, on which you will put the subordinating conjunction. The dotted line will connect the verb in the adverb clause to the modified word in the main clause.

EXAMPLE   Before she bought her stereo, she researched the market.

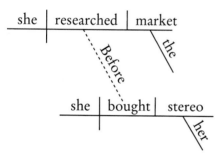

PRACTICE **Diagraming Complex Sentences: Adverb Clauses**

Diagram each sentence.

1. You must speak to the manager if you want a raise.

2. If I were you, I would take advantage of the offer.

3. The building addition will be completed before the school year ends.

4. Our dog howls whenever the tornado siren sounds.

5. Although I put them in the dryer, my jeans are still too big.

NOUN CLAUSES

Diagram the main clause and place the noun clause on a stilt in its appropriate position. You must identify the function of the introductory word of the noun clause. It may have a function within the noun clause, or it may simply connect the noun clause to the main clause. If the latter is the case, place the introductory word on a line of its own above the verb in the noun clause, connecting it to the verb with a dotted vertical line. If it has a function within the clause, diagram it appropriately.

Noun Clause as Subject

EXAMPLE   Whoever enjoys surfing will like this beach.

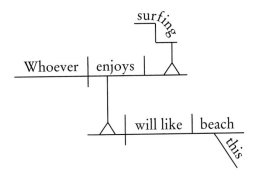

PRACTICE **Diagraming Noun Clauses as Subjects**

Diagram each sentence.

1. What I told you is a secret.
2. Why the alarm did not ring is still unknown.

3. Whoever wrote the editorial made some excellent points.

4. That the salsa needed jalapeños was obvious to Pilar.

5. Which candidate won the election was a matter of complete indifference to him.

Noun Clause as Direct Object

EXAMPLE   I heard that Sheila is moving to Nebraska.

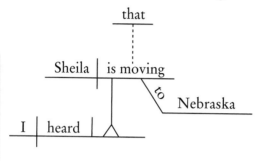

PRACTICE | **Diagraming Noun Clauses as Direct Objects**

Diagram each sentence.

1. For dessert I ordered what you had yesterday.

2. One can merely wonder what next year's weather pattern will be.

3. I can tell which way the wind is blowing.

4. Tonight the cruise director will tell us what port we will visit tomorrow.

5. Ask someone where the telephone is.

Noun Clause as Object of a Preposition

EXAMPLE   This service provides meals for whoever needs them.

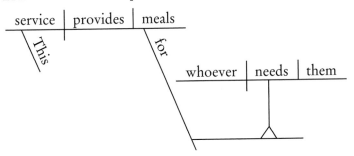

Diagram each sentence.

1. Give your uniform to whoever is collecting them in the locker room.
2. This gift is for what you did for me.
3. No one is here except whoever is staffing the lighthouse.
4. The teacher became inquisitive about what was making that incessant noise.
5. Today our professor will lecture about economic forecasts and what we talked about yesterday.

COMPOUND-COMPLEX SENTENCES

A **compound-complex sentence** has two or more main clauses and at least one subordinate clause.

Diagram a compound-complex sentence like you would diagram a compound sentence.

EXAMPLE People who train dogs for a living attend dog shows, and if they win, they receive money.

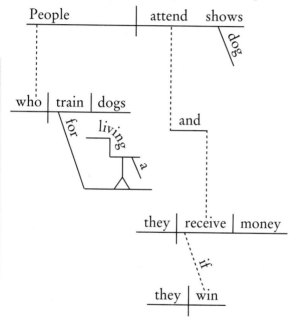

PRACTICE **Diagraming Compound-Complex Sentences**

Diagram each sentence.

1. When night falls in the islands, work ceases and the world grows still.
2. We the public elect the best candidates, and we hope that they will lead in an exemplary manner.

3. I have not noticed any improvement in myself since I began jogging with the dog, but the dog is really becoming fit.

4. Think before you speak, and you will offend no one.

5. When dawn breaks, the noise is continual in New York City; taxis screech, horns honk, and sirens blare.

POSTTEST Diagraming Sentences

Diagram each sentence.

1. Adina, why are you crying?
2. There are too many home accidents.
3. To obey the laws is a civic responsibility.
4. The law office is on the third floor.
5. The bald eagle is a symbol of power.
6. Talk to me while I iron these clothes.
7. You will see his apartment; it is up the stairs to the left.
8. Saint John, one of the Caribbean islands, is primarily a nature preserve.
9. Swimming in salt water, she was aware of her buoyancy.
10. She makes extra money by selling her homemade jellies.
11. My friend Joe said that spring in Maine is delightful.
12. Its bark stripped by lightning, the old tree managed somehow to survive.
13. The child's kite nose-dived into the water, but his brother retrieved it before the waves tore it apart.
14. The alarm jangled, and Leyla jumped out of bed.
15. Ollie, our pup, loves grapes and other fruit.
16. That I remembered their address is a miracle.
17. The superintendent is the one to hear this complaint.
18. A leaping fire in the fireplace made the room cozy.
19. Polished to perfection, a red Corvette was presented to Mark McGwire.
20. When the winter holidays arrive, people prepare special foods, and they decorate their homes.

Capitalizing

• • • • • • • • • • • • • •

PRETEST Correcting Errors in Capitalization

Rewrite any incorrect sentences, correcting errors in capitalization. If a sentence is correct, write C.

1. He attends a Canadian High School.
2. Molly has one persian cat named mickey.
3. It is hard to answer the question, "what do you want to do with your life?"
4. The first *air force one* has been retired to the dayton, ohio, air force museum.
5. Is mardi gras a holiday in the north?
6. He said he would be leaving by noon.
7. [*Letter form*] Sincerely Yours, mr. Sanders
8. The newest addition to the department is Matthew Hardy, doctor of philosophy.
9. Have the atlanta braves won the world series?
10. Tina loves to help her mother in the kitchen.
11. The south is preparing for a hit by luigi, a hurricane.
12. The southern Cross, a constellation, can be seen only in the Southern hemisphere.

13. I asked dad to help me with some Algebra problems.

14. In her freshman year, Sandra took ecology 101.

15. The world was shocked by the death of Diana, princess of Wales.

16. Have you read *Crime and punishment* by dostoyevsky?

17. Juan's Peace Corps assignment was a stint in Romania.

18. I can remember my mother saying, "always pay your bills before you pay yourself."

19. The Chicago bulls' home court is the united center.

20. "To build a fire" is a spellbinding story by Jack London.

21. The teacher said We would not have a test, but she added emphatically, "there will be a paper due."

22. My aunt works on the fifth floor of a department store.

23. Brad is going to a junior college. (this is a two-year institution.)

24. How may I help you, congressman Reynolds?

25. Last night's movie was sponsored by Atlantic Bell telephone company.

10.1 CAPITALIZING SENTENCES AND QUOTATIONS

The use of capitalization across the English-speaking world varies. In business writing particularly, people capitalize terms according to company style, which may vary from the rules in this chapter. However, for your own writing, mastering these rules will enable you to express yourself clearly in any situation.

Rule 1 Capitalize the pronoun *I* and the first word of a sentence.

EXAMPLE   Today I am graduating.

EXAMPLE   What are your plans for the summer?

Rule 2 Capitalize the first word of a sentence in parentheses that stands by itself. Don't capitalize a sentence within parentheses that is contained within another sentence.

EXAMPLE   When spring arrives, I will plant flowers. (There are five flower beds in my yard.)

EXAMPLE   I read that book (it was over four hundred pages long) in a week.

Rule 3 Capitalize the first word of a complete sentence that follows a colon. Lowercase the first word of a sentence fragment that follows a colon.

EXAMPLE   She took her dog to the vet: He needed his yearly vaccinations.

EXAMPLE   The photographer needed supplies: film, a zoom lens, and chemicals for developing photographs.

Rule 4 Capitalize the first word of a direct quotation that is a complete sentence. A **direct quotation** gives the speaker's exact words.

EXAMPLE   Jone asked, "Will you take care of my cat while I am on vacation?"

Unless it begins a sentence, don't capitalize the first word of a direct quotation that cannot stand as a complete sentence.

EXAMPLE   Rottweillers are "commonly used as guard dogs," but more importantly, they make loving companions.

Rule 5 Do not capitalize an indirect quotation. An **indirect quotation** does not repeat a speaker's exact words and should not be enclosed in quotation marks.

EXAMPLE   She says she will be late.

An indirect quotation is often introduced with the word *that*.

EXAMPLE   He said that the party will begin at seven.

Rule 6 In a traditional poem, the first word of each line is capitalized.

EXAMPLE   The rain set early in tonight,
          The sullen wind was soon awake,
          It tore the elm tops down for spite,
          And did its worst to vex the lake;
          —from "Porphyria's Lover" by Robert Browning.

PRACTICE   **Capitalizing Sentences and Quotations**

Copy the sentences, correcting any errors in capitalization. If a sentence is correctly capitalized, write C.

1. Patrick Henry said, "Give me liberty or give me death."
2. I was confused when my mother said, "you can buy some new shoes, but you can't wear them now."
3. The caller repeated that he was not soliciting money.
4. when will the Williams be leaving for their vacation?
5. The commencement speaker's speech (The title is yet to be announced) is scheduled to begin in thirty minutes.
6. I often visit Miami: my aunt lives there.
7. I listed everything I needed: camera, film, and clothes.
8. The mayor promised that She would find aid for the flood victims.
9. We will be traveling on a Carnival cruise ship. (carnival has many ships with different itineraries.)
10. I stopped my sister's boyfriend cold by asking, "just what are your intentions?"

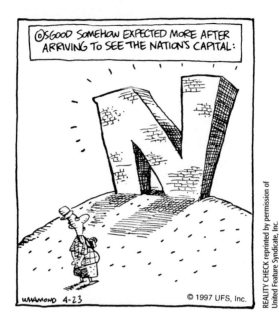

10.2 CAPITALIZING LETTER PARTS AND OUTLINES

Rule 1 Capitalize the first word in the salutation and the closing of a letter. Capitalize the title and the name of the person addressed.

EXAMPLES   Dear Miss Jones,
           Dear Sir or Madam:
           Dear General Motors:

EXAMPLES   Best regards,
           Yours truly,
           Sincerely yours,

Rule 2 In a topic outline, capitalize the Roman numerals that label main topics and the letters that label subtopics. Don't capitalize letters that label subdivisions of a subtopic. Capitalize the first word in each heading and subheading.

EXAMPLE

    I. Main topic

       A. Subtopic

          1. Division of a subtopic

             a. Subdivision of a subtopic

             b. Subdivision of a subtopic

    II. Main topic

PRACTICE   **Capitalizing Letter Parts**

Write the letter of the correctly capitalized line in each pair.

1. a. Love always,
    b. love always,

2. a. Dear director:
    b. Dear Director:

3. a. Your Friend,
    b. Your friend,

4. a. Dear president of the board of Education:
    b. Dear President of the Board of Education:

5. a. With warm regards,
    b. With Warm regards,

Rewrite the partial outline, correcting any errors in capitalization.

I. Public service jobs
   a. Career jobs
      1. government
         A. federal
         b. State
         c. local
      2. Private Sector
   B. Volunteer jobs
      1. Hospital

10.3 CAPITALIZING PROPER NOUNS AND PROPER ADJECTIVES

A **proper noun** names a particular person, place, thing, or idea. **Proper adjectives** are formed from proper nouns.

Rule 1 Capitalize both proper nouns and proper adjectives.

EXAMPLES	PROPER NOUNS	PROPER ADJECTIVES
	Australia	Australian vacation
	Victoria	Victorian England
	Christianity	Christian organization

In proper nouns and adjectives made up of more than one word, capitalize all words except articles, coordinating conjunctions, and prepositions of fewer than five letters.

EXAMPLES	PROPER NOUNS	Struthers High School
		Parent Teacher Association
		War of 1812
EXAMPLES	PROPER ADJECTIVES	Struthers High School alumni
		Parent Teacher Association member

Note: Many proper nouns do not change form when used as adjectives.

Rule 2 Capitalize the names of people and pets and the initials that stand for their names.

EXAMPLES   Barbara Walters   Rover   W. E. B. Du Bois

Note: Foreign names are often compounded with an article, a preposition, or a word meaning "son of" or "father of." These names often follow different rules of capitalization. The capitalization also depends on whether you are using the full name or just the surname, so be sure to look up the names in a reference source for proper capitalization.

EXAMPLES   **FULL NAME**   **SURNAME ONLY**

            Charles de Gaulle   de Gaulle

            Vincent van Gogh   van Gogh

            Ludwig van Beethoven   Beethoven

            Aziz ibn Saud   Ibn Saud

Capitalize nicknames.

EXAMPLES   Catherine the Great   Bogie   the Cos

Enclose nicknames in quotation marks when they are used with a person's full name.

EXAMPLE   Michael "Air" Jordan   Thomas "Stonewall" Jackson

Rule 3 Capitalize adjectives formed from the names of people.

EXAMPLE   Copernicus   Copernican system

EXAMPLE   Jefferson   Jeffersonian writings

EXAMPLE   King George   Georgian architecture

Rule 4 Capitalize a title or an abbreviation of a title used before a person's name.

EXAMPLES   **M**rs. Handel
                     Mr. Peabody
                     Ms. Mason

EXAMPLES   **P**ope Theodore I
                     Dr. Hsai
                     President Carter

EXAMPLES   **R**epresentative Jones
                     King George V
                     Chief Geronimo

Capitalize a title used in direct address.

EXAMPLE   I feel much better, **D**octor.

In general, don't capitalize a title that follows a person's name.

EXAMPLE   Ronald Reagan, **p**resident of the United States, served two terms.

Do not capitalize a title that is simply being used as a common noun.

EXAMPLE   George Bush served as his **v**ice **p**resident.

EXAMPLE   To be **e**mperor of the **u**niverse would be a hard job.

Rule 5 Capitalize the names and abbreviations of academic degrees that follow a person's name. Capitalize *Jr.* and *Sr.*

EXAMPLES   Julie Schenk, **D**octor of **P**hilosophy
                     Eli Washington, **M.B.A.**
                     Jon O'Neill **J**r.

Rule 6 Capitalize a word showing family relationship when it is used either

- **before a proper name** or
- **in place of a proper name**

EXAMPLE   When Cousin Tina arrived, the children were delighted.

EXAMPLE   I hope Mom made peach cobbler.

Don't capitalize a word showing family relationship if it is preceded by a possessive noun or pronoun.

EXAMPLE   Carol's mom is a good baker.

EXAMPLE   Your cousin has a swimming pool.

Rule 7 Capitalize the names of ethnic groups, nationalities, and languages.

EXAMPLE	**ETHNIC GROUPS**	Basque, Asian, Indian
EXAMPLE	**NATIONALITIES**	German, Nigerian, Canadian
EXAMPLE	**LANGUAGES**	Greek, Arabic, Hebrew

Rule 8 Capitalize the names of organizations, institutions, political parties and their members, government bodies, business firms, and teams.

EXAMPLES

ORGANIZATIONS	National Geographic Society World Wildlife Fund
INSTITUTIONS	New York University Austin Metropolitan Library Fairfield Union High School
POLITICAL PARTIES AND MEMBERS	Socialist Party/Socialist Democratic Party/Democrat
GOVERNMENT BODIES	Tennessee Valley Authority Peace Corps Bureau of the Census
BUSINESS FIRMS	Bank One, Incorporated Illinois Central Railroad Ameritech
TEAMS	Dallas Cowboys Pittsburgh Pirates

Note: Don't capitalize words such as *court, school,* and *university* unless they are part of a proper noun.

EXAMPLE I left school at three o'clock.

EXAMPLE I attend Lancaster High School.

Note: When referring to a specific political party or party member, words such as *democrat* and *republican* should be capitalized. However, when used to describe a way of thought or an ideal, such words should be lowercase.

EXAMPLE Are they members of the Republican or the Democratic Party (or party)?

EXAMPLE We discussed republican theories last night.

EXAMPLE How does a democratic government work?

Note: Capitalize brand names of products but not the nouns following them.

EXAMPLES Lay's™ potato chips   Bayer™ aspirin

Rule 9 Capitalize the names of roads, parks, towns, cities, counties, townships, provinces, states, regions, countries, continents, other land forms and features, and bodies of water.

EXAMPLES

Third Avenue	Jersey City	Everglades National Park
Saguaro County	Nebraska	the Midwest
Taiwan	Asia	Jervis Bay
Ozark Plateau	Lake Superior	Galápagos Islands

Note: Capitalize words such as *city, island,* and *mountains* only when they are part of a proper name.

Capitalize compass points, such as *north, south, east,* and *west,* when they refer to a specific region or when they are part of a proper name. Don't capitalize them when they indicate direction.

EXAMPLE	REGIONS/PROPER NAMES	DIRECTIONS
	the **S**outh	**s**outh of the city
	East **H**aven	driving **e**ast

Capitalize *northern, southern, eastern,* and *western* when they refer to hemispheres and cultures.

EXAMPLES **N**orthern **H**emisphere   **E**astern culture

Capitalize adjectives that are formed from place names.

EXAMPLES **A**frican art   **T**ibetan monks

Rule 10 Capitalize the names of planets and other astral bodies.

EXAMPLES	**S**aturn	**N**eptune	**U**ranus
	Beta **C**rucis	**C**astor	**O**rion

Rule 11 Capitalize the names of monuments, buildings, bridges, and other structures.

EXAMPLES	**S**tatue of **L**iberty	**W**ashington **B**ridge
EXAMPLES	**C**hrysler **B**uilding	**M**idtown **T**unnel
EXAMPLES	**G**reat **W**all of **C**hina	**O**tago **H**arbor

Rule 12 Capitalize the names of ships, planes, trains, and spacecraft. Note that these names are italicized, but the abbreviations before them are not.

EXAMPLES *Enola Gay*   *Sputnik 1*   *Santa Maria*
USS *Constitution*

Rule 13 Capitalize the names of historical events, special events, and holidays and other calendar items.

Historical events require capitalization, as do some historical periods. However, most historical periods are not capitalized. It is best to check a dictionary or other reference source for the proper capitalization of historical periods.

EXAMPLE	HISTORICAL EVENTS	Spanish Civil War, World War I, Louisiana Purchase
EXAMPLE	HISTORICAL PERIODS	Dark Ages, Renaissance, Ice Age, fifteenth century, the sixties, classical period

Note: Historical periods using numerical designations are lowercase unless they are part of a proper name.

The names of special events should be capitalized.

EXAMPLES   Chicago World's Fair   Kentucky Derby   Super Bowl

The names of holidays and other calendar items require capitalization.

EXAMPLES	Inauguration Day	Groundhog Day
EXAMPLES	Tuesday	September

Note: Names of the seasons—*spring, summer, winter, fall*—are not capitalized.

Rule 14 Capitalize the names of deities and words referring to deities, words referring to a revered being, religions and their followers, religious books, and holy days and events.

EXAMPLES

NAMES OF AND WORDS REFERRING TO DEITIES	Holy Spirit	Vishnu	Joseph
WORDS REFERRING TO A REVERED BEING	the Prophet	the Beloved Apostle	
RELIGIONS	Catholicism	Amish	Judaism
FOLLOWERS	Jew	Muslim	Rastafarian
RELIGIOUS BOOKS	Analects	Upanishads	Talmud
RELIGIOUS HOLY DAYS AND EVENTS	Ramadan	Advent	Hanukkah

Note: When referring to ancient Greek or Roman deities, don't capitalize the words *god, gods, goddess,* and *goddesses.*

Rule 15 Capitalize only those school courses that name a language, are followed by a number, or name a specific course. Don't capitalize the name of a general subject.

EXAMPLES **Portuguese**   **foreign language**

EXAMPLES **Women's Studies 152**   **women's studies**

Rule 16 Capitalize the first word and the last word in the titles of books, chapters, plays, short stories, poems, essays, articles, movies, television series and programs, songs, magazines, newspapers, cartoons, and comic strips. Capitalize all other words except articles, coordinating conjunctions, and prepositions of fewer than five letters.

EXAMPLES

To the Lighthouse   the *London Times*
You Can't Take It with You   *Much Ado About Nothing*
Dog Fancy   "Lady Be Good"

Note: It is common practice not to capitalize or italicize articles preceding the title of a newspaper or a periodical.

Rule 17 Capitalize the names of documents, awards, and laws.

EXAMPLES **Fifth Amendment**   **India Act**

EXAMPLES **Academy Award**   **Articles of Confederation**

Capitalizing Proper Nouns and Proper Adjectives

Copy the sentences, correcting errors in capitalization.

1. Tennis finals will be held on memorial day.

2. The Empire State building is in New York city.

3. In elizabethan England, some people had their houses built in the shape of an *E* to honor queen Elizabeth I.

4. Do you live North or South of Springfield?

5. At a chicago railway station, we boarded the amtrak for Washington.

6. The english barons forced king john to sign the magna carta on june 15, 1215.

7. We ate at friendship house, a restaurant east of Gulfport, Mississippi.

8. When we visit London in the Spring, we often take a leisurely walk through Hyde park.

9. The reverend Fred Jerrold, minister of the first methodist church, spoke.

10. The germans and the irish were among the settlers of the United States.

11. My Mother drives a Toyota camry.

12. On labor day, the golf course at the troy country club will be open.

13. The mayor of dallas, texas, spoke at the meeting of the rotary club.

14. In 1862 president Abraham Lincoln signed the homestead act.

15. I have not seen uncle Bob since the Fourth Of July.

16. Langston Hughes's poem "the negro speaks of rivers" is one of my favorites.

17. Ernest Hemingway, the famous american writer, once wrote for The *Kansas City Star,* a daily newspaper published in Kansas city, Missouri.

18. Next year Central high school will offer russian, journalism, and economics.

19. Zora Neale Hurston wrote an autobiography called *Dust Tracks On A Road.*

20. I took the recipes from *good housekeeping* and *woman's day* magazines.

PRACTICE **Correcting Errors in Capitalization**

Rewrite each item, correcting any errors in capitalization.

1. Dear mr. peterson,
I would like to thank you for all the help you gave me in english class at Oakdale high school. I am looking forward to my first year at the university of cincinnati, where I plan to study Poetry.
yours sincerely,
edward allen

2. I. music
    A. Classical Music
        1. baroque
            a. Vivaldi
            B. Handel
        2. Romantic
            A. Beethoven
            b. Brahms

3. George Harris, mom's brother, works for the department of the interior.

4. A reprint of "the Man With The Hoe" hangs in the office of our High School.

5. My father helps me in chemistry I, latin, and algebra II.

6. Dickens's *oliver twist* and Twain's *The adventures of huckleberry finn* both contain young male protagonists.

7. My father's favorite poem is "the lake isle of innisfree."

8. John f. Kennedy was President from 1961 to 1963.

9. Samuel Johnson, an english writer, once said, "no man but a blockhead ever wrote, except for money."

10. Martin Luther King jr. won the nobel prize in 1964.

SUMMARY OF CAPITALIZATION RULES

NAMES AND TITLES OF PEOPLE

CAPITALIZE	DO NOT CAPITALIZE
D. H. Lawrence	an **a**uthor
Miss **J**ones, **Ph. D.**	a **n**eighbor
Pope **J**ohn **P**aul II	a **r**eligious **l**eader
General **S**herman	a **g**eneral
Great-aunt **L**ouise	my **g**reat-aunt

ETHNIC GROUPS, NATIONALITIES, AND LANGUAGES

Latino	an **e**thnic **g**roup
South **A**frican	a **n**ationality
Swahili	a **l**anguage

ORGANIZATIONS, INSTITUTIONS, POLITICAL PARTIES AND THEIR MEMBERS, GOVERNMENT BODIES, BUSINESS FIRMS, AND TEAMS

League of **W**omen **V**oters	an **o**rganization
Metropolitan **M**useum of **A**rt	an **a**rt **m**useum
Republican **P**arty / **R**epublican	**r**epublican theories
Supreme **C**ourt	a **c**ourt
Coca-**C**ola **C**ompany	a soft-drink **c**ompany
Nebraska **C**ornhuskers	a football **t**eam

NAMES OF PLACES

Perry **S**treet	a **s**treet
Badlands **N**ational **P**ark	a **p**ark
the **S**outh	**s**outh of the border
Amazon **R**iver	a **r**iver
Mojave **D**esert	a **d**esert

Summary of Capitalization rules, continued

PLANETS AND OTHER HEAVENLY BODIES	
CAPITALIZE	DO NOT CAPITALIZE
Uranus	a planet
North Star	a star
MONUMENTS, BUILDINGS, BRIDGES, AND OTHER STRUCTURES	
Tomb of the Unknowns	a tomb
World Trade Center	a building
Brooklyn Bridge	a bridge
Hadrian's Wall	a wall
SHIPS, PLANES, TRAINS, AND SPACECRAFT	
Santa Maria	a ship
Spirit of Saint Louis	a plane
Columbia	a spacecraft
HISTORICAL EVENTS, SPECIAL EVENTS, AND CALENDAR ITEMS	
World War II	a war
World Series	a baseball game
Labor Day	a holiday
January, June	winter, summer
Wednesday	a day of the week
RELIGIOUS TERMS	
Allah	a deity
the Beloved Apostle	a revered being
Protestantism / Protestant	a religion / a religious follower
Bhagavad Gita	a religious book
Easter Sunday	a religious holiday

Summary of Capitalization rules, continued

SCHOOL COURSES	
CAPITALIZE	DO NOT CAPITALIZE
Russian	a foreign language
Statistics 152	statistics
TITLES OF WORKS	
Lonesome Dove	a book
"Everyday Use"	a short story
Vanity Fair	a magazine
the *Chicago Tribune*	a newspaper
DOCUMENTS, AWARDS, AND LAWS	
Articles of Confederation	a document
Nobel Prize	an award
First Amendment	a law

PRACTICE Proofreading

Rewrite the following passage, correcting the errors in capitalization. There are ten errors. Some sentences are correct.

Langston Hughes

[1]Langston Hughes was born in 1902 in missouri. [2]He published one of his most famous poems, "The Negro Speaks Of Rivers," when he was only nineteen. [3]Hughes moved North to New York City in 1921 to attend Columbia University. [4]A year later he became a cook on a ship bound for africa.

[5]After returning to the United States, Hughes won a poetry prize sponsored by *opportunity* magazine. [6]While Hughes was working in a hotel, he was discovered by a poet named Vachel lindsay. [7]Lindsay praised his

poems and told him, "hide and write and study and think." [8]Hughes then won a scholarship to Lincoln university in Pennsylvania; he graduated in 1929.

[9]Hughes's first book of poems, *The weary Blues,* was published in 1926 and won him recognition as a talented writer. [10]In the late 1930s, Hughes became known for his journalistic writing. [11]He covered the Spanish Civil War for an African American newspaper. [12]He also wrote for a newspaper called The *Chicago Defender.*

POSTTEST Correcting Errors in Capitalization

Rewrite any incorrect sentences, correcting errors in capitalization. If a sentence is correct, write C.

1. When president Jefferson purchased the louisiana territory from France, he moved the western boundary of the United States to the rocky mountains.
2. My Mother said, "In the morning we will have waffles."
3. The bill of rights is a document that is prized by Americans.
4. Bert is taking greek and psychology 101.
5. For your free sample of waldorf cereal, write to the continental food corporation.
6. The woman told us, "My Aunt once rode a train called the *flying hamburger.*"
7. The United States patent office has granted my father a patent for his extension ladder.
8. She quoted her favorite line of poetry from Wordsworth, "I wandered lonely as a cloud."
9. My favorite novel by the french writer Albert Camus is *The plague.*
10. New zealanders and australians are fierce competitors in rugby.
11. [*letter form*] Dear senator Ashley:
12. The Egyptian City Alexandria is named for Alexander the great.

13. The wildcats of Edgemont High will play in the high school bowl on Thanksgiving Day.

14. For two years after world war II, uncle George was stationed in Japan.

15. Is the composer of "autumn in my heart" the music critic for the *daily news*?

16. Tonight the school will hold an auction in wilson hall.

17. The superintendent said that he cannot change the dismissal time because of the bus schedule.

18. Both the baptists and the catholics have churches on Elm Street, near the museum of modern art.

19. Benjamin Franklin, the american statesman and philosopher, once wrote, "there never was a good war or a bad peace."

20. In the Koran, the supreme being is allah.

21. [*letter form*] very sincerely yours,

22. the title of my essay is "the second Monday of the week."

23. We called doctor Radzinsky when my brother Ray's temperature spiked.

24. The special on abc was sponsored by write well pens.

25. The north star is a directional guide in the northern hemisphere.

Chapter 11

Punctuation, Abbreviations, and Numbers

● ● ● ● ● ● ● ● ● ● ● ● ● ● ●

PRETEST **Correcting Errors in Punctuation**

Rewrite each sentence, correcting any errors in punctuation.

1. Her snapshot not his received first prize but his pleases me more.

2. The train leaves the Saint Charles Missouri station at 1230 PM.

3. The chill penetrating wind pursued him down the street pelted his back unmercifully and drove him into a sheltered doorway.

4. I asked the bank teller what I should do about my lost check?

5. Jay who knew the route well directed the man who was driving the car.

6. On the harbor, sail many brightly colored yachts.

7. That's a quotation from Bacons essay Of Studies isnt it?

8. On July 25 1985 we arrived at Port Alegre meaning "Happy Port" Brazil.

9. I've made three reports Adam Bede, a novel Dover Beach, a poem and Hamlet, a play.

10. Where the two toll roads intersect the traffic is heavy this intersection is called The Whirlpool.

11. Cars buses and trucks, must progress slowly in the congested traffic.

12. Well your solution is self evident you will have to cut your expenses.

13. Many students have trouble spelling the word success.

14. "The faculty reception, Soraya said will be in the Monarch Suite."

15. I'm going to visit I've forgotten the name of the city!

16. A steep narrow gravel road led to the camp.

17. The yacht Meteor is favored to win.

18. Bill Jones' bicycle was beside the porch but the Joneses car was gone.

19. Look in the dictionary under p not n for pneumatic.

20. Although Jerry helps with everyone elses work he often neglects his own.

Rewrite each item, correcting any errors in the use of abbreviations and numbers.

21. The 20th century saw dramatic progress in technology.

22. I gave four % of my salary to charity last year.

23. Daniel L Klein Ph D has recently moved his office to Washington, DC.

24. TS Eliot wrote a book of poems that inspired the theatrical production *Cats.*

25. The earthquake occurred at 5.32 am on September 3, 1993.

26. Does class begin at 7 or 8 o'clock?

27. Julius Caesar invaded Britain in fifty-five bc.

28. James Rodriguez MD and Roberto Diaz DDS share an office.

29. I hope to get fifty $ from my grandfather for my birthday.

30. One third of a tablespoon is one teaspoon. In a recipe, these measures are written as 1/3 tablesp and one teasp.

There are three punctuation marks used at the ends of sentences: the period, the exclamation point, and the question mark.

11.1 THE PERIOD

Use a period at the end of a declarative sentence—a statement—and at the end of an imperative sentence—a polite command or a request.

| EXAMPLE | **DECLARATIVE SENTENCE** | The banjo is a folk instrument. |
| EXAMPLE | **IMPERATIVE SENTENCE** | Please play me a song on your banjo. |

11.2 THE EXCLAMATION POINT

Use an exclamation point to show strong feeling and to indicate a forceful command.

EXAMPLES	**EXCLAMATORY SENTENCE**	What a great movie that was!
		How lovely you look!
		Woe is me!
EXAMPLES	**FORCEFUL COMMAND**	Don't you dare go without me!
		Look out!
		Help!

Use an exclamation point after an interjection that expresses a strong feeling.

EXAMPLES Ow!   Wahoo!   Oh, boy!

11.3 THE QUESTION MARK

Use a question mark at the end of a direct question.

EXAMPLE   Was Aaron Copland an American composer?

EXAMPLE   Did Copland write *Appalachian Spring*?

Don't use a question mark after an indirect question (one that has been reworded so that it is part of a declarative sentence).

EXAMPLE   My friend asked whether Aaron Copland wrote *Appalachian Spring*.

EXAMPLE   She wondered what folk tune is the central melody in *Appalachian Spring*.

Rewrite each item, adding the correct end punctuation.

1. Is this called teal blue
2. Help
3. Please report promptly when your number is called
4. Wow What a great catch
5. The director asked me why I wanted to join the health club
6. What time are you leaving
7. Kristi asked me when I would visit her
8. On Friday (what a day) our cousins from Belgium arrived
9. Ask the operator what the number is
10. Did you feel a trembling in the house a few minutes ago

11.4 THE COLON

COLONS TO INTRODUCE

Use a colon to introduce a list, especially after a statement that uses such words as *these, namely, the following,* or *as follows.*

EXAMPLE   The kinds of fiction in which justice prevails include **these:** fairy tales, Westerns, and detective stories.

EXAMPLE   Listen to a recording of one of **the following** concert vocalists: Justino Diaz, Martina Arroyo, or Jessye Norman.

Don't use a colon to introduce a list if the list immediately follows a verb or a preposition. In other words, check to be sure that the words preceding the colon make up a complete sentence.

GRAMMAR/USAGE/MECHANICS

Three important composers from the United States **are** Aaron Copland, Scott Joplin, and Arthur Cunningham. **[The list follows the verb *are* and acts as the sentence's predicate nominative. Don't use a colon.]**

What kinds of music are most popular **in** South America, Asia, Africa, and Oceania? **[The list follows the preposition *in* and acts as the object of the preposition. Don't use a colon.]**

Use a colon to introduce material that illustrates, explains, or restates the preceding material.

Note: A complete sentence following a colon should be capitalized.

The cause of the fire was obvious: Children had been playing with butane lighters.

The joyous news was announced to the patiently waiting crowd: The queen had given birth to a healthy daughter.

Use a colon to introduce a long or a formal quotation. A formal quotation is often preceded by such words as *this, these, the following,* or *as follows.*

Patrick Henry, speaking before the Virginia Convention, closed his memorable speech with **these** words: "I know not what course others may take; but as for me, give me liberty or give me death!"

Poetry quotations of more than one line and prose quotations of more than four or five lines are generally written below the introductory statement and are indented on the page.

EXAMPLE   Walt Whitman responded to critics with **the following** lines:

> Do I contradict myself?
> Very well, then I contradict myself,
> (I am large. I contain multitudes.)

OTHER USES OF COLONS

- Use a colon between the hour and the minute of the precise time.
- Use a colon between the chapter and the verse in biblical references.
- Use a colon after the salutation of a business letter.

EXAMPLES   6:40 A.M.   2:15 P.M.   Exodus 3:4   Matthew 2:5

EXAMPLE   Greetings:

EXAMPLE   Dear Ford Motor Company:

EXAMPLE   Dear Sir or Madam:

EXAMPLE   Dear Volunteers:

PRACTICE   Colons

Rewrite each sentence below, correcting any errors in the use of colons.

1. The following countries, as well as others, belong to the United Nations England, Spain, France, and Russia.
2. [*Letter form*] Dear Members
3. The quarter-finals will begin at 130 P.M. on Thursday. They will be held at the following four locations, Bellwood, Homewood, Stiverson, and Shelby.
4. Camden College will accept Hal's application, He ranks high in his class.
5. The first three runners to cross the finish line were: Judd, Ben, and Samir.

Chapter 11 Punctuation, Abbreviations, and Numbers   **323**

6. She read the following from A. E. Housman
When I was one-and-twenty,
I heard a wise man say,
"Give crowns and pounds and guineas
But not your heart away. . . .

7. From the Bible's John 8, 32, he quoted the following sentence, "And ye shall know the truth, and the truth shall make you free."

8. Lisa will be a good manager, She is very responsible.

9. Our study is in these three areas short stories, poetry, and essays.

10. Dear Sir By the 530 P.M. deadline, I received applications from the following Tico Jiminez, Pedro Vasquez, and Lorenzo White.

11.5 THE SEMICOLON

SEMICOLONS TO SEPARATE MAIN CLAUSES

Use a semicolon to separate main clauses that are not joined by a comma and a coordinating conjunction (*and, but, or, nor, so, yet,* or *for*).

EXAMPLE   I love jazz, **and** the blues are my favorite kind of jazz.

EXAMPLE   I love jazz; the blues are my favorite kind of jazz.

EXAMPLE   George Gershwin wrote music during the Jazz Age; his compositions were influenced by jazz.

Use a semicolon to separate main clauses that are joined by a conjunctive adverb (such as *however, therefore, nevertheless, moreover, furthermore,* and *subsequently*) or by an expression such as *for example* or *that is.*

In general, a conjunctive adverb or an expression such as *for example* is followed by a comma.

EXAMPLE   George Gershwin wrote popular as well as traditional music; **in fact,** he combined the two forms in pieces such as *Rhapsody in Blue.*

EXAMPLE   The jazz-opera *Porgy and Bess* is generally considered to be Gershwin's masterpiece; **consequently,** Gershwin enthusiasts call its hit songs "Summertime" and "It Ain't Necessarily So" gems.

SEMICOLONS AND COMMAS

Use a semicolon to separate the items in a series when one or more of the items already contain commas.

EXAMPLE   Three important jazz musicians of the twentieth century were Louis Armstrong, a trumpet player; Duke Ellington, a composer; and Sarah Vaughan, a singer.

Use a semicolon to separate two main clauses joined by a coordinating conjunction when one or both of the clauses already contain several commas.

EXAMPLE   Arthur Mitchell, as a leading dancer with the New York City Ballet, danced in such works as *A Midsummer Night's Dream, Agon,* and *Western Symphony;* but he is also famous as the founder of the Dance Theater of Harlem, an internationally acclaimed dance company.

PRACTICE Semicolons

Rewrite each sentence below, correcting errors in the use of semicolons.

1. We visited friends in Akron, Ohio, Ann Arbor, Michigan, and Chicago, Illinois.

2. This will be a year of difficult decisions for you for example, you must decide on a career.

3. Write what you really think don't let others sway your thinking.

4. This road map is several years old, however, it is adequate for our needs.

5. Ms. Lippman, a banker, Mrs. Ballard, an office manager, and Mr. Laird, an accountant, spoke to us yesterday.

11.6 THE COMMA

As you study the rules for comma usage, keep in mind that to *separate* elements means to place a comma between two equal elements. To *set off* an element means to put a comma before and after it. Of course, you never place a comma at the beginning or the end of a sentence.

COMMAS IN A SERIES

Use commas to separate three or more words, phrases, or clauses in a series.

EXAMPLE   Langston Hughes wrote poetry, drama, screenplays, and popular songs.

EXAMPLE   We hung party decorations in the gym, in the halls, and around the courtyard.

EXAMPLE   Some movies make audiences laugh, others make them cry, and still others amaze them with state-of-the-art special effects.

Note: The comma before the *and* is called the serial comma. Some authorities do not recommend it. However, many sentences may be confusing without it. We recommend that you always insert the serial comma for clarity.

EXAMPLE   **UNCLEAR**   Michelle, Susan and Henry are going to the store. [This sentence might be telling Michelle that Susan and Henry are going to the store.]

CLEAR	Michelle, Susan, and Henry are going to the store. [This sentence clearly states that three people are going to the store.]

When all items in a series are connected by conjunctions, no commas are necessary.

EXAMPLE   Langston Hughes's poetry is insightful and expressive and powerful.

EXAMPLE   You won't want the orange or the green or the red.

Nouns that are used in pairs to express one idea (*pen and ink, spaghetti and meatballs, thunder and lightning*) are usually considered single units and should not be separated by commas. If such pairs appear with other nouns or groups of nouns in a series, however, they must be set off from the other items in the series.

EXAMPLE   I like oil and vinegar, salt and pepper, and croutons on my salad.

EXAMPLE   Swimming and diving pools, football and baseball fields, and tennis and volleyball courts can be found in the park.

COMMAS AND COORDINATE ADJECTIVES

Place a comma between coordinate adjectives that precede a noun.

Coordinate adjectives modify a noun equally. To determine whether adjectives are coordinate, try to reverse their order or put the word *and* between them. If the sentence still sounds natural, the adjectives are coordinate.

EXAMPLE   Hea is a happy, intelligent, graceful child.

Don't use a comma between adjectives preceding a noun if the adjectives sound unnatural with their order reversed or with *and* between them. In general, adjectives that describe size, shape, age, and material do not need to be separated by commas.

EXAMPLE Julia wore a long blue wool scarf.

Commas may be needed between some of the adjectives before a noun and not between others.

EXAMPLE It was a cozy, clean, old-fashioned living room.

In the preceding sentence, *and* would sound natural between *cozy* and *clean* and between *clean* and *old-fashioned,* but it would not sound natural between *old-fashioned* and *living.*

COMMAS AND COMPOUND SENTENCES

Use a comma between the main clauses in a compound sentence.

Place a comma before a coordinating conjunction *(and, but, or, nor, for, so,* or *yet)* that joins two main clauses.

EXAMPLE The Marx Brothers were a comedy team, **but** each brother did work on his own.

EXAMPLE Groucho Marx made wisecracks, **and** his brother Harpo played music.

PRACTICE Commas in a Series, with Coordinate Adjectives, and in Compound Sentences

Rewrite each item below, correcting any errors in the use of commas.

1. Carlo's impromptu class theme had a humorous unexpected ending.
2. Mr. Thomas spoke in a strong resonant voice when he asked Harry Michelle and Juan to be quiet.
3. A triangular, state flag hangs from the mast of their new white sailboat.

4. Ham, and cheese and peanut butter, and jelly are two of the most common sandwich fillings.

5. Bill closed his locker I grabbed my bag and we hurried to join the others.

COMMAS AND NONESSENTIAL ELEMENTS

Use commas to set off participles, infinitives, and their phrases if they are not essential to the meaning of the sentence.

EXAMPLE   The children, **exhilarated,** ripped open their presents.

EXAMPLE   Mari made her way down the street, **happily calling out to her neighbors.**

EXAMPLE   I have no idea, **to tell the truth,** what he meant by that remark.

Don't set off participles, infinitives, and their phrases if they are essential to the meaning of the sentence.

EXAMPLE   The most famous documentary film **directed by Robert J. Flaherty** is *Nanook of the North.* **[adjective phrase]**

EXAMPLE   Flaherty made the film **to show the realities of Inuit life. [adverb phrase]**

EXAMPLE   **To film *Nanook of the North*** was a difficult undertaking. **[infinitive phrase as subject]**

Use commas to set off a nonessential adjective clause.

A nonessential clause can be considered an extra clause because it gives optional information about a noun. Because it is an extra clause that is not necessary, it is set off by commas.

EXAMPLE   My cousin Ken, **who lives in California,** works as a film editor. **[The adjective clause *who lives in California* is nonessential.]**

Don't set off an essential adjective clause. Because an essential adjective clause gives necessary information about a noun, it is needed to convey the exact meaning of the sentence.

EXAMPLE The person **who actually films a movie** is called the camera operator. [The adjective clause *who actually films a movie* is essential. It tells *which* person.]

EXAMPLE The director first interviewed the actors, **who were very talented.** [This clearly states that all the actors were very talented.]

EXAMPLE The director first interviewed the actors **who were very talented.** [This clearly states that the director first interviewed those actors who were very talented and then interviewed other actors.]

Use commas to set off an appositive if it is not essential to the meaning of a sentence.

A nonessential appositive can be considered extra information; it calls for commas.

EXAMPLE James Wong Howe, **a famous camera operator,** was born in China.

EXAMPLE Howe first worked for Cecil B. DeMille, **a director of many Hollywood films.**

EXAMPLE *The Ten Commandments,* **a classic film from the 1950s,** is one of DeMille's most successful films.

A nonessential appositive is sometimes placed before the noun or pronoun to which it refers.

EXAMPLE **A camera operator for Cecil B. DeMille,** James Wong Howe was important to the film industry. [The appositive, *A camera operator for Cecil B. DeMille,* precedes the noun it identifies, *James Wong Howe.*]

An essential appositive gives necessary information about a noun and is not set off with commas.

James Wong Howe operated the camera for Martin Ritt's film *The Molly Maguires.* **[If a comma were placed before the essential appositive, *The Molly Maguires,* the sentence would say that this was Ritt's only film.]**

PRACTICE **Commas and Nonessential Elements**

Rewrite each sentence below, correcting any errors in the use of commas.

1. The computer, that I bought, is an IBM.
2. The temperature at game time thirty-seven degrees made sitting in the bleachers miserable.
3. Yesterday was a bad day to put it mildly.
4. The crowd subdued by their candidate's poor showing soon dispersed.
5. Janet whose name was called first was absent.

COMMAS WITH INTERJECTIONS, PARENTHETICAL EXPRESSIONS, CONJUNCTIVE ADVERBS, AND ANTITHETICAL PHRASES

Use commas to set off the following:

- interjections (such as *oh, well, alas,* and *good grief*)
- parenthetical expressions (such as *in fact, on the other hand, for example, on the contrary, by the way, to be exact,* and *after all*)
- conjunctive adverbs (such as *however, moreover, therefore,* and *consequently*)

EXAMPLE **Indeed,** Francis Ford Coppola is a talented scriptwriter.

EXAMPLE He wrote the screenplay for *Patton,* **for example.**

EXAMPLE He is also a gifted director; **after all,** he won an Academy Award for his direction of *The Godfather.*

GRAMMAR/USAGE/MECHANICS

EXAMPLE   **In fact,** Coppola comes from an artistic family.

EXAMPLE   Talia Shire is Francis Ford Coppola's sister; **moreover,** she is a talented actor.

Use commas to set off an antithetical phrase. An antithetical phrase uses a word such as *not* or *unlike* to qualify what precedes it.

EXAMPLE   Augusta, **not Bangor,** is the capital of Maine.

EXAMPLE   **Unlike Kansas,** Colorado is very mountainous.

PRACTICE   **Commas with Interjections, Parenthetical Expressions, Conjunctive Adverbs, and Antithetical Phrases**

Rewrite each sentence below, correcting any errors in the use of commas.

1. Maroon not red is the color of Julia's bridesmaids' dresses.
2. By the way what is your phone number?
3. Our dinner plans were canceled; consequently we ate leftovers from the preceding night.
4. On the contrary the show will be presented as scheduled.
5. Good grief that's the last thing I need to hear today.

COMMAS WITH OTHER ELEMENTS

Set off two or more introductory prepositional phrases or a single long one with a comma.

EXAMPLE   **During the winter in New England,** snowstorms are common. [two prepositional phrases—*During the winter* and *in New England*]

EXAMPLE   **Above one thousand twinkling holiday lights,** the snowy mountains drowsed. [one long prepositional phrase—*Above one thousand twinkling holiday lights*]

You need not set off a single short introductory prepositional phrase, but it's not wrong to do so.

EXAMPLE **In 1862** Victor Hugo published *Les Misérables.*

or

In 1862, Victor Hugo published *Les Misérables.*

Don't use a comma if the introductory prepositional phrase is immediately followed by a verb.

EXAMPLE On the rug by the fireplace slept a large white dog.

Use commas to set off introductory participles and participial phrases.

EXAMPLE **Smiling,** I watched Whoopi Goldberg's award-winning performance in *Ghost.* **[introductory participle]**

EXAMPLE **Beginning as a comic actor,** Sally Field graduated into more serious roles. **[introductory participial phrase]**

Use commas after all introductory adverbs and adverb clauses.

EXAMPLE **Finally,** the lights dimmed and the movie started. **[introductory adverb]**

EXAMPLE **Although the usher tried to hush the noisy children,** I could not hear the dialogue. **[introductory adverb clause]**

Also use commas to set off internal adverb clauses that interrupt the flow of a sentence.

EXAMPLE Denzel Washington, **before he became a movie star,** appeared in the television series *St. Elsewhere.* **[*before he became a movie star* interrupts the flow of the sentence.]**

In general, don't set off an adverb clause at the end of a sentence unless the clause is parenthetical or the sentence would be misread without the comma.

GRAMMAR/USAGE/MECHANICS

EXAMPLE Denzel Washington appeared in the television series *St. Elsewhere* before he became a movie star. **[no comma needed]**

EXAMPLE We held our car wash, **although it was raining.** **[nonessential adverb clause needs comma]**

PRACTICE Commas with Other Elements

Rewrite each sentence below, correcting any errors in the use of commas.

1. In the middle of the desert they came upon a green oasis.
2. Battling back after a bout with cancer Scott Hamilton returned to the ice.
3. On the table in the dining room, was my birthday gift.
4. Before you turn out the lights make sure that the doors are locked.
5. That tiny insect seen through a microscope is actually very colorful.

ADDITIONAL USES OF COMMAS

Use commas to set off a title when it follows a person's name.

EXAMPLE Henry VIII, **king of England,** had six wives.

EXAMPLE Lucia Sanchez, **Ph.D.,** will chair the new committee.

Set off the name of a state or a country when it's used after the name of a city. Set off the name of a city when it's used after a street address. Don't use a comma after the state if it's followed by a ZIP code.

EXAMPLE Paris, **France,** is the setting of some of Hemingway's novels.

EXAMPLE   The company is located at 840 Pierce Street, Friendswood, Texas 77546.

In a date, set off the year when it's used with both the month and the day. Don't use a comma if only the month and the year are given.

EXAMPLE   On October 12, 1492, Christopher Columbus landed on the island now called San Salvador.

EXAMPLE   It was July 1776 when the Declaration of Independence was signed.

Use commas to set off the parts of a reference that direct the reader to the exact source.

EXAMPLE   We performed Act 1, Scene 1, of William Shakespeare's *Julius Caesar.*

Use commas to set off words or names in direct address.

EXAMPLE   **Mona,** can you meet me this afternoon?

EXAMPLE   You, **my dear,** are leaving at once.

EXAMPLE   Thank you for the book, **Mrs. Gomez.**

Use commas to set off tag questions.

A tag question (such as *shouldn't I?* or *have you?*) suggests an answer to the question that precedes it.

EXAMPLE   *Bye Bye Birdie* starred Chita Rivera, **didn't it?**

EXAMPLE   Chita Rivera was not in the film version of *Bye Bye Birdie,* **was she?**

Place a comma after the salutation of an informal letter. Place a comma after the closing of all letters. In the inside address, place a comma between the city and state and between the day and year.

EXAMPLE 23 Silver Lake Road
Sharon, Connecticut 06069
February 15, 2000

EXAMPLE Dear Cousin Agnes,

EXAMPLE Best wishes,

PRACTICE **Additional Uses of Commas**

Rewrite each sentence below, correcting any errors in the use of commas.

1. Torremolinos Spain is a place I'd like to visit.
2. Friends and family thank you for your help.
3. These jeans are the ones you like best aren't they?
4. President Kennedy was shot in November, 1963 in Dallas Texas.
5. Mr. Lee General Manager hired a new assistant.

MISUSE OF COMMAS

In general, don't use a comma before a conjunction that connects a compound predicate or a compound subject.

EXAMPLE INCORRECT Our school never wins the championship, but always has a spectacular loser's party. **[compound predicate]**

CORRECT Our school never wins the championship but always has a spectacular loser's party.

EXAMPLE INCORRECT The cheerleaders with their little trampoline, and the band members with their instruments make a lively display. **[compound subject]**

CORRECT The cheerleaders with their little trampoline and the band members with their instruments make a lively display.

Don't use only a comma to join two main clauses unless they are part of a series of clauses. Such a sentence punctuated with a comma alone is called a *run-on sentence* (or a *comma splice* or a *comma fault*). To join two clauses correctly, use a coordinating conjunction with the comma, or use a semicolon.

EXAMPLE   **INCORRECT**   The navigator Juan Rodríguez Cabrillo sighted land in 1542, the history of California entered a new chapter.

           CORRECT   The navigator Juan Rodríguez Cabrillo sighted land in 1542, **and** the history of California entered a new chapter.

           CORRECT   The navigator Juan Rodríguez Cabrillo sighted land in 1542; the history of California entered a new chapter.

Don't use a comma between a subject and its verb or between a verb and its complement.

EXAMPLE   **INCORRECT**   What she considered an easy ballet step to master, was quite difficult for me.

           CORRECT   What she considered an easy ballet step to master was quite difficult for me.

EXAMPLE   **INCORRECT**   Popular tourist attractions in Florida include, Disney World, Palm Beach, and the Everglades.

           CORRECT   Popular tourist attractions in Florida include Disney World, Palm Beach, and the Everglades.

EXAMPLE   **INCORRECT**   Their motto was, "All for one and one for all."

           CORRECT   Their motto was "All for one and one for all."

Rewrite each sentence below, correcting any errors in the use of commas.

1. My favorite movies are, *The Wizard of Oz,* and *Big.*
2. Gordon Parks's photographs appeared in *Life* magazine for years, he captured the intensity of the human condition.
3. Cool nights, and warm sunny days, make fall a pleasant time of year.
4. Whichever restaurant you choose, will be fine by me.
5. The company's total sales increased during the last year but profits were lower than expected.

"Sorry, but I'm going to have to issue you a summons for reckless grammar and driving without an apostrophe."

Rewrite each sentence below, correcting any errors in the use of commas.

1. Please take down the following address: C. Allen Jenks Ph.D. 459 North Sixth Street Richmond Virginia 23204.
2. Your story was printed in three school papers: the *Signal* the *Bugle* and the *Echo.*
3. [*Letter forms*] Dear Mom   Sincerely yours
4. The western sky dark and threatening hurried our steps.
5. We did not know the answers to the third and fourth questions but we knew the answers to the first and second.
6. Well when I looked in the refrigerator the banana cream pie was gone.
7. I finally found my favorite sweatshirt torn to shreds by my puppy whose name appropriately enough is Mr. Pest.
8. Donna our papers aren't due until Friday are they?
9. On our walk through Sutton Park I found the wildflower I've been wanting but of course one cannot pick a flower in a state park.
10. One starless frigid night I heard a noise by the picture window and shined a flashlight on a doe huddled against the pane for warmth.

11.7 THE DASH

On a typewriter, indicate the dash with two hyphens (--). If you're using a computer, you may make a dash with a certain combination of keystrokes. Refer to the manual of your word-processing program for instructions.

Don't place a comma, a semicolon, a colon, or a period before or after a dash.

DASHES TO SIGNAL CHANGE

Use a dash to indicate an abrupt break or change in thought within a sentence.

EXAMPLE "I think the answer is—I've forgotten what I was going to say."

EXAMPLE All of us—I mean most of us—look forward to vacations.

DASHES TO EMPHASIZE

Use a dash to set off and emphasize extra information or parenthetical comments.

EXAMPLE Operatic soprano Dame Kiri Te Kanawa—she is the Maori superstar who sang at the wedding of the Prince and Princess of Wales in 1981—published *Land of the Long White Cloud: Maori Myths and Legends* in 1989.

Don't overuse dashes in your writing. Dashes are most often found in informal or personal letters. In formal writing situations, use subordinating conjunctions (such as *after, until, because,* and *unless*) or conjunctive adverbs (such as *however, nonetheless,* and *furthermore*), along with the correct punctuation, to show the relationships between ideas.

PRACTICE Dashes

Rewrite each sentence, correcting errors in the use of the dash.

1. His answer and it did surprise us was a reluctant consent.

2. Then slowly stir in the salt, pepper, mustard, are you listening?

3. Of course—the appointment will have to be put to a vote.

4. My shoes, my very best ones, too, were spotted with asphalt.

5. Yo Yo Ma, he is a famous cellist, will perform in a concert with our local symphony orchestra.

11.8 PARENTHESES

PARENTHESES TO SET OFF SUPPLEMENTAL MATERIAL

Use parentheses to set off supplemental, or extra, material.

Commas and dashes as well as parentheses can be used to set off supplemental material; the difference between the three marks of punctuation is one of degree. Use commas to set off supplemental material that is closely related to the rest of the sentence. Use parentheses to set off supplemental material that is not important enough to be considered part of the main statement. Use dashes to set off and emphasize any material that interrupts the main statement.

EXAMPLE   Mary Jane Canary (Calamity Jane) knew Wild Bill Hickok.

EXAMPLE   The ASL (Amateur Storytellers League) entertains listeners at their monthly meetings.

A complete sentence within parentheses is not capitalized and needs no period if it is contained within another sentence. If a sentence within parentheses is not contained within another sentence—that is, if it stands by itself—both a capital letter and end punctuation are needed.

EXAMPLE	Mary Jane Canary (she was known as Calamity Jane) was a good friend of Wild Bill Hickok's.
EXAMPLE	Paul Bunyan is a famous figure in the folklore of the United States. (You can learn all about him at the Paul Bunyan Center in Minnesota.)

PARENTHESES WITH OTHER MARKS OF PUNCTUATION

Place a comma, a semicolon, or a colon *after* the closing parentheses.

EXAMPLE	The writer Bret Harte is associated with the West (his stories include "The Luck of Roaring Camp" and "The Outcasts of Poker Flat"), but this celebrated western author was actually born in Albany, New York.

Place a question mark or an exclamation point *inside* the parentheses if it is part of the parenthetical expression.

EXAMPLE	Owatonna is the name of a Native American princess (a member of the Santee nation?) who lived hundreds of years ago.
EXAMPLE	A novel based on the life of Sacagawea (what a fascinating person she must have been!) was published recently.

Place a period, a question mark, or an exclamation point *outside* the parentheses if it is part of the entire sentence.

EXAMPLE	The code of laws that governed Iroquois society was the Great Binding Law (known as the Iroquois Constitution).

EXAMPLE   How surprised I was to learn that the British call corn *maize* (which comes from the West Indian name for corn)!

PRACTICE   **Parentheses**

Rewrite each sentence, adding parentheses and any other necessary punctuation for clarity.

1. The AHS American Horticultural Society offers free seeds to its members each year.
2. The Bicycle Derby it is an annual event is held in August.
3. Our first game it will be held at home is with Oak Ridge High School.
4. I was working I was cleaning the drains when Martha called me in to dinner.
5. Joseph Macklin have you heard of him has won the Good Will Award.

11.9 BRACKETS AND ELLIPSIS POINTS

BRACKETS

Use brackets to enclose information that you have inserted into a quotation for clarity.

EXAMPLE   We cannot be free until they [all Americans] are.
                                                    —James Baldwin

Use brackets to enclose a parenthetical phrase that already appears within parentheses.

EXAMPLE   The name *Oregon* comes from the French word *ouragan* (which means "hurricane" [referring to the Columbia River]).

Rewrite the following sentences, adding brackets where they are needed.

1. The paper continues, "Everyone who knows him Watson is impressed."

2. Our grandfather, proud of his heritage, swore, "I love them the Irish all!"

3. The new citizen exclaimed, "It freedom is my prize possession!"

4. The movie critic said, "It *To Kill a Mockingbird* is one of the best films of all time."

5. Sandro Piotti (he is from Milan the city called the "fashion capital of the world") is a snappy dresser.

ELLIPSIS POINTS

Use a series of three spaced periods, called ellipsis points, to indicate the omission of material from a quotation.

Use three spaced periods if the omission is at the beginning of the sentence. If the omission is at the middle or the end of the sentence, include any punctuation immediately preceding the omitted material (for instance, a comma, a semicolon, or a period) plus the three spaced periods. When it is necessary to use a period, do not leave any space between the last word and the first ellipsis point, which is the period.

EXAMPLE   "Listen, my children, and you shall hear. . . ."
                                                        —Henry Wadsworth Longfellow

If the remaining material becomes the end of the sentence, replace the internal punctuation mark with a period, followed by three ellipsis points.

EXAMPLE	ORIGINAL QUOTATION	She spoke sullenly, careful to show no interest or pleasure, and he spoke in a fast bright monotone.
		—Joyce Carol Oates
	QUOTATION WITH OMISSION	She spoke sullenly, careful to show no interest or pleasure....
		—Joyce Carol Oates

PRACTICE Ellipsis Points

Rewrite the following passage from Abraham Lincoln's Gettysburg Address, *adding ellipses points in place of the underlined material.*

<u>Four score and seven years ago</u> our fathers brought forth <u>on this continent</u>, a new nation, conceived in Liberty, <u>and dedicated to the proposition that all men are created equal</u>.

Now we are engaged in a great civil war, <u>testing whether that nation, or any nation so conceived and so dedicated, can long endure</u>. We are met on a great battlefield of that war. We have come to dedicate a portion of that field, as a final resting place for those who here gave their lives that that nation might live. <u>It is altogether fitting and proper that we should do this</u>.

11.10 QUOTATION MARKS

QUOTATION MARKS WITH DIRECT QUOTATIONS

Use quotation marks to enclose a direct quotation.

Place quotation marks around the quotation only, not around purely introductory or explanatory remarks. Generally separate such remarks from the actual quotation with a comma. (For the use of colons to introduce quotations, see page 322.)

EXAMPLE "Weave us a garment of brightness," says a Native American song.

EXAMPLE   Phil Rizzuto, in an observation famous for its optimism, said, "They still can't steal first base."

EXAMPLE   The first verse of the national anthem of the United States begins with the words "Oh, say, can you see. . . ." and ends with ". . . and the home of the brave."

Do not use a comma after a quotation that ends with an exclamation point or a question mark.

EXAMPLE   "Look at me! Look at my arm. I have ploughed and planted, and gathered into barns, and no man could head me! And ain't I a woman?" said Sojourner Truth when she addressed the Ohio Women's Rights Convention in 1851.

When a quotation is interrupted by explanatory words such as *he said* or *she wrote,* use two sets of quotation marks.

Separate each part of the quotation from the interrupting phrase with marks of punctuation before and after the phrase. If the second part of the quotation is a complete sentence, begin it with a capital letter and use a period, not a comma, after the interrupting phrase.

EXAMPLE   "Writing free verse," Robert Frost begins a famous poetry definition, "is like playing tennis with the net down."

EXAMPLE   "The Lord prefers common-looking people," Abraham Lincoln once said. "That is why he makes so many of them."

Don't use quotation marks in an indirect quotation.

EXAMPLE   **ORIGINAL QUOTATION**   Toni Morrison said, "I write the kind of books I want to read."

INDIRECT QUOTATION   Toni Morrison said she writes the kind of books she wants to read.

Use single quotation marks around a quotation within a quotation.

The teacher said to her students, "Benjamin Franklin once wrote, 'Lose no time; be always employed in something useful.'"

In writing dialogue, begin a new paragraph and use a new set of quotation marks every time the speaker changes.

"Are you going to pass this collection of abalone shells on to your children?" I said.

"No," he said. "I want my children to collect for themselves. I wouldn't give it to them."

"Why?" I said. "When you die?"

Mr. Abe shook his head. "No. Not even when I die," he said. "I couldn't give the children what I see in these shells. The children must go out for themselves and find their own shells."

—Toshio Mori

QUOTATION MARKS WITH OTHER MARKS OF PUNCTUATION

Always place a comma or a period *inside* closing quotation marks.

Nadine Gordimer said in a lecture, "The creative act is not pure."

"Literature is a state of culture," Juan Ramón Jiménez said; "poetry is a state of grace."

Always place a semicolon or a colon *outside* closing quotation marks.

EXAMPLE The Greek writer Nikos Kazantzakis said, "My entire soul is a cry"; his meaning escaped me until I read the rest of the quotation, in which he explained, "and all my work is a commentary on that cry."

EXAMPLE According to Rousseau, "*Vivre ce n'est pas respirer, c'est agir*": "Living is not breathing but doing."

Place the question mark or the exclamation point *inside* the closing quotation marks when it is part of the quotation.

EXAMPLE We read Leonard Bernstein's essay "What Makes Music American?"

EXAMPLE The toddler cried, "No! Cookie *my*!"

Place the question mark or the exclamation point *outside* the closing quotation marks when it is part of the entire sentence.

EXAMPLE When did he say, "We'll be there at nine sharp"?

EXAMPLE How I hate to make a hurried phone call only to hear "Please hold"!

If both the sentence and the quotation at the end of the sentence need a question mark (or an exclamation point), use only one punctuation mark, and place it *inside* the closing quotation marks.

EXAMPLE What was the name of the French poet who asked, "Where are the snows of yesteryear?"

EXAMPLE How astounded we were to hear little Timmy pipe up, "I know! It was François Villon!"

Don't use a comma after a quotation that ends with a question mark or an exclamation point.

EXAMPLE "That's a surprise!" my mother said, smiling.

QUOTATION MARKS WITH TITLES, UNUSUAL EXPRESSIONS, AND DEFINITIONS

Use quotation marks to enclose titles of short works, such as short stories, short poems, essays, newspaper articles, magazine articles, book chapters, songs, and single episodes of a television series.

EXAMPLE "Abalone, Abalone, Abalone" [short story]

EXAMPLE "Dream Variations" [short poem]

EXAMPLE "A Chicano in China" [essay]

EXAMPLE "Bald Eagle Coming Off Endangered Species List" [newspaper article]

EXAMPLE "Ahab" [book chapter]

EXAMPLE "The Star-Spangled Banner" [song]

EXAMPLE "Lions and Tigers and Bears, Oh, My!" [episode in a television series]

Note: For the use of italics with longer titles, see page 351.

Use quotation marks to enclose unfamiliar slang and other unusual or original expressions.

EXAMPLE "Groovy" was a word of high praise in the late 1960s.

EXAMPLE In the late 1990s, "fresh" and "fly" were complimentary adjectives.

Be careful not to overuse quotation marks with unusual expressions. Generally, use quotation marks only the first time you use the unusual expression in a piece of writing.

Use quotation marks to enclose a definition that is stated directly.

EXAMPLE *Ukulele* comes from the Hawaiian words for "jumping flea."

The word *beige* in French means "of the natural color of undyed wool."

PRACTICE Quotation Marks

Rewrite each item, correcting errors in the use of quotation marks and other punctuation.

1. Julia asked when does the party begin?
2. Unchained Melody has become a classic.
3. "Greetings, welcomed the college president. I know you're all happy to be here today."
4. She said "that all was well at home."
5. Why, he asked, weren't we told in time that a tornado had been sighted.
6. I enjoy the works of Joan Didion, particularly her essay On the Mall.
7. Ben Jonson wrote the poem On My First Son after his son Benjamin died.
8. The third chapter of the book is titled American Foreign Relations.
9. The best poem I've ever read, he said, is W. H. Auden's The Unknown Citizen.
10. Why does my mother say, Do you know how lucky you are.

11.11 ITALICS (UNDERLINING)

Italic type is a special slanted type that is used in printing. *(This sentence is printed in italics.)* Indicate italics on a typewriter or with handwriting by underlining. (<u>This sentence is underlined</u>.) When you are using a computer, learn the special keystrokes for italics by referring to your software manual.

ITALICS WITH TITLES

Italicize (underline) the following: titles of books, long poems, plays, films, television series, paintings, sculptures, and long musical compositions. Also italicize (underline) the names of ships, airplanes, spacecraft, newspapers, magazines, and court cases.

A "long poem" or a "long musical composition" is any poem or musical composition published under its own title as a separate work.

EXAMPLES

The Invisible Man [book]

A Raisin in the Sun [play]

Nature [television series]

David [sculpture]

USS *Intrepid** [ship]

Apollo 9 [spacecraft]

Psychology Today [magazine]

Leaves of Grass [long poem]

Casablanca [film]

Christina's World [painting]

Ninth Symphony [long musical composition]

Spruce Goose [airplane]

St. Louis Post-Dispatch [newspaper]

Brown v. *Board of Education of Topeka Kansas* [court case]

*Don't italicize abbreviations such as USS in the name of a ship.

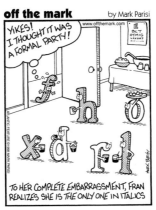

off the mark by Mark Parisi

www.offthemark.com

YIKES! I THOUGHT IT WAS A FORMAL PARTY!

TO HER COMPLETE EMBARRASSMENT, FRAN REALIZES SHE IS *THE ONLY ONE* IN ITALICS

off the mark © Mark Parisi. Reprinted with permission of Atlantic Feature Syndicate.

GRAMMAR/USAGE/MECHANICS

Italicize (underline) and capitalize articles (*a, an, the*) written at the beginning of a title only when they are a part of the title itself. It is common practice not to italicize (underline) the article preceding the title of a newspaper or a magazine. Do not italicize the word *magazine* unless it is a part of the title of a periodical.

EXAMPLE

The Old Man and the Sea   *A Night at the Opera*

but

the *Arabian Nights*   the *New Yorker* magazine

ITALICS WITH FOREIGN WORDS

Italicize (underline) foreign words and expressions that are not used frequently in English.

EXAMPLE   James always ends his letters to me with the words **hasta la vista.**

Don't italicize (underline) a foreign word or expression that is commonly used in English. Consult a dictionary; if a foreign word or expression is a dictionary entry word, don't italicize (underline) it.

EXAMPLE   The health spa offers courses in **judo** and **karate.**

ITALICS WITH WORDS AND OTHER ITEMS USED TO REPRESENT THEMSELVES

Italicize (underline) words, letters, and numerals used to represent themselves—that is, words used as words, letters used as letters, and numerals used as numerals.

EXAMPLE   To make your essays read more smoothly, connect ideas with conjunctive adverbs such as **therefore** and **however.**

EXAMPLE   The *t* and the *v* sometimes stick on this typewriter.

EXAMPLE   Should I use the dollar sign (*$*) or spell out the word?

PRACTICE Italics (Underlining)

Rewrite each item, correcting errors in the use of italics (underlining).

1. Affreux means "awful" or "frightful."
2. The submarines Nautilus and Skate have crossed the North Pole under ice.
3. Necessary, which is often misspelled, has one c.
4. Anna is studying advertisements in Time, Ebony, and Vogue.
5. My brother watched the movie Jurassic Park nine times.

11.12 THE APOSTROPHE

APOSTROPHES TO SHOW POSSESSION

Use an apostrophe and *-s* for the possessive form of a singular indefinite pronoun.

Do not use an apostrophe with other possessive pronouns.

EXAMPLE   somebody**'s** hat

EXAMPLE   each other**'s** books

EXAMPLE   no one**'s** business

but

EXAMPLE   **its** engine

EXAMPLE   **whose** mail

EXAMPLE   The responsibility is **theirs.**

EXAMPLE   The rewards are **yours.**

EXAMPLE   The car is **ours.**

Use an apostrophe and -*s* to form the possessive of a singular noun, even one that ends in *s*.

EXAMPLES	the child**'s** toys	Ray Charles**'s** music
EXAMPLES	the bus**'s** muffler	Wallace Stevens**'s** poetry
EXAMPLES	the duchess**'s** plans	Harpo Marx**'s** sweet smile
EXAMPLES	the lynx**'s** habitat	Peru**'s** mountains

There are some exceptions to this rule, however. To form the possessive of ancient proper nouns that end in *es* or *is*, the name *Jesus,* and expressions with such words as *conscience* and *appearance,* just add an apostrophe.

EXAMPLES	Ulysses**'** journey	Hercules**'** cradle
EXAMPLES	Iris**'** apple of discord	Jesus**'** parables
EXAMPLES	Xerxes**'** army	her conscience**'** voice

Use an apostrophe alone to form the possessive of a plural noun that ends in *s*.

EXAMPLES	the Girl Scouts**'** badges	the teachers**'** cafeteria
EXAMPLES	the Hugheses**'** vacation	the tennis rackets**'** grips

Use an apostrophe and -*s* to form the possessive of a plural noun that does not end in *s*.

EXAMPLES	the children**'s** surprise	her teeth**'s** crowns
EXAMPLES	the women**'s** decision	his feet**'s** arches

Put only the last word of a compound noun in the possessive form.

EXAMPLES	my sister-in-law**'s** computer
	the foster child**'s** happiness
EXAMPLES	my great-grandfather**'s** watch
	my pen pal**'s** photograph

If two or more persons (or partners in a company) possess something jointly, use the possessive form for the last person named.

EXAMPLE	my father and mother**'s** house
EXAMPLE	Lerner and Loewe**'s** musicals
EXAMPLE	Lord and Taylor**'s** department store
EXAMPLE	Procter and Gamble**'s** e-mail address

If two or more persons (or companies) possess an item (or items) individually, put each one's name in the possessive form.

EXAMPLE	Julio**'s** and Emma**'s** test scores
EXAMPLE	the Murphys**'** and the Ramirezes**'** houses
EXAMPLE	the winner**'s** and losers**'** times

Use a possessive form to express amounts of money or time that modify a noun.

The modifier can also be expressed as a hyphenated adjective. In that case, no possessive form is used.

EXAMPLE	two hours' drive	*but*	a two-hour drive
EXAMPLE	eighty cents' worth		an eighty-cent loaf
EXAMPLE	five miles' walk		a five-mile walk

APOSTROPHES IN CONTRACTIONS

Use an apostrophe in place of letters that are omitted in contractions.

A **contraction** is a single word made up of two words that have been combined by omitting letters. Common contractions combine a subject and a verb or a verb and the word *not*.

EXAMPLE	I'd	*is formed from*	I had, I would
EXAMPLE	you're		you are
EXAMPLE	who's		who is, who has
EXAMPLE	it's		it is, it has
EXAMPLE	won't		will not
EXAMPLE	can't		cannot

Use an apostrophe in place of the omitted numerals of a year.

EXAMPLES   the summer of '62   the '92 election results

PRACTICE   Apostrophes

Rewrite each sentence, correcting errors in the use of the apostrophe.

1. Whos the owner of the 89 car in the parking lot?
2. Id like to know why you took Linus hat.
3. Youre making a cake for Harrys' party, arent you?
4. My fathers high school had a girls entrance and a boys entrance.
5. Phyllis' enthusiasm is evident even when she read's the newspaper.
6. If this billfold isnt your's, whose is it? It isnt her's or John's.
7. Do lady's styles change more often than mens', or does it just seem so?
8. Isnt your father-in-laws house nearby?
9. Jeremy Willis' summers were always spent at his grand-mother's and grandfathers' ranch in Wyoming.
10. Two dollars worth of gasoline isnt anyones idea of a thrilling prize.

11.13 THE HYPHEN

HYPHENS WITH PREFIXES

A hyphen is not ordinarily used to join a prefix to a word. There are a few exceptions, however. If you are in doubt about using a hyphen, consult a dictionary. Also keep in mind the following guidelines:

Use a hyphen after any prefix joined to a proper noun or a proper adjective. Use a hyphen after the prefixes *all-*, *ex-* (meaning "former"), and *self-* joined to any noun or adjective.

EXAMPLES	pre-Raphaelite	ex-senator
EXAMPLES	all-purpose	self-sealing

Use a hyphen after the prefix *anti-* when it joins a word beginning with *i*. Also use a hyphen after the prefix *vice-*, except in *vice president.*

EXAMPLES anti-inflammatory

vice-consul

but vice president

Use a hyphen to avoid confusion between words beginning with *re-* that look alike but are different in meaning and pronunciation.

EXAMPLE	re-cover the sofa	*but*	recover a loss
EXAMPLE	re-store the supplies		restore confidence
EXAMPLE	re-lease the car		release the captives

HYPHENS WITH COMPOUNDS AND NUMBERS

Use a hyphen in a compound adjective that precedes a noun.

In general, a compound adjective that follows a noun is not hyphenated.

EXAMPLE   a plum-colored shirt
but
The shirt is plum colored.

EXAMPLE   the well-liked performer
but
The performer is well liked.

Compound adjectives beginning with *well, ill,* or *little* are usually not hyphenated when they are modified by an adverb.

EXAMPLE   an ill-tempered man
but
a rather ill tempered man

Do not hyphenate an expression made up of an adverb that ends in *-ly* and an adjective.

EXAMPLE   a badly torn blanket

EXAMPLE   a perfectly balanced mobile

Hyphenate any spelled-out cardinal number (such as *twenty-one*) or ordinal number (such as *twenty-first*) up to *ninety-nine* or *ninety-ninth.*

EXAMPLE   I counted **twenty-seven** birds at the feeder.

EXAMPLE   The **twenty-seventh** bird was a goldfinch.

EXAMPLE   Most people have **thirty-two** teeth.

EXAMPLE   The **thirty-second** day of the year is February first.

Hyphenate a fraction that is expressed in words.

one-half teaspoon   one-quarter of the pie
a two-thirds majority

Hyphenate two numerals to indicate a span.

1899–1999   pages 152–218

When you use the word *from* before a span, use *to* rather than a hyphen. When you use *between* before a span, use *and* rather than a hyphen.

from 1899 **to** 1999   **between** 2:45 **and** 3:15 P.M.

HYPHENS TO DIVIDE WORDS AT THE END OF A LINE

Words are generally divided between syllables or pronounceable parts. Because it is often difficult to decide where a word should be divided, consult a dictionary.

In general, if a word contains two consonants occurring between two vowels or if it contains double consonants, divide the word between the two consonants.

con-sonant   per-sistent   pul-ley   scis-sors

If a suffix has been added to a complete word that ends in two consonants, divide the word after the two consonants. Remember, the object is to make the hyphenated word easy to read and understand.

dull-est   reck-less   steward-ship   fill-ing

Rewrite each sentence, correcting errors in the use of hyphens. Then make a list of all the italicized words, showing where each would be divided if it had to be broken at the end of a line. Don't consult a dictionary; divide each word as you have been taught in this lesson.

1. I need twenty six dollars for the blouse, which is *yellow* colored.

2. The flower like structure on a *dogwood* tree is actually a bract, not a true flower.

3. *Sometimes* one's thoughts become self fulfilling prophecies.

4. If you would add one fourth teaspoon of *cinnamon* to the pie recipe, I think it would be just right.

5. Our *citizenship* class meets tomorrow between 1:00–3:15 P.M.

11.14 ABBREVIATIONS

Abbreviations are shortened forms of words.

Abbreviations save space and time and prevent unnecessary wordiness. Most abbreviations require periods. If you are unsure of how to write an abbreviation, consult a dictionary.

Use only one period, not two, if an abbreviation that has a period occurs at the end of a sentence that would ordinarily take a period of its own.

If an abbreviation that has a period occurs at the end of a sentence that ends with a question mark or an exclamation point, use the abbreviation's period *and* the question mark or the exclamation point.

EXAMPLE   He awoke at 5:00 A.M.

EXAMPLE   Did he really awake at 5:00 A.M.?

CAPITALIZING ABBREVIATIONS

Capitalize abbreviations of proper nouns.

EXAMPLES Thurs.   U.S.A.   U.S. Army   Sept.

Abbreviations of organizations and government agencies are often formed from the initial letters of the complete name. Such abbreviations, whether pronounced letter by letter or as words, do not use periods and are written with capital letters.

EXAMPLES UN   NASA   ABC   IRS   NBA

When abbreviating a person's first and middle names, leave a space after each initial.

EXAMPLES Robert E. Lee   W. H. Auden   J. S. Bach

Capitalize the following abbreviations related to dates and times.

A.D. (*anno Domini*, "in the year of the Lord" [since the birth of Christ]); place before the date: A.D. 5

B.C (before Christ); place after the date: 1000 B.C.

B.C.E. (before the common era, equivalent to *B.C.*); place after the date: 164 B.C.E.

C.E. (common era; equivalent to *A.D.*); place after the date: 66 C.E.

A.M. (*ante meridiem*, "before noon"); place after exact times: 7:45 A.M.

P.M. (*post meridiem*, "after noon"); place after exact times: 2:30 P.M.

POSTAL ABBREVIATIONS

In ordinary prose, spell out state names. On envelopes, however, abbreviate state names using the two-letter abbreviations approved by the United States Postal Service.

A complete list of these abbreviations can be found in the Ready Reference section on pages 90–91.

Alabama	**AL**
Florida	**FL**
Louisiana	**LA**
Nebraska	**NE**
Rhode Island	**RI**

The two-letter form for the District of Columbia, for use on envelopes only, is **DC.** In ordinary prose, however, use periods to write **Washington, D.C.**

EXAMPLE   We visited **Washington, D.C.,** on our vacation.

ABBREVIATIONS OF TITLES AND UNITS OF MEASURE

Use abbreviations for some personal titles.

Titles such as *Mrs., Mr., Ms., Sr.,* and *Jr.* and those indicating professions and academic degrees *(Dr., Ph.D., M.A., B.S.)* are almost always abbreviated. Titles of government and military officials and members of the clergy are frequently abbreviated when used before a full name.

EXAMPLES	Maria García, **M.F.A.**	**Mr.** Christopher Reeve
EXAMPLES	Victoria Proudfoot, **M.D.**	Lydia Stryk, **Ph.D.**
EXAMPLES	**Mrs.** Hillary Clinton	**Dr.** Jonas Salk
EXAMPLES	Douglas Fairbanks **Jr.**	Paul Chin, **D.V.M.**

Abbreviate units of measure used with numerals in technical or scientific writing. Do not abbreviate them in ordinary prose.

The abbreviations that follow stand for both singular and plural units.

U.S. SYSTEM		METRIC SYSTEM	
ft.	foot	**cg**	centigram
gal.	gallon	**cl**	centiliter
in.	inch	**cm**	centimeter
lb.	pound	**g**	gram
mi.	mile	**kg**	kilogram
oz.	ounce	**km**	kilometer
pt.	pint	**l**	liter
qt.	quart	**m**	meter
tbsp.	tablespoon	**mg**	milligram
tsp.	teaspoon	**ml**	milliliter
yd.	yard	**mm**	millimeter

For more information on abbreviations, see pages 85–92 in the Ready Reference.

PRACTICE Abbreviations

Rewrite each sentence, correcting errors in the use of abbreviations.

1. The road was built in 395 ad.
2. The flight to New Orleans, LA, leaves shortly after noon.
3. The US government funds N.A.S.A.
4. I need 6 yds. of fabric for the draperies I'm making.
5. The science text was edited by GH Rawlings.
6. Washington DC is a favorite destination for students in the eastern United States.
7. The Greek playwright Sophocles wrote *Antigone* in BC 441.
8. Did you correctly list the professor's name as Roberto Guerrera, Phd?
9. Alfred the Great became king of England in 871 AD.
10. The grandfather of Andrew Garner is Jerome B Garner sr.

11.15 NUMBERS AND NUMERALS

In nontechnical writing, some numbers are spelled out, and some are expressed in figures. Numbers expressed in figures are called numerals.

NUMBERS SPELLED OUT

In general, spell out cardinal numbers (such as *twenty*) and ordinal numbers (such as *twentieth*) that can be written in one or two words.

EXAMPLE   We needed **twenty-two** tickets for the whole family.

EXAMPLE   There were **fifteen hundred** people in line.

Spell out any number that occurs at the beginning of a sentence. (Sometimes, it is better to revise the sentence to move the spelled-out number.)

EXAMPLES

Two hundred twenty-five singers performed.

BETTER   There were 225 singers in the performance.

Nineteen ninety-eight was the year my dog was born.

BETTER   My dog was born in 1998.

NUMERALS

In general, use numerals to express numbers that would be written in more than two words.

EXAMPLE   There were **220** marching in the band.

EXAMPLE   We worked **150** hours of community service.

Very large numbers are often written as a numeral followed by the word *million* or *billion*.

EXAMPLE   The area of Canada is roughly **3.85 million** square miles.

If related numbers appear in the same sentence and some can be written out while others should appear as numerals, use all numerals.

EXAMPLE   This year the number of women marathon runners increased from **78** to **432.**

Use numerals to express amounts of money, decimals, and percentages. Spell out the word *percent,* however.

EXAMPLE   She owed me **$2.75.**

EXAMPLE   The bottle holds **1.5** quarts of shampoo.

EXAMPLE   The bank paid **6** percent interest.

Amounts of money that can be expressed in one or two words, however, should be spelled out.

EXAMPLES   **forty-six** cents   **twenty-two thousand** dollars

Use numerals to express the year and day in a date and to express the precise time with the abbreviations A.M. and P.M.

EXAMPLE   Newfoundland became Canada's tenth province on March **31, 1949.**

EXAMPLE   The movie was scheduled to begin at **7:05 P.M.**

Spell out expressions of time that do not use A.M. or P.M.

EXAMPLE   The movie starts at **seven** o'clock.

To express a century when the word *century* is used, spell out the number. Likewise, to express a decade when the century is clear from the context, spell out the number.

EXAMPLE The **twentieth** century saw the beginnings of rock-and-roll music in the **fifties.**

When a decade is identified by its century, use numerals followed by an *-s*.

EXAMPLE The baby boom reached its peak in the **1950s.**

Use numerals for numbered streets and avenues above ninety-nine and for all house, apartment, and room numbers. Spell out numbered streets and avenues of ninety-nine and below.

EXAMPLE The office is near **Fifth** Avenue, at **4** West **347th** Street, Suite **220.**

PRACTICE Numbers and Numerals

Rewrite each item, correcting errors in the use of numbers and numerals.

1. The soda costs 70 cents.
2. 3,076 was the population of Sandersburg.
3. 51% constitutes a majority.
4. By 10 o'clock, I had seen almost 100 trucks go by.
5. Queen Victoria of England reigned for more than half of the 19th century.
6. 5th and 6th Streets are closed for repaving, but Lincoln Avenue is still open.
7. I felt lucky to get this coat for forty-nine dollars and sixty-five cents.
8. The ball game is on the sports channel tonight from 8:00 to 10:30.
9. Dinner is at six P.M., and there will be a snack at 9 P.M.
10. Hawaii became the 50th state of the United States in 1959.

Rewrite the following passage, correcting the errors in spelling, capitalization, grammar, and usage. Add any missing punctuation. There are ten errors. Some sentences are correct.

Frederick Douglass

[1]Frederick Douglass who was born enslaved in Maryland, became one of the most famous advocates for African American rights. [2]Douglass taught hisself to read and write as a child. [3]His childhood experiences were retold in his first autobiography, Narrative of the Life of Frederick Douglass. [4]The story of Douglass' boyhood introduced readers to the horrors of slavery and convinced many people to support the abolition of slavery.

[5]After escaping to Massachusetts, Douglass became a speaker a newspaper editor, and a diplomat. [6]He established The *North Star,* an antislavery newspaper. [7]He published this newspaper from 1847–1860.

[8]Douglass became a consultant to President Abraham Lincoln during the Civil War. [9]He worked to enlist African American soldiers in the Northern Army and his sons were included in the ranks. [10]Witnessing the soldiers' unfair treatment Douglass spoke to President Lincoln on behalf of the soldiers.

[11]Throughout his life Douglass worked to make sure African Americans were given rights and protections. [12]He was also a passionate supporter of womens rights.

POSTTEST Correcting Errors in Punctuation

Rewrite each sentence, correcting any errors in punctuation.

1. "Quick Call the fire department!", she shouted.
2. Tim asked whether a tall dignified and well dressed woman had come to the house that day?

GRAMMAR/USAGE/MECHANICS

3. No George I meant the attendance office not the business office.

4. Starches not sweets are my downfall.

5. [*Letter forms*] Dear Mr. President

Dear Dad

Your loving daughter

6. In last months issue of the Homemaker magazine, there is an interesting article called Two for Tea.

7. Does the word camporee have one r in it? Its a strange looking word.

8. Mrs Jo Brooks she teaches history at our school moved to California in the winter of 80.

9. André sold his yacht the Sea Breeze.

10. We shouted Happy Birthday! Then someone asked How old are you.

11. These self winding watches are on sale at Mr. Smiths Pharmacy. (They are inexpensive copies of Rolex watches).

12. Plutarch the Greek author of the biographical collection Parallel Lives wrote "The virtues of these great men serve me as a sort of looking glass".

13. Mr. Sanchez hammered away at us, Learn to spell! Learn to spell! Learn to spell!

14. What I consider great music, is loud and annoying to my mother.

15. The following states have filed their election returns— Maine Georgia Utah and South Dakota.

16. Raising his eyebrows Doug my sleepy roommate drawled Well I don't think we should leave before 1100 AM do you

17. Shakespeare wrote the play Julius Caesar before he wrote the play Macbeth.

18. I meant to go to the store to get eggs, however by the time I had finished work the store was closed.

19. Gesundheit said Al is a German word meaning health.

20. We covered the sofa last year but the cover is torn consequently we will have to recover it this year.

POSTTEST **Correcting Errors in the Use of Abbreviations and Numbers**

Rewrite each item, correcting any errors in the use of abbreviations and numbers.

21. "Did you watch the special program on N.B.C.?" asked Emily.

22. Mr. Kelly announced that the parade would begin promptly at 1000 AM on January 1 2000.

23. In fact, he donates 5% of his salary to various charities.

24. When Sally listed her expenses, she found that one half of her income was needed for her car.

25. AntonioC DiGuilio MD has moved his practice to 512 Burton Place Trenton New Jersey.

26. 10 helpers have enrolled; however, I'm sure we could use 25 assistants.

27. There has been a one fourth cut in all prices at the department store.

28. My savings account has grown to four thousand one hundred twenty-three dollars.

29. Two of the old coins in my uncle's collection are dated 1239 AD.

30. The 20th century saw the invention of computers.

Chapter 12

Sentence Combining

● ● ● ● ● ● ● ● ● ● ● ● ● ● ●

PRETEST **Combining Sentences**

Read each group of sentences below. Combine the sentences in the way that seems best to you.

1. The dinner had been planned for eight o'clock. The dinner was canceled.
2. I tried to call you. You weren't home.
3. I opened the window. A breeze fanned the curtain.
4. I have enrolled in an exercise program. I want to get in shape.
5. Leo Tolstoy wrote *Anna Karenina* and *War and Peace.* Both of these are novels. Tolstoy was Russian.

6. Harry is going to plant tulips. He is going to plant daffodils. He is an avid gardener.

7. Someone broke into the car. The doctor's medical bag has been stolen.

8. The huge seaside mansion can house thirty-five people. It was built as a retreat.

9. Put your coat on the hook. The hook is near the door.

10. He was growing angry. He left without receiving a reply.

11. Esperanto is an artificial language. It was proposed many years ago as an international language.

12. Rubies and emeralds are very expensive. They are precious stones.

13. I am meeting Susan and Jack for lunch. Susan is a consultant. Jack is a taxi driver. We will lunch at a café. It is on the corner of Henderson and Blackberry.

14. This redwood towers over other trees. It is hundreds of years old.

15. I held my tongue for an hour. I could stand the silence no longer.

16. Worry consumes a lot of energy. It is also useless.

17. We are supporting our representative. We think he should be the next president.

18. Pearl S. Buck wrote several novels about China. She had lived in China for many years.

19. A sirocco is a hot, dry wind. It originates over the Libyan deserts. It blows across the Mediterranean, picking up moisture as it moves.

20. Sugar is a sweetener. Honey is another one.

12.1 TIPS FOR SENTENCE COMBINING

A distinctive writing style is one way of communicating your personality. Developing a clear, expressive writing style requires practice, of course. By writing regularly in your journal and by trying out different kinds of writing—poems, essays, stories, letters to the editor—you practice a range of skills. Another excellent approach for developing style is sentence combining.

The process of combining short sentences into more complex ones is the focus of this chapter. Your goal, though, is not to make long sentences, but to make good ones. Sometimes you'll find that longer, complex sentences let you express your ideas clearly and precisely. At other times, shorter is better.

Sentence combining is easy and fun. Here are some suggestions that have worked for other high school students—suggestions you might try as you explore your style.

1. **Whisper sentences to yourself.** This is faster than writing, and it helps you decide on the best sentence to write down.

2. **Work with a partner.** By trying out sentences on a partner and hearing your partner's ideas, you will often discover new, interesting ways to solve specific challenges. Feel free to borrow ideas.

3. **Use context when choosing sentences for a paragraph.** Each paragraph has an emerging context: the sentences you have already combined. Reading this context aloud helps you decide on the best next sentence.

4. **Compare your sentences with those of other students.** Seeing how others have solved combining tasks broadens your awareness of sentence options. Keep asking yourself, "Which do I prefer?"

5. **Look for stylistic patterns in your writing.** Calculate the average number of words per sentence; study your sentence openers; listen to rhythms in your style. Try new patterns to stretch yourself.

6. **Take risks.** It makes good sense to take risks and make mistakes as you combine sentences. Mistakes provide feedback. As you learn from them, you develop a personal style, a voice. You come to know yourself as a writer.

The point of sentence combining is to improve your revising and editing skills. Practice in combining sentences helps you see that sentences are flexible tools for thought, not rigid structures cast in concrete. The simple fact that you feel confident in moving sentence parts around increases your control of revising and editing. To acquire this sense of self-confidence—based on your real competence in combining and revising sentences—try strategies like these:

1. **Vary the length of your sentences.** Work for a rhythmic, interesting balance of long and short sentences, remembering that short sentences can be dramatic.

2. **Vary the structure of your sentences.** By using sentence openers occasionally and by sometimes tucking information into the middle of a sentence, you can create stylistic interest.

3. **Use parallelism for emphasis.** Experiment with repeated items in a series—words, phrases, clauses.

4. **Use interruption for emphasis.** Commas, colons, semicolons, dashes, parentheses—all of these are useful in your stylistic toolkit.

5. **Use unusual patterns for emphasis.** That you might sometimes reverse normal sentence patterns may never have occurred to you, but it can strengthen your writing.

You'll use these four main strategies when you combine sentences:

- deleting repeated words
- adding connecting words
- rearranging words
- changing the form of words

12.2 COMBINING SENTENCES BY INSERTING WORDS

When two sentences talk about the same idea, sometimes you can effectively combine them simply by taking a word or words from one sentence and inserting them into the other sentence. Occasionally the word or words you are inserting must change their form.

ORIGINAL VERSION	COMBINED VERSION
Sharks detect electrical fields The electrical fields are faint.	Sharks detect **faint** electrical fields. **[no change]**
A homing pigeon can hear wind sounds. The wind sounds have low frequencies. The sounds are thousands of miles away.	A homing pigeon can hear **low-frequency** wind sounds **thousands of miles away.** **[The noun phrase** *low frequencies* **has changed to the compound adjective** *low-frequency*.**]**

Read each group of sentences below. Combine the sentences by inserting a word or words in the way that seems best to you.

1. The dancers performed a ballet. It was a Russian ballet. The dancers performed gracefully.
2. My brother spies on me. He is annoying. He does it every day.
3. The clock struck twelve. It was a big old grandfather clock. It struck slowly.
4. The athlete ran in the marathon. She was determined. She ran twenty-six miles.
5. The woman wore a raincoat and carried an umbrella. The raincoat was tan, and the umbrella was black.
6. The baby played in the sand. The sand was wet. The baby played happily.
7. I drove the car to Pittsburgh. I drove carefully. The car was old.
8. The students waited for their exam results. They were nervous, so they waited anxiously.
9. The gentlemen strolled through the park. They strolled leisurely. The park was in their neighborhood.
10. The detectives examined the evidence. They examined it carefully. They were puzzled.

12.3 COMBINING SENTENCES BY INSERTING PHRASES

Another way to combine sentences is to insert a phrase from one sentence into another sentence. Sometimes you can use the phrase unchanged; at other times, you must make the words into a phrase. The most useful phrases for this purpose are prepositional phrases, appositive phrases, and participial phrases.

GRAMMAR/USAGE/MECHANICS

PREPOSITIONAL PHRASES

ORIGINAL VERSION	COMBINED VERSION
Bobolinks sense subtle distortions. The distortions are in the earth's magnetic field.	Bobolinks sense subtle distortions **in the earth's magnetic field.** [no change]
They use this information to navigate. The information helps them map their location.	They use this information **like a map** to navigate. [**The second sentence is changed into a prepositional phrase.**]

Note: For more information on prepositional phrases, see pages 146–148.

PRACTICE **Combining Sentences by Inserting Prepositional Phrases**

Read each group of sentences below. Combine the sentences by inserting prepositional phrases in the way that seems best to you.

1. You will need the address I gave you. You'll need it for your application.

2. The cookies are ready to bake. They are on the cookie sheet.

3. John F. Kennedy was assassinated. It happened in Dallas, Texas. The year was 1963.

4. My aunt Mary makes quilts. She has won several prizes.

5. The tarantula is a large, hairy spider. It has a poisonous bite.

6. Sophocles wrote *Antigone.* He wrote it in 441 B.C.

7. It was late afternoon. We lit our campfire then.

8. This table is very unsteady. It has only three legs.

9. We went to dinner. The dinner was at a fancy restaurant. The restaurant was in Austin.

10. Pick up the books on your way out. They are on the kitchen table.

APPOSITIVE PHRASES

ORIGINAL VERSION	COMBINED VERSION
Charles Dickens was born in 1812. He was a British novelist.	Charles Dickens, **a British novelist,** was born in 1812.
	or
	British novelist Charles Dickens was born in 1812.

Note: For more information on appositive phrases, see pages 148–149.

PRACTICE Combining Sentences by Inserting Appositive Phrases

Read each group of sentences below. Combine the sentences by inserting appositive phrases in the way that seems best to you.

1. I ordered the soup. It was a clam chowder.

2. The doctor treated poor patients in her free time. She is a compassionate person.

3. We booked passage on a ship that sails out of Oslo. It is a Norwegian liner.

4. Joan Didion wrote *Slouching Towards Bethlehem* and *Run River. Slouching Towards Bethlehem* is a collection of essays. *Run River* is a novel.

5. One of John Philip Sousa's marches is often played on the Fourth of July. The march is called "Stars and Stripes Forever."

6. The bald eagle and the peregrine falcon are predatory birds. They have been on the endangered species list.

7. The backpacker took only one change of clothing. He took a pair of jeans and a sweatshirt.

8. Mrs. Brown will take care of my younger brother next year. She is an English nanny.

9. Two yard chores must be done routinely. These are mowing and weeding.

10. Basic math skills are taught in elementary school. These skills are addition, subtraction, multiplication, and division.

PARTICIPIAL PHRASES

ORIGINAL VERSION	COMBINED VERSION
Dickens's novels were immensely popular in the nineteenth century. They contained a hidden agenda.	**Containing a hidden agenda,** Dickens's novels were immensely popular in the nineteenth century.
	or
	Dickens's novels, **containing a hidden agenda,** were immensely popular in the nineteenth century.
Dickens's novels opposed many human rights violations of the time. They were crowded with memorable characters.	Dickens's novels, **crowded with memorable characters,** opposed many human rights violations of the time.
	or
	Crowded with memorable characters, Dickens's novels opposed many human rights violations of the time.

Note: For more information on participial phrases, see pages 150–151.

Read each group of sentences below. Combine the sentences by inserting participial phrases in the way that seems best to you.

1. The baker preheated the oven. He turned it to 350°.

2. The farmer hummed to herself. She did this while she baled the hay.

3. The gymnast received a gold medal. She smiled at the cheering crowd.

4. The contract arrived in less than an hour. It was delivered by a courier service.

5. The basketball court is in excellent shape. It is maintained by the city's Parks and Recreation Department.

6. This blue and yellow plaid rug won't wear out. It is woven from yarn-dyed cotton.

7. The tires on my car are almost worthless. They are pocked by rocks and gravel.

8. My grandmother is very tired. She has nursed her friend around the clock.

9. The waiter forgot to place the customer's order. He was exhausted after a long day at work.

10. Thousands attended the festival. It was considered a huge success.

12.4 COMBINING SENTENCES USING COORDINATING CONJUNCTIONS

To combine sentences that have equally important ideas, you can form a compound sentence by using a coordinating conjunction *(and, but, or, so, nor, for, yet)* or a pair of correlative conjunctions *(both . . . and, just as . . . so, not only . . . but (also), either . . . or, neither . . . nor, whether . . . or).* As an alternative to using conjunctions to join the independent clauses, you could use a semicolon with or without a conjunctive adverb, such as *however, consequently,* and *furthermore.*

ORIGINAL VERSION	COMBINED VERSION
Jan flexed her knees at the top of the ski slope. She took several deep breaths.	Jan flexed her knees **and** took several deep breaths at the top of the ski slope.
The car had a costly sound system. Its rocker panels were badly rusted, though.	The car had a costly sound system, **but** its rocker panels were badly rusted.
We will steam off the old wallpaper. Alternatively, we will paint over it.	We will **either** steam off **or** paint over the old wallpaper.
The waiter was slow, arrogant, and grumpy. For those reasons, I did not leave a tip.	The waiter was slow, arrogant, and grumpy; **accordingly,** I did not leave a tip.

Note: For more information on coordinating conjunctions, see page 122.

PRACTICE Combining Sentences Using Coordinating Conjunctions

Read each group of sentences below. Combine the sentences using coordinating conjunctions in the way that seems best to you.

1. We must rehearse more often. The play will be a failure.
2. Judson was a man with strong opinions. He expressed them colorfully.
3. The highway is closed for five miles. The detour is an excellent road.

4. Someone has taken my sandwiches. Maybe I forgot to pack them.

5. The play has been selected. The cast will be announced soon.

6. The administrator is a clear-thinking individual. She is also an eloquent speaker.

7. Frederique will buy a birthday present for her mother. As an alternative, she will make one.

8. Our football team didn't win the state championship. Our basketball team didn't win either.

9. I am interested in other cultures, and I love to read. For these reasons, I will be majoring in French literature.

10. Many people believe in the existence of the island of Atlantis. Searchers have never found it.

12.5 COMBINING SENTENCES USING SUBORDINATION IN ADVERB CLAUSES, ADJECTIVE CLAUSES, AND NOUN CLAUSES

Sometimes the ideas in two sentences are not equally important. Instead, one idea is more important than the other. You can combine these kinds of sentences by making the less important idea into a subordinate clause.

ADVERB CLAUSES

One kind of subordinate clause is an adverb clause. An adverb clause is introduced by a subordinating conjunction and modifies a verb, an adjective, or another adverb in the main clause. Following are some subordinating conjunctions you might use to show the relationship between the two clauses.

SUBORDINATING CONJUNCTIONS

FOR EXPRESSING TIME RELATIONSHIPS	after, as, as soon as, before, since, so long as, until, when, whenever, while
FOR EXPRESSING PLACE RELATIONSHIPS	as far as, where, wherever
FOR EXPRESSING CAUSE-AND-EFFECT RELATIONSHIPS	as, because, since, so (that)
FOR EXPRESSING CONDITIONAL RELATIONSHIPS	although, as if, as long as, as though, considering (that), if, inasmuch as, in order that, provided (that), since, than, so (that), though, unless, whereas

In the following examples, some of the techniques you have already seen are used along with subordinating conjunctions to combine several sentences into one. Study the examples to see how the techniques can be used together.

ORIGINAL VERSION	COMBINED VERSION
His destination was a truck stop. The truck stop was familiar. He would have breakfast there.	His destination was a familiar truck stop **where** he would have breakfast.
The cook poured water into the skillet of venison sausage patties. The patties were sputtering. Venison should cook slowly.	The cook poured water into the skillet of sputtering venison sausage patties **because** venison should cook slowly.
Her stylish shoes pinched her feet cruelly. The shoes were tight. In spite of the pain, she danced every dance with a smile. The smile was blissful.	**Although** her stylish but tight shoes pinched her feet cruelly, she danced every dance with a blissful smile.

Note: For more information on using subordinating conjunctions in adverb clauses, see page 168.

Read each pair of sentences below. Using adverb clauses, combine the sentences in the way that seems best to you.

1. My grandmother moved to this country from Ireland. This happened long before I was born.
2. We are going to the amusement park. There we will ride the roller coasters.
3. Congress will take a recess until January. This will mean that politicians will have time to campaign.
4. First the city workers trimmed the trees. Then they repaired the power lines.
5. The doctor was paged. He left immediately.
6. The dieter lost ten pounds. He lost the weight by eating lots of fruits and vegetables and exercising regularly.
7. People in this country saved aluminum foil and grease during World War II. They did this after the United States entered the war.
8. You were skiing in Nevada. At that time, I was swimming in the warm waters around Saint Thomas.
9. I receive an allowance. My mother gives it to me if I complete my homework and do my chores.
10. There is now heightened awareness about the dangers of smoking. This is the result of a massive campaign by the government and several health agencies.

ADJECTIVE CLAUSES

An adjective clause is a subordinate clause that modifies a noun or a pronoun in the main clause. To combine ideas using an adjective clause, replace the subject of one sentence with the word *who, whose, which,* or *that.*

ORIGINAL VERSION	COMBINED VERSION
My father taught me about the Australian Aborigines. My father was born in Australia.	My father, **who was born in Australia,** taught me about the Australian Aborigines.
	or
	My father, **who taught me about the Australian Aborigines,** was born in Australia.
Oodgeroo Noonuccal was a poet and an Aboriginal rights activist. Her name is pronounced OO-juh-roo nuh-NUCK-ul	Oodgeroo Noonuccal, **whose name is pronounced OO-juh-roo nuh-NUCK-ul,** was a poet and an Aboriginal rights activist.
Her 1964 collection of poems was called *We Are Going.* It made her the first Aboriginal writer to be published in English.	Her 1964 collection of poems, **which made her the first Aboriginal writer to be published in English,** was called *We Are Going.*
	or
	Her 1964 collection of poems, **which was called *We Are Going,*** made her the first Aboriginal writer to be published in English.

PRACTICE **Combining Sentences Using Subordination: Adjective Clauses**

Read each group of sentences below. Using adjective clauses, combine the sentences in the way that seems best to you.

1. Alice Walker is an American writer, and she wrote *The Color Purple.* This novel was made into a movie.
2. Quito is the capital of Ecuador. Quito is a large city that has been damaged by earthquakes several times.

3. Mount Vesuvius is the only active volcano on the European continent. This volcano was responsible for the burying of Pompeii.

4. The phoenix was a mythical bird. After burning, it rose again from its own ashes.

5. The *Wall Street Journal* is a daily newspaper. It contains financial news.

6. Charlotte Brontë wrote *Jane Eyre.* She was one of three sisters who wrote novels.

7. In 1929 the muralist Diego Rivera married Frieda Kahlo. Kahlo was a Mexican painter.

8. Fluoride is a chemical compound. It has been effective in preventing tooth decay.

9. One poet is known for his creative punctuation and lack of ordinary capitalization. His name is E. E. Cummings.

10. Peter will enlist in the army. He is a talented athlete and a diligent student. He will enlist next year.

NOUN CLAUSES

A noun clause is a subordinate clause used as a noun. To combine ideas using a noun clause, begin one sentence with one of the words in the following chart. (It will probably be necessary to change some other words in the sentence.) Then put the noun clause you have made into another sentence.

WORDS THAT CAN INTRODUCE NOUN CLAUSES			
how	whatever	which	whoever, whomever
that	when	whichever	whose
what	where	who, whom	why

ORIGINAL VERSION	COMBINED VERSION
I wish I knew something. My notebook is somewhere.	I wish I knew **where my notebook is.** [noun clause acting as direct object]
Give someone the prize. The runner who finishes first is the winner.	Give **whoever is first** the prize. [noun clause acting as indirect object]
A news story should begin with something. It should get the reader's attention.	A news story should begin with **whatever will get the reader's attention.** [noun clause as object of the preposition *with*]
You want to wear clothes that are too big for you. This desire makes no sense to me.	**Why you want to wear clothes that are too big for you** makes no sense to me. [noun clause acting as subject]

PRACTICE Combining Sentences Using Subordination: Noun Clauses

Read each group of sentences below. Using noun clauses, combine the sentences in the way that seems best to you.

1. The squirrels have been especially active this fall. I do not know the reason for their activity.
2. My sister made a mess of our bedroom three days after I'd cleaned it. This upsets me terribly.
3. Where is Mykonos? I do not know.
4. Give someone the book. The person who wants to read it next should get it.
5. You mentioned meeting someone. Please give him an invitation to the reception.
6. Why are snowflakes in patterns? I wonder about that.

7. These notebooks were left here. I don't know the owner.
8. Our class is going to be remembered. I am certain of that.
9. Someone took my lunch money. I wish that this person would return it to me.
10. My brother charms everyone he meets. I do not know how he does this.

PRACTICE **Combining Sentences Using Subordination**

Read each group of sentences below. Using subordination, combine the sentences in the way that seems best to you.

1. The rain had passed. Then the clouds parted.
2. You were exhausted. In spite of this, you persisted.
3. Maria was born in Mexico. She is a talented musician and a good friend.
4. What do you want for your birthday? Give me some idea.
5. I introduced you to this man. Here he is.
6. *Arrivederci* is an Italian word. Most Americans know this.
7. Sometimes I am lonely. During these times, I turn on the radio.
8. The owner of a local nursery is going out of business. She is selling all of her plants very inexpensively.
9. Judge Diaz decided the case. It had been pending for a long time.
10. Stephen Crane wrote "The Open Boat." He was an American author. The story is based on his own experiences after the sinking of the *Commodore.*

PRACTICE Proofreading

The following passage is about the writer Alice Walker.
Rewrite the passage, combining sentences that are closely
related in meaning.

Alice Walker

Alice Walker was born in Georgia. Her parents were poor share-croppers. They were African American. Walker graduated at the top of her high school class. She won a scholarship to Spelman College. The college was located in Atlanta, Georgia. Walker attended Spelman for two years. She transferred to Sarah Lawrence College in New York. She earned her degree from Sarah Lawrence College.

After college Walker returned to Mississippi. There she taught writing and African American literature. She also worked to improve welfare rights and to increase voter registration among African Americans in the South.

Walker's first published work was an essay on the Civil Rights movement. It was published in 1966. Most of her acclaim as a writer has come from her novels. Her novels reveal the injustice of the racism and sexism faced by African American women. Walker's third novel won the Pulitzer Prize. It was called *The Color Purple.* It was made into an award-winning movie.

POSTTEST Combining Sentences

Read each group of sentences below. Combine the sen-
tences in the way that seems best to you.

1. *Aloha* is a Hawaiian word. It means "hello." It also means "goodbye."
2. I am often late for school. This is caused by my missing the bus.

3. People should write personal notes by hand. This is a time-consuming activity.

4. Robert E. Lee was a Confederate general. He was widely respected.

5. Dinah's brother enjoys sculling. So does her dad.

6. My father travels to Europe. He is a stockbroker. He goes on business. He goes four times a year.

7. The cardinal is the state bird of Ohio. It is also the state bird of several other states.

8. There are three vegetables in the soup. They are tomatoes, okra, and corn.

9. Senator Diamond reached the hotel. Mr. Barnes was waiting for him.

10. Their colors are maroon and gold. They are very attractive.

11. We had an hour to wait before the theater opened. We went window-shopping.

12. Some towels are oversized. I like those.

13. Larry and his family went to Paris last summer. They visited the Louvre Museum and the Eiffel Tower.

14. At noon the sun disappeared behind a cloud. It did not reappear until the next day.

15. Niagara Falls can be viewed from two countries. One is Canada and the other is the United States.

16. Count Basie played great music. He played during the Big Band era.

17. Copper Mountain is in Colorado. It is a skiing area close to the town of Frisco.

18. The wedding cake was a marble cake with white icing. It had three tiers.

19. There are huge floats in the Rose Bowl Parade. Many of them are made with flowers.

20. Row houses are totally separate inside but attached on the outside. There are many of these in Baltimore.

Chapter 13

Spelling and Vocabulary

● ● ● ● ● ● ● ● ● ● ● ● ● ●

13.1 SPELLING RULES

The following rules, examples, and exceptions will help you master the spelling of many words. However, not all words follow the rules. When you're not sure how to spell a word, the best thing to do is check a dictionary.

Spelling *ie* and *ei*

An easy way to learn when to use *ie* and when to use *ei* is to memorize a simple rhyming rule. Then learn the common exceptions to the rule.

RULE	EXAMPLES
"WRITE *I* BEFORE *E*	achieve, believe, brief, chief, die, field, friend, grief, lie, niece, piece, pier, quiet, retrieve, sieve, tie, tier, yield
EXCEPT AFTER *C*	ceiling, conceit, conceive, deceit, deceive, receipt, receive
OR WHEN SOUNDED LIKE *A*, AS IN *NEIGHBOR* AND *WEIGH*."	eight, eighth, eighty, freight, neigh, reign, sleigh, veil, vein, weigh, weight

Some exceptions: *either, caffeine, foreign, forfeit, height, heir, leisure, neither, protein, seize, species, their, weird;* words ending in *cient* (ancient) and *cience* (conscience); plurals of nouns ending in *cy* (democracies); the third-person singular form of verbs ending in *cy* (fancies); words in which *i* and *e* follow *c* but represent separate sounds *(science, society)*

GRAMMAR/USAGE/MECHANICS

Words Ending in *cede, ceed,* and *sede*

The only English word ending in *sede* is *supersede.* Three words end in *ceed: proceed, exceed,* and *succeed.* You can remember these three words by thinking of the following sentence:

If you **proceed** to **exceed** the speed limit, you will **succeed** in getting a ticket.

All other words ending with the "seed" sound are spelled with cede: *concede, intercede, precede, recede, secede.*

Spelling Unstressed Vowels

Listen to the vowel sound in the second syllable of the word *or-i-gin.* This is an unstressed vowel sound, and it can be spelled in many ways. Dictionary respellings use the schwa (ə) to indicate an unstressed vowel sound.

To spell a word that has an unstressed vowel sound, think of a related word in which the syllable containing the vowel sound is stressed.

The word *original,* for example, should help you spell the word *origin.* The chart shows some other examples.

SPELLING UNSTRESSED VOWELS

UNKNOWN SPELLING	RELATED WORD	WORD SPELLED CORRECTLY
leg_l	le**ga**lity	legal
fant_sy	fan**tas**tic	fantasy
host_le	hos**til**ity	hostile
opp_site	op**pose**	opposite
def_nite	de**fine**	definite

Adding Prefixes

Adding prefixes is easy. Keep the spelling of the root word and add the prefix. If the last letter of the prefix is the same as the first letter of the word, keep both letters.

un- + happy = unhappy

dis- + appear = disappear

re- + enlist = reenlist

mis- + spell = misspell

co- + operate = cooperate

il- + legal = illegal

un- + natural = unnatural

im- + migrate = immigrate

GRAMMAR/USAGE/MECHANICS

Adding Suffixes

When you add a suffix beginning with a vowel, double the final consonant if the word ends in a **single consonant preceded by a single vowel** *and*

- the word has one syllable

mud + -y = muddy   sad + -er = sadder

put + -ing = putting   stop + -ed = stopped

- the word is stressed on the last syllable and the stress remains on the same syllable after the suffix is added

occur + -ence = occurrence

regret + -able = regrettable

begin + -ing = beginning

repel + -ent = repellent

commit + -ed = committed

refer + -al = referral

Don't double the final consonant if the word is not stressed on the last syllable or if the stress shifts when the suffix is added.

murmur + -ed = murmured

refer + -ence = reference

Don't double the final letter if the word ends in *s, w, x,* or *y: buses, rowing, waxy, employer.*

Don't double the final consonant before the suffix *-ist* if the word has more than one syllable: *druggist* but *violinist, guitarist.*

Adding suffixes to words that end in *y* can cause spelling problems. Study the following rules and note the exceptions.

When a word ends in **a vowel and *y*,** keep the *y*.

play + -s = plays
obey + -ed = obeyed
buy + -ing = buying
employ + -er = employer
joy + -ful = joyful
joy + -less = joyless

joy + -ous = joyous
annoy + -ance = annoyance
enjoy + -ment = enjoyment
enjoy + -able = enjoyable
boy + -ish = boyish
coy + -ly = coyly

SOME EXCEPTIONS: gay + -ly = gaily, day + -ly = daily, pay + -d = paid, lay + -d = laid, say + -d = said

When a word ends in **a consonant and *y*,** change the *y* to *i* before any suffix that doesn't begin with *i*. Keep the *y* before suffixes that begin with *i*.

carry + -es = carries
dry + -ed = dried
easy + -er = easier
merry + -ly = merrily
happy + -ness = happiness
beauty + -ful = beautiful
fury + -ous = furious
defy + -ant = defiant
vary + -ation = variation

deny + -al = denial
rely + -able = reliable
mercy + -less = merciless
likely + -hood = likelihood
accompany + -ment =
   accompaniment
carry + -ing = carrying
baby + -ish = babyish
lobby + -ist = lobbyist

SOME EXCEPTIONS: shy + -ly = shyly, dry + -ly = dryly, shy + -ness = shyness, dry + -ness = dryness, biology + -ist = biologist, economy + -ist = economist, baby + -hood = babyhood

Usually a **final silent *e*** is dropped before a suffix, but sometimes it's kept. The following chart shows the basic rules for adding suffixes to words that end in silent *e*.

ADDING SUFFIXES TO WORDS THAT END IN SILENT *E*

RULE	EXAMPLES
Drop the *e* before suffixes that begin with a vowel.	care + -ed = cared dine + -ing = dining move + -er = mover type + -ist = typist blue + -ish = bluish arrive + -al = arrival desire + -able = desirable accuse + -ation = accusation noise + -y = noisy
Some exceptions	mile + -age = mileage dye + -ing = dyeing
Drop the *e* and change *i* to *y* before the suffix *-ing* if the word ends in *ie*.	die + -ing = dying lie + -ing = lying tie + -ing = tying
Keep the *e* before suffixes that begin with *a* and *o* if the word ends in *ce* or *ge*.	dance + -able = danceable change + -able = changeable
Keep the *e* before suffixes that begin with a vowel if the word ends in *ee* or *oe*.	see + -ing = seeing agree + -able = agreeable canoe + -ing = canoeing hoe + -ing = hoeing
Some exceptions (There can never be three of the same letter in a row.)	free + -er = freer free + -est = freest
Keep the *e* before suffixes that begin with a consonant.	grace + -ful = graceful state + -hood = statehood like + -ness = likeness care + -less = careless sincere + -ly = sincerely

See next page for some exceptions.

RULE	EXAMPLES
Some exceptions	awe + -ful = awful
	argue + -ment = argument
	true + -ly = truly
	due + -ly = duly
	whole + -ly = wholly
Drop *le* before the suffix *-ly* when the word ends with a consonant and *le*.	possible + -ly = possibly
	sparkle + -ly = sparkly
	gentle + -ly = gently

Don't drop any letters when you add *-ly* to a word that ends in a single *l*. When a word ends in *ll*, drop one *l* when you add the suffix *-ly*.

real + -ly = really   chill + -ly = chilly
cool + -ly = coolly   full + -ly = fully

Don't drop any letters when you add the suffix *-ness* to a word that ends in *n*.

stubborn + -ness = stubbornness   mean + -ness = meanness

Compound Words

Keep the original spelling of both parts of a compound word.

Remember that some compounds are one word, some are two words, and some are hyphenated. Check a dictionary when in doubt.

foot + lights = footlights   fish + hook = fishhook
busy + body = busybody   with + hold = withhold
book + case = bookcase   book + keeper = bookkeeper
light + house = lighthouse   heart + throb = heartthrob

GRAMMAR/USAGE/MECHANICS

Spelling Plurals

To form the plural of **most nouns,** you simply add -*s*. Remember that simple plural nouns never use apostrophes.

The following chart shows other basic rules.

GENERAL RULES FOR PLURALS

NOUNS ENDING IN	TO FORM PLURAL	EXAMPLES
ch, s, sh, x, z	Add -*es*.	lunch → lunches loss → losses dish → dishes box → boxes buzz → buzzes
a vowel and *y*	Add -*s*.	boy → boys turkey → turkeys
a consonant and *y*	Change *y* to *i* and add -*es*.	baby → babies penny → pennies
a vowel and *o*	Add -*s*.	radio → radios rodeo → rodeos
a consonant and *o*	Usually add -*es*.	potato → potatoes tomato → tomatoes hero → heroes echo → echoes
	Sometimes add -*s*.	zero → zeros photo → photos piano → pianos

NOUNS ENDING IN	TO FORM PLURAL	EXAMPLES
f or *fe*	Usually change *f* to *v* and add *-s* or *-es*.	wife → wives knife → knives life → lives leaf → leaves half → halves shelf → shelves wolf → wolves thief → thieves
	Sometimes add *-s*.	roof → roofs chief → chiefs cliff → cliffs giraffe → giraffes

The plurals of **proper names** are formed by adding *-es* to names that end in *ch, s, sh, x,* or *z.*

EXAMPLE   The **Woodriches** live on Elm Street.

EXAMPLE   There are two **Jonases** in our class.

Just add *-s* to form the plural of all other proper names, including those that end in *y.* Remember that the rule of changing *y* to *i* and adding *-es* doesn't apply to proper names.

EXAMPLE   The **Kennedys** are a famous American family.

EXAMPLE   I know three **Marys.**

EXAMPLE   The last two **Januarys** have been especially cold.

To form the plural of a **compound noun written as one word,** follow the general rules for plurals. To form the plural of **hyphenated compound nouns** or **compound nouns of more than one word,** usually make the most important word plural.

EXAMPLE   The two women's **fathers-in-law** have never met.

EXAMPLE   The three **post offices** are made of brick.

EXAMPLE   There have been three **surgeons general** in this decade.

EXAMPLE   The list of **poets laureate** in Great Britain is a short list.

EXAMPLE   The general presided over two **courts martial** today.

Some nouns have **irregular plural forms** that don't follow any rules.

man → men   tooth → teeth
woman → women   mouse → mice
child → children   goose → geese
foot → feet   ox → oxen

Some nouns have the same singular and plural forms. Most of these are the names of animals, and some of the plural forms may be spelled in more than one way.

deer → deer   species → species
sheep → sheep   fish → fish *or* fishes
head (of cattle) → head   antelope → antelope *or* antelopes
Sioux → Sioux   buffalo → buffalo *or* buffaloes
series → series   *or* buffalos

Learning to Spell New Words

You can improve your spelling by improving your study method. Try the following method to learn to spell new words. You can also improve your spelling by thoroughly learning certain common but frequently misspelled words.

1. Say It
Look at the printed word and say it aloud. Then say it again, pronouncing each syllable correctly.

2. Visualize It
Picture the word in your mind. Avoid looking at the printed word on the page. Try to visualize the word letter by letter.

3. Write It
Look at the printed word again, and write it two or three times. Then write the word without looking at the printed spelling.

4. Check It
Check your spelling. Did you spell the word correctly? If not, repeat each step until you can spell the word easily.

Get into the habit of using a dictionary to find the correct spelling of a word.

Using a Computer to Check Spelling

A spelling checker is a useful computer tool. If you have misspelled any words, a spelling checker can find them for you. Not only will it save you time, but it will also show you words you need to learn to spell.

Although spelling checkers are handy, they can't do the whole job. When a spelling checker finds a misspelled word, it searches the computer's dictionary for words spelled in a similar way. *You* must choose the correct word from the options the computer gives you.

Furthermore, a spelling checker can't check for sense. If you type *right* instead of *write*, the spelling checker won't highlight the error because both right and write are correctly spelled words. You still need to know correct spellings.

PRACTICE **Spelling Rules**

Find the misspelled word in each group and write it correctly.

1. yield, freight, concieve
2. exceed, procede, precede
3. sincerely, responsiveness, engagement
4. sheriffes, scarves, thieves
5. headdresses, dining rooms, brother-in-laws
6. realy, plainness, occurring
7. illiterate, mispell, preenroll
8. buyer, steadiness, studing
9. patios, bunchs, delicacies
10. sheeps, feet, children

13.2 SPELLING DIFFICULT WORDS

Some words are more difficult to spell than others, and not all words follow basic spelling rules. Each person has an individual list of "problem" words. One useful strategy for learning difficult words is to develop a list of words that you frequently misspell and study them often.

A list of frequently misspelled words follows. Use it for quick reference.

FREQUENTLY MISSPELLED WORDS

abdomen
absence
abundant
academically
accelerator
accept
accessible
accidentally
acclimated
accommodate
accompaniment
accomplishment
acknowledge
acknowledgment
acquaintance
adequately
admission
admittance
adolescent
advantageous
advertisement
adviser
aerate
aerial
against
alcohol
allegiance
alliance
allot
allotting
all right
a lot
anonymous
answer

apologetically
apparatus
apparent
arctic
arousing
arrangement
atheistic
attendant
ballet
bankruptcy
beautiful
beginning
behavior
bibliography
biscuit
blasphemy
boulevard
buffet
bureau
bureaucrat
burial
business
cafeteria
calendar
camouflage
canceled
canoe
capitalism
carburetor
caricature
cataclysm
catastrophe
cemetery
changeable

chassis
choir
circumstantial
coliseum
colleague
colonel
coming
commercial
competition
complexion
concede
conceivable
connoisseur
conscience
conscientious
conscious
consciousness
consistency
controlling
controversy
convenient
cruelty
curriculum
decadent
decathlon
deceitful
deference
definite
deodorant
descend
descendant
descent
desirable
detrimental

devastation	exuberant	idiomatic
develop	familiarize	immediate
devise	fascinating	incidentally
dilemma	fascism	independent
diligence	February	inevitable
diphtheria	feminine	influential
disastrous	financier	ingenious
disciple	fission	innocent
discipline	foreign	inoculate
discrimination	forfeit	institution
disease	forty	intellectual
diseased	fulfill	interference
dissatisfied	fundamentally	irresistible
division	funeral	jewelry
efficiency	gaiety	knowledge
eighth	galaxy	knowledgeable
elementary	gauge	laboratory
eligible	genius	larynx
embarrass	government	legitimate
embarrassed	grammatically	leisure
emperor	guarantee	leisurely
emphasize	guidance	library
endeavor	harassment	license
enormous	height	livelihood
entertainment	hereditary	luxurious
entrance	hindrance	magistrate
environment	hippopotamus	magnificence
espionage	horizontal	maintenance
essential	hospital	malicious
exceed	humorous	manageable
except	hygiene	maneuver
exhibition	hypocrisy	marital
exhilaration	hypocrite	marriageable
expensive	ideally	martyrdom

GRAMMAR/USAGE/MECHANICS

mathematics
mediocre
melancholy
melodious
metaphor
miniature
mischievous
misspell
molasses
mortgage
mosquito
municipal
muscle
naive
necessary
necessity
negligence
negotiable
neighborhood
neurotic
newsstand
niece
nucleus
nuisance
nutritious
occasion
occasionally
occur
occurrence
occurring
omission
omitting
opportunity
orchestra

original
outrageous
pageant
pamphlet
parallel
paralysis
parliament
pastime
peasant
pedestal
perceive
permanent
permissible
personnel
perspiration
persuade
pharmacy
physical
physician
picnic
picnicking
pilot
playwright
pneumonia
politician
possessed
precede
preferable
presence
prestige
presumption
prevalent
privilege
procedure

proceed
propaganda
propagate
prophecy
prophesy
psychoanalysis
questionnaire
realtor
rebellion
receipt
receive
recognize
recommend
recommendation
reference
referred
rehearsal
reminiscent
remittance
repetitive
representative
responsibility
restaurant
reveal
rhythm
rhythmical
ridiculous
salable
schedule
seize
separate
separation
sergeant
significance

Frequently Misspelled Words, continued

sincerely	symmetrical	undoubtedly
souvenir	synonymous	unmistakable
specimen	technique	unnecessary
sponsor	technology	unscrupulous
statistics	temperament	usually
strategic	tendency	vaccine
stubbornness	theory	vacuum
succeed	tolerance	valedictory
succession	tortoise	variety
sufficient	traffic	vaudeville
superintendent	tragedy	vehicle
supersede	transparent	vengeance
suppress	truly	versatile
surprise	twelfth	villain
susceptible	unanimous	Wednesday

THE FAR SIDE   By GARY LARSON

Primitive spelling bees

Find each misspelled word and write it correctly.

1. That's the twelvth unecessary phone call you've made to the personnel office.
2. Did you complete the questionaire from the supertendent about vehicle registration?
3. Can we perswade you to play an accompaniment on the piano during the rehersal of our tradgedy?
4. "Devision is my weakest skill in mathmatics," he said apologeticly.
5. Will you sieze the opportunity to taste this nutricious minature biscuit?
6. Ommitting the last name of your aquaintance undoubtedly embarassed her.
7. The victim was in a horzontal position when he arrived at the hospital after the disasterous accident.
8. My presumption is that independant people accept responsability for their actions.
9. Do you know the correct prosdure for operating a vaccuum cleaner in a commersial establishment?
10. The calender shows that the guideance office will be closed this comeing Wensday.

13.3 EXPANDING YOUR VOCABULARY

Increasing your vocabulary improves your reading and writing skills and your chances of scoring well on standardized tests. The following tips suggest ways to expand your vocabulary and remember new words you encounter.

1. **Notice** new words when you're reading or listening. Write the words and their meanings in a notebook.

2. **Check** the meaning and pronunciation of a new word in a dictionary. Use the original context— surrounding words that are familiar—to understand the word's meaning and use.
3. **Relate** the new word to words you already know. Associate its spelling or meaning with a familiar word that will make the new word easier to remember.
4. **Verify** your understanding of the new word with someone else. A teacher, a parent, or a friend may be able to tell you if you correctly understand the meaning of the word.
5. **Practice** using the new word in your writing and conversation. Try to use the new word at least once a day for a week. Using a word repeatedly is the best way to remember it.

LEARNING FROM CONTEXT

You can often figure out the meaning of an unfamiliar word by looking for clues in the words and sentences around it. These surrounding words and sentences are called the context.

USING SPECIFIC CONTEXT CLUES

Writers often give clues to the meaning of unfamiliar words. Sometimes they even tell you exactly what a word means. The following chart shows five types of specific context clues. It also lists clue words to look for. Finally, the chart gives examples of sentences with unfamiliar words whose meanings you should be able to figure out from the context. In the examples, the clue words are in bold type. The unfamiliar words and the helpful context are in italic type.

INTERPRETING CLUE WORDS IN CONTEXT

TYPE OF CONTEXT CLUE	CLUE WORDS	EXAMPLES
Definition The meaning of the unfamiliar word is stated in the sentence.	also known as in other words or that is which is which means	The course emphasized *demography*, **which is** *the study of human populations.* The lecturer was *verbose;* **that is,** he was *wordy.*
Example The meaning of the unfamiliar word is explained through familiar examples.	for example for instance including like such as	Osbert served as the old duke's *amanuensis;* **for example,** *he took dictation and copied manuscripts.* *Miscreants* of all kinds, **including** *pickpockets, thieves, and vandals,* roamed the streets of Victorian England.
Comparison The unfamiliar word is similar to a familiar word or phrase.	also identical like likewise resembling same similarly too	Joan's friend testified to her *veracity.* Her teacher, **too,** said Joan's *truthfulness* was evident to all who knew her. Consuela suffered from *acrophobia;* her father **also** had a *fear of heights.*
Contrast The unfamiliar word is the opposite of a familiar word or phrase.	although unlike however on the contrary	**Unlike** his *despondent* opponent, Kwami appeared *hopeful, happy,* and *sure* he would win.

TYPE OF CONTEXT CLUE	CLUE WORDS	EXAMPLES
Contrast, *continued*	on the other hand though but	Martin always *grouses* about doing his chores, **but** his sister does her work *without complaining.*
Cause and Effect The unfamiliar word is explained as part of a cause-and-effect relationship.	as a result because consequently therefore thus	Maria felt the stranger was being *intrusive* **because** he *asked too many* personal questions. Otis has a *loquacious* nature; **consequently,** the teacher is constantly telling him to stop talking.

GRAMMAR/USAGE/MECHANICS

USING GENERAL CONTEXT

Sometimes there are no special clue words to help you understand an unfamiliar word. However, you can still use the general context. That is, you can use the details in the words or sentences around the unfamiliar word. Read the following sentence:

EXAMPLE Ramon was in a *jocund* mood, laughing and joking with his friends.

Even if you don't know the meaning of *jocund,* you do know that it must be an adjective describing *mood.* From other details in the sentence (*laughing and joking*), you may guess correctly that *jocund* means "merry, cheerful, carefree."

Use context clues to figure out the meaning of the italicized word. Write the meaning. Then write definition, example, comparison, contrast, cause and effect, *or* general *to tell what type of context clue you used to define the word.*

1. At the fall of Berlin, *anarchy,* or complete disorder, reigned until Allied forces took control.
2. That song, for instance, has no good qualities; it is *devoid* of melody, rhythm, and interesting lyrics.
3. A glass of warm milk before bedtime often has a *soporific* effect; consequently, you may fall asleep more easily.
4. Like decayed leaves, other *decomposed* vegetable matter makes good fertilizer.
5. The general's caution contrasted with the *temerity* of his fierce warriors.
6. Because this room is small, you don't need to speak in a *stentorian* voice to be heard.
7. The small boat was filling with water. The passengers watched their belongings splash into the sea as they *jettisoned* everything on board that was not nailed down.
8. Although the weather was calm and peaceful, dark clouds were gathering *portentously* on the horizon.
9. We expect *decorum* from our students; we hope our visitors will also behave properly.
10. In the nineteenth century, some writers used a *pseudonym* to conceal their identities. Charlotte Brontë at first used the pen name Currer Bell.

13.4 ROOTS, PREFIXES, AND SUFFIXES

You can often figure out the meaning of an unfamiliar word by analyzing its parts. The main part of a word is its root. When the root is a complete word, it's sometimes called a base word. A root or base word can be thought of as the "spine" of a word. It gives the word its backbone of meaning.

A root is often combined with a prefix (a word part added to the beginning of a word), a suffix (a word part added to the end of a word), or another root. Prefixes and suffixes change a word's meaning or its part of speech.

Although the English language borrows words from many other languages, a large number of words we use have their origins in Latin and Greek roots. Knowing some of these Latin and Greek roots will help you analyze many unfamiliar words and determine their meanings.

EXAMPLE

encryption

Prefix	The prefix *en-* means "to put into."
Root	The root *crypt* means "hidden" or "secret." The word *encrypt,* therefore, means "to put into a hidden or secret form."
Suffix	The suffix *–ion* changes *encrypt* from a verb to a noun meaning "the state of being encrypted."

The word *encryption,* then, means "something that has been put into a secret code," in other words, "a coded message." Although this word's parts add up to its meaning in a fairly clear way, sometimes an analysis of a word's parts doesn't yield the word's meaning so readily. Use a dictionary to check your analysis.

GRAMMAR/USAGE/MECHANICS

ROOTS

When you're trying to determine the meaning of an unfamiliar word, think of words that might share a root with it. The meanings of these other words might give you clues to the meaning of the unfamiliar word. The following chart lists some common roots and some words that share them. Keep in mind that one or more letters in a root may change when the root is combined with other word parts.

ROOTS		
ROOTS	**WORDS**	**MEANINGS**
ac or *ag* means "do"	action	act or process of doing
	agenda	list of things to do
agri or *agro* means "field"	agriculture	science of cultivating the soil
	agronomy	study of crop production and soil management
am means "love" or "friend"	amicable	friendly
	amorous	relating to love
anima means "life" or "mind"	animate	having life
	unanimous	being of one mind
anthrop means "human beings"	anthropology	study of human beings
	misanthrope	one who hates or distrusts human beings
aqua means "water"	aquarium	tank of water in which living animals are kept
	aqueduct	structure for moving water
arch means "rule" or "government"	anarchy	absence of government
	archives	government records

ROOTS	WORDS	MEANINGS
astr or *astro* means "star"	astronaut	traveler among the stars
	astronomy	study of stars
audio means "hear"	audience	group that hears a performance
	audiometer	device for measuring hearing
aut or *auto* means "self"	autistic	absorbed in the self
	autobiography	story of a person's life written by that person
bene means "good"	beneficial	good, helpful
	benevolent	inclined to do good
bibli or *biblio* means "book"	bibliography	list of books related to a particular subject
	bibliophile	lover of books
bio means "life"	autobiography	story of a person's life written by that person
	biology	study of living things
brev means "short" or "brief"	abbreviate	shorten a word or phrase
	brevity	shortness of expression
cand means "shine" or "glow"	candle	molded mass of wax that may be burned to give light
	incandescent	bright, glowing
capit means "head"	capital	place where the head of government sits
	decapitate	remove the head
ced means "go"	proceed	go forward
	recede	go back
cent means "hundred"	centimeter	one hundredth of a meter
	century	one hundred years

Chapter 13 Spelling and Vocabulary **413**

ROOTS	WORDS	MEANINGS
chron or *chrono* means "time"	chronological synchronize	arranged in time order cause to happen at the same time
cid or *cide* means "kill"	germicide homicide	agent that destroys germs killing of one human being by another
circ means "circle"	circumference circus	distance around a circle entertainment usually held in a circular area
cis means "cut"	incision incisor	surgical cut tooth adapted for cutting
cline means "bend," "lean," or "slope"	decline incline	slope downward lean forward
cogn means "know"	cognition recognize	knowledge; awareness know someone or something
corp means "body"	corps corpse	body of military troops dead body
cracy means "government"	democracy technocracy	government by the people government by technical experts
cred means "believe" or "trust"	credible incredible	believable unbelievable
crypt or *crypto* means "hidden" or "secret"	cryptic cryptogram	having a hidden meaning communication in secret code
culp means "blame" or "guilt"	culpable culprit	guilty one who is guilty
cur or *curs* means "run"	current	water running in a stream or electricty running through a wire

GRAMMAR/USAGE/MECHANICS

ROOTS	WORDS	MEANINGS
cur or *curs,* continued	cursory	rapidly performed or produced
cycl means "circle" or "wheel"	bicycle cyclone	two-wheeled vehicle storm that rotates in a circle
dec or *deca* means "ten"	decade decathlon	ten years athletic contest consisting of ten events
dem or *demo* means "people"	democracy epidemic	rule by the people affecting many people
di means "two"	dichotomy dichromatic	division into two groups having two colors
dict means "say"	contradict dictate	say the opposite of speak for another to record
duc or *duct* means "lead" or "draw"	conductor deduct	one who leads take away from a total
ectomy means "surgical removal"	appendectomy mastoidectomy	surgical removal of the appendix surgical removal of part of the mastoid bone or process
equi means "equal"	equilateral equitable	having sides of equal length dealing equally with all
err means "wander" or "err"	aberration erratic	result of straying from the normal way inconsistent, irregular
eu means "good" or "well"	eulogize euphoria	praise feeling of well-being

GRAMMAR/USAGE/MECHANICS

ROOTS	WORDS	MEANINGS
exo means "outside" or "outer"	exoskeleton	outer supportive covering of an animal, as an insect or mollusk
	exotic	outside the ordinary
fac or *fec* means "make" or "do"	effective	done well
	factory	place where things are made
ferous means "bearing" or "producing"	coniferous	bearing cones, as a pine tree
	somniferous	producing sleep
fid means "faith" or "trust"	confidant	person one trusts
	fidelity	faithfulness
fin means "end" or "limit"	define	limit the meaning of
	infinite	having no end
fix means "fasten"	fixate	fasten one's attention intently
	fixative	substance that fastens or sets
frac or *frag* means "break"	fracture	break
	fragile	easily broken
fus means "pour" or "melt"	effusive	demonstrating an excessive pouring out of talk or affection
	fusion	joining by melting
gen means "class," "kind," "descent," or "birth"	general	affecting a whole class
	generate	start or originate
geo means "earth," "ground," or "soil"	geocentric	measured from the center of the earth
	geology	study of the earth

ROOTS	WORDS	MEANINGS
grad or *gress* means "step" or "go"	egress gradual	way to go out proceeding by steps or degrees
gram or *graph* means "writing"	autograph telegram	written signature written message sent over a distance
grat means "pleasing" or "thanks"	congratulate gratuity	express sympathetic pleasure something given voluntarily to show thanks for service
hetero means "different"	heterogeneous heteronym	made up of different kinds of things or people word spelled like another word but different in meaning and pronunciation, for example, *bow*
homo means "same"	homogeneous homophone	made up of the same kinds of things or people word pronounced like another word but different in meaning and spelling, for example, *to, too,* or *two*
hydr or *hydro* means "water"	dehydrate hydrant	remove water large pipe used to draw water
ject means "throw"	eject trajectory	throw out path of something thrown

GRAMMAR/USAGE/MECHANICS

ROOTS	WORDS	MEANINGS
jud means "judge"	judicious	using good judgment
	prejudice	judgment formed without sufficient knowledge
junct means "join"	conjunction	word that joins other words
	junction	place where two things join
jur or *jus* means "law"	jurisprudence	system of law
	justice	determination of rights according to the law
lect or *leg* means "read"	lectern	stand used to support a book or paper for reading
	legible	capable of being read
like means "resembling"	businesslike	resembling the conduct of a business
	childlike	resembling the behavior of a child
loc means "place"	local	relating to a place
	location	position, site, or place
locut or *loqu* means "speak" or "speech"	locution	style of speaking
	loquacious	talkative
log or *logo* means "word," "thought," or "speech"	dialogue	speech between two people
	monologue	speech by a single person
logy means "science" or "study"	biology	science of living things
	genealogy	study of ancestors
luc means "light"	lucid	suffused with light; clear
	translucent	permitting the passage of light

GRAMMAR/USAGE/MECHANICS

ROOTS	WORDS	MEANINGS
macro means "large"	macrocosm	world; universe
	macroscopic	large enough to be observed with the naked eye
magn means "large" or "great"	magnificent	large and grand
	magnify	make larger
mal means "bad" or "badly"	maladjusted	badly adjusted
	malice	desire to see another suffer
man means "hand"	manual	done by hand
	manuscript	document written by hand or typed
meter or *metr* means "measure"	metric	relating to meter
	thermometer	instrument for measuring heat
micr or *micro* means "small"	micrometer	device for measuring very small distances
	microwave	a short electromagnetic wave
milli means "thousand"	millimeter	one thousandth of a meter
	million	one thousand times one thousand
mis or *mit* means "send"	remiss	failing to respond
	transmit	send across a distance
mon means "warn"	admonish	express warning or disapproval in a gentle way
	premonition	forewarning
mon or *mono* means "one"	monarchy	rule by one person
	monochromatic	having one color

GRAMMAR/USAGE/MECHANICS

ROOTS	WORDS	MEANINGS
morph or *morpho* means "form"	metamorphosis morphology	change in physical form study of the form and structure of animals and plants
mort means "death"	mortal mortician	subject to death one who prepares the dead for burial
neo means "new"	neologism neonatal	new word, usage, or expression affecting the newborn
nym means "name"	anonymous pseudonym	not named or identified fictitious or pen name
octa or *octo* means "eight"	octagon octopus	figure with eight sides creature with eight limbs
omni means "all"	omniscient omnivorous	knowing all eating both animal and vegetable matter
oper means "work"	opera operative	musical and dramatic work working
pan means "all" or "whole"	panacea Pan-American	remedy for all problems relating to the whole of North and South America
path or *pathy* means "feeling" or "suffering"	pathology sympathy	study of disease inclination to feel like another
ped means "child" or "foot"	pediatrician quadruped	physician who cares for children animal having four feet
pend or *pens* means "hang" or "weigh"	pendant	something hanging or suspended

GRAMMAR/USAGE/MECHANICS

ROOTS	WORDS	MEANINGS
pend or *pens,* continued	suspense	feeling that leaves one hanging or unsure of an outcome
phil or *phile* means "loving" or "fondness"	bibliophile philanthropist	lover of books one who loves human beings
phobia means "fear"	acrophobia hydrophobia	fear of heights fear of water
phon or *phono* means "sound," "voice," or "speech"	phonics phonograph	method of teaching relationships between sounds and letters instrument for playing recorded sound
physi or *physio* means "nature" or "physical"	physiognomy physiotherapy	natural features of the face believed to show temperament and character physical therapy
poly means "many"	polyglot polygon	composed of numerous language groups a many-sided figure
pon or *pos* means "place" or "put"	exponent position	symbol placed above and to the right of a mathematical expression place where something is situated
port means "carry"	portable porter	capable of being carried one who carries
prehend means "seize" or "grasp"	apprehend comprehend	arrest by seizing grasp the meaning of
prim means "first"	primary	first in order of time or development

GRAMMAR/USAGE/MECHANICS

ROOTS	WORDS	MEANINGS
prim, continued	primitive	characteristic of an early stage of development
prot or *proto* means "first" or "beginning"	proton prototype	elementary particle original model
pseudo means "false"	pseudoclassic pseudonym	pretending to be classic fictitious or pen name
psych or *psycho* means "mind"	psychology psychotherapy	study of the mind therapy for the mind
punctus means "point"	punctual puncture	on time hole or wound made by a pointed instrument
quadr or *quadri* means "four"	quadrangle quadrilateral	four-sided enclosure having four sides
rect means "right" or "straight"	rectangle rectitude	figure with four right angles quality of being correct in judgment or procedure
reg means "rule" or "direct"	regular regulate	according to rule direct according to rule
rupt means "break"	interrupt rupture	stop or hinder by breaking in break
sang means "blood"	consanguinity sanguine	blood relationship marked by high color and cheerfulness; confident; optimistic
sci means "know"	omniscient science	knowing all things knowledge about the natural world
scope means "a means for viewing"	microscope	a means for viewing small things

GRAMMAR/USAGE/MECHANICS

ROOTS	WORDS	MEANINGS
scope, continued	telescope	a means for viewing things at a distance
scrib or *script* means "write"	prescribe	write an order for medicine
	prescription	written order for medicine
secu or *sequ* means "follow"	sequel	installment that follows a previous one
	sequence	series in which one item follows another
sens or *sent* means "feel" or "sense"	sensation	feeling
	sentence	group of words that makes sense
sol or *solv* means "dissolve" or "solve"	solution	that which solves a problem
	solvent	that which dissolves
son means "sound"	resonant	continuing to sound
	sonorous	full of sound
soph means "wise" or "clever"	sophisticated	having wise and clever knowledge of the ways of the world
	sophomore	student in the second year of high school or college (a combination of wise and foolish)
spec or *spect* means "look" or "watch"	perspective	way of looking at something
	spectator	one who watches an event
spir means "breath" or "breathe"	inspire	exert an influence on
	respiration	breathing
strict or *string* means "bind"	constrict	draw together
	stringent	strict; severe

GRAMMAR/USAGE/MECHANICS

ROOTS	WORDS	MEANINGS
tact or *tang* means "touch"	contact	touching of two things or people
	tangible	capable of being touched
tele means "far off" or "distant"	telephone	instrument for hearing sound at a distance
	television	instrument for viewing pictures at a distance
terr means "earth"	extraterrestrial	being from beyond earth
	terrain	physical features of a tract of land
therm or *thermo* means "heat"	thermal	relating to heat
	thermometer	instrument for measuring heat
trac means "draw" or "pull"	extract	pull out
	traction	friction caused by pulling across a surface; pulling force
tri means "three"	triangle	figure with three angles
	triathlon	athletic contest consisting of three events
vac means "empty"	evacuation	process of emptying out
	vacant	empty
ven or *vent* means "come"	intervene	come between
	venue	place related to a particular event
verb means "word"	verbal	having to do with words
	verbose	wordy
vers or *vert* means "turn"	avert	turn away
	reverse	turn back
vid or *vis* means "see"	evident	plain to see
	visible	capable of being seen

GRAMMAR/USAGE/MECHANICS

ROOTS	WORDS	MEANINGS
viv means "live" or "alive"	revive	bring back to life
	vivacious	full of life; lively
vit means "life"	vital	necessary to the maintenance of life
	vitamin	substance necessary for the regulation of life processes
voc or *vok* means "call" or "call forth"	evoke	call forth
	vocation	job a person feels called to do
vol or *volv* means "roll"	evolve	develop
	revolution	rotation

PREFIXES

Prefixes are word parts added to the beginning of a root or a base word to change its meaning. They are important tools for understanding and learning new words. The following chart shows common prefixes and their meanings. Notice that some prefixes have more than one meaning and that some prefixes convey the same meaning as others.

PREFIXES

PREFIXES	WORDS	MEANINGS
a- means "without" or "not"; it can also mean "on," "in," or "at"	abloom	in bloom
	aboard	on board
	amoral	without morals
	atypical	not typical

Chapter 13 Spelling and Vocabulary **425**

PREFIXES	WORDS	MEANINGS
ant- or *anti-* means "against" or "opposing"	antacid	agent that works against acidity
	antiwar	opposing war
ante- means "before"	antecedent	going before
	antediluvian	before the biblical flood
be- means "cause to be"	befriend	act as a friend to
	belittle	cause to seem little or less
bi- means "two"	bimonthly	once every two months or twice a month
	bisect	divide into two equal parts
cat- or *cata-* means "down"	catacomb	subterranean cemetery
	catastrophe	final stage of a tragedy
circum- means "around" or "about"	circumference	distance around a circle
	circumstance	surrounding condition
	circumvent	avoid by going around
co- means "with" or "together"	coworker	person one works with
	cowrite	write together
col-, com-, con-, or *cor-* means "together" or "with"	collaborate	work with others
	companion	one who accompanies another
	confer	consult with others
	correspond	exchange letters with another
contra- means "against"	contradict	speak against
	contrary	opposite
counter- means "opposite" or "opposing"	counterbalance	oppose with an equal weight or force
	counterclockwise	opposite of clockwise

PREFIXES	WORDS	MEANINGS
de- means "do the opposite of," "remove," or "reduce"	de-emphasize	do the opposite of emphasize
	defrost	remove frost
	devalue	reduce the value of
dia- means "through" or "across"	diameter	length through the center of a circle
	diaphragm	a membrane stretching across an area
dis- means "not" or "absence of"	dishonest	not honest
	distrust	absence of trust
e- or *ex-* means "out"; *ex-* also means "former"	eject	throw out
	exceed	go beyond
	ex-president	former president
en- means "cause to be" or "put into"	enlarge	cause to be made large
	enthrall	put into thrall
extra- means "outside" or "beyond"	extralegal	outside of legal means
	extraordinary	beyond the ordinary
for- means "so as to involve prohibition or exclusion"	forgive	give up feelings of resentment
	forgo	give up pleasure or advantage
hemi- means "half"	hemicycle	structure consisting of half a circle
	hemisphere	half a sphere
hyper- means "excessive" or "excessively"	hyperbole	excessive exaggeration
	hypersensitive	excessively sensitive
il-, im-, in-, or *ir-* means "not" or "into"	illegal	not legal
	illuminate	bring light into
	immature	not mature
	immigrant	one who moves into a country

GRAMMAR/USAGE/MECHANICS

Chapter 13 Spelling and Vocabulary **427**

PREFIXES	WORDS	MEANINGS
il-, im-, in-, or *ir-,* continued	inconvenient insight irregular irrigate	not convenient power of seeing into 　a situation not regular bring water into
inter- means "among" 　or "between"	international interscholastic	among nations between schools
intra- means "within"	intramural intrastate	within the walls (of a 　school) within a state
intro- means "in" or "into"	introspection introvert	looking within oneself one who is turned inward
mis- means "bad," "badly," "wrong," or "wrongly"	misspell mistreat	spell wrong treat badly
non- means "not"	nonallergenic nonconformist	not causing allergies one who does not 　conform
over- means "exceed," "surpass," or "excessive"	overeat overqualified	eat to excess qualified beyond the 　normal requirements
para- means "beside" or "beyond"	paramedic paranormal	one who works beside 　a physician beyond the normal
peri- means "around"	perimeter periscope	distance around a 　plane figure instrument for looking 　around
post- means "after"	postgame postwar	after the game after the war
pre- means "before"	precede premonition	go before advance warning

PREFIXES	WORDS	MEANINGS
pro- means "in favor of," "forward," "before," or "in place of"	pro-American proceed prologue pronoun	in favor of America go forward introduction before the main text word that takes the place of a noun
re- means "again" or "back"	recall replay	call back play again
retro- means "back," "backward," or "behind"	retroactive retrogress	effective as of a prior date move backward
semi- means "half" or "partly"	semicircle semisweet	half a circle partly sweet
sub- means "under" or "less than"	subhuman submarine	less than human underwater
super- means "over and above"	superabundant superhuman	having more than an abundance over and above what is normal for a human being
sym- or *syn-* means "with" or "together"	symbiosis synchronize	living together of two dissimilar organisms make happen at the same time
trans- means "across"	transmit transport	send across carry across
un- means "not" or "do the opposite of"	unhappy untie	not happy do the opposite of tie
uni- means "one"	unicycle unified	one-wheeled vehicle joined into one

GRAMMAR/USAGE/MECHANICS

SUFFIXES

Suffixes are word parts added to the end of a root or a base word to change its meaning and sometimes its part of speech. The following chart shows common suffixes and their meanings. Notice that some suffixes have more than one meaning and that some suffixes convey the same meaning as others. Notice also that the spelling of a root often changes when a suffix is added. Furthermore, more than one suffix may be added to many words.

SUFFIXES

SUFFIXES	WORDS	MEANINGS
-able or -ible means "capable of," "fit for," or "tending to"	agreeable	tending to agree or able to be agreed with
	breakable	capable of being broken
	collectible	fit for collecting
-age means "action," "process," or "result"	breakage	action or process of breaking
	marriage	action, process, or result of marrying
	wreckage	result of wrecking
-al means "relating to" or "characterized by"; it can also mean "action," "process," or "result"	fictional	relating to fiction
	rehearsal	action or process of rehearsing
-an or -ian means "one who is of or from"; it can also mean "relating to"	Bostonian	one who lives in Boston
	Elizabethan	relating to the reign of Queen Elizabeth I

SUFFIXES	WORDS	MEANINGS
-ance, -ancy, -ence, or *-ency* means "action," "process," "quality," or "state"	dependency performance persistence vacancy	state of being dependent action or process of performing quality of persisting state of being vacant
-ant means "one who or that which"; it can also mean "being"	contestant observant	one who participates in a contest being observing
-ar means "relating to" or "resembling"; it can also mean "one who"	liar molecular spectacular	one who lies relating to molecules resembling a spectacle
-ard or *-art* means "one who"	braggart dullard	one who brags one who is dull
-ary means "person or thing belonging to or connected with"; it can also mean "relating to or connected with"	complimentary functionary	relating to a compliment person who serves a particular function
-ate means "of," "relating to," or "having"; it can also mean "cause to be"	activate collegiate	cause to be active relating to college
-cy means "state," "quality," "condition," or "fact of being"	accuracy bankruptcy infancy	quality of being accurate condition of being bankrupt state of being an infant
-dom means "state of being"	boredom freedom	state of being bored state of being free

GRAMMAR/USAGE/MECHANICS

SUFFIXES	WORDS	MEANINGS
-ee means "receiver of action" or "one who"	escapee trainee	one who escapes receiver of training
-eer means "one who"	auctioneer engineer	one who runs an auction one who is concerned with engines
-en means "made of or resembling"; it can also mean "cause to be or become"	golden strengthen	made of or resembling gold cause to be strong
-ent means "one who"	resident superintendent	one who resides in a place one who superintends
-er means "one who" or "native or resident of"; it can also mean "more"	New Yorker reporter sooner stronger	resident of New York one who reports more soon more strong
-ery or *-ry* means "character," "art or practice," "place," or "collection"	bakery cookery jewelry snobbery	place for baking art or practice of cooking collection of jewels character of being a snob
-ese means "originating in a certain place or country"; it can also mean "resident of" or "language of"	Japanese	originating in Japan; resident of Japan; language of Japan
-esque means "in the manner or style of" or "like"	picturesque statuesque	in the manner or style of a picture like a statue

SUFFIXES	WORDS	MEANINGS
-et or *-ette* means "small" or "group"	islet kitchenette quartet	small island small kitchen group of four
-fold means "multiplied by"	fourfold	multiplied by four
-ful means "full of" or "tending to"; it can also mean "amount that fills"	fearful forgetful spoonful	full of fear tending to forget amount that fills a spoon
-fy or *-ify* means "make or form into," "make similar to," or "become"	fortify glorify solidify	make similar to a fort make glorious become solid
-hood means "state," "condition," "quality," or "character"	childhood likelihood statehood	state of being a child quality of being likely condition of being a state
-ic or *-ical* means "having the qualities of," "being," "like," "consisting of," or "relating to"	angelic athletic atomic historical	like an angel having the qualities of an athlete consisting of atoms relating to history
-ile means "tending to" or "capable of"	contractile infantile	capable of contracting tending to be like an infant
-ine means "of," "like," or "relating to"	Alpine crystalline marine	relating to the Alps like crystal of the sea
-ion or *-ation* means "act or process," "result," or "state or condition"	pollution selection sensation	result of polluting process of selecting state or condition of feeling something

GRAMMAR/USAGE/MECHANICS

SUFFIXES	WORDS	MEANINGS
-ish means "like," "inclined to," "somewhat," or "having the approximate age of"	bookish	inclined to be interested in books
	foolish	like a fool
	reddish	somewhat red
	thirtyish	about thirty
-ism means "act, practice, or process," "prejudice," "state or condition," "doctrine or belief," or "conduct or behavior"	criticism	act of criticizing
	heroism	conduct or behavior of a hero
	Mormonism	belief in the doctrines of the Mormon faith
	parallelism	state of being parallel
	racism	prejudice against a race of people
-ist means "one who"	violinist	one who plays a violin
-ite means "native or resident of"	Brooklynite	native or resident of Brooklyn
-ity means "quality," "state," or "condition"	humanity	condition of being human
	purity	quality of being pure
	sanity	state of being sane
-ive means "performing or tending toward"	active	tending toward action
	excessive	tending toward excess
-ize means "cause to be," "become," or "make"	Americanize	become American
	modernize	make modern
	sterilize	cause to be sterile
-less means "without"	hopeless	without hope
-ly means "like"; it can also mean "in a manner" or "to a degree"	easily	in an easy manner
	friendly	like a friend
	partly	to a partial degree

SUFFIXES	WORDS	MEANINGS
-ment means "result," "action," or "condition"	amazement	condition of being amazed
	astonishment	result of being astonished
	development	act of developing
-ness means "state," "condition," or "quality"	darkness	condition of being dark
	goodness	state of being good
	heaviness	quality of being heavy
-or means "one who or that which"	elevator	that which raises people or goods to a higher level
	inventor	one who invents
-ory means "place of or for"; it can also mean "relating to" or "characterized by"	contradictory	characterized by contradiction
	observatory	place for observing
	sensory	relating to the senses
-ose means "full of" or "having"	grandiose	having grand ideas
	verbose	full of words; wordy
-ous means "full of," "having," or "characterized by"	courageous	characterized by courage
	gracious	having grace
	joyous	full of joy
-ship means "state, condition, or quality," "office, dignity, or profession," or "art or skill"	ambassadorship	office of an ambassador
	friendship	state of being a friend
	horsemanship	art or skill of horseback riding
-some means "characterized by"; it can also mean "group of"	foursome	group of four
	troublesome	characterized by trouble
-th or *-eth* is used to form ordinal numbers	seventh	ordinal for *seven*
	twentieth	ordinal for *twenty*

GRAMMAR/USAGE/MECHANICS

SUFFIXES	WORDS	MEANINGS
-ty means "quality," "condition," or "state"	novelty	quality or condition of being novel
	safety	state of being safe
-ure means "act," "process," "state," or "result"	composure	state of being composed
	erasure	result of erasing
	exposure	act of exposing
-ward means "toward" or "in a certain direction"	afterward	at a later time
	homeward	toward home
-y means "characterized by or full of," "like," or "tending or inclined to"; it can also mean "state, condition, or quality" or "instance of an action"	chatty	tending or inclined to chat
	homey	like home
	inquiry	instance of inquiring
	jealousy	state, condition, or quality of being jealous
	juicy	full of juice
	waxy	characterized by wax

GRAMMAR/USAGE/MECHANICS

Use the following roots, prefixes, and suffixes to make a list of ten words you know or combinations you think might be words. Use at least one root, prefix, or suffix from the chart in each word you write. Check your words in a dictionary.

PREFIXES	ROOTS	SUFFIXES
bi-	aut, auto	-able, -ible
circum-	bio	-al
col-, com-, con-, cor-	cur, curs	-ent
de-	duc, duct	-ic, -ical
il-,im-,in-, ir-	grad, gress	-ile
inter-	gram, graph	-ion, -ation
pre-	ject	-ity
pro-	mis, mit	-ive
re-	mort	-ment
retro-	oper	-or
trans-	ped	-y
	port	
	scrib, script	
	spec, spect	

Part Three

● ● ● ● ● ● ● ● ● ● ● ● ●

Composition

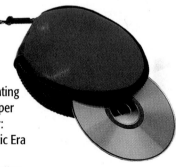

Chapter 14

The Writing Process

• • • • • • • • • • • • • • • •

Writing is a process done in different stages: prewriting, drafting, revising/editing, and publishing/presenting. These stages are recursive; that is, they do not necessarily follow one another in order; you can go back and forth among steps, repeating those that you need to until you end up with the result you want.

Calvin and Hobbes   **by Bill Watterson**

CALVIN AND HOBBES © Watterson. Reprinted
with permission of UNIVERSAL PRESS SYNDI-
CATE. All rights reserved.

The Writing Process

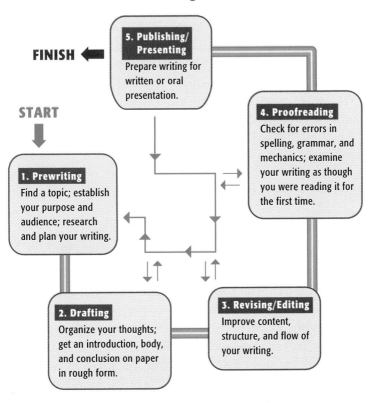

5. Publishing/Presenting
Prepare writing for written or oral presentation.

FINISH ←

START

1. Prewriting
Find a topic; establish your purpose and audience; research and plan your writing.

4. Proofreading
Check for errors in spelling, grammar, and mechanics; examine your writing as though you were reading it for the first time.

2. Drafting
Organize your thoughts; get an introduction, body, and conclusion on paper in rough form.

3. Revising/Editing
Improve content, structure, and flow of your writing.

STAGE 1: PREWRITING

During Prewriting, you decide what you want to write about by exploring ideas, feelings, and memories. Prewriting is the stage in which you not only decide what your topic is, but

- you refine, focus, and explore your topic
- you gather information about your topic
- you make notes about what you want to say about it
- you also think about your audience and your purpose

COMPOSITION

Your audience is whoever will read your work. Your purpose is what you hope to accomplish through your writing.

After you've decided on a topic and explored it, making notes about what you will include, you will need to arrange and organize your ideas. This is also done during the Prewriting stage, before you actually draft your paper.

There are many techniques you can use to generate ideas and define and explore your topic.

CHOOSING AND EXPLORING YOUR TOPIC

Keeping a Journal

Many writing ideas come to us as we go about our daily lives. A journal, or log, can help you record your thoughts from day to day. You can then refer to this record when you're searching for a writing topic. Every day you can write in your journal your experiences, observations, thoughts, feelings, and opinions. Keep newspaper and magazine clippings, photos, songs, poems, and anything else that catches your interest. They might later suggest questions that lead to writing topics. Try to add to your journal every day. Use your imagination. Be creative and don't worry about grammar, spelling, or punctuation. This is your own personal record. It is for your benefit only, and no one else will read it.

Freewriting

Freewriting means just what it says: writing freely without worrying about grammar, punctuation, spelling, logic, or anything. You just write what comes to your mind. Choose a topic and a time limit and then just start writing ideas as they come to you. If you run out of ideas, repeat the same word over and over until a new idea occurs to you. When the time is up, review what you've written. The ideas that most interest you are likely to be the ones that will be most worth writing about. You can use your journal as a place for freewriting, or you can just take a piece of paper and start the process. The important thing is to allow your mind to follow its own path as you explore a topic. You'll be surprised where it might lead you.

1. Let your thoughts flow. Write ideas, memories, anything that comes to mind.
2. Don't edit or judge your thoughts; just write them down. You can evaluate them later. In fact, evaluating your ideas at this point would probably dry up the flow. Accepting any idea that comes is the way to encourage more ideas.
3. Don't worry about spelling, punctuation, grammar, or even sense; just keep writing.

Brainstorming

Brainstorming is another free-association technique that you can use to generate ideas. It is often most effective to brainstorm with others because ideas can spark new ideas. Start with a key word or idea and list other ideas as they occur to you. Don't worry about the order; just let your ideas flow freely from one to the next.

Clustering

Write your topic in the middle of a piece of paper. As you think about the topic, briefly write down everything that comes to mind. Each time you write something, draw a circle around it and draw lines to connect those circles to the main idea in the center. Continue to think about the secondary ideas and add offshoots to them. Draw circles around those related ideas and connect them to the secondary ideas.

Clustering

Collecting Information

Whether you're deciding on your topic or exploring a topic you've already chosen, you need to discover as many facts as possible about your topic or possible topic.

Asking Questions To discover the facts you need, begin by writing down a list of questions about your topic. Different questions serve different purposes, and knowing what kind of question to ask can be as important as knowing how to ask it clearly. The chart that follows will help you categorize your list of questions.

KINDS OF QUESTIONS	
PERSONAL QUESTIONS	ask about your responses to a topic. They help you explore your experiences and tastes.
CREATIVE QUESTIONS	ask you to compare your subject to something else or to imagine observing your subject as someone else might. Such questions can expand your perspective on a subject.
ANALYTICAL QUESTIONS	ask about structure and function: How is this topic constructed? What is its purpose? Analytical questions help you evaluate and draw conclusions.
INFORMATIONAL QUESTIONS	ask for facts, statistics, or details.

FoxTrot

by Bill Amend

Library Research If your topic requires information you do not already have, your school or public library is the best place to find it.

Library Research TIP

1. Search for books by title, author, and subject, using either the card catalog or the online computer system.
2. Use the subject heading for each listing as a cross-reference to related material.
3. Browse among other books in the section where you locate a useful book.
4. Jot down the author, title, and call number of each book you think you will use.
5. Record the titles of books that don't provide help (so you won't search for them again).
6. Examine each book's bibliography for related titles.
7. Try to be an independent researcher but ask a librarian for help if you cannot locate much information on your topic.

If you do your research on the Internet, evaluate your sources carefully and always find at least one more source to verify each point. The reliability of Internet information varies a great deal. It's probably a good idea to use print sources to verify information you find on the Internet, if that is possible.

Observing One good starting point for exploring a topic is simply to observe closely and list the details you see. After you've listed the details, arrange them into categories. The categories you choose depend on the details you observe and your writing goal. For example, you might want to organize your details using spatial order, chronological order, or order of importance.

Interviewing   Get your information directly from the source: interview someone. By asking questions, you can get the specific information you need or want. Follow these steps:

BEFORE THE INTERVIEW	Make the appointment.
	Research your topic and find out about your source.
	Prepare four or five basic questions.
DURING THE INTERVIEW	Ask informational questions (who, what, where, when, why, and how).
	Listen carefully.
	Ask follow-up questions.
	Take accurate notes (or tape-record with permission).
AFTER THE INTERVIEW	Write a more detailed account of the interview.
	Contact your source to clarify points or to double-check facts.

IDENTIFYING PURPOSE AND AUDIENCE

Purpose

Before you start to write, you must determine the primary purpose for your writing: to inform or explain, to persuade, to amuse or entertain, to narrate, or to describe. Sometimes you might want to accomplish more than one purpose, so you will have a primary purpose and a secondary purpose. To determine the primary purpose, answer these questions:

1. Do I want to tell a story?
2. Do I want to describe someone or something?
3. Do I want to inform my readers about the topic or to explain something about it?

4. Do I want to persuade my readers to change their minds about something or take some action?

5. Do I want to amuse or entertain?

Audience

Your audience is anyone who will be reading your writing. Sometimes you write just for yourself. Most often, however, you write to share information with others. Your audience might include a few friends or family members, your classmates, the population at large, or just your teacher. As you write, consider these questions:

1. Who will my audience be? What do I want to say to them?

2. What do my readers already know about my topic?

3. What types of information will interest my audience?

ARRANGING AND ORGANIZING IDEAS

Once you have gathered your information and ideas, you can choose from many kinds of details—examples, facts, statistics, reasons, and concrete and sensory details—to support your main idea. As a writer, you need to organize these details and put them in order. Your purpose and main idea will determine which kinds of supporting details you include as well as the order in which you arrange them. Some possible patterns of organization include

- chronological order (by time)
- spatial order (relationships based on space, place, or setting)
- order of importance
- cause and effect (events described as reason and result, motive and reaction, stimulus and response)
- comparison and contrast (measuring items against one another to show similarities and differences)

COMPOSITION

The technique you choose to organize details might be as simple as making a list or an outline that shows how the details will be grouped under larger subtopics or headings. You can also organize details visually by making a chart or a diagram similar to the Clustering diagram on page 445. You might better be able to see a plan for organizing your paper when you see the relationships among the parts of your topic.

STAGE 2: DRAFTING

When you write your draft, your goal is to organize the facts and details you have accumulated into unified paragraphs. Make sure each paragraph has a main idea and does not bring in unrelated information. The main idea must be stated in a topic sentence, and it must be supported by details that explain and clarify it. Details can be facts and statistics, examples or incidents, or sensory details.

Writing a draft, or turning your ideas into paragraphs, is a stage in the Writing Process and a tool in itself. During Prewriting, you started to organize your details. You will continue to do this as you write your draft because you might find links between ideas that give new meanings to your words and phrases. Continue to organize your details using one of the methods discussed in Prewriting.

To make your sentences interesting, be sure to vary the length of sentences. Don't use too many short, choppy sentences when you can incorporate some of your ideas in subordinate clauses or compound or complex sentences.

Writing Tip

Your composition should consist of three parts: the introduction, the body, and the conclusion (see the outline on page 486). Begin your paper with an **introduction** that grabs the reader's interest and sets the tone. The introduction usually gives the reader a brief explanation of what your paper is about and often includes the **thesis.** The thesis states your paper's main idea or what you're trying to prove or support.

Each paragraph in the **body,** or main part, of your paper should have a topic sentence that states what the paragraph is about. The rest of the paragraph should include details that support the topic sentence. Similarly, each topic sentence should support the thesis, or main idea of the paper.

End your paper with a good **conclusion** that gives a feeling of "completeness." You might conclude your paper in any of the following ways:

- Summarize what you've said in the body of your paper.
- Restate the main idea (using different words).
- Give a final example or idea.
- Make a comment on or give a personal reaction to the topic.
- End with a quotation that sums up or comments on the topic.
- Call for some action (especially in persuasive papers).

STAGE 3: REVISING/EDITING

The purposes of Revising are to make sure that your writing is clear and well organized, that it accomplishes your goals, and that it reaches your audience. The word *revision* means "seeing again." You need to look at your writing again, seeing it as another person might. You might read your paper very carefully, you might tape-record yourself reading your paper aloud, or you might share your

COMPOSITION

writing with another student, a small group of students, or your teacher. After evaluating your work, you might want to move things around or change them completely. You might want to add or cut information. Mark these changes right on your draft and then incorporate them.

The revision stage is the point at which you can

- improve paragraphs
- implement self-evaluation and peer evaluation
- check content and structure
- make sure the language is specific, descriptive, and nonsexist
- check unity and coherence
- check style and tone

Writing Tip

When you are writing about people in general, people who may be either male or female, use nonsexist language. That is, use words that apply to all people, not specifically to males or females. For example, instead of *mailman*, which is gender-specific, you could use the term *mail carrier*.

Traditional nouns for males and females in the same occupation (for instance, *poet* and *poetess*) are no longer encouraged. The noun *poet* now refers to both males and females. Refer to the following list for other gender-neutral terms to use in your writing.

Use	Instead of
actor	actress
Briton	Englishman
businesspeople	businessman/woman
chairperson, chair, moderator	chairman/woman
a member of the clergy	clergyman
craftspeople	craftsmen
crewed space flight	manned space flight
fisher	fisherman
flight attendant	stewardess
Framers, Founders	Founding Fathers

Writing Tip (continued)

Use	Instead of
handmade, synthetic, manufactured	manmade
homemaker	housewife
humanity, human beings, people	mankind
it/its (in reference to ships, countries)	she/her/hers, he/his
land of origin, homeland	mother country
letter carrier/mail carrier	mailman
police officer	policeman
representative	congressman/woman
server	waiter or waitress
supervisor	foreman
watch, guard	watchman
worker	workman
workforce	manpower

Masculine pronouns (such as *he, him, his*) were once used to refer to mixed groups of people. Females were understood to be included. That is, a sentence like *A reporter must check his facts* was understood to apply to both male and female reporters. Now everyone is encouraged to use gender-neutral wording. Some gender-neutral possibilities for that sentence are *Reporters must check their facts, A reporter must check the facts,* and *A reporter must check his or her facts.* (See page 245.)

STAGE 4: PROOFREADING

The purposes of Proofreading are to make sure that you've spelled all words correctly and that your sentences are grammatically correct. Proofread your writing and correct mistakes in capitalization, punctuation, and spelling. Refer to the following chart for Proofreading symbols to help you during this stage of the Writing Process.

COMPOSITION

Proofreading Marks		
Mark	**Meaning**	**Example**
∧	Insert	My gran^d^mother is eighty-six years old.
℘	Delete	She grew up on a dair~y~y farm.
# ∧	Insert space	She milked#cows every morning.
◡	Close up space	She fed the chickens in the barn ⌒ yard.
≡	Capitalize	≡times have changed.
/	Make lowercase	Machines now do the /Milking.
◯ *Sp*	Check spelling	Chickens are fed (automatically.) *Sp*
◡	Switch order	Modern farms are ⌒like⌒ more factories.
ℋ	New paragraph	ℋLast year I returned to the farm.

STAGE 5: PUBLISHING/PRESENTING

This is the stage at which you share your work with others. You might read your work aloud in class, submit it to the school newspaper, or give it to a friend to read. There are many avenues for Presenting your work.

Chapter 15

Modes of
Writing

• • • • • • • • • • • • • •

15.1 DESCRIPTIVE WRITING

Descriptive writing helps the reader experience the subject described. This type of writing requires

- strong observation skills
- precise, informative word choice
- effective organization of details

BEFORE YOU WRITE

Choose a Subject Your descriptive writing may take the form of a character sketch, which is a quick profile that reveals a person's personality and physical appearance. Instead, you may wish to describe an object, an event, or a setting. As you look for people, objects, settings, or incidents to describe in your writing, ask yourself the following questions:

- What is most striking about this subject?
- What memories does this person, object, event, or setting evoke?

- How can I express my impressions of this subject in my writing?
- What aspects of my subject do I want my reader to experience?

Choose a Vantage Point The vantage point is the angle from which the actions are witnessed. You may either write from a stationary vantage point, a fixed position from which to view a scene, or from a moving vantage point. Choosing a vantage point selects and limits the details available to you. You should, therefore, determine your purpose before you choose your vantage point. Note how the purpose of describing a baseball game changes the choice of a vantage point in the chart below.

PURPOSE	VANTAGE POINT
To describe for the reader how it feels to be a baseball player	Dugout; locker room
To show the reader the thrill of watching a baseball game	Stands

Keep these questions in mind as you describe an event:
- Is my vantage point clearly defined and consistent?
- Can I see, hear, smell, taste, or touch the things I am describing from my vantage point?
- Is the passage of time logical and believable?

Writing Tip

When you begin writing, be sure to alert the reader if you shift vantage points. Begin a new paragraph or say something like "Meanwhile, at Sue's house . . ."

Observe and Take Notes Once you decide what you will describe and from which vantage point you will describe it, you will need to capture striking, image-creating details through direct observation and note taking. Videotape, sketch, or jot down notes on your subject to refer to as you write. If you are describing an event that has already occurred, you may "observe" the scene using your memory or photographs.

WRITE A UNIFIED, COHERENT, AND VIVID DESCRIPTION

Create a Topic Sentence The topic sentence states the main idea of your writing. It may entice or tantalize readers, set the stage for the description that follows, or focus the reader's attention in a particular direction. Each paragraph in your writing should have a topic sentence.

Include Details That Support the Topic Sentence A unified paragraph uses only those supporting details that reinforce the main idea of the topic sentence.

> *Main Idea: Except for an occasional gust of fretful wind that flattened the high, corn-like grass, nothing uttered— nothing in the valley stirred.*
>
> *Supporting Details:* • *drone of grasshoppers was dead*
> • *birds left sky unmarked*

Use Sensory Details Well-chosen words based on the five senses—sight, smell, hearing, touch, and taste—can draw your reader into a description. Be aware, however, that too many strong sensory details can numb your reader. Pick a few good details and let these carry the description.

Organize Details Noting details is only one part of your job as a writer. Equally important is the task of selecting and arranging details to achieve the effects you want. You may organize your details in four ways: by order of impression, by order of importance, by spatial order, or by chronological order.

- **Order of Impression** organizes details in the order in which you notice or experience them. If you want to create a "you are there" impression in your writing, use order of impression.
- **Order of Importance** organizes details by their significance or importance. If you want to show that some details are more significant than others, use order of importance.
- **Spatial Order** presents details by their location. If you want readers to visualize details as they truly exist in relationship to one another, use spatial order.
- **Chronological Order** gives details in the order in which they occurred. Use chronological order to describe an event or a process.

Use Transitions to Achieve Coherence Use transitional words and phrases to achieve coherence and to show

- movement in time (*when, before, soon, first, second*)
- movement in space (*beyond, farther, in front of*)
- movement in importance (*in fact, especially, above all*)

Use Descriptive Language You can bring energy to your writing by using specific, action-packed words. Stay away from overused modifiers, such as *good, bad, really,* and *very.* Use exact verbs to evoke a mood and strong mental images. To choose just the right verb, use a thesaurus, which is a collection of synonyms. Keep in mind, however, that synonyms are not always interchangeable. For example, you wouldn't write "The horse *jogs*" when you mean "The horse *gallops*." Use a dictionary to find the exact meanings of words.

PEANUTS reprinted by permission of United
Feature Syndicate, Inc.

Use Analogies An analogy is an extended comparison between two things that are usually considered dissimilar but share common features. An analogy makes an extended comparison, supported point by point with examples and details. It can last through several paragraphs or an entire essay.

CREATING SUCCESSFUL ANALOGIES
1. Find a minimum of three similarities between the ideas you are comparing.
2. Use specific details and examples to support your comparisons.
3. Write a topic sentence that establishes the basis of the comparison.
4. Decide on a logical order for the points of the analogy and use transitions, such as *similarly* and *also,* to link them clearly.

Produce a Mood The overall feeling, or mood, of a piece of writing is constructed through the details chosen and the language used to describe these details. The mood of a piece will depend on your purpose. Do you want your reader to get a sense of excitement? Calm? Sadness? Changing the mood of a description can alert the reader to a change in feeling toward the subject or to a shift in the action.

GUIDELINES FOR DESCRIPTIVE WRITING
1. Gather vivid details that will help you describe a person or re-create a scene or an experience for your readers.
2. Decide which kind of organization will be more appropriate for your subject—spatial order, chronological order, order of importance, or order of impression.
3. Write a topic sentence for each paragraph.
4. Use appropriate transitions to make the organization and relationships among ideas clear.
5. Use descriptive language and analogies to make your writing vivid and interesting.

15.2 NARRATIVE WRITING

When you write a narrative, you tell a story of an event.

- A **fictional narrative** is a story from a writer's imagination.
- A **nonfiction narrative,** such as a biography or a history, is about events that really happened.

Fictional and nonfiction narratives have the same basic elements: character, plot, point of view, theme, and setting.

DEVELOP YOUR NARRATIVE

Set the Scene Use the details of setting to create mood and develop readers' expectations about character and action. The elements of setting are **time, place, weather, culture,** and **historical period.** As you write, consider how each element of setting can contribute to your narrative.

Reveal Character Use interesting dialogue and vivid description to make your characters as lifelike as possible.

- **Use Interesting Dialogue** Dialogue gives the reader important information about the characters. What characters say and how they say it reveal personality and show relationships among characters. Use language that reflects the age, background, and personality of each character.

- **Use Vivid Description** A description that reveals character has more impact than one that merely tells what you think. Notice how the specific observation that follows is more interesting and descriptive than the general statement:

General statement: "Bob is soft-hearted and impractical."

Specific observation: "Bob can't pass a musician on the street without giving away all his change, so he never has a quarter for the telephone."

Writing Tip

Answer these questions as you describe the characters in your narrative:

- How do the characters look, move, and speak?
- How do the characters behave toward others?
- How do others react to the characters?
- What personality traits do the characters have?
- What overall impression should my descriptions convey?

Convey a Mood Writers use word choice and description to create moods in their stories. Notice how two different moods can be created for the same desert setting:

TWO MOODS OF THE DESERT	
UPBEAT: LOCATION IS INVITING	rich golds of the sunset, aroma of mesquite on the fire, clear music of mission bells
NEGATIVE: LOCATION IS HOSTILE	sharp needles of cacti, parched streambed, threatening hiss of a snake

Communicate a Theme The theme of a story is the insight into human life that the writer conveys through the narrative. One way to express the theme of your narrative is through your description of the setting. Ask yourself how you can create mood and hint at theme through scenery, props, color, and sound. Then use concrete, evocative words to describe these details.

Choose a Point of View Once you have decided on the characters, plot, and setting, you must choose the point of view from which you will tell the story.

- **First-person point of view:** The narrator is a character in the story; he or she uses the pronoun *I.*
- **Third-person point of view:** The narrator is not a character in the story but an observer of it. Using this point of view, you may choose a **third-person limited narrator,** who sees the world through the eyes of one character and knows and relays the thoughts and actions of only this character. Alternatively, you may choose a **third-person omniscient narrator,** who knows and relays the thoughts and actions of all of the characters.

Remember that the point of view you choose significantly affects the story. It can give the story a bias, or it can limit what the audience knows until the very end. Think carefully about the point of view and how it will affect the development of the plot.

ORGANIZE YOUR NARRATIVE

Construct a Plot A narrative is comprised of a series of events. Plot is the writer's arrangement of events to dramatize a particular conflict or theme. When you begin to organize the information you have decided to include in your story, review the basic plot structure diagram that follows.

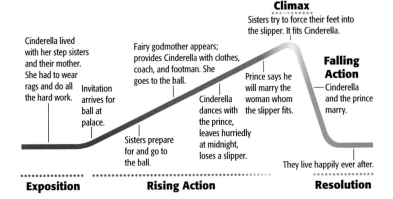

Climax
Sisters try to force their feet into the slipper. It fits Cinderella.

Cinderella lived with her step sisters and their mother. She had to wear rags and do all the hard work.

Invitation arrives for ball at palace.

Fairy godmother appears; provides Cinderella with clothes, coach, and footman. She goes to the ball.

Sisters prepare for and go to the ball.

Cinderella dances with the prince, leaves hurriedly at midnight, loses a slipper.

Prince says he will marry the woman whom the slipper fits.

Falling Action
—Cinderella and the prince marry.

They live happily ever after.

Exposition   **Rising Action**   **Resolution**

Most plots develop in five stages.

- **Exposition** is background information about the characters and setting. This sets the scene for the conflict that follows.
- **Rising action** develops the conflict.
- **Climax** is the point of highest interest, conflict, or suspense in the story.
- **Falling action** shows what happens to the characters after the climax.
- **Resolution** shows how the conflict is resolved or the problem solved.

Establish Conflict Conflict is the heart of narrative writing. It sets the plot in motion and causes changes in the characters.

- In an **external conflict,** a character struggles with another character or an element of nature.
- In an **internal conflict,** a character struggles to make a decision or to act in a certain way.

Order Time in Your Narrative Writers don't always begin a narrative with the event that happened first, because this event is not always the one that best sets the mood or introduces the conflict. You can manipulate your readers' perceptions of time. You can use flashbacks to show the complicated relationship between past and present; you can use fantasies, dreams, and flash-forwards to offer glimpses of events to come.

- **Chronological narratives** describe events in the order in which they occur.
- **Flashbacks** interrupt chronological narratives to relate events that occurred in the past.

Writing Tip

Some writers use a character's musings and memories to introduce a flashback; others have characters relate past events to a first-person narrator.

Few, if any, narratives take place in real time. A ten-day train ride may be described in only one sentence, while a ten-minute conversation may take several pages to describe.

Build Narrative Suspense Suspense is the uncertainty about the outcome of a story—what makes a reader's pulse quicken. Add suspense to a narrative to give readers a pressing desire to read on to the end.

Use any of the following techniques to create suspense in your narrative:

- Construct an eerie setting.
- Use delaying tactics. Slow down time at a crucial moment with precise descriptions, flashbacks, or scene changes.
- Use foreshadowing—a hint of what is to come.

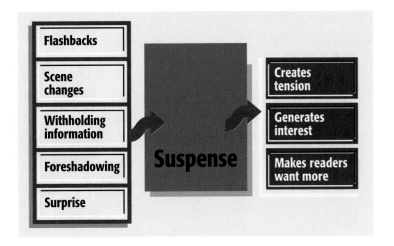

15.3 EXPOSITORY WRITING

Giving directions, explaining an idea or a term, comparing one thing to another, and explaining how to do something are all forms of expository writing. The purpose of expository writing is to inform your readers or to explain something to them. Effective expository writing

- gives the reader a logical step-by-step path through new information
- allows writers to share information and explanations directly with the reader

USE EXPOSITORY WRITING TO
• explain a process
• show a cause-and-effect relationship
• compare and contrast
• identify problems and propose solutions
• build and support a hypothesis

EXPLAIN A PROCESS

This type of expository writing allows you to explain either how to do something or how something happens.

Consider Your Audience As you write your explanation, you should keep your audience's background knowledge in mind. Answer the following questions:

- How much does my audience know about the process?
- How much detail are they likely to need?
- Which terms, if any, will I need to define?

Understand the Process To explain a process, the writer must first understand the steps involved in the process and then present these steps in order.

Writing Tip

Effective instructions are straightforward, precise, and clearly organized. Obscure language or garbled logic can confuse your reader.

Write the Essay Follow the three steps below to write an essay that explains a process.

- **Prewriting:** Research by reading, watching others, or performing the process.
- **Drafting:** Arrange the steps of the process in chronological order. Break one step into two if more detail is needed. Omit unnecessary steps.
- **Revising:** Reread the explanation. Make sure you've included all necessary details and signaled separate steps with transition words. Reorder steps as necessary.

COMPOSITION

CAUSE AND EFFECT

In cause-and-effect writing, you give reasons and explanations for events, conditions, or behavior. Whenever you explain "why" in writing, you will use some form of cause-and-effect exposition. Cause-and-effect relationships can

- start with one cause and lead to one effect
- start with one cause and lead to several effects
- start with several causes and lead to one effect
- start with several causes and lead to several effects
- start with one cause that leads to an effect, which in turn leads to another effect, resulting in a chain of events

Plan Your Essay When planning a cause-and-effect essay,

1. identify the event or condition you want to explain
2. ask yourself the following questions:
   - Who or what was responsible?
   - Who or what was affected?
3. list and explain the causes and the effects
4. answer the questions in the following chart to be sure you have not drawn any faulty conclusions

FAULTY CAUSE-AND-EFFECT RELATIONSHIPS	
• HAVE YOU ASSUMED A CAUSE-AND-EFFECT RELATIONSHIP WHEN THERE IS NONE?	*My mother knows everyone; therefore, I can get into any college in the country.*
• HAVE YOU ASSUMED ONLY ONE CAUSE WHEN MANY CAUSES MAY BE APPROPRIATE?	*The team lost the pennant because of the umpire's bad call.*
• HAVE YOU INCORRECTLY ASSUMED A CAUSAL RELATIONSHIP BETWEEN TWO EVENTS THAT FOLLOWED EACH OTHER?	*Unemployment skyrocketed once he began his term as governor. He should claim responsibility for the horrible state of the economy.*

Write Your Essay Follow these steps to write a cause-and-effect essay.

1. Compose a thesis statement that clearly states your topic. Include this thesis statement in your introduction.
2. Organize and write your essay. Cause-and-effect essays need a logical structure, so you might begin with a cause and then present its effect. You can also reverse this order—you might begin with an effect and trace it back to its original cause.
3. Summarize your arguments in your conclusion.

COMPARE AND CONTRAST

A compare-and-contrast essay expresses the essential differences and similarities between two subjects. Compare-and-contrast essays should be carefully constructed around thesis statements to explain the similarities and differences between items or events. The thesis gives the essay a shape—it determines what information belongs in the essay.

Choose a Method of Organization Some writers choose to organize their compare-and-contrast essays according to subject. Using this method, writers will discuss all the details about one subject first and then all the details about the next subject. Then they will compare and contrast the subjects. Other writers prefer to organize details by feature. They will select one feature of the subjects at a time and list all the similarities and differences for both subjects.

IDENTIFY PROBLEMS AND PROPOSE SOLUTIONS

When writing about a problem and its solutions, define the problem carefully and try to present a range of possible solutions.

1. Begin your essay by gathering information at the library, on the Internet, or from interviews or observation.

2. Ask yourself such questions as the following:
   - What is the nature and extent of the problem?
   - What are its causes?
   - How does it affect people?

3. Draw on different types of information to explain the dimensions of a problem.
   - Use personal anecdotes to help your readers relate a problem to their own lives.
   - Use statistics to help you present an overview of a problem.

4. Present solutions. Most problems have more than one possible solution. Examine the advantages and disadvantages of proposed solutions carefully and systematically. Be realistic when you explain solutions—it may be that no solution will completely solve a problem.

BUILD A HYPOTHESIS

A **hypothesis** is a statement of a belief that you assume to be true.

	THE STEPS TO BUILDING A HYPOTHESIS
STEP 1	Decide on the issue or question you want to explore. For example, you might build a hypothesis to explain a foreign policy decision or a chemical reaction.
STEP 2	Identify what you are trying to explain.
STEP 3	Collect data and consult experts.
STEP 4	Compare and contrast data to identify patterns or trends.
STEP 5	Decide on the most reasonable hypothesis based on the data.
STEP 6	Test the conclusion for acceptance, modification, or rejection.

COMPOSITION

Present Your Data After you have tested your hypothesis, you can begin writing. Follow these steps when you begin your essay.

1. Present your hypothesis in a thesis statement. This statement should be part of an introductory paragraph that tells how and why your topic and thesis are important.

2. Develop your explanation in the body of your essay by supporting each point with specific examples, facts, or expert testimony.

3. Summarize your main points in your concluding paragraph. Draw a conclusion by evaluating the evidence you've assembled or by expressing a judgment or a realization.

15.4 PERSUASIVE WRITING

Persuasive writing is used to motivate readers—to change their minds about a topic, to convince them to buy a product, or to get them to vote for a certain candidate or issue. The main reason for persuasive writing is to convince readers to take action, in whatever form that might be. To make a persuasive argument, you must

- state your opinion clearly as early in the essay as possible
- support your position with facts, reasons, and examples
- choose a presentation that is designed to appeal to your audience

CHOOSE A TOPIC

You are writing to convince your reader to agree with your opinion. Choose an argument about which you and others feel strongly.

KNOW YOUR AUDIENCE

A particular topic or issue may be insignificant to one group of people and yet be of great interest to another group. Make a list of information about your audience, including their likes and dislikes, their biases, and what they probably know about the subject. Keep this list in mind when constructing your argument.

CONSTRUCT AN ARGUMENT

Begin by clearly expressing your opinion in a thesis statement. Compare the thesis statements in the following chart.

SAMPLE THESIS STATEMENT		
Not So Good	**Better**	**Best**
In a democracy, all citizens are allowed to participate.	*Democratic rule requires participation; therefore, everyone should vote.*	*Low voter turnout is undermining our democracy; we must encourage greater participation through voter information.*
(Not an opinion, just a statement of fact)	(Vague)	(Well-defined position, specific solution)

To test your thesis, summarize the opposing view. If you cannot state an opposing view, you probably do not have a strong point to make.

Next gather evidence to support your thesis and develop a strategy for presenting it. You may choose to begin your essay by analyzing and refuting the arguments of the opposing side. You might choose to present information in one of the following ways:

- **decreasing order of importance,** placing the most important evidence first
- **increasing order of importance,** placing the most important evidence last

Increasing order of importance can fail if you don't hold the audience's attention until the end. An attention-getting introduction and a strong middle are essential to this strategy.

EVALUATE THE EVIDENCE

To support your argument, you must choose and evaluate a variety of evidence. Each type of evidence you use adds a different kind of support to your position.

- **Factual information and concrete details,** such as statistics, observations, scientific reports, and historical perspectives, are convincing because they are verifiable.
- **Opinions** are effective if they are from a respected authority or are deduced from factual evidence.
- **Examples, anecdotes, and analogies** can bring your subject to life or illuminate a point.
- **Reasons** guide your audience through the logic of your position.

The wider your range of supporting evidence, the stronger your arguments. However, collecting mountains of evidence does not guarantee that you'll have a strong argument. You need to judge the quality of the evidence. The following questions can help you analyze your research:

- Does the evidence come from a reliable, unbiased, up-to-date source?
- Is the evidence consistent with what you or authorities on the subject believe to be true?
- Does the evidence address all sides of the issue, taking all objections into account?

Sift Fact from Opinion A strong persuasive argument supports opinions with relevant facts. Recognizing the difference between fact and opinion can help you more clearly define your position. It can also guide you in presenting facts and opinions appropriately in your writing.

Follow these guidelines to help you determine whether the "facts" you read and hear are actually opinions in disguise.

RECOGNIZING FACTS AND OPINIONS	
RECOGNIZING FACTS	RECOGNIZING OPINIONS
Can the statement be verified?	**Is the statement based on personal preference or belief?**
Facts can be proven or measured; you can check them in reference works. Sometimes you can observe or test them yourself.	Often, although not always, opinions are open to interpretation and contain phrases such as "I believe" or "in my view."

COMPOSITION

Evaluate Facts and Opinions To evaluate the strength of an argument, you need to do more than distinguish between fact and opinion. You also need to determine whether facts are relevant and whether they tell the whole story.

Opinion, as well as fact, should be evaluated carefully. Informed opinions, based on facts and on the experiences of eyewitnesses or experts, carry the most weight.

Use Inductive and Deductive Reasoning Both inductive and deductive reasoning involve using facts to arrive at conclusions, but they work in different ways. When you use inductive reasoning, you

1. begin with a series of facts
2. study the facts, looking for a connection among them
3. draw a conclusion or a generalization

We rely on this kind of reasoning for much of our knowledge.

Inductive reasoning proceeds logically from limited facts or observations to a general conclusion. An inductive argument will hold up only if the evidence is accurate and the conclusion follows reasonably from the evidence. Check your reasoning by asking whether you can draw another conclusion from the evidence.

EVALUATE INDUCTIVE REASONING
1. What are the specific facts or evidence from which the conclusion is drawn?
2. Is each fact or piece of evidence accurate?
3. Do the facts form a representative and sufficiently large sample?
4. Do all of the facts or the evidence lead to the conclusion?
5. Does the argument contain any logical fallacies?

FoxTrot

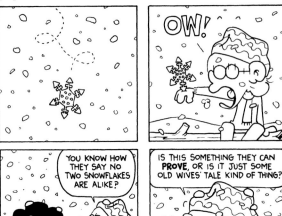

When you use deductive reasoning, you

1. begin with a generalization

2. apply that generalization to a specific example

3. arrive at a conclusion

Deductive reasoning may involve a **syllogism,** which consists of a major premise, or a general statement; a minor premise, or a related fact; and a conclusion based on the two.

SYLLOGISM	
START WITH A GENERALIZATION OR MAJOR PREMISE.	A diet high in fat is unhealthful.
STATE A RELATED FACT OR MINOR PREMISE.	A typical teenager's diet is high in fat.
DRAW A CONCLUSION BASED ON THE TWO.	A typical teenager's diet is unhealthful.

COMPOSITION

Note: A syllogism is valid if it follows the rules of deductive reasoning. It is true if the statements are factually accurate. A syllogism, then, can be valid but untrue. For example:

Major premise: Basketball players are the best athletes. [This can't be proved true.]

Minor premise: Michael Jordan is the best basketball player. [This, too, can be debated.]

Conclusion: Therefore, Michael Jordan is the best athlete. [This conclusion is valid according to the premises, but it isn't necessarily true.]

EVALUATE DEDUCTIVE REASONING
1. What are the major premise, the minor premise, and the conclusion?
2. Is the major premise a universal statement?
3. Are both premises true?
4. Does the conclusion follow logically from the major and the minor premises?
5. Does the argument contain any logical fallacies?

Recognize Logical Fallacies Faulty reasoning involves errors called logical fallacies. Learning to recognize your own and others' logical fallacies will strengthen your skills in persuasive writing. Listed are some of the most common types of flaws.

- A **red herring** statement diverts attention from the issue at hand. A senator who is attacked for irregular attendance might describe her charitable work to prove she is productive. However, she has not addressed the criticism about the missed meetings.

- **Circular reasoning** is an argument that apparently leads to a logical conclusion but actually takes you back to where you started. The statement "Shaquille O'Neal is a great basketball player because he has so much talent" sounds true, but the statement doesn't prove anything; it merely repeats the point in different words. To say that talent makes O'Neal great is just another way of saying he's a great basketball player.

- **Bandwagon Reasoning** The term "jumping on the bandwagon" means doing or thinking something because everyone else is doing or thinking it. This type of reasoning provides no evidence to support a decision or a viewpoint.

Anticipate Objections When you present an argument, anticipate objections to your view and then try to answer those objections. A good strategy for handling opposition is to make concessions—to admit that some point in your argument is weak or to agree with some part of your opponent's argument.

Research Paper Writing

● ● ● ● ● ● ● ● ● ● ● ● ● ● ●

When you write a research paper, you collect factual information from a variety of sources, analyze and organize this information, and present it to your readers in a clear and interesting way.

Follow these steps to write a research paper:

- Choose a topic that interests you.
- Narrow the topic to fit your paper's length.
- Perform extensive research to gather information about the topic.
- Organize your research and write an outline.
- Form a thesis statement and support the thesis with the information you gathered in your research.
- Compile a list of works cited.

16.1 PREWRITING

CHOOSE A TOPIC

Researching and writing will be easier if you are curious about the topic you choose, so try to find a topic that interests you. Keep in mind how much information will be manageable given the length of your research paper. If the topic is too broad, you'll have too much information. Narrow your topic until you feel you can cover it adequately in your paper.

TOO BROAD	NARROW	NARROWER
Sports	Tennis	The History of Wimbledon
Dance	Ballet	Romantic Ballet
History	History of Art	Art in the Romantic Era

> ### Research TIP
>
> If your teacher assigns a topic, do some preliminary research at the library or on the Internet to find an aspect of this topic that appeals to you.

Decide on a Central Idea

After choosing a topic, you need to decide on your paper's central idea, which will guide your selection of research questions. Identify three to seven research questions, each question focusing on one aspect of the topic. Ask the *whats, whys,* and *hows* about your topic. As you begin to find answers, you'll come up with more sharply focused questions. Feel free to modify your central idea as you learn more about the topic.

QUESTIONS FOR A RESEARCH PAPER ABOUT THE ROMANTIC ERA
• What were the beliefs of the Romantics?
• Why did Romantics believe in these things?
• How did artists, musicians, and poets of the Romantic Era express these beliefs in their works?
• Which artists are considered Romantics?
• What did these artists have in common? How were they different?

FIND INFORMATION ON YOUR TOPIC

Use two types of sources—primary and secondary.

- A **primary source** is first-hand information that has not been evaluated or analyzed by someone else. A witness to an event, letters and original documents from the historical era you are studying, and interviews with experts on your topic are considered primary sources.
- A **secondary source** is information that has been organized, evaluated, and analyzed by someone else. An article analyzing a witness's comments would be a secondary source. Most books and magazine articles are considered secondary sources.

Technology Tip
The Internet can be a valuable tool for finding both primary and secondary sources. Evaluate Internet sources carefully; not all Internet sites contain accurate information. To make certain that the sources are valid, find another source that contains the same information.

Take Notes

Once you have found some sources, you can begin taking notes and collecting information. Taking notes efficiently and accurately is one of the most important steps in writing a good research paper. You will probably take many more notes than you will use, but at this point, it is better to have too much information than too little.

Prepare Note Cards Read your sources thoroughly for information, ideas, statements, and statistics that relate to your research topic and to your main idea. When you find something you can use, write it on a three-by-five note card, with one piece of information per card, and record the number of that source's bibliography card. There are three ways to record the information you find.

- **Paraphrase:** Write the information in your own words.

- **Quote Directly:** Copy the information exactly as it appears in the text. Use quotation marks to indicate when you quote directly.

- **Summarize:** Write a brief summary of the information, focusing on key points and concepts.

Develop a Working Bibliography Assemble a record of the books, articles, Internet sites, and other sources you consult. This record is your working bibliography. When you find a useful source, record the publishing data on a three-by-five index card. This way you can easily find and use the information later. Complete bibliography cards will also help you write your list of works cited.

Different types of sources need different data on their bibliography cards, as the following samples illustrate. Examples of other kinds of sources can be found in the List of Works Cited on pages 494–495.

Number Your Sources Number each card. This number will later serve as an easy way to identify the source. You can also write brief notes indicating the type of information in the source.

Types of Bibliography Cards

EXAMPLE   Book

> 1
>
> Kerner, Mary. *Barefoot to Balanchine: How to Watch Dance.* New York: Doubleday, 1990.

EXAMPLE   Internet Source

> 3
>
> Wordsworth, William. *Literary Ballads.* Comp. Thomas Gannon. London: Routledge, 1991. *Favorite Quotations from William Wordsworth.* 25 May 1995. Preface. University of South Dakota. 15 July 1998
> <http://www.usd.edu/~tgannon/txts/wordquot.txt>.

Avoid Plagiarism Presenting the ideas or statements of another writer without crediting the original source is plagiarism. Plagiarism occurs when

- a writer directly quotes a source without using quotation marks or paraphrases a source too closely, substituting only a few words of his or her own. Even if credit is given to the source, this use of information is still considered plagiarism.
- a writer summarizes a source's ideas or observations without giving credit

© 1998, Washington Post Writers Group.
Reprinted with permission.

Research TIP

To avoid paraphrasing a source too closely, look away from the source while you take notes. After you have finished paraphrasing, reread the source to make sure that you have used your own words.

Read Sources Critically As you do research, evaluate each source for bias. If a source's bias detracts from the objectivity of your paper, you may not want to use it unless you present one or more opposing views. To detect bias, ask yourself whether you think the source is treating the topic fairly or not. Does the author make unqualified assertions?

Are the views of the author often disputed? Answering these questions will help you choose the best sources.

Calvin and Hobbes by Bill Watterson

CHOOSE A METHOD OF ORGANIZATION

How can you decide on the best way to arrange the ideas in your notes? You have a number of options, depending on the nature of your information.

- **Chronological:** Arrange the information according to when it happened. This organization is often used in papers describing historical changes.
- **Cause and Effect:** Arrange items in causal order to show how one idea or event directly determines another. This organization is often used in papers exploring why something happened.
- **Cumulative:** Arrange items according to how important or how familiar to the reader each one is. This organization is often used in papers evaluating results.

Develop an Outline

An outline is a summary of the main points and the ideas that support them. As you take notes, look for ways to classify the facts and the ideas you find. Begin to group the note cards as you classify them. As you make decisions about how to organize your cards, you are developing the information you need to write a working outline. You will continue to write and revise this outline as you conduct research. The following tip will help you write your working outline, which will eventually become the formal outline you will use when you write your first draft.

Outlining TIP

1. Look for similarities among notes; group note cards on similar topics together. Use each group as a main topic in your outline.

2. Within groups, cluster similar note cards into subgroups that elaborate on the main topic. Use these subgroups as the subheadings in your outline.

3. Arrange main topics to build on your central idea. Under each topic, arrange subheadings so they elaborate on the heading, or main topic, in a logical way.

4. As you continue your research and learn more, revise your outline. Subdivide information in subheadings into outline entries as well.

5. Set aside note cards that don't fit under any of your headings, but don't throw them away.

6. Before you begin your first draft, prepare a formal outline.

Title of Paper

I. Introduction
   Central idea (thesis statement)

II. Heading (main topic)
   A. Subheading (supporting detail)
      1. sub/subheading
      2.
   B. Subheading (supporting detail)
      1.
      2.

III. Heading (main topic)

IV. Heading (main topic)

V. Conclusion

Body —

Make Smooth Transitions: Note how the writer of the following outline organizes the information to provide smooth transitions between the headings. For example, the writer places "natural settings" at the end of heading III and at the beginning of heading IV; doing so gives the writer an effective way to connect the two paragraphs.

Art in the Romantic Era: How Writers,
Dancers, Musicians, and Artists Were
Influenced by Romantic Philosophy.

I. Introduction
   Artists, poets, musicians, and dancers
   all shared common elements of
   Romantic thought.
II. Definition and history of Romantic Era
   A. History of the term
   B. Shared beliefs
      1. Emotional over intellectual
      2. New forms
      3. Love of nature
III. Romanticism in Literature
   A. William Wordsworth; Samuel Taylor
      Coleridge
      1. Emotions
      2. Reaction against Classicists
   B. New forms
      1. Wordsworth
      2. William Blake
   C. Natural settings
IV. Romanticism in the visual arts
   A. Natural settings
   B. Personal feelings
      1. Comparison to poets
      2. New techniques
V. Romanticism in music
   A. Personal feelings
   B. Shared goals of Romantic composers
VII. Conclusion

16.2 DRAFTING

DEVELOP A THESIS STATEMENT

Until now, you have guided your research and outline according to a central idea about your topic. Now you should turn your central idea into a **thesis statement**—that is, a concise idea you will try to prove, expand on, or illustrate in your writing. Your thesis statement gives your writing a focus from start to finish.

THREE STEPS TO CONSTRUCTING A THESIS STATEMENT
1. Examine your central idea and refine it to reflect the information that you gathered in your research. The information you find may be very different from what you expected to find.
2. Consider your approach to the topic. What is the purpose of your research? Are you proving or disproving something? Illustrating a cause-and-effect relationship? Offering a solution to a problem? Examining one aspect of your topic thoroughly?
3. Revise your central idea to reflect your approach and polish your wording to form a concise thesis statement.

USE YOUR OUTLINE AND NOTES

Using the structure of your formal outline, you will be able to transform your piles of note cards into the basis for a first draft. Look at your outline again to be sure you're satisfied with the way each idea leads to the next. Then begin drafting.

DRAFTING TIP

1. Try to draft as smoothly and logically as possible without getting stalled on details. Don't worry about finding the perfect word or phrase; you can revise later.
2. Use your outline as a map to help guide you in your writing. The outline should remind you of what comes before or after a particular idea.
3. Write at least one paragraph for each heading, or main topic, in your outline. Each paragraph should have a topic sentence and supporting details.
4. When you use data from a note card, write the number of that card near the data in the text to help you document the idea later.

Write the Introduction and Conclusion

Your paper's introduction and conclusion work together to frame your research paper. A good introduction should grab your reader's attention and make him or her want to read on. The introduction can be a good place to use a special bit of information you have found in your research, perhaps a little-known fact, a vivid description, or a funny anecdote that you want to highlight. Your conclusion should alert the reader that you are wrapping up. You might summarize your main points or mention any new questions your paper raises.

TRAITS OF EFFECTIVE INTRODUCTIONS AND CONCLUSIONS	
Introduction	**Conclusion**
Contains a clear, concise thesis statement	Restates the thesis statement
Grabs and keeps the reader's interest	Reviews the main points of the paper
Identifies your approach to the topic	Notes the significance of the research
Presents a bit of enticing background information on unfamiliar subjects	Identifies possible implications for the future (if appropriate)

RESEARCH PAPER FORMAT

Use the following format for your research paper:

- At the top, bottom, and both sides of each page, leave margins of one inch.
- Double-space every line, including the title if it is more than one line long.
- Unless you are told to include a cover page, put your name, your teacher's name, the name of the course, and the date on four lines at the start of page one, even with the left margin.
- Center the title on the next line.
- For all but the first page, put the first line of text one inch from the top edge of the paper.
- Put your last name and the page number at the upper right corner of each page, one-half inch from the top and even with the right margin. Number all pages, even the first, consecutively.
- Indent each paragraph's first line one-half inch from the left margin.
- If you use a set-off quotation, indent each line of it one inch from the left margin.

- At the end of your research paper, on a new page, begin your list of works cited. Center the title, *Works Cited,* an inch from the top of the page. Begin each entry even with the left margin. If an entry is more than one line long, indent the next line or lines one-half inch from the left margin.

16.3 CITING SOURCES

Document Information You need to name the sources of words, ideas, and facts that you borrow. Readers should be able to distinguish your ideas from those of your sources. Documenting your sources enables your reader to check the source personally and to judge how believable or important a piece of information is. Documentation also decreases the chance of plagiarism.

What to Document You should document your information

- whenever you use someone's exact words
- whenever you paraphrase a particular idea or series of ideas
- whenever you use information that is not generally known or found in most books on the subject

You do not need to document the following information:

- widely known proverbs, famous quotations, and simple definitions
- information that is common knowledge or is found in most sources about the topic

Use Parenthetical Documentation Cite sources in the text of your report by inserting the author's last name and a page reference in parentheses after the information that requires citation.

COMPOSITION

- **Name in Text:** If you mention the author in the text (for example, if the text reads "As Ferguson points out, . . ."), then you can merely insert the page number in parentheses.

- **Two or More Authors:** For two authors, insert both authors and the page numbers in parentheses: (Smith and Brown 42). If the source has more than two authors, just give the last name of the first author listed, followed by *et al.* ("and others") and the page number: (Wold et al. 42).

- **More than one work by the same author:** Use the author's name, a shortened version of the title, and give the page number: (Longyear, Romanticism in Music 12).

- **No author or editor:** Use a shortened version of the title and give the page number: (Brittanica 160).

- **No page numbers:** Use *n. pag.* in place of a page reference: (Clark n. pag.).

- **More than one source at the same time:** Include both sources, and separate them with a semicolon: (Wold et al. 42; Brittanica 160).

- **Author quoted in another source:** Use the abbreviation *qtd. in* for "quoted in" and the author and page number of the source: (qtd. in Longyear 33).

Use Quotations

You may quote from a source in the following ways:

1. You may quote one word or part of a sentence, including it in a sentence of your own.

   This ideal differed greatly from the thoughts of eighteenth-century poets, who felt that poetry was "primarily an imitation of human life" (Abrams 5).

2. You may quote a complete sentence, which you should introduce in your own words.

The Romantics favored natural settings over newly industrial cities such as London. In his poem "The Tables Turned," Wordsworth wrote, "Come forth into the light of things, Let Nature be your teacher" (Bartlett 372).

3. You may omit words or sentences from a quotation by using ellipses in place of the omitted words or sentences. Place brackets around words you have inserted in place of the omitted words or sentences. Be careful not to change the meaning of the original sentences.

Composers wrote works that they felt would appeal to the public or "satisfy . . . [their] intense feeling for expression" (Wold et al. 253).

4. You may use a quotation of more than four lines by starting a new line and indenting the quote. In this case, you do not need to use quotation marks.

Which Page Numbers Should I Include? Page numbers in parenthetical documentation indicate the pages from which the information is taken. Page numbers in works cited entries are for the page span of the entire newspaper or magazine article or anthologized work.

Compile a List of Works Cited

From your bibliography cards, record the publishing information about the source in the form of a list of works cited. This list should appear on a new page at the end of your report. Write the information about the sources in the order in which you wrote it on your bibliography card. List the sources in alphabetical order by authors' last names, or if no author is given, by title.

The following chart shows the proper bibliographic style for various sources. The style is based on the recommendations of the Modern Language Association. If your teacher asks you to use a different style to document your sources, you can still refer to this chart to be sure you have included everything necessary.

A LIST OF WORKS CITED

TYPE OF CITATION	EXAMPLE
Book with Single Author	Kerner, Mary. <u>Barefoot to Balanchine: How to Watch Dance</u>. New York: Doubleday, 1990.
Book with Two Authors	Collier, Peter and Robert Lethbridge. <u>Artistic Relations: Literature and the Visual Arts in Nineteenth-Century France</u>. New Haven: Yale University Press, 1994.
Book with Three or More Authors	Wold, Milo, et al. <u>An Introduction to Music and Art in the Western World</u>. Dubuque: Brown and Benchmark, 1996.
Articles in a Periodical	Furst, Lilian. "Poetic Madness and the Romantic Imagination." <u>Nineteenth-Century Literature</u> Vol. 52 June 1997: 110–112.
Encyclopedia Article	"Romanticism." <u>The New Encyclopaedia Brittanica: Micropaedia</u>. 15th ed. 1998.

TYPE OF CITATION	EXAMPLE
Internet Site with a Print Version	Wordsworth, William. <u>Literary Ballads</u>. London: Routledge, 1991. <u>Favorite Quotations from William Wordsworth</u>. Comp. Thomas Gannon. 25 May 1995. Preface. University of South Dakota. 15 July 1998 <http://www.usd.edu/~tgannon/txts/word quot.txt>.

Not all sources fit the categories listed in the preceding chart. To cite such sources, refer to the *MLA Handbook for Writers of Research Papers* and adapt one of the above entries, arranging the information in the following order:

Author information should appear at the beginning of the entry, with the author's last name first.

- If the source has two or more authors, reverse only the first author's name.
- If no author is listed, list the editor. If no editor is listed, begin with the title.
- If you use more than one work by the same author, you do not need to repeat the author's name for each entry. Instead, use three hyphens followed by a period to begin the entry.

Title information follows any author information and lists the title of the article, essay, or other part of the book first if applicable, then the title of the book.

COMPOSITION

Publication information follows the author and title and, as needed, lists the editor's name, edition number, volume number, and series name. List the city of publication, publisher's name, and the publication date. (Note: This information may not be available on Internet sources. Just include the information given at the site.) If appropriate, list page numbers. If a newspaper or magazine article does not appear on consecutive pages, include the first page number and a plus sign (10+).

Citing Online Sources

You will not need to include everything from the following list in a single citation; most sources don't offer all this information. If you cannot find all the information needed for a particular source, provide as much information as is available.

1. Author, editor, or compiler of the source
2. Title of an article, poem, or short work (in quotation marks); or title of a posting to a discussion line or forum followed by the phrase *Online posting*
3. Title of a book (underlined)
4. Editor, compiler, or translator of the text (if not mentioned earlier)
5. Publication information for any print version of the text
6. Title of the scholarly project, database, periodical, or professional or personal site (underlined). If the professional or personal site has no title, use a description such as *Home page.*
7. Editor or director of the scholarly project or database
8. Version number of the source, or for a journal, the volume number, issue number, or other identifying number
9. Date of electronic publication, of the last update, or of the posting

10. Total number of pages (if they are numbered)
11. Name of the institution or organization sponsoring or associated with the Internet site
12. Date when you accessed the source
13. Electronic address of the source (in angle brackets)

16.4 REVISING/EDITING

When you revise your first draft, you can improve your choice of words, your transitions, and—most important—the way you present your ideas. Use the following chart to help you revise your draft.

SOLVING REVISION PROBLEMS	
Problem	**Solution**
My first draft needs a clearer focus.	Review your thesis statement; delete or rewrite anything in the paper that doesn't support it.
My argument should be easier to follow.	Add transitions and rearrange and add ideas to make the paper more coherent; delete irrelevant information.
My paragraphs do not flow smoothly from one to another.	Add or change transitions between paragraphs; rearrange paragraphs in a more logical order.
My introduction doesn't connect well with the rest of my paper.	Add transitions or rewrite the introduction to conform with the purpose and the main idea.
My sentences sound repetitive.	Vary sentence structure. Use precise, lively language. Find synonyms for repeated words.

16.5 PROOFREADING

After you have revised your paper, proofread it several times, looking for a different kind of flaw each time. Read your paper once for sense, looking for mistakes in usage, omitted words, and transposed elements. Read again for typing, spelling, and punctuation errors. Finally, proofread your citations, cross-checking your bibliography cards, note cards, and first draft as necessary. Use the following checklist to help you catch any remaining problems.

FINAL PROOFREADING CHECKLIST
❏ Are words omitted?
❏ Do typing errors exist?
❏ Are grammar and usage correct?
❏ Is punctuation correct?
❏ Are all words spelled correctly and consistently?
❏ Are proper names capitalized?
❏ Are unfamiliar words defined or explained?
❏ Is each source properly documented?

16.6 PUBLISHING/PRESENTING YOUR RESEARCH PAPER

Your teacher will probably ask you to make a cover sheet for your research paper, containing the title of the paper as well as your name and other identifying information. Center your name and the date under the title. Your teacher may also ask you for other materials to check the extent of your research and the construction of your paper. You may be asked to include a clean copy of your formal outline.

Your teacher may ask you to include a summary statement. This is a brief restatement of your thesis statement, no more than two sentences long and inserted before your report.

SAMPLE RESEARCH PAPER

Dorothea Brooke

Mr. Garcia

English III

March 15, 2000

Art in the Romantic Era: How Writers,

Dancers, Musicians, and Artists Were Influenced

by Romantic Philosophy

"Every intellectual product must be judged from the point of view of the age and the people in which it was produced."

—Walter Pater (qtd. in <u>Familiar Quotations</u>)

Until the nineteenth century, painters, sculptors, writers, and musicians in England received most of their income from wealthy patrons (lords, ladies, and sometimes kings and queens) or from the church. This system of patronage began to change in the early nineteenth century. Artists no longer received an income from the church and the

COMPOSITION

aristocracy; instead composers gave performances, poets and novelists sold copies of their works, and painters and sculptors sold their artworks (Wold et al. 244–245). These artists had to cater to the tastes of an entirely new audience—the general public—who now had the income and the education to enjoy artistic pursuits. This new audience gave artists a new freedom; with a wider audience to which to appeal, they could experiment with new forms and express emotions that had once been considered off-limits. The time was right for the birth of a new movement—and this new movement was Romanticism. Romantic artists believed in the individual, and each looked for individual ways to express his or her ideals. However, the writers, visual artists, and composers of this time shared common elements of Romantic thought, such as a love of nature, an interest in new forms, and an emphasis on expressing spontaneity and emotion.

The thesis statement clearly states the main idea of the paper.

The Romantic Era was named after the medieval romances that had become popular at the end of the eighteenth century. These romances were tall tales of heroic individuals who battled evil creatures and returned home victorious. The Romantics of literature did not tell these tall tales, but they did place an emphasis on the individual. Unlike their predecessors, the Classicists, who had favored intellectual pursuits and material goods, the Romantics favored emotions, spontaneous thought, and nature. If Classicism was the Age of Reason, then this was the Age of Emotion.

The Romantic Era began in the 1790s, when William Wordsworth published a book of poems called *Lyrical Ballads*. In the preface to the second edition, he summed up the ideals of the Romantics when he described poetry as "the spontaneous overflow of powerful feelings" (qtd. in <u>Favorite Quotations</u>). This ideal differed greatly from the thoughts of eighteenth-century poets, who had felt

COMPOSITION

that poetry was "primarily an imitation of human life" (Abrams 5). To the Romantics, feelings were more important than intellectual thoughts; in fact, Romantics felt it was impossible to think deeply without emotion. Wordsworth's friend Samuel Taylor Coleridge expressed this idea when he wrote, "Deep thinking is attainable only by a man of deep feeling" (Abrams 7).

Romantic poets chose new, freer forms and natural settings to express their emotions and ideas. Wordsworth felt that the Classicists had imposed artificial limits on poetry. He rejected the highly stylized language and heroic topics of the seventeenth century. Instead, he wrote in the *Lyrical Ballads* that he had decided to "choose incidents and situations from common life, and to relate or describe them . . . in a selection of the language really used by men" (qtd. in <u>Favorite Quotations</u>). William Blake, another Romantic poet, wrote from "Inspiration and Vision" (Abrams 5).

> The topic sentence of each paragraph supports or explains the thesis statement; the rest of the paragraph supports or explains the topic sentence.

Romantic poets often wrote about their emotions, which they felt most acutely in nature. They favored natural settings over newly industrialized cities such as London. In his poem "The Tables Turned," Wordsworth wrote, "Come forth into the light of things, Let Nature be your teacher" (Bartlett 372). Wordsworth's poems tell of the great joy and serenity people can find in natural settings.

Many of the visual artists of the nineteenth century shared the Romantic poets' love of nature. Instead of finding inspiration in history or in classical literature as artists before them had often done, many Romantic artists were inspired by nature. Painters such as J. M. W. Turner and John Constable became famous for their sweeping landscapes and seascapes; they used shading, lighting, and bold colors to express the magnificence of natural settings (Brittanica 161).

The artists of this era also expressed their personal feelings in their art—and their personal feelings

COMPOSITION

could take the form of joy, rage, or violence. William Blake (who was both a poet and a painter) expressed the ideals of the Romantics with bold, sometimes violent paintings. Probably because they no longer had to cater to aristocratic tastes, Romantic artists were less concerned with depicting things as they really were and more with expressing their feelings toward their subjects. Turner "used rapid brush techniques to create the spirit of the object rather than a mere photographic likeness" (Wold et al. 248). Just as the poets used new, freer forms to express their emotions, Romantic artists expressed their feelings using light and shadow in new ways.

The music of this time also reflected changes in form and function. Romantic music is intense and passionate because composers began to express their feelings in their works. They shared a belief that "musical tension is necessary to achieve . . . [an] emotional response" (Wold et al. 253). Released from aristocratic patronage, composers such as Ludwig van Beethoven and Franz Schubert wrote works that they felt would appeal to the public or "satisfy . . . [their] intense feeling for expression" (Wold et al. 253). Like the Romantic poets, many composers of this era shared a love of nature; Beethoven, for example, wrote a "Pastoral" symphony that celebrated nature. The work was not meant to depict nature, however; he described it as having "more of an expression of feeling than painting" (qtd. in Longyear 12).

Each Romantic composer, artist, poet, and dancer was an individual, but together they produced a body of work that shares elements of the Romantic philosophy—a love of nature, a spontaneous response to life, and a reaction against the ideals of the Classicists. Romantic works—such as Wordsworth's poems, Blake's paintings, and Beethoven's music—can be distinguished by their passion, their emotion, and their intensity of feeling.

The conclusion might restate the thesis statement, summarize the main points, or mention new questions the paper raises.

COMPOSITION

Works Cited

Abrams, M. H., ed. <u>The Norton Anthology of English Literature</u>. New York: W. W. Norton and Company, 1993.

Bartlett, John. "Walter Pater." <u>Familiar Quotations: A Collection of Passages, Phrases, and Proverbs Traced to Their Sources in Ancient and Modern Literature</u>. Boston: Little, Brown, and Company: 16th ed. 1992.

---. "William Wordsworth." <u>Familiar Quotations: A Collection of Passages, Phrases, and Proverbs Traced to Their Sources in Ancient and Modern Literature</u>. Boston: Little, Brown, and Company: 16th ed. 1992.

Longyear, Rey M. <u>Nineteenth-Century Romanticism in Music</u>. Englewood Cliffs: Prentice Hall, 1988.

"Romanticism." <u>The New Encyclopaedia Brittanica: Micropaedia</u>. 15th ed. 1998.

Wold, Milo, et al. <u>An Introduction to Music and Art in the Western World</u>. Dubuque: Brown and Benchmark, 1996.

Wordsworth, William. <u>Literary Ballads</u>. London: Routledge, 1991. <u>Favorite Quotations from William Wordsworth</u>. Comp. Thomas Gannon. 25 May 1995. Preface. University of South Dakota. 15 July 1998 <http://www.usd.edu/~tgannon/txts/wordquot.txt>.

Calvin and Hobbes

by Bill Watterson

COMPOSITION

Chapter 17

Business Writing

17.1 WRITING A COVER LETTER

Often the first contact you have with a potential employer is the cover letter you include with your résumé. Many employers read the cover letter before they look at the résumé. It is important, therefore, that you make a good impression in the cover letter. One way to do this is to make sure your letter is completely free of errors. The tone of your letter should be more personal than that of the résumé. However, keep your letter clear and direct, because most employers don't have time to read long, rambling letters.

A résumé describes your background concisely and somewhat impersonally. A cover letter allows you to add details about your background in a more relaxed and personal way. Each time you submit a résumé, you should include a cover letter.

Résumés are written for specific positions, but not often for specific employers. A cover letter, on the other hand, allows you to point out how your qualifications will make you an asset to a specific employer's company. Although you might send a copy of the same résumé to several potential employers, each cover letter should be unique, written especially for that company.

Cover letters must include all the parts of a business letter: the heading, inside address, salutation, body, closing, your signature, and your typed name.

GATHERING INFORMATION

Before you start writing a cover letter, find out as much as you can about the employer and the position you're seeking. Many employers have Web pages that describe their organizations. You might find out that the company is developing a new product, upgrading its services, or facing a challenging competitor. Then you can use your cover letter to show you are familiar with the company and its goals. Potential employers will be impressed that you made an effort to learn about them.

If possible, you also need to find the name of the person at the company who will review your résumé and cover letter. You should address your cover letter to this person. He or she might be the supervisor of the human resources department or the manager of the department where you would work. To find out this person's name and title, call the company and ask. Be sure to get the correct spellings.

If you cannot find out the name of a specific person, use clues from the ad to write a salutation similar to one of these:

> Dear Human Resources Department:
> Dear Supervisor, Accounts Payable:
> Dear Manager of Support Services:
> Dear Hiring Coordinator:

ORGANIZING YOUR LETTER

Your cover letter should include about four paragraphs. In the first paragraph, state the specific job you are seeking and how you found out about it. Be sure to include the job title; writing "I am applying for the job you advertised in Sunday's newspaper" will not be sufficient if the company has advertised more than one job opening. By expecting the reader to guess which job you want, you are giving him or her a reason to eliminate you from consideration for any position.

The next two paragraphs are the heart of your letter. Here you will explain how you meet the requirements in the newspaper ad or Internet listing and why you are the person to hire for this opening.

Explain how you meet the job requirements. Study the position requirements carefully. Think about how your background and knowledge match those requirements. Your cover letter is an opportunity to sell yourself, so add details to show why you're qualified for this specific job. For example, if the job opening calls for an "articulate" person, describe your experience on the debate team or as a telephone surveyor for a volunteer group.

Emphasize ways you can contribute to the position, not what you expect to gain from the job. Avoid this type of statement: "I know this job could help me develop my abilities and lead to a challenging position in management." This comment suggests that you are more focused on what the company can do for you than on what you can offer the company.

Do not apologize for being unable to meet a requirement in an ad. Describe only the relevant experience, training, or abilities you do have. The requirements listed in ads describe ideal candidates for the job, but many companies are willing to be flexible if you can meet most of their needs.

Show you're the person for the job. You might also be a valuable employee because of special courses you have taken at school, your volunteer work, or your natural abilities. Use your cover letter to show that you are familiar with the employer and have these unique qualifications but be careful not to overstate your abilities. Employers are not eager to hire inexperienced applicants who believe they know everything.

In the last paragraph of your cover letter, ask for an interview and explain when you would be available for it. Then repeat your phone number, making it easy for the employer to call you.

If you are applying for a position in sales, where employees are expected to be somewhat aggressive, you might tell the employer that you will call in a few days to check on the status of your application. However, most employers don't welcome calls from job applicants, so it's usually best to wait for someone to call you.

COVER LETTER ESSENTIALS

- Write to a specific person.
- Name the title or number of the job you want.
- Explain how you meet the job requirements.
- Show why you're the person to hire.
- Ask for an interview.

WRITING THE LETTER

Getting Started

The next page shows a sample cover letter. Notice that it includes all the parts of a business letter.

754 Harbor View Drive
Wheaton, IL 98767
March 16, 1999

Joseph Simpkins, Personnel Director
Simpkins Publishing Company
72 Central Avenue
Wheaton, IL 98767

Dear Mr. Simpkins: [Write to a specific person.]

[Name the job you want and how you know about it.]

Please consider me for the summer internship (Job number 132-I) described in your Web site.

I am currently a senior at Robertson High School and plan to major in journalism at the University of Illinois this fall. I believe this makes me eligible for the internship. [Explain how you meet the job requirements.]

[Show your knowledge of the employer.] This past year I served as editor of our high school's weekly newspaper and often incorporated information from your paper's "Facts and Figures" column into my articles. During my journalism class, we often analyzed the techniques your staff used in both news stories and features. I would really appreciate an opportunity to help your staff gather information for their stories, proofread, and perhaps write some short articles.

[Explain specific ways you can contribute to the organization.]

[Ask for an interview.] Please call me for an interview any day after 3:00 P.M. I would be glad to bring my file of clippings from the school newspaper. I could begin the internship any time after graduation, which is on June 3. I look forward to hearing from you.

Sincerely,

Karen Carbone

Karen Carbone

Another Kind of Cover Letter

Many job openings are advertised, but most are not. Unadvertised jobs are called the "hidden job market." You find out about these openings through friends, family members, neighbors, and school staff. Just explain what type of position you want; then ask them to let you know if they hear about an opening that might suit you.

Your cover letter will change somewhat if you are seeking an unadvertised position. You may have to convince the reader to create a job for you, or, with some luck, your qualifications may fit a job position that is vacant but has not yet been advertised.

Reprinted by permission of Sidney Harris

"HE MAY HAVE A PH.D. IN ELEMENTARY PARTICLE PHYSICS, BUT HE'S HAVING AN AWFUL LOT OF TROUBLE WITH THE APPLICATION FORM."

17.2 WRITING A RÉSUMÉ

As you enter the job market, sooner or later you will need a résumé. A résumé is a combination of carefully

COMPOSITION

selected information about you, presented as concisely and neatly as possible, with the goal of convincing an employer to invite you for an interview.

To write an effective résumé, think about how it will be used. Employers may receive hundreds—even thousands—of résumés. The human resources department, sometimes just one person, has to eliminate most of the résumés and choose a few promising people to interview. On the first pass, this person may spend less than twenty seconds scanning each résumé.

What kinds of résumés get eliminated immediately?

- *The messy ones.* Some people submit résumés that are hand-written or coated with correction fluid. Type yours on a typewriter or use a personal computer. If you spot a mistake, type or print your résumé again.
- *The long ones.* While you're in high school, one page offers enough space to describe your accomplishments. After you've been working for ten or more years, you might need two pages.
- *The ones that are hard to read.* Narrow margins, tiny printing, and no white space discourage the résumé reader and often lead to rejection.
- *The flashy ones.* Unless you're applying to be a model or a perfomer, don't include a picture of yourself. Neon-colored paper or "cute" graphics will get noticed, but they won't usually get you an interview.

The résumé on the next page is simple and effective. You can place information in other positions, of course, as long as your résumé is still easy to skim. Make sure it looks neat, has plenty of white space, and is free of typing or spelling errors. The questions and answers following the sample résumé will help you further polish your own résumé.

Jeremy Jacobs
903 East Oak Street
Aurora, IL 98765
Phone: 312-555-2345
E-Mail: jjacobs@email.com

Include your full name, address, phone number, and e-mail address.

Objective   To obtain a position as Head Lifeguard

Qualification Summary

- Gained knowledge and skills as a lifeguard and as a supervisor during the past two summers

- Certified Water Safety Instructor

Experience

Summers, 1998 and 1997

HIGH LAKES POOLS, Aurora, Illinois
Lifeguard
In 1997, recognized by the city for saving a child's life. In 1998, supervised two other guards.

Be consistent. For example, if you type one company name in capital letters, type them all that way.

7/97-6/98

AURORA COMMUNITY CENTER, Aurora, Illinois
Swim Coach (volunteer position)
Coached a team of nine- and ten-year-olds to a city championship.

Line up the columns vertically.

Education   Completed my junior year at Westfield High School.
Selected for Honor Roll three of four grading periods.
Captain of school swim team

Certifications   Certified as a Water Safety Instructor and lifeguard; also certified in standard first aid and CPR.

Make your headings stand out and use any headings that make sense.

References Available

COMPOSITION

Do I have to include an objective?

An objective is often used to indicate the kind of job you are seeking. Some objectives are too vague, such as this one: "A challenging position with a progressive company that will allow me to advance in my field." Prospective employers will look for résumés from people who have a clearer idea of the job they want.

In place of an objective, you might start your résumé by simply naming your career field, or you could write a qualification summary. This short section at the beginning of your résumé sums up what you offer in several bullet points. Here you can point out your strengths, including those you developed as a volunteer, without tying them directly to a job you've held. A qualification summary can highlight the skills you have, even though you might not have much employment experience.

Should I put my education or my work experience next?

If you have taken courses that will help you on the job you're applying for, put your education first and list those courses. If you have some work experience in the field in which you're applying, put your employment history first.

How can I best describe my work experience?

Start with the job you have now or your most recent job and work backwards. Include the employer, its city and state, your job title, and the dates you worked there. Make it easy for the reader to see at a glance where you've worked and what you did there.

Under each position, don't just list the responsibilities anyone would have in that job. Explain what you did that made you a valuable employee. For example, if you work for a fast-food restaurant, the reader can guess that you take orders and cook burgers. Instead, name any promotions or awards you have received. Do you supervise other workers?

Are you responsible for opening or closing the restaurant? Mention any skills or knowledge you have gained that will help you do the job for which you're applying.

Subjects are not used in good job descriptions. Each statement starts with a verb, so choose a strong verb that will add strength to your résumé. For example:

Weak:	Was asked to balance the cash drawer
Strong:	Balanced the cash drawer
Weak:	Was a clown at children's parties
Strong:	Established my own company to provide entertainment at children's parties

By permission of Mell Lazarus and Creators Syndicate.

Should I explain why I quit a job?

No! Leave that for the interview and don't bring it up then unless the interviewer asks.

Should I include my volunteer experience, hobbies, or interests?

No—if they are common and likely to appear on many of the résumés the employer receives. Yes—if they have helped prepare you for the new job or they show that you are a well-rounded person who contributes to the community. You can combine paid and unpaid work under a heading such as Experience; you can include hobbies and interests under the heading Personal.

Can I exaggerate a little?

No! If you didn't increase the sales where you work all by yourself, don't claim credit for it. Instead, you could say "Significantly contributed to a 10 percent increase in sales." If you don't actually supervise the other people on your team, don't say you do. Truth has a way of coming out, especially during job interviews. Exaggeration can cost you a job.

Should I list references on my résumé?

You can, if you are sure they will help you make a good impression on the employer. Alternatively, you can take a list of references with you to your interview. In any case, make sure you ask your references ahead of time for permission to list their names.

As you write your résumé, select information about your experience, education, and skills that will convince the résumé reader to call you to set up an interview.

17.3 MAKING A PRESENTATION

Most people are required to give an oral presentation at some point in their lives. You have probably already given several yourself, as book reports in English class or oral reports in social studies class. After you graduate, you might be asked to make oral presentations in college or other training programs. When you begin working, you might help a team prepare a presentation for another department or for a client. Confidence in giving oral presentations will get you noticed and appreciated in the workplace.

Knowing how to plan an effective oral presentation will give you this confidence. Here are the steps you will learn in this lesson:

1. Consider your topic and your purpose.
2. Analyze your audience.
3. Choose the form of your presentation.
4. Decide what to say.
5. Organize your presentation.
6. Create visuals for a multimedia presentation.
7. Practice giving your presentation.
8. Look professional and speak effectively.

CONSIDER YOUR TOPIC AND YOUR PURPOSE

First, find out what the audience needs to know about the topic. Is your goal to inform them? If so, you might need to narrow a topic that is too broad. Perhaps your purpose is to persuade the audience to change their opinions on your topic. To succeed, you must analyze the audience's needs and viewpoints so you can motivate them to act or, at least, to think differently about the topic.

If you're not thoroughly familiar with the topic, do some research. Look for information at the library and on the Internet. The more you know about your topic, the easier it will be to narrow it and to organize your presentation. You must feel confident and knowledgeable about your topic to make an effective presentation.

ANALYZE YOUR AUDIENCE

Consider how your audience might respond to your topic. Audience members who are familiar with the topic might already have strong opinions on it. You will need to respect their opinions, even if you intend to convince your audience to adopt a new point of view. If the audience have heard this topic many times before, you might have to think of a new approach to rekindle their interest.

If the topic is relatively new to this audience, consider the following:

- What, if anything, do the members of the audience already know about your topic?
- Can you use technical terms? If so, will you have to define them?
- What is the audience's educational level?
- What interests or experiences do they have that will help them relate to this unfamiliar topic?
- How can you show them that the topic is important in their everyday lives?

In a work setting, you will also need to know whether your audience will be mostly co-workers, mostly management, or a combination of the two. Are your listeners the decision-makers or the ones who carry out decisions? Will they accept your recommendations, or will you have to support your arguments with statistics and experts' opinions?

Answering these questions will help you decide what your presentation should include to meet the audience's needs and to accomplish your own goals.

CHOOSE THE FORM OF YOUR PRESENTATION

Will your audience play an active or a passive role in your presentation? Here are two possible forms you may choose for your presentation:

A traditional speech or lecture In this approach, you provide information on a topic and answer questions from the audience afterward. This approach is often used because it is a direct way to share information. However, the audience has only a passive role: sitting and listening.

An interactive presentation This approach is more like a conversation and is effective with a smaller audience. You provide basic information and then ask the audience questions. Here are some possible goals for this type of presentation:

- to get the audience's feedback on an issue
- to convince the audience to act on an issue
- to help a group work together to solve a problem
- to encourage the audience to ask questions that will help them explore and understand the topic
- to guide the audience to see how they can apply a certain concept or technique in their everyday lives

Interactive presentations get the audience more involved, but the presenter must be able to keep discussions on track and quickly adjust the questions to meet the audience's needs and interests.

DECIDE WHAT TO SAY

Learning more about your topic and analyzing your audience will help you decide what to include in your presentation. The length of your presentation will also help determine the amount of information you include. Instead of saying a little about many aspects of the topic, focus on two or three main points that will be meaningful to your audience. Your audience will not remember lots of facts and statistics, but they are likely to remember two or three points if you offer interesting examples and solid evidence to support them.

"'What I Did Last Summer,' by Scott Sweningen, as told to Samantha Gerhart."

COMPOSITION

ORGANIZE YOUR PRESENTATION

Plan an opening that will grab the audience's attention and introduce your topic. Here are some possibilities:

Tell a story You may want to begin with a true story about yourself or others but make sure it won't embarrass anyone. Instead you could tell a story that "sounds true" and helps you introduce your presentation. For example: "I had a friend once who was a slave. He was a slave to his anger. It controlled everything he did. . . ."

Ask a question Get the audience thinking about the topic by asking a question. For example, you might ask, "When was the last time you felt really angry?"

Offer a surprising fact Get the audience's attention with a fact that challenges their ideas. For example: "You make yourself angry. No one else can do it; only you have that power!"

Tell a joke Tell a joke only if you're good at it. Choose one that relates to your topic and make sure it does not insult any person or group of people. Most libraries have books of jokes written especially for speakers to use. After you choose a joke, try it on friends first to see if they think it's funny, doesn't insult anyone, and isn't too silly. Telling a joke can relax both the audience and you, but you do risk embarrassing yourself if the joke flops.

After deciding how to begin your presentation, make an outline that organizes your main points into a logical order. Be sure to include examples, quotations, or statistics to back up each point. Here are some organizational patterns:

- **Chronological:** Explain a series of events or steps in the order they occurred.

- **Priority:** Persuade your audience by arranging the reasons they should do something from least to most important.
- **Problem/Cause/Solution:** Describe a problem, explain why it happened (or will happen), and offer a solution (which usually involves some action by the audience).
- **Compare and Contrast:** Show how two events, people, or objects are similar and different; use this organization to help the audience understand an unfamiliar concept or to convince them that one course of action is better than another. A variation on this organization is the pro/con pattern, in which you give both the advantages and the disadvantages of a certain action.
- **Categories:** Divide the topic into categories and explain each one. For example, you might use this approach to explain several anger management techniques.

The ending of your presentation is as important as the beginning. Here are two effective endings:

- Summarize your main points and then go back to your opening statement. Finish your story, repeat your question, or refer to the fact or joke you used. Going back to the beginning gives the audience a sense of closure.
- Repeat your strongest point and then ask the audience to do something specific in response, such as trying a technique that same day.

After organizing your presentation into an outline, write the main points on separate note cards. On each note card, include any important details you want to mention, along with any quotations or statistics you think will be effective. Use words and phrases, not sentences. You are not going to read these cards aloud, just use them to remind yourself of what you planned to say. Number the cards so you can keep them in order during your presentation.

COMPOSITION

Four responses to anger

1. turning it inward – "It's my fault."

2. avoiding it – leaving the room

3. blaming others – "It's their fault."

4. resolving the problem – identifying what's wrong and making changes

CREATE VISUALS FOR A MULTIMEDIA PRESENTATION

Multimedia simply means "involving several media or channels of communication." Speaking is one channel of communication, and visuals are another. Some people prefer the auditory channel and like to listen to new information, while others prefer the visual channel and would rather read or view new information. This second group will certainly appreciate your use of visuals.

Visuals explain your points and help keep the audience interested. A series of visuals can serve as an outline for your presentation and reduce the number of note cards you need. Visuals have two other important benefits: they give the audience something to look at besides you, and they provide something for you to do with your hands! In addition, using visuals makes you look professional and well organized.

Visuals can be as simple as a list printed on poster board or as complex as animated computer graphics. Visuals can include charts, tables, graphs, maps, models, samples, videotapes, drawings, photographs, or diagrams. They can be presented on handouts, poster board, or overhead slides or transparencies. They might be created by hand or by computer.

When designing visuals

- Explain only one point per visual. Keep the visual simple so your audience can grasp the point right away. If necessary, explain a complicated point with a series of visuals or with overlays on a basic transparency.

- Give every visual an informative title that stresses the point you want to make. For example, instead of "Causes of Anger," you could use "Stress Is a Major Cause of Anger."

- Use a font with 14-point type or larger so your audience can read labels and explanations. Do not use all upper case. IT'S MUCH HARDER TO READ!

- Don't try to include every detail of your presentation in the visuals, just the main points.

- Avoid clutter, such as too many colors, fonts, clip art graphics, or borders. Three colors and two fonts are enough. Choose art that closely relates to your topic. You might use the same border on all your visuals to tie them together.

- Don't forget to proofread. Otherwise, a transparency might display a misspelled word or other error in three-inch letters.

PRESENTATION TIP

Keep your visuals simple; use
- one idea for each visual
- no more than 5–7 lines of type per visual
- no more than 6–8 words per line
- no more than 35 words total

COMPOSITION

Using Computer Software

Many software packages have been developed to aid in school and business presentations. Several programs can create slides and transmit them directly from a computer to an overhead projector. They allow you to make words, paragraphs, or graphics appear and disappear on the slide. You can also add sound effects and fade the picture between slides. Using a chart or graph, you can make lines or bars "grow," or you can separate one bar into several bars.

Evaluate your visuals by looking at them from the audience's point of view. Are they
- easy to understand?
- interesting?
- relevant?
- neat and uncluttered?

Using some computer programs, you can design visuals that a service center, such as a camera store, can convert into 35-mm slides for use in a projector. You can also use computer programs to design overhead transparencies or handouts for the audience. Some programs allow you to write notes to use during your presentation, with the appropriate slide or overhead printed right on the page.

Using Visuals

- Before using the visuals you've prepared, check your equipment. Check it again just before the presentation to make sure it works. A program that worked at home may not work in another setting. A power surge may have scrambled the computer. The bulb on the over-head projector may have burned out. Be ready with another way to share the information in case of disaster.

- Don't show a visual until you're ready to talk about it. Then display it until you are ready for the next visual. Turning equipment on and off can annoy an audience. Glaring white screens can also be distracting.
- Face your audience and stand to one side of the visual. Do explain your visuals but don't read them to the audience.

PRACTICE GIVING YOUR PRESENTATION

Use your visuals as you rehearse your speech so that you will feel comfortable with them. After your opening, tell the audience the points you will cover to let them know what to expect. Practice making smooth transitions between your points so your presentation will flow well.

Ask a few friends or family members to listen to your presentation and give you feedback on both the content and your delivery. Instead, you might prefer to videotape yourself and do your own critique. Watch and listen for times when your words were difficult to understand or you didn't clearly explain what you meant. Were any points a little dry and boring? If so, find more interesting examples to liven them up.

Check your timing and make adjustments if your presentation is too long or short. Remember that you might speak more quickly in front of a larger audience. Be careful not to practice so many times that you memorize your presentation. You want it to be fresh and interesting for you and the audience.

LOOK PROFESSIONAL AND SPEAK EFFECTIVELY

As you know, a carefully planned presentation can be ruined by a panicked speaker. But if you feel nervous before

COMPOSITION

speaking to a group, congratulations! You're just like ninety-nine percent of speakers. That doesn't mean you won't do well. Admit to yourself that you're feeling a little jittery and use that energy to do your best.

Getting Ready

Get a good night's sleep and arrive at the location at least a half hour ahead of time so you don't have to rush. To prevent hiccups, avoid carbonated beverages for several hours before your presentation. Also, don't drink any more caffeine than you usually do.

To help yourself relax just before the presentation, take several deep breaths. Next, tighten and relax your muscles, working from your toes to the top of your head. Then take a few more deep breaths for good measure. Finally, gather your notecards in your hand and take your place, with your visuals waiting for you. Pause and smile at the audience. Remember that they want you to do well. Don't apologize for being nervous. Begin!

Using Your Body Effectively

- Stand up straight, but in a relaxed way.
- Maintain eye contact with the audience. Pretend you are talking to just one person but focus on a different person in a different area of the audience every minute or so. (According to several studies, audiences believe that speakers who look at them are better informed, more experienced, friendlier, and more sincere than speakers who do not make eye contact.)
- Use gestures when they're appropriate. They help show your enthusiasm and interest in your topic.
- Move around. Unless you're standing on a stage or must stay close to a microphone, try walking among the audience members. It will bring you closer to them, physically and emotionally.

Using Your Voice Effectively

- Speak clearly and slowly. Let your voice rise and fall naturally, as if you were having a conversation. Try not to rush.
- Speak loudly enough to reach people in the back of the room. However, if you're using a microphone, let it carry your voice. Don't shout.
- Show enthusiasm in your voice. Get excited about your topic. Your audience will "catch" your excitement because enthusiasm is contagious.

PUTTING IT ALL TOGETHER

Now you know how to do well on your next presentation. If you still feel nervous about it, imagine the worst thing that could happen. Here are some disasters that might come to your mind:

- You'll forget what you were going to say. (No, you won't. Your notecards and your visuals will keep you on track.)
- You'll mispronounce a word. (If a word is giving you problems, check a dictionary, ask someone how to say it, or use another word.)
- Your presentation will be boring. (Not after all the thought you've put into it! You know your audience and your topic well. You're going to start with an interesting story, and you've found good examples to support your main points. You have also created excellent visuals.)

So when *is* your next presentation? Are you looking forward to it now? You will as soon as you follow the steps you just learned. Remember: If you have prepared and carefully considered your audience's needs, you will be an impressive, effective speaker.

Part Four

● ● ● ● ● ● ● ● ● ● ● ● ●

Resources

Knowledge is of two kinds: we know a subject ourselves, or we know where we can find information on it.

—Samuel Johnson

Chapter 18

The Library
or Media Center

• • • • • • • • • • • • • •

Although you've probably been in a library, you might not realize all the resources the library has to offer or how to find them. This chapter will guide you through the library and help you understand how and where to find what you need.

CIRCULATION DESK

At the circulation desk, you'll find a librarian who can answer your questions and check out your books. In addition to a circulation desk, some libraries have computers you can use to check out your own books. Larger libraries might station additional librarians at many of the following locations.

CATALOG

A computer or card catalog will tell you which books are available in the library and where to find them. You'll learn more about using both kinds of catalogs on pages 535–541.

STACKS

The stacks, or rows of book shelves, are called the "adult section" in some libraries, but you don't have to be an adult to use these books. The stacks are usually divided into sections for fiction (novels and short stories that are works of the imagination) and nonfiction (books based on fact about subjects such as history and science).

YOUNG ADULT AND CHILDREN'S SECTION

Young readers, including high school students, can find excellent resources in the young adult and children's section. Fiction, nonfiction, and biographies are usually grouped separately, with picture books for very young readers in their own section. All of these books are listed in the library's computer or card catalog.

REFERENCE AREA

The reference area might include encyclopedias, dictionaries, almanacs, yearbooks, atlases, and other reference materials. Books in this area can be used only in the library. By not allowing people to check out these books, the library ensures that all reference materials will always be available for anyone who needs to consult them.

NEWSPAPERS AND PERIODICALS

In the newspaper and periodical section, you can read local newspapers as well as papers from major cities in the United States and perhaps from other countries. You can also browse through periodicals, which include magazines and journals. You probably cannot check out the currrent issues, but you can usually take older issues home to read. The young adult and children's section might have its own periodicals area. You'll learn more about finding specific articles in newspapers and periodicals on pages 547–549.

AUDIO-VISUAL MATERIALS

The audio-visual section of the library may stock software programs, audiocassettes and compact discs (CDs) of your favorite music, books on tape, videos, and slides for you to borrow and enjoy at home.

COMPUTER AREA

Many of today's libraries offer the use of personal computers for research on the Internet or for writing reports and papers. You may have to reserve a computer ahead of time, and the library might set a time limit on your use of it. Many library computer areas also have software programs for you to use there, such as a résumé-writing program, an accounting program, or even a program to teach you how to type. For a small fee per page, you can usually print the articles you've located or the papers you've written.

STUDY AREAS

Many libraries now have desks or small rooms set aside for quiet study. You might need to reserve them ahead of time.

SPECIAL COLLECTIONS

Some libraries set aside a special room or section for collections of rare books, manuscripts, and items of local interest, including works by local students.

The size of some university libraries can be pretty intimidating to first-year students.

Using Print Resources

● ● ● ● ● ● ● ● ● ● ● ● ● ●

Imagine how frustrating it would be if you had to walk up and down the stacks in a library, looking for a book that might—or might not—be anywhere on the shelves! To make life easier, libraries use cataloging systems to keep track of what's available and arrange books on the shelves according to their content.

19.1 UNDERSTANDING CATALOGING SYSTEMS

Whether you want information on a particular subject, books by a certain author, or a specific book, the catalog will help you find what you're looking for. Many libraries now use computerized catalogs, but some still rely on paper card catalogs. You should be able to use both kinds of tools. Then no matter what library you enter, its catalog will be at your service.

COMPUTER CATALOGS

Computer systems vary, so before you use one for the first time, read the instructions posted beside the computer or printed on the screen. Most catalog programs begin by asking whether you want to search by author, title, or subject. If you use the author's name, type the last name first, followed by a comma and the first name, as in *Johnson, Samuel.* (Some systems will allow you to type *Samuel Johnson* or even just *Johnson*, although in the latter case you'll have to search through a list of all the authors named Johnson to find the one you want.) If you search by title, enter the title but start with the first important word, ignoring *A, An,* and *The.* For a subject search, you'll use a **keyword,** a word or phrase that describes your topic. Whenever you search a computer database, including the Internet, to find books, articles, or other media, the keyword you choose will greatly affect the results you get.

Search TIP

1. **Be specific.** A general keyword, such as *animal,* will get you a long list of sources, sometimes called **matches** or **hits.** However, few of them will be helpful to you. If you use a more specific keyword, such as *dachshund,* you won't have to read screen after screen of possible sources, trying to find a few that might be helpful.

2. **Use Boolean search techniques,** which offer different ways to combine words. You can use these techniques to look for books in a computer catalog, to find articles in magazine databases (described later), or to locate information on the Internet (also described later).

Named for George Boole, a nineteenth-century English mathematician, Boolean techniques use the words *and, or, not,* and sometimes *near* or *adj.*

and: If you combine two keywords with *and* (such as *genetics and disorders)*, the computer will list only sources that contain both words. This kind of search results in far fewer hits, but a much higher percentage of them will relate to your topic. (Some programs use + in place of *and: genetics + disorders.)*

or: If you want information on either one of two related topics, link them with *or,* as in *alligators or crocodiles.* This technique tells the computer to conduct two searches at once.

not: To eliminate a category of information from a search, use *not.* For example, if you want information about genetic disorders but not Down's Syndrome, you can enter *genetic and disorders not Down.*

near *or* adj: Some computer programs allow you to use *near* or *adj* (adjacent) to locate sources, usually articles, that have two keywords used near each other. For example, you might use *genetics near laboratory* as your keywords. One program may list only those sources in which the keywords are within eight words of each other. Another program might allow the keywords to be fifteen words apart. This search technique has

RESOURCES

an advantage over linking words with *and,* a method that can generate a long list of articles in which both words appear but never in connection with each other.

Not all computer programs recognize Boolean techniques; some will treat *and, or, not, near,* or *adj* as part of your keyword/phrase. For some other computer programs, you must begin a Boolean search with *b/,* as in *b/genetics and experiments.*

3. **Use quotation marks.** Enclosing a phrase in quotation marks (for instance, *"experimenting with DNA"*) tells the computer to find every book or article with exactly those words.

4. **Try truncating.** If you **truncate,** or shorten, your keyword by using an asterisk (*), the computer will search for all words that begin with the letters before the asterisk. For example, using *experiment** as a keyword will tell the computer to list books or articles containing such words as *experiment, experimental, experimented, experimenting,* and *experiments.* By truncating your keyword, you make sure the computer doesn't overlook various forms of the word.

   You can also truncate when you aren't sure how to spell a word. For example, you could use *Azer** as a keyword if you couldn't remember how to spell Azerbaijan, a country in southeastern Europe.

5. **Use a "wildcard"** by inserting a question mark *(?)* into certain words. For example, if you aren't sure whether to use *woman* or *women,* enter *wom?n.*

Now that you know how to choose keywords, here is an example of their use. To use a computer catalog, you type in the author's name, the book title, or a keyword or phrase, and the screen will list any related sources available at that library. Let's say you type the keywords *credit card safety*. The screen will then show you a list similar to the one below. If the catalog program is connected to a printer, you could print this list.

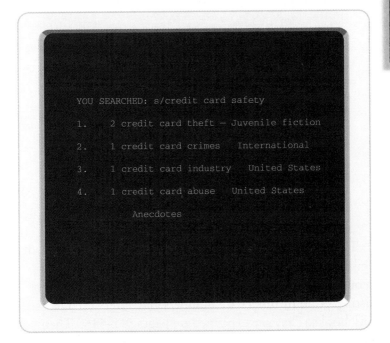

```
YOU SEARCHED: s/credit card safety

1.    2 credit card theft — Juvenile fiction

2.    1 credit card crimes   International

3.    1 credit card industry   United States

4.    1 credit card abuse   United States

         Anecdotes
```

The first listing (1) tells you that the library has two books about credit card theft in the juvenile fiction category. Books listed in this category will be novels or collections of short stories that are appropriate for young readers. The second listing (2) tells you that the library has one book about international credit card crimes. This book isn't marked fiction, so it's nonfiction; it isn't marked juvenile, so it's for adults. To find out more about this book, enter the number of its listing, 2. The next screen might give you the following information.

CALL NO: 364.163 DAV

AUTHOR: Davisson, Judith

MAIN TITLE: Identities for Rent: how
international thieves can be you for a day
/ by Judith Davisson.

PUBLISHER: New York: Atheneum Books, c1995

LOCATION	STATUS	UNITS
1. ADULT NON-FICTION	Available	364.163 DAV

The status column indicates that no one has checked out this book, so it should be filed on a shelf. To find it, you would write down its call number, shown at the top of the listing. (**Call numbers** are numbers and letters used to classify books. They are explained on pages 541–546.) Then you would go to the location listed (the adult non-fiction stacks), find the shelf with call numbers between 360 and 370, and look down the rows for the book marked 364.163 DAV. The books are in numerical and alphabetical order.

If someone had checked out this book, the status column would state the date when it was due back at the library. If the library had several copies of the book, the status of each copy would be stated. Some catalog entries also include the number of pages in the book; whether it has illustrations, an index, a glossary, or a bibliography; and what kind of medium it is, such as a book or videotape. Many entries list additional headings you could enter into the catalog as keywords to find more information about the same topic.

The computer instructions will tell you how to move forward and backward as you search through the library's listings. For example, you might enter *ns* (next screen) or *f* (forward) to see more of a listing. To go backward, you might enter *ps* (previous screen) or *b* (backward).

CARD CATALOGS

Card catalogs are stored in long, narrow drawers. The drawers hold two or three small cards for every book in the library, arranged alphabetically. Fiction books have two cards each, one listing the book by its author and one listing it by its title. Nonfiction books have three cards each, listing the book by its author, title, and subject.

The cards list the same information as the computer catalog, although they don't, of course, tell you whether someone has checked out the book. A library may divide its card catalog into two categories: subject cards and author/title cards. Often cards are cross-referenced, listing other available books on the same subject or a related topic. A card catalog might also have separate cross-reference cards, filed alphabetically and listing related topics.

19.2 LOCATING BOOKS

The purpose of call numbers is to help you locate books. Most school and community libraries use call numbers based on the Dewey decimal system, while many college

and university libraries use call numbers based on the
Library of Congress system.

DEWEY DECIMAL SYSTEM

The Dewey decimal system, created in 1876 by a librarian
named Melvil Dewey, divides nonfiction books into the ten
categories listed below.

DEWEY DECIMAL CATEGORIES OF NONFICTION

NUMBERS	CATEGORY	EXAMPLES OF SUBCATEGORIES
000-099	General Works	encyclopedias, bibliographies, newspapers, periodicals
100-199	Philosophy	ethics, psychology, personality
200-299	Religion	theology, mythology, bibles
300-399	Social Sciences	sociology, education, government, law, economics
400-499	Language	dictionaries, foreign languages, grammar guides
500-599	Sciences	chemistry, astronomy, biology, mathematics
600-699	Technology	medicine, engineering, business
700-799	Arts	painting, music, theater, sports
800-899	Literature	poetry, plays, essays
900-999	History	ancient history, biography, geography, travel

Let's say you wanted to know more about Samuel Johnson,
a seventeenth-century British author and dictionary writer.
You would begin by entering his name as a keyword in a
computer catalog or by looking under the *J*s in a card catalog.

The library might have many books about Johnson and his work, but the call numbers of these books could fall into different categories on the Dewey decimal chart, depending on their content. For example, one book listed by a computer catalog is *The Samuel Johnson Encyclopedia* by Pat Rogers. The 800 category, Literature, is broken down into subcategories; for example, 810 is American literature and 820 is English literature. Samuel Johnson was an English author, so this book has a call number of 820.

The more specific the topic, the more specific the call number. Some call numbers have decimals added to make them even more specific. We saw this earlier in *Identities for Rent*, which had a call number of 364.163 DAV.

Many libraries add the first three letters of the author's last name to the call number, in this case DAV for Davisson. Thus, in some libraries, the call number for *The Samuel Johnson Encyclopedia* would be 820 ROG (for Rogers).

Let's say our library also has a book titled *The Making of Johnson's Dictionary, 1746–1773* by Allen Reddick. Since this book is more about language than about Johnson, it's classified in the 400 category, Language, with a call number of 423. Another book is titled *Dr. Johnson's London,* by Dorothy Marshall. This historical account falls in the 900 category, History, so it has a call number of 942.1.

Research TIP

All libraries that use the Dewey decimal system use the same chart to assign call numbers to books. However, two librarians may put the same book into different categories. For this reason, the same book may have different call numbers in different libraries.

Biographies Our library has another book called *Everybody's Boswell: the Life of Samuel Johnson* by James Boswell. It has a call number of *B*, which stands for biography. Many libraries group their biographies together, with one biography section in the adult stacks and one in the young adult and children's section. Biographies are shelved alphabetically according to the last name of the subject of the book. *Everybody's Boswell: The Life of Samuel Johnson* will be in the *J* section of the biographies.

The library also has another biography of Johnson: *The Personal History of Samuel Johnson* by Christopher Hibbert. Two books about the same person will be shelved alphabetically by the author's last name. So Boswell's book will be before Hibbert's book in the *J* section of the biographies.

Fiction Most libraries that use the Dewey decimal system identify fiction with the call number *F* or *Fic.* The second line of the call number consists of the first three letters of the author's name or of the author's entire last name. Fiction is shelved alphabetically by the authors' last names. Books by the same author are shelved alphabetically by the first word in each title (not counting *A, An,* and *The*). Many public libraries have separate sections for some categories of fiction, such as mysteries or science fiction. In that case, usually a mark or label on the book's spine shows its inclusion on these special shelves. Within the mystery or science fiction section, books are shelved alphabetically by author's last name.

Reference Books Reference books, such as encyclopedias and current yearbooks, have an *R* or *Ref* preceding their call numbers. This label will alert you that you cannot check out these sources and must use them in the library. An *OV* or another symbol added to a call number indicates that the book is oversized and kept in a section of the library with taller shelves. (Ask the librarian where this section is.)

LIBRARY OF CONGRESS SYSTEM

The Library of Congress system divides books into twenty-one categories, each represented by a letter as shown in the chart below. Like the Dewey decimal system, the Library of Congress system has subcategories, which are identified by a second letter. For example, N is the category for fine arts. You would look under NA for books about architecture, NB for sculpture, ND for painting, and so on. Numbers added to the letter combinations identify more specific categories.

LIBRARY OF CONGRESS CATEGORIES

LETTER	CATEGORY	LETTER	CATEGORY
A	General Works	N	Fine Arts
B	Philosophy and Religion	P	Language and Literature
C–F	History	Q	Science
G	Geography and Anthropology	R	Medicine
H	Social Sciences	S	Agriculture
J	Political Science	T	Technology
K	Law	U	Military Science
L	Education	V	Naval Science
M	Music	Z	Bibliography and Library Science

In one library using the Library of Congress system, Pat Rogers' book, *The Samuel Johnson Encyclopedia,* has a call number of PR 3532.R64. *P* represents the general category of Literature, while *R* indicates a work by a British author.

The second *R* in the call number is from the author's name, Rogers.

Note that in the Library of Congress system, biographies are not filed separately but with the other books. Therefore, the call numbers of the biographies for Johnson begin with *PR*, indicating a British author.

FINDING INFORMATION IN NONFICTION BOOKS

Being familiar with the content and purpose of the parts of books will help you quickly determine whether a source will be useful to you. Not every book contains all the sections described below.

Information about a book

To find information about a book, check the following parts:

The **title page** contains the book title, author's name, and usually the publisher.

The **copyright page**, which is usually printed on the back of the title page, gives the publication or copyright date. Check the copyright date to determine how current the information is.

The **table of contents** lists the main topics covered to help you decide whether the book has the information you're seeking.

The **foreword**, **introduction**, or **preface**, which is written by the author or an expert in the same field, may explain the purpose of the book or the author's outlook on the subject.

Information in a book

To find information in a book, check the sections below:

The **index** lists alphabetically the people, places, events, and other significant topics mentioned in the book and gives the pages where you can find references to them.

The **glossary** lists terms in the book alphabetically and defines them, taking into account the intended readers. (Books for young children define basic terms; those for adults define terms that would be unfamiliar to most adult readers.)

The **bibliography** suggests additional research sources that are appropriate for the intended readers of the book. It may also include the sources of the information in the book.

The **appendix** contains additional information related to the book, such as maps, charts, illustrations, or graphs.

The **afterword** or **epilogue** is used by some authors to make a final statement about the book, discuss implications, or offer additional findings.

19.3 LOCATING ARTICLES IN NEWSPAPERS AND OTHER PERIODICALS

If you need current information from newspapers, magazines, or journals, the two tools described below may make your search easier.

COMPUTER DATABASES

Many libraries subscribe to databases holding collections of magazine, journal, and newspaper articles that you can access using the library computers. Most of these databases allow you to search by topic, by type of publication, or by specific publication. Some programs also allow you to select the years you want to search. You might choose to browse through all the magazines or all the newspapers in the database that cover a certain period of time, or you could narrow your search to a specific magazine or newspaper, such as the *New York Times.* Some databases allow you to review the table of contents of one issue of a magazine and read any of the articles that interest you.

If you enter a keyword that describes your topic, the database will list the title of each article on that topic along with the author, the publication, the date, and a short description of the article. You can select any titles that seem especially relevant and read either a short summary or the whole article on the computer screen. For a small fee, you can print a copy of articles that you want to take home with you.

What kinds of articles you will find depends on the database you use. If you search using the keywords *genetic disorders,* for example, one database might list articles on this subject from publications such as *Time, Newsday, Rocky Mountain Press,* and *USA Today.* If you enter the same keywords in a more academically oriented database, you might find articles from the *Journal of the National Cancer Institute* and *Biological Bulletin.* Don't check just one database and assume you've seen all the articles that are available.

READERS' GUIDE TO PERIODICAL LITERATURE

Not every library can afford to subscribe to computer databases, but nearly every library stocks the paper edition of *Readers' Guide to Periodical Literature.* This guide includes the titles of articles from nearly two hundred magazines and journals, with both subjects and authors listed alphabetically and cross-referenced. It's also available on a compact disc that you can search using a computer.

An update of the paper index is published every two weeks, and information about all the articles for the year is reprinted in a hardbound book at the end of the year. One index provided the following listing under *credit card crimes.*

CREDIT CARD CRIMES
> *See also*
> Credit cards—Security measures
> Identity theft
Are your theft fears overblown? S. Medintz. il
> *Money* v27 no6 p137-9 Je '98

RESOURCES

If the article "Are Your Theft Fears Overblown?" in *Money* sounds interesting, you must locate the June 1998 issue of this magazine and turn to page 137. (The *il* indicates that the article is illustrated.)

Libraries often keep issues for the current year in their newspapers and periodicals section. Issues from the previous one to five years may be stored in a different area, and older issues may be on **microfilm** (a roll or reel of film) or **microfiche** (a sheet of film). Both types of film must be inserted into special projectors that enlarge the images so you can read them. You can usually make photocopies of these articles to take home.

Not every book or article in the library or on its databases offers unbiased, valuable, reliable information. The following steps will help you avoid sources that offer irrelevant, outdated information or biased opinions.

1. **Evaluate the author of each source of information** and read any biographical information about him or her. Consider whether the author is an expert in a certain field or simply someone who has opinions about it.

2. **Evaluate the information itself,** starting with whether it is directly related to your topic. If it's only loosely related and you try to include it in your report, your work may seem unorganized and disjointed.

3. **Evaluate the author's reasoning.** Are the "facts" in a source actually unsupported opinions or exaggerations? Does the author seem to make too many assumptions? Does he or she overgeneralize from one situation to another?

4. **Check the publication date.** Are certain statistics now out of date? Is it likely that the findings have been contradicted by more recent research? Information on many topics, such as Mark Twain's childhood, may be the same whether it was published last week or twenty years ago. However, you must use up-to-date information when discussing topics that are still being researched or debated.

5. **Gather information** on the same topic from several sources. This way, you'll be more likely to become familiar with different opinions on the issue or topic. Then compare and contrast facts from each source. If three sources agree and one disagrees, the latter source may be mistaken—unless it's more current than the other sources.

19.4 USING OTHER REFERENCE SOURCES

GENERAL REFERENCE SOURCES

General reference sources are easy to locate and easy to use. They also provide detailed information on thousands of topics. Following are some excellent examples of these sources.

TYPE OF REFERENCE	EXAMPLES
General Encyclopedias These encyclopedias usually consist of many volumes. Subjects are arranged alphabetically, with an index and cross-referencing to help you find related topics. Many encyclopedia publishers offer yearly updates.	*World Book Encyclopedia* *Encyclopædia Britannica* *Collier's Encyclopedia* *Grolier Encyclopedia* *Encarta Encyclopedia* (Some encyclopedias are also available on compact discs; *Encarta Encyclopedia* is available only on a CD-ROM. CD-ROMs are described in Accessing Electronic Resources, page 569.)
Specialized Encyclopedias Each of these references focuses on a certain subject. Most provide specialized information, while some, such as *Books in Print,* tell you where to look for the information you seek. You might be surprised at the number of specialized encyclopedias that are available.	*Encyclopedia of World Art* *Van Nostrand's Scientific Encyclopedia* *Encyclopedia of World Crime* *Encyclopedia of the Opera* *Encyclopedia of the Third Reich* *Encyclopedia of Vitamins, Minerals, and Supplements* *Encyclopedia of Western Movies* *Encyclopedia of the Geological Sciences* *Books in Print*
Almanacs and Yearbooks These references are published frequently to provide up-to-date facts and statistics.	*Information Please Almanac* *World Almanac and Book of Facts* *Guinness Book of Records* *Statistical Abstract of the United States*
Atlases Atlases can be historical or current; they contain maps and statistics about countries and continents, climates, exports and imports, and the spread of world cultures, among other topics.	*Hammond World Atlas* *Cambridge Atlas of Astronomy* *Historical Atlas of the United States* *Goode's World Atlas* *National Geographic Atlas of the World* *Atlas of World Cultures*

TYPE OF REFERENCE, *continued*	EXAMPLES
Literary and Other Biographical Works These references include brief histories of notable people, living or dead, and are usually organized by fields instead of by names.	*Contemporary Authors* *American Authors 1600–1900* *European Authors 1000–1900* *Cyclopedia of Literary Characters* *Webster's New Biographical Dictionary* *Dictionary of American Biography* *Current Biography* *Biographical Dictionary of World War I (and II)* *Biographical Dictionary of Scientists (by field)* *Biographical Dictionary of Artists*
Government Documents Some large libraries hold the federal government documents that are available to the public. These pamphlets, journals, and reports offer information on agriculture, population, economics, and other topics.	*Monthly Catalog of United States Government Publications* *United States Government Publications Catalog* (both also available on compact discs and online)
Books of Quotations The indexes of these references help you look up quotations by certain people and by subject. The quotation from Samuel Johnson at the beginning of Part Four was taken from *The Harper Book of Quotations*. It was included in the category titled "Knowledge."	Bartlett's *Familiar Quotations* *The Harper Book of Quotations* *The Oxford Dictionary of Quotations* *The International Thesaurus of Quotations*

PLANNING LIBRARY RESEARCH

1. Start early. If you wait, other students may check out the sources you want to use.

2. Begin with the general reference sources rather than those that deal with specific fields or topics. A general source will offer an overview of your topic. It may

provide all the information you need, or it may guide you to additional sources.

3. List the sources you want to check and mark each one off your list after you've examined it so you won't check the same source twice.

4. Take careful notes and include the title, author, publisher, publication date, and page number of each source. (See page 481 for more information about compiling source cards.)

5. Talk with the librarian about your project, its purpose, its length, and the kinds of sources you have been asked to use. Describe what you've done so far and be ready with specific questions you'd like answered. Librarians can often suggest valuable references you haven't considered and perhaps help you locate them.

19.5 MAKING THE MOST OF WORD RESOURCES

When you're visiting a library's reference department, your goal is to go right to the information you need. Hunting aimlessly through the shelves and finding only irrelevant information is a waste of your time, no matter how interesting the information might be. This section will show you the uses and benefits of the different reference books that are available.

KINDS OF DICTIONARIES

Maybe you never stopped to think about it, but there are many kinds of dictionaries. Most of the dictionaries you've seen at school and in public libraries are general dictionaries, each including words from general English for a general reader. Then there are specialized dictionaries that define only words used in a particular field or profession, art or craft.

General Dictionaries

General dictionaries fall into these three categories:

School dictionaries contain fewer than 90,000 entries. They focus on common words and offer easy-to-understand definitions.

College dictionaries have about 150,000 entries. These references are used in homes, schools, and businesses. They answer most questions about spelling and definitions.

Unabridged dictionaries contain more than 250,000 entries and often fill several volumes. They are generally located in libraries and include extensive definitions and word histories.

Specialized Dictionaries

Specialized dictionaries list words used in a particular field. Following are some examples of the many kinds of specialized dictionaries:

Dictionary of Sports Idioms
Dictionary of Inventions and Discoveries
Facts on File Dictionary of 20th-Century Allusions
Dictionary of Italian Literature
Dictionary of Occupational Titles
Dictionary of Medical Folklore
Dictionary of Historic Nicknames

WORD ENTRIES IN GENERAL DICTIONARIES

Any one page in a dictionary probably *contains* a few thousand words, but it probably *defines* only a few dozen. A word entry discusses the meanings and the various forms of the entry word or headword, which is the word in bold-faced type that begins the word entry. When you look up a word in a dictionary, you are looking for its word entry.

Finding Words

Words are listed alphabetically in dictionaries, usually with no regard to hyphenated words or open compounds, as in this example:

soften
soft-focus
soft pedal
softshell

Words beginning with the abbreviation *St.* are listed as if the abbreviation were spelled out. So *St. Louis encephalitis* comes before the word *saintly.*

As you search for a word, don't forget to use the guide words at the top of every page. Guide words are the first and last entry words on the page. If the word you seek doesn't fall between these words alphabetically, it won't be on that page.

Search TIP

When you can't find the word you're looking for, consider these possibilities:

1. The word might have silent consonants, such as the *k* in *knight,* the *b* in *doubt,* or the *gh* in *blight.*

2. A consonant in the word might have an unusual spelling. For example, the *k* sound can be spelled with a *k (kindness), c (concur, lecture), ck (mackerel),* or *ch (chrysanthemum, chrome).*

3. A vowel in the word might have an unusual spelling, such as the first vowel sound in *beautiful* and *eerie.*

4. Your dictionary might not be large enough. An unusual word might not be listed in a school dictionary, for example.

Understanding Word Entries

Let's analyze a sample word entry to see what kinds of information it offers.

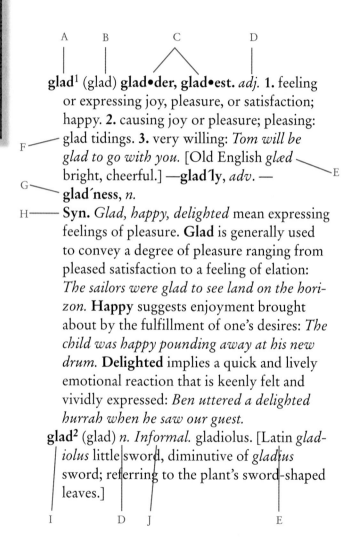

A   B   C   D

glad[1] (glad) **glad•der, glad•est.** *adj.* **1.** feeling or expressing joy, pleasure, or satisfaction; happy. **2.** causing joy or pleasure; pleasing: glad tidings. **3.** very willing: *Tom will be glad to go with you.* [Old English *glæd* bright, cheerful.] —**glad′ly,** *adv.* — **glad′ness,** *n.*

F

E

G

H——**Syn.** *Glad, happy, delighted* mean expressing feelings of pleasure. **Glad** is generally used to convey a degree of pleasure ranging from pleased satisfaction to a feeling of elation: *The sailors were glad to see land on the horizon.* **Happy** suggests enjoyment brought about by the fulfillment of one's desires: *The child was happy pounding away at his new drum.* **Delighted** implies a quick and lively emotional reaction that is keenly felt and vividly expressed: *Ben uttered a delighted hurrah when he saw our guest.*

glad[2] (glad) *n. Informal.* gladiolus. [Latin *gladiolus* little sword, diminutive of *gladius* sword; referring to the plant's sword-shaped leaves.]

I   D J   E

A. The Entry Word: The boldfaced word at the beginning of the entry is the entry word. If this word can be divided at the end of a line, the divisions will be indicated by a raised dot. The word *explicate,* for example, is written ex•pli•cate; this means you can divide the word after *ex* or after *expli.* In the sample word entry, *glad* has only one syllable and therefore cannot be divided. The entry word also tells you when a compound word should be written as one word (as in *handbag*), when it should be hyphenated (as in *hand-me-down*), and when it should be written as two words (as in *hash brown*).

B. Pronunciation: The correct way to say the word is shown immediately after the entry word and indicated in three ways: accent marks, phonetic symbols, and diacritical marks. In entry words with more than one syllable, accent marks indicate which syllable should be stressed. To check the meaning of the other marks and symbols, look at the pronunciation key that is usually located at the bottom of the page.

C. Inflected Forms: Plural forms of nouns, adjective forms, and forms of verbs in other tenses are included in an entry. In this case, we see that the comparative and superlative forms of *glad* are *gladder* and *gladdest.*

  When two spellings are connected with *or,* they are equally acceptable. However, when they are joined with *also,* the first spelling is preferred. For example, the dictionary shows the plural of *alga* as "**algae** *also* **algas.**"

D. Parts of Speech: Abbreviations in italics indicate the part of speech of the entry word and other forms of the word. At the beginning of this entry, we see that *glad* is usually used as an adjective, but later we learn that the same spelling can be used as a noun.

E. **Etymology:** Many entries include the history of the word, or etymology. The entry for *glad¹* indicates that this word is based on an Old English word. The entry for *glad²* shows this word comes from Latin.

F. **Definitions:** If an entry has more than one meaning, each meaning is numbered. Definitions might be listed by frequency (starting with the one used most often) or chronologically (starting with the first definition given to that word). Example sentences using the entry word are often included in definitions to make meanings clearer.

G. *Derived words:* A definition may end with a variation of the entry word, preceded by a dash and followed by its part of speech. In the example, the derived words *gladly* and *gladness* are shown. When the meaning of the variation is taken from the entry word, the variation is not defined. If the pronunciation changes, it is given for each variation. Phrases that include the entry word are defined because their meanings tend to be different from that of the entry word by itself.

H. **Synonyms:** Many entries list words with similar meanings along with examples so you'll know when to use each word. Understanding small differences in meaning will keep you from using words incorrectly. Some dictionaries also include antonyms in entries.

I. **Homographs:** Homographs are words that are spelled the same but have different meanings and histories. Homograph entries are listed separately and are followed by small numbers. *Glad* has two homographs pronounced the same. (When homographs vary in pronunciation, their entries make that clear.) As you can see, the homographs of *glad* have quite different definitions and completely different etymologies.

J. Usage Label: Some entries also provide information on how words are used in different contexts. The entry *glad²* is labeled *Informal*. The following chart describes some usage guidelines you might encounter in a dictionary entry. Words that are often misused, such as *aggravate* and *complected*, may be followed by an entire paragraph explaining their usage.

TYPE OF INFORMATION	DESCRIPTION	EXAMPLE FROM AN ENTRY
Capitalization	indicates that a word should be capitalized under certain conditions	**pilgrim** . . . *n* . . . **3.** *cap:* one of the English colonists settling at Plymouth in 1620
Out-of-Date Usage	identifies meanings that are obsolete (no longer used) or used only in special contexts	**play** . . . *n* . . . **1.b** *archaic:* GAME, SPORT
Special Field Usage	uses a phrase or label to indicate a definition used only in a particular field	**break** . . . *n* . . . **5.d** *mining:* FAULT, DISLOCATION
Informal	advises that the word be avoided when speaking and writing formally	**bloom•ing** . . . *adj* . . . **3.** *Informal.* complete, utter: *a blooming idiot.*
Regional Usage	explains how a word is used in a certain geographical area	**pet•rol** . . . *n.* *British.* gasoline

TYPE OF INFORMATION	DESCRIPTION	EXAMPLE FROM AN ENTRY
Usage Note	offers general guide-lines for using a word in a certain situation; often preceded by a dash and by the abbreviation *usu.* for *usually* or the words *called also.*	**fire away** *vi* . . . – usu. used as an imperative. **hun•dred•weight** *n* . . . –called also *long-hundredweight.*

OTHER KINDS OF INFORMATION IN GENERAL DICTIONARIES

When did Genghis Khan live? What does *de mal en pis* mean? You can find out by looking in the back of your dictionary.

Biographical Names

This section lists the spelling and pronunciation of the names of thousands of notable people. It also includes each person's birth and death dates, nationality, and field or title.

Geographical Names

In the geographical names section, you can find the correct spelling, pronunciation, and location of countries, regions, cities, mountains, rivers, and other geographical features.

Abbreviations and Symbols for Chemical Elements

Check this section if you are confused by the abbreviation *PAT* (point after touchdown) or want to learn that *Fe* is the chemical symbol for iron.

Foreign Words and Phrases

The foreign words and phrases section defines unusual phrases, such as *Ars longa, vita brevis* (Art is long; life is short). Commonly used foreign phrases, such as *déjà vu,* are listed with the regular word entries.

Signs and Symbols

This section provides the symbols used in astronomy, business, math, medicine, weather forecasting, and other fields.

Style Handbook

Use the style section to check your punctuation or capitalization and for help with documentation of sources and ways to address people in certain positions, such as government officials.

THESAURUSES

A thesaurus, one kind of specialized dictionary, lists synonyms. The synonyms can be arranged categorically (traditional style) or alphabetically (dictionary style).

Traditional Style

To use a thesaurus arranged in the traditional style, begin by looking in the index for the word for which you want a synonym. For example, if you looked in the index under *require,* you might find these choices:

require entail 76.4
necessitate 637.9
lack 660.6
demand 751.4
oblige 754.5
charge 844.14
obligate 960.11

RESOURCES

Let's say that *demand* seems like a good word to replace *require* in the report you're writing. You could simply use *demand,* or you could look in the front of the book under 751.4 for more choices. Guide numbers at the top of each page, similar to a dictionary's guide words, help you find the number you want quickly. On the page with the guide numbers 748.16–751.7, you find that word 751 is *demand.* Under this word are numbered paragraphs, each with possible synonyms for *demand.* The most commonly used words are printed in boldface type. Because *demand* can be a noun or a verb, the synonyms are separated into those two categories. You locate paragraph 751.4:

> VERBS **4. demand, ask,** make a demand; **call for,** call on *or* upon one for, come upon one for, appeal to for; cry for, clamor for; **require, exact,** require at the hands of; **requisition,** make *or* put in requisition, lay under contribution.

You decide that *exact* is an even better choice than *demand,* but you also read the other entries under *demand,* as those words are closely related. You notice that the thesaurus also includes synonyms in other languages, such as French and Latin. Some synonyms are marked *[coll.],* meaning "colloquial" or "informal." A page in the front or back of the thesaurus explains the other abbreviations that are used.

Dictionary Style

Looking up a word in a thesaurus organized alphabetically is just like looking up a word in a dictionary. Using the guide words at the top of the page, you locate the entry for the word *require:*

REQUIRE

Verb. **1.** [To need] want, feel the necessity for, have need for; see NEED. **2.** [To demand] exact, insist upon, expect; see ASK.

For more choices, you check *ask,* one of the capitalized words:

ASK

Verb. request, query, question, interrogate, examine, cross-examine, demand, pose *or* raise *or* put a question, inquire, frame a question, order, command, challenge, pry into, scour, investigate, hunt for, quiz, grill, *needle, *sound out, *pump, *put through the third degree.

Antonym: see ANSWER, REFUTE, REJOIN.

Checking the front of the book, you learn that an asterisk (*) indicates that a term is colloquial or slang.

STYLE GUIDES

Should you capitalize a title when it follows a person's name? Should you write *87* or *eighty-seven?* You can find a number of style guides, such as *The Chicago Manual of Style,* that will answer these questions. Style guides are reference books with detailed indexes that allow you to look up specific questions. The answers in one style guide may contradict the answers in another guide, so everyone working on the same project should agree to use the same style guide. Perhaps some of your teachers have asked you to follow a certain style guide in your writing.

Accessing Electronic Resources

• • • • • • • • • • • • • • •

The Internet is an increasingly important source of information for people of all ages worldwide, but CD-ROMs and other electronic resources not connected to the Internet also offer vast amounts of information.

20.1 USING THE INTERNET

The Internet is a computer-based, worldwide information network. The Internet uses telephone and cable lines and satellites to link personal computers worldwide. The World Wide Web, or WWW, is a set of programs and rules that determine how files are created and displayed on the Internet. To understand the difference, try this analogy: if the Internet were one computer, the WWW would be a program that runs on that computer. As you research a topic, the Internet and World Wide Web allow you to identify, retrieve, and study documents without leaving your home, school, or library. You can also use electronic mail, or e-mail, to communicate with others interested in a specific topic or to experts on that topic.

GAINING ACCESS

Your library computers can probably link you directly to the Internet at no cost to you. If you are using a computer at home, you'll need a **modem,** a device that connects your computer to a telephone or cable line. You must also subscribe to an **Internet service provider.** This service will connect you to the Internet for a fee.

UNDERSTANDING ADDRESSES

The information on the Internet is organized by locations, or sites, each with its own address. A Web address is also called a **Uniform Resource Locator,** or URL. Most addresses begin with *http://,* which stands for "hypertext transfer protocol" and identifies a way in which information is exchanged among computers connected by the Internet. The last part of an address, or its suffix, indicates the type of site it is. Here are some of the suffixes in use:

SUFFIX	TYPE OF SITE
.com	commercial
.edu	educational
.gov	government
.mil	military
.net	network organization or Internet service provider
.org	organization

USING BROWSERS

Each Internet service provider uses a specific **browser,** a program that locates and displays Web pages. Some browsers display only the text, or words, on a Web page;

most will display both text and **graphics** (pictures, photos, and diagrams). Browsers also allow you to print or download part or all of a Web site. (**Downloading** means copying information from Internet files onto a computer hard drive or a diskette.) Browsers permit you to move from page to page within a site or to jump from one site to a related site. Names of current browsers include Netscape Navigator and Internet Explorer.

ACCESSING WEB SITES

Let's say you are now connected to the Internet. If you want to see the information offered at a certain site, you can enter the site's address on the computer screen and be transferred there. You can also access specific reference sources this way, such as the *New York Times* or *Encyclopædia Britannica.* Some of these sources are free, but to gain access to others, you must subscribe and pay a fee in addition to the cost of the online service. A screen will explain any extra charges that are involved and let you choose whether to continue.

USING SEARCH ENGINES AND SUBJECT DIRECTORIES

If you don't have a specific address in mind, you can search by keyword with the help of a search engine or a subject directory.

Technology Tip

Be sure to read the Search Tip on pages 536–538, which provides information about using keywords. A keyword that is too general may generate hundreds of thousands of possible Web sites. It will take you a long time to search them and find a few helpful sources.

FoxTrot

by Bill Amend

Search Engines Search engines are a type of software that uses your keyword to compile lists of related Web sites. Internet service providers use certain search engines, but you can switch to a different one by entering its address. Many kinds of search engines are available, and they offer slightly different services. Some print the first sentence or two of the information offered at each Web site, while other search engines list only the site's title and address. Some search engines offer to list additional Web sites similar to those already on your screen.

Subject Directories Subject directories are a kind of software that provides an excellent place to start a search if you haven't selected a specific topic yet. A subject directory first lists general topics. After you choose one, the directory offers a list of possible subtopics from which to select. The directory then offers several more lists of subtopics for you to consider, allowing you to further narrow your topic. Finally, it provides a page of links to Web sites that are related to the specific topic you have now chosen.

MOVING AROUND WEB SITES

Often a word or phrase within the text of a Web page or at the end of the file will provide a link to a related Web site. These special words or phrases are called **hyperlinks.** They may be underlined or printed in a different color to make them easy to spot. When you click your mouse on a hyperlink, you'll immediately be transferred to another Web site. To get back, you can click on the back arrow or a similar symbol at the top of the computer screen.

Many Web sites are not checked for accuracy, so you must evaluate each site yourself. Begin by reviewing the Evaluating Tip on pages 549–550; this tip applies to Internet sources too.

1. Determine whether a Web site actually relates to your topic. A search engine will use every possible meaning of your keyword or phrase to compile a list of hundreds or thousands of sites. You may find that your keyword is also the name of a computer game or a sports team.

2. Pay particular attention to the source of the information in a Web site. (You may have to press the "move back" key several times to identify the organization sponsoring a site.) If a site is a personal Web page or if you cannot figure out its source or author, be sure to find another source to verify the information you find.

3. Evaluate the accuracy and fairness of the information. Is it based on more than one source? Are dissenting opinions included? After doing some of your own research elsewhere, are you aware of important information that was omitted from the site? Does the site include a bibliography and links to other sites? The answers to these questions can help you decide whether to use that source.

20.2 USING CD-ROMS AND DVDS

Technological advances create new research opportunities every day, so any discussion of the resources available quickly becomes out-of-date. Still, two resources are likely to be used for many years to come: CD-ROMs (Compact Disc-Read-Only Memory) and DVDs (Digital Video Discs). They can be used with a personal computer at home, at school, or at a library.

CD-ROM databases store both visual and audio information, such as photographs, maps, samples of different kinds of music, sound clips of famous speeches, and bird calls. Some CD-ROMs offer short videos of historical events and animated, narrated sequences that explain, for example, how acid rain forms or how airplanes fly.

One CD-ROM can store the same information as seven hundred diskettes; therefore, many dictionaries, encyclopedias, and other reference sources are now available as CD-ROMs. Many manufacturers offer yearly or monthly updates. To read a CD-ROM, your computer must have a CD-ROM drive. To broadcast sound effects, it must have speakers and a sound card.

Similar to a CD-ROM, a DVD has a larger storage capacity, enough space to store a full-length movie. DVDs require a DVD drive, which can also read CD-ROMs. (CD-ROM drives, however, cannot read DVDs.)

Library computer catalogs are another example of electronic resources that are not part of the Internet. Some of the databases available at the library are actually on CD-ROMs purchased by the library; other databases accessible from library computers are part of the Internet.

Knowledge often means knowing how to find information. Now you have knowledge. You can use it to find out more about the world and to take your place in it.

Answers

● ● ● ● ● ● ● ● ● ● ● ● ● ● ● ● ●

CHAPTER 1
PARTS OF SPEECH

PLURAL NOUNS, PAGE 98
1. reasons
2. pictures
3. melons
4. persons or people
5. glasses
6. keyboards
7. juries
8. democracies
9. ratios
10. children

POSSESSIVE FORMS OF NOUNS, PAGE 99
1. the tomato's color
2. the restaurant's prices
3. the professor's lecture
4. the post office's location
5. the sun's temperature
6. the men's business cards
7. the books' covers
8. the secretaries' computers
9. the trees' leaves
10. the meetings' agendas

COMMON AND PROPER NOUNS, PAGE 100
1. Rocky Mountains: proper; Colorado: proper
2. Cats: common, concrete; mischief: common, abstract
3. spirit: common, abstract; goodwill: common, abstract; Special Olympics: proper
4. John: proper; tomatoes: common, concrete; summer: common, concrete
5. Henry: proper; aunts: common, concrete; Paris: proper

COLLECTIVE NOUNS, PAGE 101
1. committee, S
2. jury, P
3. police, P
4. orchestra, S
5. herd, S
6. audience, P
7. family, S
8. band, P

9. team, P
10. crowd, S; team, S

PERSONAL PRONOUNS, PAGE 104

1. their: third person, plural, possessive
2. he: third person, singular
3. their: third person, plural, possessive
4. her: third person, singular, possessive
5. Ours: first person, plural, possessive
6. We: first person, plural
7. its: third person, singular, possessive
8. your: second person, plural, possessive
9. they: third person, plural
10. I: first person, singular

PRONOUNS, PAGE 108

1. itself, reflexive
2. anybody, indefinite
3. This, demonstrative
4. whom, interrogative
5. herself, intensive
6. whom, relative
7. someone, indefinite
8. neither, indefinite
9. Which, interrogative
10. that, demonstrative

TRANSITIVE AND INTRANSITIVE VERBS, PAGE 110

1. takes: transitive, criticism
2. prefer: transitive, plants
3. worked: intransitive
4. gains: transitive, respect
5. doubts: transitive, himself, herself
6. sets: intransitive
7. rises: intransitive
8. settled: intransitive
9. speaks: transitive, languages
10. repeats: transitive, itself

VERBS AND VERB PHRASES, PAGE 112

1. Should make: transitive
2. will be going: intransitive
3. see: transitive
4. Could be: linking
5. seem: linking
6. Redeem: transitive
7. has been: linking
8. has been making: transitive
9. will be leaving: intransitive
10. charted: transitive

ADJECTIVES, PAGE 113

1. apple: pie; delicious: pie
2. Several: trees; large: trees
3. Strong: winds

4. His: arm; left: arm; soft: cast

5. good: use; throwaway: items

6. devastating: poliovirus

7. my: shoes; dress: shoes

8. Quiet: music; soothing: music

9. good: stylist; that: cowlick; stubborn: cowlick

10. Fifty: years; short: time

ADJECTIVES THAT COMPARE, PAGE 115

1. better
2. taller
3. best
4. most complicated
5. most likely *or* likeliest
6. more difficult
7. sandiest
8. sweetest
9. better
10. worse

PROPER ADJECTIVES, PAGE 116

1. the Mexican soil
2. the Vesuvian eruption
3. the Dutch people
4. the Spanish language
5. the Atlantic coastline
6. the Greek islands
7. a Chinese citizen
8. the largest Russian lake
9. the British legislature
10. the French food

ADVERBS, PAGE 118

1. often: shops (verb)
2. thoroughly: disgusted (adjective)
3. Seldom: can select (verb)
4. properly: set (verb)
5. rather: brisk (adjective)
6. barely: is working (verb)
7. too: fast (adverb); fast: grows (verb)
8. Lately: have been (verb)
9. somewhat: dismayed (adjective)
10. unusually: good (adjective)

ADVERBS THAT COMPARE, PAGE 119

1. faster, fastest
2. more carelessly, most carelessly
3. earlier, earliest
4. more frequently, most frequently
5. higher, highest
6. more deeply, most deeply
7. more recently, most recently
8. more delicately, most delicately
9. more poorly, most poorly
10. lower, lowest

PREPOSITIONAL PHRASES, PAGE 121

1. of a (circle), from one (side), to the (other)
2. Because of the power (outage)
3. During my study (period), about my (schedule)
4. On the (outskirts), of (town)
5. In spite of the (heat), through the (afternoon), into the (evening)
6. In the (fifties), to the (music), of the big (bands)
7. of the (sea), to the (horizon)
8. Without a (guide)
9. in the shallow (waters), around coral (reefs)
10. In the (beginning), of (summer), to the (rear), of our (house)

COORDINATING AND CORRELATIVE CONJUNCTIONS, PAGE 123

1. or, coordinating
2. either . . . or, correlative
3. Neither . . . nor, correlative
4. or, coordinating
5. and, coordinating
6. Both . . . and, correlative
7. not only . . . but also, correlative
8. but, coordinating
9. Whether . . . or, correlative
10. nor, coordinating

SUBORDINATING CONJUNCTIONS, PAGE 125

1. where
2. If
3. how
4. Unless
5. as if
6. Where
7. Because
8. inasmuch as
9. Provided that
10. When

CONJUNCTIVE ADVERBS, PAGE 126

Answers will vary. Possible sentences follow.

1. My older sister lives in Germany; however, she visits us every spring.
2. Hillary is a sports enthusiast; consequently, she often attends football games.
3. Joseph is a talented musician: He plays the piano; furthermore, he composes music for school plays.

4. Our French teacher is strict; nevertheless, he is always fair.
5. Charles enjoys swimming; however, his favorite pastime is reading.
6. I love the Pre-Raphaelites; consequently, my friend Manuel gave me a book about Dante Gabriel Rossetti.
7. Tom Hanks starred in *Splash*; also, he starred in *Sleepless in Seattle*.
8. My brother went away to school; however, I decided to attend the local community college.
9. Danielle volunteers at the library; furthermore, she organizes fundraisers at the elementary school.
10. I tidy my desk every night; still, I often misplace my pencils.

INTERJECTIONS, PAGE 127
1. Oh, no
2. Thank goodness
3. Whew
4. Ha
5. Yippee
6. Wow
7. Alas
8. Ah
9. Fantastic
10. Hey

PARTS OF SPEECH, PAGE 128

Sentences will vary. Possible sentences follow.

1. (This) store has great books. adjective
   (This) is where we live. demonstrative pronoun
2. The plane is (fast). adjective
   The dog runs (fast). adverb
3. He looked (outside) the house. preposition
   The cat went (outside). adverb
4. (Those) shoes are blue. demonstrative adjective
   I will buy (those). demonstrative pronoun
5. I will hang the (picture) on the wall. noun
   I (picture) myself in Austria next fall. verb
6. He draws (well). adverb
   I feel (well). adjective
7. Blue is my favorite (color). noun
   Some people (color) their hair. verb

8. He looked (over) the gate. preposition
   He looked (over). adverb

9. We went to the store, (but) it was closed. coordinating conjunction
   All (but) a few remained. preposition

10. He wished upon a (star). noun
    Who will (star) in the new action movie? verb

PROOFREADING, PAGE 128

1. American (capitalization of proper adjective)
2. no error
3. children's (possessive form of plural noun)
4. Edwards (capitalization of proper noun)
5. his (no apostrophe with possessive pronoun)
6. congregation were (plural collective noun)
7. were (subject-verb agreement)
8. an (indefinite article *an* used before vowel sound)
9. its (no apostrophe with possessive pronoun)
10. best (superlative form of good)
11. no error

12. themselves (reflexive pronoun—no such word as *theirselves*)

CHAPTER 2 PARTS OF THE SENTENCE

SIMPLE SUBJECTS AND SIMPLE PREDICATES, PAGE 133

1. members <u>have been striving</u>
2. assortment <u>is</u>
3. Elena <u>has been studying</u>
4. woodchuck <u>slept</u>
5. Grains <u>clung</u>
6. family <u>had agreed</u>
7. sandpipers <u>hopped</u>
8. friends <u>will be visiting</u>
9. sound <u>could be heard</u>
10. road <u>came</u>

COMPLETE SUBJECTS AND COMPLETE PREDICATES, PAGE 134

1. CP
2. CS
3. CP
4. CP
5. CP
6. CS
7. CP
8. CS
9. CS
10. CS

COMPOUND SUBJECTS AND COMPOUND PREDICATES, PAGE 136

1. CP bird; flew, disappeared
2. CS cheese, walnuts; are
3. CS Richie, sister; learned
4. CP brother; washed, waxed, filled
5. CS flowers, sunshine; make
6. CS,CP teacher, principal; will give, (will) direct
7. CS Sima, friend; jog
8. CS Peanuts, Linus, Peppermint Patty; are
9. CS sunrise, sunset; was
10. CS Blue, white, red; are

SIMPLE SUBJECTS AND SIMPLE PREDICATES, PAGE 137

1. deer; stood
2. (you); pass
3. classroom; is
4. effects; were
5. siren; was blaring
6. (you); Dip, lower
7. rain; came
8. you; Did see
9. scrap; remained
10. (you); Print

COMPLEMENTS, PAGE 141

1. William Shakespeare, PN
2. Claude, DO; leader, OC

3. lifeguard, PN
4. Li, Nancy, DO; co-captains, OC
5. terrifying, PA
6. tourists, IO; sense, DO
7. eggs, DO
8. technique, DO
9. baby, DO; Vincenzo, OC
10. predictable, PA

PROOFREADING, PAGE 142

1. published. (end punctuation)
2. Wheatley's (apostrophe with possessive noun); received (spelling)
3. Boston (capitalization of proper noun)
4. an enslaved (indefinite article *an* before a vowel sound)
5. no error
6. no error
7. occurred (spelling)
8. freedom, and *or* freedom. She *or* freedom; she (run-on sentence)
9. no error
10. African American (capitalization of proper adjective)
11. By (capitalization of first word in a sentence)
12. no error

13. alone at age thirty-one. *or* She was thirty-one. (fragment)
14. no error

CHAPTER 3
PHRASES

PREPOSITIONAL PHRASES, PAGE 148

1. In the morning, water, ADV
2. of water, glasses, ADJ
3. of the day's events, summary, ADJ
4. to yourself, keep, ADV
5. in a rainbow, can be seen, ADV
6. of change, pocketful, ADJ
7. For my family, would do, ADV
8. under the front porch, ground, ADJ
9. at a fast food restaurant, stopped, ADV
10. Across the street, lives, ADV

APPOSITIVES AND APPOSITIVE PHRASES, PAGE 149

1. Liam, friend
2. an elm and a maple, trees
3. a championship bout, match
4. Our best mechanic, Don
5. the contest director, Mr. Arcaro
6. a good source of Vitamin C, potato
7. An oil refinery, plant
8. *To Kill a Mockingbird*, novel
9. A valuable player, Rocco
10. five minutes of spectacular fireworks, finale

PARTICIPLES AND PARTICIPIAL PHRASES, PAGE 151

1. gathering, clouds
2. Born in Italy, Dino
3. Having learned German as a child, I
4. made of cork, shoes
5. Refreshed after a long night's sleep, golfer
6. Newly clipped and groomed, poodle
7. fallen, apples
8. Dreaming of sun and surf, women
9. charred, furniture
10. being a realist, Maria

GERUNDS AND GERUND PHRASES, PAGE 153

1. Seeing all her grandchildren, subject
2. fishing, direct object
3. Constant complaining, subject

4. his singing, indirect object
5. conserving energy, object of a preposition
6. jumping in mud puddles, appositive
7. practicing every day, object of a preposition
8. mowing the lawn, predicate nominative
9. reading the morning paper, direct object
10. exercising for an hour every morning, appositive

INFINITIVES AND INFINITIVE PHRASES, PAGE 155

1. to wash dishes, noun
2. to make out your schedule, adjective
3. To eat properly, noun
4. to build in the spring, noun
5. (to) plan the program, adverb
6. to help me with difficult math problems, adverb
7. to hear in the auditorium, adverb
8. (to) help you, adverb
9. to go home, noun
10. Bob to get the pizza, noun

VERBALS AND APPOSITIVES, PAGE 155

1. gerund
2. appositive
3. participle
4. gerund
5. gerund
6. participle
7. infinitive
8. participle
9. participle
10. appositive

ABSOLUTE PHRASES, PAGE 156

1. Their chores completed
2. its engine still smoking
3. Their wings singed by the fire
4. their hopes dashed
5. The construction completed
6. the air being cold
7. The sun having set
8. His plane approaching the airport
9. Their mouths burning from the jalapeño peppers
10. their eyes glazed and tired

PHRASES, PAGE 157

1. prepositional phrase
2. participial phrase
3. absolute phrase
4. gerund phrase
5. participial phrase
6. appositive phrase
7. participial phrase
8. infinitive phrase

9. appositive phrase
10. infinitive phrase

PROOFREADING, PAGE 158

1. no error
2. few. (end punctuation)
3. 23, 1564 (comma between day and year in date)
4. family, (comma with nonessential appositive)
5. no error
6. Anne (capitalization of proper noun)
7. Susannah, (comma in a series)
8. playwright (spelling)
9. Men, (comma with nonessential appositive)
10. Thames (capitalization of proper noun)
11. were (subject-verb agreement)
12. no error
13. no error
14. He was buried at Holy Trinity Church in Stratford. (fragment)

CHAPTER 4 CLAUSES AND SENTENCE STRUCTURE

SUBORDINATE CLAUSES, PAGE 166

1. that is now universal
2. who cleans chimneys
3. that I have
4. How a mother of triplets manages
5. when the pavement is wet
6. how shortwave radios work
7. whom the students admire; who are always fair
8. Because I like music
9. Before you take the test
10. that the customers want

MAIN CLAUSES AND SUBORDINATE CLAUSES, PAGE 166

1. We wondered when the speech would end.
2. Raisa's predicament was that she didn't have enough money.
3. How a reporter interviews is important.
4. While you are at the market, buy some fresh tomatoes.

5. <u>Because we are moving,</u> <u>our house is not a pleas-</u><u>ant sight</u>.
6. <u>Disneyland is a park</u> <u>that</u> <u>has been tremendously</u> <u>successful</u>.
7. <u>When the phone rang</u>, <u>I</u> <u>was on the front porch</u> <u>and didn't hear it</u>.
8. <u>This concert ticket will go</u> <u>to</u> <u>whoever knows the</u> <u>answer</u>.
9. <u>The leaves</u> <u>that cover our</u> <u>lawn</u> <u>are all from the huge</u> <u>sycamore tree</u>.
10. <u>Call me in the evening</u> <u>if</u> <u>you can</u>.

SUBORDINATE CLAUSES, PAGE 170

1. what I told the investiga-tor, N
2. before the game ever started, ADV
3. If you have any doubts, ADV
4. what I am supposed to say during the interview, N
5. that Sean refinished, ADJ
6. wherever you wish, ADV
7. how those pieces fit together, N
8. which runs north and south, ADJ
9. that has training wheels, ADJ

10. Why that light blinks con-stantly, N

FOUR KINDS OF SENTENCES, PAGE 172

1. E (D)
2. IT
3. IM
4. D
5. D
6. D
7. IT
8. IM
9. E (D)
10. IM

SIMPLE AND COMPOUND SENTENCES, PAGE 173

1. C
2. S
3. C
4. C
5. S
6. S
7. S
8. C
9. C
10. C

COMPLEX AND COMPOUND-COMPLEX SENTENCES, PAGE 175

1. CX, When he was in the third grade
2. CC, While you were in the shower

3. CX, what the future will bring
4. CX, that she would be here on time
5. CC, When a person hurries too much
6. CC, because he prefers the natural sciences
7. CX, Because they are both warm and comfortable
8. CC, Because bananas are so rich in potassium
9. CC, before we begin the lesson
10. CX, when it is served with ice cream

SIMPLE, COMPOUND, COMPLEX, AND COMPOUND-COMPLEX SENTENCES, PAGE 175

1. CX A soda fountain was standard equipment in a drug store when my dad was a boy.
2. S In some countries, students attend school on Saturdays.
3. C Eat well today; tomorrow, on the backpacking trip, we will have very little to eat.
4. CX Whichever tie you choose, you will have a good time at the dance.
5. C I wanted to go to the movies on Friday; however, my aunt asked me to baby-sit my nephew.
6. CC If he were wise, he would get a job, and he would save all his money.
7. CX The car should be repainted before you sell it.
8. C My friends and I enjoy sports; consequently, we attend a sporting event every week.
9. S Between the two of us, we can get this wood chopped into fireplace logs before the snowstorm.
10. S Ricardo and his band members played dance music all evening at Carlotta's wedding reception.

FRAGMENTS AND RUN-ON SENTENCES, PAGE 178

Sentences will vary. Possible sentences follow.

1. R   I picked some violets because I like a spot of color in the house.

2. R   There goes my next-door neighbor, Eduardo Munoz. Do you know him?

3. F   While we were waiting for the bus, I dropped my ticket in a puddle.

4. R   He could not answer the question, but he was not discouraged.

5. F   If you are free tomorrow night, please join us.

6. F   Show your rough draft to the teacher before you complete the assigned term paper.

7. F   Reading and basic addition are taught in the first grade.

8. R   Lee Ann repaired the sink, and she was pleased with herself.

9. R   A tornado is approaching; take cover immediately.

10. F   When a person is sound asleep, he or she is likely to dream.

PROOFREADING, PAGE 179

1. find; he *or* find. He *or* find, and he (comma splice)

2. He even *or* Hebrew, and he even (fragment)

3. no error

4. year because he wanted *or* He wanted (fragment)

5. 1642; she *or* 1642. She (run-on sentence)

6. parents' (plural possessive)

7. their (plural possessive pronoun)

8. divorce, which (nonessential clause)

9. no error

10. 1652, and *or* 1652; he *or* 1652. He (run-on sentence)

11. no error

12. friends (spelling)

13. Milton (capitalization of proper noun)

CHAPTER 5 VERB TENSES AND VOICE

PRINCIPAL PARTS OF VERBS, PAGE 186

1. spent
2. will have written
3. are replacing
4. seem
5. was asked
6. are putting
7. will be presented

8. flew

9. tried

10. went

PAST AND PAST PARTICIPLE FORMS OF VERBS, PAGE 191

	Base Form	Past Form	Past Participle
1.	drive	drove	driven
2.	do	did	done
3.	think	thought	thought
4.	steal	stole	stolen
5.	choose	chose	chosen
6.	begin	began	begun
7.	love	loved	loved
8.	say	said	said
9.	put	put	put
10.	leave	left	left
11.	grow	grew	grown
12.	let	let	let
13.	hold	held	held
14.	find	found	found
15.	wear	wore	worn
16.	dive	dived or dove	dived
17.	shake	shook	shaken
18.	break	broke	broken
19.	learn	learned	learned
20.	serve	served	served
21.	draw	drew	drawn
22.	tell	told	told
23.	rise	rose	risen
24.	pay	paid	paid
25.	read	read	read

FORMS OF VERBS, PAGE 193

1. shone
2. stung
3. hung
4. torn
5. sat
6. woven
7. worn
8. drew
9. taken
10. hanged

PRESENT TENSE, PAGE 195

Answers will vary, but some suggestions are given below.

1. The government spends huge amounts of money.
2. No one thinks that Sandy's answer is the correct one.
3. Earth revolves around the Sun.
4. Maria has a toothache.
5. Once again, a courageous athlete swims the English Channel.
6. A small generator drives the pump.
7. Bubbles burst as they float up in the air.
8. The employees wear casual attire on Fridays.
9. Maria seems unhappy about her new schedule.
10. My dad takes his multi-vitamin with juice.

FUTURE TENSE, PAGE 198

1. Donna will paint her bedroom.
   Donna is going to paint her bedroom.
   Donna is about to paint her bedroom.
   Donna paints her bedroom [tomorrow].
2. Those trees will lose their leaves.
   Those trees are going to lose their leaves.
   Those trees are about to lose their leaves.
   Those trees lose their leaves [as soon as fall arrives].
3. The streets will be repaved.
   The streets are going to be repaved.
   The streets are about to be repaved.
   The streets are repaved [next week].
4. They will drink their milkshakes.

They are going to drink their milkshakes.
They are about to drink their milkshakes.
They drink their milkshakes [in a few minutes].

5. The flight will land at Washington National Airport.

   The flight is going to land at Washington National Airport.

   The flight is about to land at Washington National Airport.

   The flight lands at Washington National Airport [next Tuesday].

PRESENT, PAST, AND FUTURE TENSE, PAGE 198

1. past
2. future
3. present
4. past
5. future
6. past
7. future
8. past
9. present
10. past

PERFECT TENSES, PAGE 201

1. has driven
2. will have worked
3. has given
4. will have been
5. have cut
6. had given
7. has read
8. has been
9. had spoken
10. will have rebuilt

TENSE OF VERBS, PAGE 201

1. past perfect
2. future perfect
3. present
4. past
5. past perfect
6. present
7. future
8. present perfect
9. future
10. present perfect

THE SIX TENSES, PAGE 202

Make sure that each of the six tenses (present, past, future, present perfect, past perfect, and future perfect) is included in the paragraphs.

PROGRESSIVE AND EMPHATIC FORMS, PAGE 204

1. present emphatic
2. present perfect progressive
3. present progressive
4. future progressive
5. past emphatic
6. past progressive
7. future perfect progressive
8. past perfect progressive
9. past emphatic
10. past progressive

VOICE OF VERBS, PAGE 207

1. The home team scored ten points.
2. A witness reported the accident.
3. The committee's report will be given by Manuela.
4. I did the dinner dishes.
5. Almost everyone in the city knows the candidate.
6. A show of hands will determine the vote.
7. These pictures were taken by a commercial photographer.
8. The winning ticket is held by someone.
9. The students read the book.
10. Members of the House of Representatives discussed the issue.

MOOD OF VERBS, PAGE 208

1. subjunctive
2. subjunctive
3. indicative
4. imperative
5. indicative
6. imperative
7. subjunctive
8. subjunctive
9. indicative
10. imperative

PROOFREADING, PAGE 209

1. no error
2. fished (consistency of verb tense)
3. kept (irregular past form)
4. written (past perfect form)
5. no error
6. taught (irregular past form)
7. worked (consistency of verb tense)
8. became (past tense used when with a specific time)
9. built (irregular past form)
10. against (spelling)
11. hoped (past perfect form)

12. hanged (past perfect form of *hang* when referring to "death by hanging.")

13. no error

14. no error

CHAPTER 6 SUBJECT-VERB AGREEMENT

SUBJECT-VERB AGREEMENT, PAGE 216

1. Have

2. sits

3. opens

4. am

5. Does

6. are

7. is

8. were

9. have

10. is

AGREEMENT WITH INTERVENING PHRASES AND CLAUSES, PAGE 218

1. computer; was

2. C

3. menu; is

4. vase; is

5. C

6. C

7. maple; grows

8. peaks; are

9. change; is

10. C

AGREEMENT WITH COMPOUND SUBJECTS, PAGE 219

1. Both trucks and buses; are

2. Neither the equipment nor the uniforms; have

3. Her attorney and confidant; is

4. Bread and butter; is

5. Neither a letter of recommendation nor good grades; guarantee

6. Either an orange or prunes; are

7. Both Florida and California; thrive

8. Peanuts and popcorn; are

9. Ham and cheese; is

10. Neither falling rocks nor icy pavement; keeps

AGREEMENT WITH SPECIAL SUBJECTS, PAGE 222

1. is

2. passes

3. feeds

4. is

5. is

6. go

7. are

8. receives
9. was
10. is

INDEFINITE PRONOUNS AS SUBJECTS 1, PAGE 224

1. tastes
2. buy
3. is
4. were
5. memorize
6. hopes
7. are
8. likes
9. is
10. have

INDEFINITE PRONOUNS AS SUBJECTS 2, PAGE 224

Sentences will vary. Possible sentences are given.

Singular Subjects

1. Anyone is allowed to join the committee.
2. Somebody knows the answer to that question.
3. No one goes there anymore.
4. Nothing was done about the vandalism.
5. Everybody loves sitcoms.

Plural Subjects

6. Both of the candidates are qualified for the position.
7. Many of the seniors attend prom.

8. Of all the students, few miss the weekly football game.
9. Others study for tests more than I do.
10. Several of her dresses are new.

Singular or Plural Subjects

11. Most of the cookies are delicious.
12. Most of the cake is gone.
13. None of the comedians are serious.
14. Some of the movie is amusing.
15. All of the students are going to the pep rally.

PHRASES AND CLAUSES AS SUBJECTS, PAGE 225

1. depends
2. is
3. makes
4. is
5. receives
6. tires
7. has
8. is
9. requires
10. is

AGREEMENT IN INVERTED SENTENCES, PAGE 227

1. are; is
2. C
3. grows; grow

4. live; lives
5. stride; strides
6. C
7. C
8. is; are
9. travel; travels
10. is; are

SUBJECT-VERB AGREEMENT, PAGE 227

1. News, travels
2. Shingles, attacks
3. dollars, does
4. pieces, are
5. Everyone, knows
6. percent, have
7. Managing restaurants, is
8. United States, has
9. person, wishes
10. All, has

AGREEMENT WITH SUBJECT, NOT PREDICATE NOMINATIVE, PAGE 228

1. Bushels, were
2. jams, are
3. subject, is
4. Beans, are
5. accomplishment, is
6. sunsets, are
7. islands, are
8. asset, is
9. special, is
10. fingers, are

AGREEMENT WITH RELATIVE PRONOUNS, PAGE 229

1. that, dog, bites
2. that, one, challenges
3. that, rooms, have
4. that, streets, are
5. that, recordings, were
6. that, one, catches
7. who, broker, sells
8. who, one, reads
9. that, Antiques, are
10. that, music, entertains

PROOFREADING, PAGE 230

1. no error
2. was (agreement with subject, not predicate nominative)
3. nineteen, and he *or* nineteen. He *or* nineteen; he (comma splice)
4. African American (capitalization of proper adjective)
5. was (subject-verb agreement with title)
6. *Son,* (comma with appositive phrase)
7. its (possessive pronoun)
8. were (subject-verb agreement in adjective clause preceded by *one of*)
9. no error

10. were (subject-verb agreement with *Some*)
11. are (subject-verb agreement)
12. are (subject-verb agreement)

CHAPTER 7
USING PRONOUNS CORRECTLY

PERSONAL PRONOUNS, PAGE 236
1. I
2. its
3. I
4. she
5. your
6. me
7. Theirs
8. We; they
9. its
10. them

PRONOUNS AS APPOSITIVES, PAGE 238
1. she; assistants; subject
2. I; leaders; subject
3. us; people; object of a preposition
4. them; people; object of a preposition
5. me; officers; indirect object
6. he; triplets; predicate nominative

7. me; student; indirect object
8. she; violinist; subject
9. me; group; direct object
10. them, us; everyone; object of a preposition

PRONOUNS AFTER *THAN* AND *AS*, PAGE 240
1. José is a better worker than I am a worker.
2. He should do better on the test than I should do on the test.
3. Our employer doesn't pay Roger as much as our employer pays me.
4. Les goes to movies more often than I go to movies.
5. The weight lifter is no stronger than I am strong.
6. The family next door hasn't planted as many trees as we have planted.
7. My sister has saved more money than I have saved.
8. I cannot swim as well as she can swim.
9. I was not as late as she was late.
10. Mr. Andrews told me more than he told her. *or* Mr. Andrews told me more than she told me.

REFLEXIVE AND INTENSIVE PRONOUNS, PAGE 241

1. I fried myself some eggs and potatoes.
2. He wrote himself a note about the bill.
3. C
4. Simon Hudson built the patio himself.
5. C
6. C
7. Please send Lois and me a postcard when you go to Italy.
8. We did ourselves a favor by staying away from the crowd in the street.
9. We bought ourselves hot dogs and chips at the baseball game.
10. At the spa, the women pampered themselves with mud baths and facials.

WHO AND *WHOM* IN QUESTIONS AND SUBORDINATE CLAUSES, PAGE 244

1. whom
2. Who
3. Whom
4. whoever
5. whom
6. whoever
7. who
8. whom
9. Whoever
10. Who

GENDER-NEUTRAL PRONOUN-ANTECEDENT AGREEMENT, PAGE 246

1. A student must buy himself or herself school supplies.

   Students must buy themselves school supplies.

   A student must buy school supplies.
2. A schoolteacher often volunteers his or her time to help students.

   Schoolteachers often volunteer their time to help students.

   A schoolteacher often volunteers time to help students.
3. A student should do his or her homework before class.

   Students should do their homework before class.

   A student should do homework before class.

4. An employee must get himself or herself to work on time.

Employees must get themselves to work on time.

Employees must get to work on time.

5. Every day, a doctor must make his or her rounds at the hospital.

Every day, doctors must make their rounds at the hospital.

Every day, a doctor must make rounds at the hospital.

AGREEMENT WITH COLLECTIVE NOUNS, PAGE 247

1. its, jury, singular
2. their, panel, plural
3. their, board, plural
4. its, band, singular
5. its, class, singular

AGREEMENT IN PERSON, PAGE 248

Sentences may vary. Possible sentences follow.

1. When one keeps an open mind, one can appreciate many points of view.

2. I bought a new encyclopedia set, which I can read to learn about many subjects.

3. Some students take the woodworking class where they learn how to make furniture.

4. When a person goes to work, he or she should be on time.

5. He watches the kinds of movies that make him weep.

GENDER-NEUTRAL AGREEMENT WITH INDEFINITE PRONOUN ANTECEDENTS, PAGE 250

Sentences may vary. Possible sentences follow.

1. Each of the seniors will receive his or her diploma.

All of the seniors will receive their diplomas.

Each of the seniors will receive a diploma.

2. Everyone must bake his or her own cake.

All must back their own cakes.

Everyone must bake a cake.

3. Everybody is entitled to his or her opinion.

People are entitled to their opinions.

Everybody is entitled to an opinion.

4. Anyone who does not do his or her homework will not pass the class.

Students who do not do their homework will not pass the class.

Anyone who does not do homework will not pass the class.

5. Everyone must pay his or her taxes.

People must pay their taxes.

Everyone must pay taxes.

CLEAR PRONOUN REFERENCE, PAGE 251

Sentences may vary. Possible sentences follow.

1. Harry phoned Sally every night for a week, but the line was always busy.

2. I hear that Pierre paints beautifully, but he'll never show me his paintings.

3. The streets in my neighborhood were flooded; the flood was caused by a hurricane.

4. I saw the local ballet company perform *Swan Lake* last night; the performance was great!

5. My friend Jean is a fantastic baker, and she often brings me a cookie for a snack.

CORRECTING UNCLEAR AND INDEFINITE PRONOUN REFERENCE, PAGE 253

Sentences may vary. Possible sentences follow.

1. Susan, who was talking to Sarah, got another phone call.

2. The weather forecasters say that the temperature will reach ninety degrees today.

3. My dad snapped at Rick, who was just goofing around.

4. In preschool children learn to play nicely with others.

5. Both the president and his aide agreed that the president would attend the meeting of world leaders.

PROOFREADING, PAGE 253

1. teachers often (incorrect use of *they* as an indefinite pronoun)

2. 1770; his *or* 1770. His (run-on sentence)

3. sent him (objective case for a personal pronoun in a compound object)

4. memories of this place *or* . . . of Hawkshead (vague pronoun reference)

5. was he (nominative case for a personal pronoun following the linking verb *be*)

6. Cambridge, (comma with appositive)

7. with whom (objective pronoun *whom* as the object of the preposition *with*)

8. they (subject of the incomplete adverb clause *as much as they published and wrote*)

9. no error

10. ; their argument was . . . (vague pronoun reference)

11. that he and Coleridge (nominative case for a compound subject)

CHAPTER 8 USING MODIFIERS CORRECTLY

THE THREE DEGREES OF COMPARISON, PAGE 260

1. Of the two track stars, Althea runs faster.

2. Of all the ornaments in the living room, this ornament is shiniest.

3. Little Danny played more calmly than the other children.

4. C

5. Of all the students in art class, Danielle is most artistic.

6. This is the better job of the two.

7. Her second idea was even worse than her first one.

8. C

9. We live farther from school than anyone else.

10. All of us tried making square knots; mine was the most nearly square.

IRREGULAR COMPARISONS, PAGE 262

1. more

2. worse

3. farther

4. worse

5. less

6. best

7. better

8. furthest

9. better

10. least

CORRECTING DOUBLE COMPARISONS, PAGE 263

1. Today is the hottest day of the summer.
2. The gargoyle over the doorway is ugliest.
3. Washing dishes is the most boring work in the house.
4. C
5. C
6. Fish used to be more abundant in the ocean than they are now.
7. I actually feel worse than I did yesterday.
8. Some days are better than others.
9. I drove farther yesterday than I did today.
10. C

CORRECTING INCOMPLETE COMPARISONS, PAGE 264

1. Jacques got better grades than anyone else in his class.
2. My handwriting is worse than the other boy's.
3. C
4. I think I learned more than anyone else at band camp.

5. In my opinion, biology is more interesting than any other subject.
6. C
7. C
8. C
9. The bedrooms in this house are smaller than the bedrooms in the first house we saw.
10. The skin of a child is usually softer than the skin of an adult.

CORRECTING ERRORS IN COMPARISON, PAGE 265

1. I am more ready for this test than I was for the last.
2. C
3. C
4. The pattern of a snowflake is even more intricate than that of a spider web.
5. The Smiths have traveled farther than the Wilsons.
6. There is no question that this watermelon is better than that one.
7. I feel better today than I did yesterday.
8. Saul polishes and cleans his car more often than anyone else.

9. Of the two weight lifters, he is definitely more muscular.
10. Of the three nurses, Michael was most thoughtful.

GOOD OR *WELL;* *BAD* OR *BADLY,* PAGE 266

1. The team's quarterback runs so well that no one can stop him.
2. I feel bad about the damage to your house.
3. Although she is generally in good health, she isn't feeling well today.
4. This soup tastes bad; I think I added too much salt.
5. It is looking bad for our outing because dark clouds are rolling in.
6. C
7. C
8. C
9. The financial situation for the newly independent country looks bad.
10. The pitcher was throwing so badly last night that he was replaced in the second inning.

COMPARATIVE AND SUPERLATIVE FORMS, PAGE 267

1. more nearly perfect, most nearly perfect
2. better, best
3. more satisfactory, most satisfactory
4. more pleasant, most pleasant
5. lazier, laziest
6. more nearly unique, most nearly unique
7. worse, worst
8. better, best
9. more fattening, most fattening
10. faster, fastest

CORRECTING DOUBLE NEGATIVES, PAGE 268

1. These situations don't ever seem to correct themselves. *or* These situations never seem to correct themselves.
2. We never have any fun on the weekend. *or* We have no fun on the weekend.
3. I have scarcely any money left to buy clothes.
4. There is hardly any food in the refrigerator.

5. If you don't attend classes, you won't get a diploma. *or* If you don't attend classes, you will get no diploma.

6. One should never do anything that would cause harm to others. *or* One should do nothing that would cause harm to others.

7. C

8. There weren't any signs of a tornado. *or* There were no signs of a tornado.

9. Make no sound because the baby is sleeping. *or* Don't make a sound because the baby is sleeping.

10. There is scarcely enough time in the day to get everything done.

CORRECTING MISPLACED AND DANGLING MODIFIERS, PAGE 271

Sentences will vary. Possible sentences are given.

1. Running a victory lap in his bare feet, the marathoner stubbed his toe on a stone.

2. The written test has only two parts.

3. Steering the ship to the north, the pilot avoided the storm.

4. Reaching California, the miners began the search for gold.

5. With pink and blue balloons, the proud father announced the birth of his twins.

6. His kite with a long tail was caught in a tree.

7. Discouraged by criticism, the candidate gave up his bid for office.

8. The teacher gave us only two assignments.

9. The car with a badly damaged engine crossed the finish line.

10. Singing in the shower, my dad couldn't hear the phone.

PROOFREADING, PAGE 272

1. most (superlative modifier)

2. more complete (comparative modifier)

3. thirteen. (end punctuation)

4. Elizabeth Barrett's health began to fail when she was at an early age. (dangling modifier)

5. matters worse, (double comparison)

6. Barrett, living in her father's house, did . . . *or* Living in her father's house, Barrett did . . . (misplaced modifier)

7. poet; Browning *or* poet. Browning (run-on sentence)

8. didn't ever forgive *or* never forgave (double negative)

9. better (comparative form of *well*)

10. that her poetry expressed . . . *or* better than any other Victorian poet. (incomplete comparison)

CHAPTER 9 DIAGRAMING SENTENCES

Diagrams can be found in the Teacher's Guide.

CHAPTER 10 CAPITALIZING

CAPITALIZING SENTENCES AND QUOTATIONS, PAGE 299

1. C

2. I was confused when my mother said, "You can buy some new shoes, but you can't wear them now."

3. C

4. When will the Williams be leaving for their vacation?

5. The commencement speaker's speech (the title is yet to be announced) is scheduled to begin in thirty minutes.

6. I often visit Miami: My aunt lives there.

7. C

8. The mayor promised that she would find aid for the flood victims.

9. We will be traveling on a Carnival cruise ship. (Carnival has many ships with different itineraries.)

10. I stopped my sister's boyfriend cold by asking, "Just what are your intentions?"

CAPITALIZING LETTER PARTS, PAGE 301

1. a
2. b
3. b
4. b
5. a

CAPITALIZING OUTLINES, PAGE 302

I. Public service jobs
  A. Career jobs
    1. Government
      a. Federal
      b. State
      c. Local
    2. Private sector
  B. Volunteer jobs
    1. Hospital

CAPITALIZING PROPER NOUNS AND PROPER ADJECTIVES, PAGE 310

1. Tennis finals will be held on Memorial Day.
2. The Empire State Building is in New York City.
3. In Elizabethan England, some people had their houses built in the shape of an *E* to honor Queen Elizabeth I.
4. Do you live north or south of Springfield?
5. At a Chicago railway station, we boarded the Amtrak for Washington.
6. The English barons forced King John to sign the Magna Carta on June 15, 1215.
7. We ate at Friendship House, a restaurant east of Gulfport, Mississippi.
8. When we visit London in the spring, we often take a leisurely walk through Hyde Park.
9. The Reverend Fred Jerrold, minister of the First Methodist Church, spoke.
10. The Germans and the Irish were among the settlers of the United States.
11. My mother drives a Toyota Camry.
12. On Labor Day, the golf course at the Troy Country Club will be open.
13. The mayor of Dallas, Texas, spoke at the meeting of the Rotary Club.
14. In 1862 President Abraham Lincoln signed the Homestead Act.
15. I have not seen Uncle Bob since the Fourth of July.

16. Langston Hughes's poem "The Negro Speaks of Rivers" is one of my favorites.

17. Ernest Hemingway, the famous American writer, once wrote for the *Kansas City Star,* a daily newspaper published in Kansas City, Missouri.

18. Next year Central High School will offer Russian, journalism, and economics.

19. Zora Neale Hurston wrote an autobiography called *Dust Tracks on a Road.*

20. I took the recipes from *Good Housekeeping* and *Woman's Day* magazines.

CORRECTING ERRORS IN CAPITALIZATION, PAGE 311

1. Dear Mr. Peterson,
   I would like to thank you for all the help you gave me in English class at Oakdale High School. I am looking forward to my first year at the University of Cincinnati, where I plan to study poetry.
   Yours sincerely,
   Edward Allen

2. I. Music
   A. Classical music
   1. Baroque
      a. Vivaldi
      b. Handel
   2. Romantic
      a. Beethoven
      b. Brahms

3. George Harris, Mom's brother, works for the Department of the Interior.

4. A reprint of "The Man with the Hoe" hangs in the office of our high school.

5. My father helps me in Chemistry I, Latin, and Algebra II.

6. Dickens's *Oliver Twist* and Twain's *The Adventures of Huckleberry Finn* both contain young male protagonists.

7. My father's favorite poem is "The Lake Isle of Innisfree."

8. John F. Kennedy was president from 1961 to 1963.

9. Samuel Johnson, an English writer, once said, "No man but a blockhead ever wrote, except for money."

10. Martin Luther King Jr. won the Nobel Prize in 1964.

PROOFREADING, PAGE 314

1. Missouri (capitalization of proper noun)
2. "The Negro Speaks of Rivers," (no capitalization of prepositions of fewer than five letters in titles)
3. north (no capitalization of compass points when they indicate direction)
4. Africa (capitalization of proper noun)
5. *Opportunity* (capitalization of magazine title)
6. Lindsay (capitalization of proper noun)
7. "Hide (capitalization of first word in a direct quotation that is a complete sentence)
8. University (capitalization of part of a proper noun)
9. *The Weary Blues* (capitalization of title)
10. no error
11. no error
12. the *Chicago Defender* (no capitalization of article preceding a newspaper title)

CHAPTER 11 PUNCTUATION, ABBREVIATIONS, AND NUMBERS

PERIODS, EXCLAMATION POINTS, AND QUESTION MARKS, PAGE 321

1. Is this called teal blue?
2. Help!
3. Please report promptly when your number is called.
4. Wow! What a great catch!
5. The director asked me why I wanted to join the health club.
6. What time are you leaving?
7. Kristi asked me when I would visit her.
8. On Friday (what a day!) our cousins from Belgium arrived.
9. Ask the operator what the number is.
10. Did you feel a trembling in the house a few minutes ago?

COLONS, PAGE 323

1. The following countries, as well as others, belong to the United Nations: England, Spain, France, and Russia.

2. Dear Members:

3. The quarter-finals will begin at 1:30 P.M. on Thursday. They will be held at the following four locations: Bellwood, Homewood, Stiverson, and Shelby.

4. Camden College will accept Hal's application: He ranks high in his class.

5. The first three runners to cross the finish line were Judd, Ben, and Samir.

6. She read the following from A. E. Housman:
When I was one-and-twenty,
I heard a wise man say,
"Give crowns and pounds and guineas
But not your heart away. . . .

7. From the Bible's John 8:32, he quoted the following sentence: "And ye shall know the truth, and the truth shall make you free."

8. Lisa will be a good manager: She is very responsible.

9. Our study is in these three areas: short stories, poetry, and essays.

10. Dear Sir: By the 5:30 P.M. deadline, I received applications from the following: Tico Jiminez, Pedro Vasquez, and Lorenzo White.

SEMICOLONS, PAGE 325

1. We visited friends in Akron, Ohio; Ann Arbor, Michigan; and Chicago, Illinois.

2. This will be a year of difficult decisions for you; for example, you must decide on a career.

3. Write what you really think; don't let others sway your thinking.

4. This road map is several years old; however, it is adequate for our needs.

5. Ms. Lippman, a banker; Mrs. Ballard, an office manager; and Mr. Laird, an accountant, spoke to us yesterday.

COMMA IN A SERIES, WITH COORDINATE ADJECTIVES, AND IN COMPOUND SENTENCES, PAGE 328

1. Carlo's impromptu class theme had a humorous, unexpected ending.

2. Mr. Thomas spoke in a strong, resonant voice when he asked Harry, Michelle, and Juan to be quiet.
3. A triangular state flag hangs from the mast of their new white sailboat.
4. Ham and cheese and peanut butter and jelly are two of the most common sandwich fillings.
5. Bill closed his locker, I grabbed my bag, and we hurried to join the others.

COMMAS AND NONESSENTIAL ELEMENTS, PAGE 331

1. The computer that I bought is an IBM.
2. The temperature at game time, thirty-seven degrees, made sitting in the bleachers miserable.
3. Yesterday was a bad day, to put it mildly.
4. The crowd, subdued by their candidate's poor showing, soon dispersed.
5. Janet, whose name was called first, was absent.

COMMAS WITH INTERJECTIONS, PARENTHETICAL EXPRESSIONS, CONJUNCTIVE ADVERBS, AND ANTITHETICAL PHRASES, PAGE 332

1. Maroon, not red, is the color of Julia's bridesmaids' dresses.
2. By the way, what is your phone number?
3. Our dinner plans were canceled; consequently, we ate leftovers from the preceding night.
4. On the contrary, the show will be presented as scheduled.
5. Good grief, that's the last thing I need to hear today.

COMMAS WITH OTHER ELEMENTS, PAGE 334

1. In the middle of the desert, they came upon a green oasis.
2. Battling back after a bout with cancer, Scott Hamilton returned to the ice.
3. On the table in the dining room was my birthday gift.

4. Before you turn out the lights, make sure that the doors are locked.

5. That tiny insect, seen through a microscope, is actually very colorful.

ADDITIONAL USES OF COMMAS, PAGE 336

1. Torremolinos, Spain, is a place I'd like to visit.

2. Friends and family, thank you for your help.

3. These jeans are the ones you like best, aren't they?

4. President Kennedy was shot in November 1963 in Dallas, Texas.

5. Mr. Lee, General Manager, hired a new assistant.

COMMAS 1, PAGE 338

1. My favorite movies are *The Wizard of Oz* and *Big*.

2. Gordon Parks's photographs appeared in *Life* magazine for years; he captured the intensity of the human condition. (*or* years, and he *or* years. He)

3. Cool nights and warm, sunny days make fall a pleasant time of year.

4. Whichever restaurant you choose will be fine by me.

5. The company's total sales increased during the last year, but profits were lower than expected.

COMMAS 2, PAGE 339

1. Please take down the following address: C. Allen Jenks, Ph.D., 459 North Sixth Street, Richmond, Virginia 23204.

2. Your story was printed in three school papers: the *Signal*, the *Bugle*, and the *Echo*.

3. Dear Mom,
   Sincerely yours,

4. The western sky, dark and threatening, hurried our steps.

5. We did not know the answers to the third and fourth questions, but we knew the answers to the first and second.

6. Well, when I looked in the refrigerator, the banana cream pie was gone.

7. I finally found my favorite sweatshirt, torn to shreds by my puppy, whose name, appropriately enough, is Mr. Pest.

8. Donna, our papers aren't due until Friday, are they?

9. On our walk through Sutton Park, I found the wildflower I've been wanting, but, of course, one cannot pick a flower in a state park.

10. One starless, frigid night, I heard a noise by the picture window and shined a flashlight on a doe huddled against the pane for warmth.

DASHES, PAGE 340

1. His answer—and it did surprise us—was a reluctant consent.

2. Then slowly stir in the salt, pepper, mustard—are you listening?

3. Of course, the appointment will have to be put to a vote.

4. My shoes—my very best ones, too—were spotted with asphalt.

5. Yo Yo Ma—he is a famous cellist—will perform in a concert with our local symphony orchestra.

PARENTHESES, PAGE 343

1. The AHS (American Horticultural Society) offers free seeds to its members each year.

2. The Bicycle Derby (it is an annual event) is held in August.

3. Our first game (it will be held at home) is with Oak Ridge High School.

4. I was working (I was cleaning the drains) when Martha called me in to dinner.

5. Joseph Macklin (have you heard of him?) has won the Good Will Award.

BRACKETS, PAGE 344

1. The paper continues, "Everyone who knows him [Watson] is impressed."

2. Our grandfather, proud of his heritage, swore, "I love them [the Irish] all!"

3. The new citizen exclaimed, "It [freedom] is my prize possession!"

4. The movie critic said, "It [*To Kill a Mockingbird*] is one of the best films of all time."

5. Sandro Piotti (he is from Milan [the city called the "fashion capital of the world"]) is a snappy dresser.

ELLIPSIS POINTS, PAGE 345

. . . our fathers brought forth . . . a new nation, conceived in Liberty. . . .

Now we are engaged in a great civil war. . . . We are met on a great battlefield of that war. We have come to dedicate a portion of that field, as a final resting place for those who here gave their lives that that nation might live. . . .

QUOTATION MARKS, PAGE 350

1. Julia asked, "When does the party begin?"
2. "Unchained Melody" has become a classic.
3. "Greetings," welcomed the college president. "I know you're all happy to be here today."
4. She said that all was well at home.
5. "Why," he asked, "weren't we told in time that a tornado had been sighted?"
6. I enjoy the works of Joan Didion, particularly her essay "On the Mall."
7. Ben Jonson wrote the poem "On My First Son" after his son Benjamin died.
8. The third chapter of the book is titled "American Foreign Relations."
9. "The best poem I've ever read," he said, "is W. H. Auden's 'The Unknown Citizen.'"
10. Why does my mother say, "Do you know how lucky you are?"

ITALICS (UNDERLINING), PAGE 353

1. *Affreux* means "awful" or "frightful."
2. The submarines *Nautilus* and *Skate* have crossed the North Pole under ice.
3. *Necessary*, which is often misspelled, has one *c*.
4. Anna is studying advertisements in *Time*, *Ebony*, and *Vogue*.
5. My brother watched the movie *Jurassic Park* nine times.

APOSTROPHES, PAGE 356

1. Who's the owner of the '89 car in the parking lot?
2. I'd like to know why you took Linus's hat.

3. You're making a cake for Harry's party, aren't you?

4. My father's high school had a girls' entrance and a boys' entrance.

5. Phyllis's enthusiasm is evident even when she reads the newspaper.

6. If this billfold isn't yours, whose is it? It isn't hers or John's.

7. Do ladies' styles change more often than men's, or does it just seem so?

8. Isn't your father-in-law's house nearby?

9. Jeremy Willis's summers were always spent at his grandmother and grandfather's ranch in Wyoming.

10. Two dollars' worth of gasoline isn't anyone's idea of a thrilling prize.

HYPHENS, PAGE 360

1. I need twenty-six dollars for the blouse, which is yellow colored.

2. The flower-like structure on a dogwood tree is actually a bract, not a true flower.

3. Sometimes one's thoughts become self-fulfilling prophecies.

4. If you would add one-fourth teaspoon of cinnamon to the pie recipe, I think it would be just right.

5. Our citizenship class meets tomorrow between 1:00 and 3:15 P.M.

6. yel-low

7. dog-wood

8. some-times

9. cin-namon

10. citizen-ship

ABBREVIATIONS, PAGE 363

1. The road was built in A.D. 395.

2. The flight to New Orleans, Louisiana, leaves shortly after noon.

3. The U.S. government funds NASA.

4. I need six yards of fabric for the draperies I'm making.

5. The science text was edited by G. H. Rawlings.

6. Washington, D.C. is a favorite destination for students in the eastern United States.

7. The Greek playwright Sophocles wrote *Antigone* in 441 B.C.

8. Did you correctly list the professor's name as Roberto Guerrera, Ph.D.?
9. Alfred the Great became king of England in A.D. 871.
10. The grandfather of Andrew Garner is Jerome B. Garner Sr.

NUMBERS AND NUMERALS, PAGE 366

1. The soda costs seventy cents.
2. Three thousand seventy-six was the population of Sandersburg. *or* The population of Sandersburg was 3,076.
3. Fifty-one percent constitutes a majority.
4. By ten o'clock, I had seen almost one hundred trucks go by.
5. Queen Victoria of England reigned for more than half of the nineteenth century.
6. Fifth and Sixth Streets are closed for repaving, but Lincoln Avenue is still open.
7. I felt lucky to get this coat for $49.65.
8. The ball game is on the sports channel tonight from eight to ten-thirty.

9. Dinner is at 6:00 P.M., and there will be a snack at 9:00 P.M.
10. Hawaii became the fiftieth state of the United States in 1959.

PROOFREADING, PAGE 367

1. Douglass, who (comma with nonessential adjective clause)
2. himself (reflexive pronoun)
3. *Narrative of the Life of Frederick Douglass* (italicize book title)
4. Douglass's (apostrophe and -*s* to form possessive of a singular noun)
5. speaker, (comma to separate three items in a series)
6. the *North Star* (no capitalization of article preceding a newspaper title)
7. from 1847 to 1860. (no hyphen with the word *from* before a span)
8. no error
9. Army, (comma in a compound sentence)
10. treatment, (comma to set off a participial phrase)
11. no error

12. women's (apostrophe and -*s* to form the possessive of a plural noun that does not end in *s*)

9. The gentlemen strolled leisurely through their neighborhood park.

10. The puzzled detectives carefully examined the evidence.

CHAPTER 12
SENTENCE COMBINING

COMBINING SENTENCES BY INSERTING WORDS, PAGE 375

Answers will vary. Sample answers are given.

1. The dancers gracefully performed a Russian ballet.

2. My annoying brother spies on me every day.

3. The big old grandfather clock slowly struck twelve.

4. The determined athlete ran twenty-six miles in the marathon.

5. The woman wore a tan raincoat and carried a black umbrella.

6. The baby played happily in the wet sand.

7. I carefully drove the old car to Pittsburgh.

8. The nervous students waited anxiously for their exam results.

COMBINING SENTENCES BY INSERTING PREPOSITIONAL PHRASES, PAGE 376

Answers will vary. Sample answers are given.

1. You will need the address I gave you for your application.

2. The cookies on the cookie sheet are ready to bake.

3. John F. Kennedy was assassinated in Dallas, Texas, in 1963.

4. My aunt Mary has won several prizes for her quilts.

5. The tarantula is a large, hairy spider with a poisonous bite.

6. Sophocles wrote *Antigone* in 441 B.C.

7. In the late afternoon, we lit our campfire.

8. This table with only three legs is very unsteady.

9. We went to dinner at a fancy restaurant in Austin.
10. Pick up the books on the kitchen table on your way out.

COMBINING SENTENCES BY INSERTING APPOSITIVE PHRASES, PAGE 377

Answers will vary. Sample answers are given.

1. I ordered the soup, a clam chowder.
2. The doctor, a compassionate person, treated poor patients in her free time.
3. We booked passage on a ship, a Norwegian liner, that sails out of Oslo.
4. Joan Didion wrote *Slouching Towards Bethlehem*, a collection of essays, and *Run River*, a novel.
5. One of John Philip Sousa's marches, "Stars and Stripes Forever," is often played on the Fourth of July.
6. The bald eagle and the peregrine falcon, predatory birds, have been on the endangered species list.
7. The backpacker took only one change of clothing, a pair of jeans and a sweatshirt.
8. Mrs. Brown, an English nanny, will take care of my younger brother next year.
9. Two yard chores, mowing and weeding, must be done routinely.
10. Basic math skills, addition, subtraction, multiplication, and division, are taught in elementary school.

COMBINING SENTENCES BY INSERTING PARTICIPIAL PHRASES, PAGE 379

Answers will vary. Sample answers are given.

1. The baker preheated the oven, turning it to 350°.
2. Baling the hay, the farmer hummed to herself.
3. Smiling at the cheering crowd, the gymnast received a gold medal.
4. Delivered by a courier service, the contract arrived in less than an hour.
5. Maintained by the city's Parks and Recreation Department, the basketball court is in excellent shape.

6. Woven from yarn-dyed cotton, this blue and yellow plaid rug won't wear out.

7. The tires on my car, pocked by rocks and gravel, are almost worthless.

8. My grandmother is very tired, having nursed her friend around the clock.

9. Exhausted after a long day at work, the waiter forgot to place the customer's order.

10. Attended by thousands, the festival was considered a huge success.

COMBINING SENTENCES USING COORDINATING CONJUNCTIONS, PAGE 380

Answers will vary. Sample answers are given.

1. We must rehearse more often, or the play will be a failure.

2. Judson was a man with strong opinions, and he expressed them colorfully.

3. The highway is closed for five miles, but the detour is an excellent road.

4. Either someone has taken my sandwiches, or I forgot to pack them.

5. The play has been selected, and the cast will be announced soon.

6. The administrator is both a clear-thinking individual and an eloquent speaker.

7. Frederique will either buy or make a birthday present for her mother.

8. Neither our football team nor our basketball team won the state championship.

9. I am interested in other cultures and I love to read, so I will be majoring in French literature.

10. Many people believe in the existence of the island of Atlantis; however, searchers have never found it.

COMBINING SENTENCES USING SUBORDINATION: ADVERB CLAUSES, PAGE 383

Answers will vary. Sample answers are given.

1. Long before I was born, my grandmother moved to this country from Ireland.

2. We are going to the amusement park, where we will ride the roller coasters.
3. Congress will take a recess until January so that the politicians have time to campaign.
4. After the city workers trimmed the trees, they repaired the power lines.
5. When the doctor was paged, he left immediately.
6. Because he ate lots of fruits and vegetables and exercised regularly, the dieter lost ten pounds.
7. After the United States entered World War II, people in this country saved aluminum foil and grease.
8. While you were skiing in Nevada, I was swimming in the warm waters around Saint Thomas.
9. If I complete my homework and do my chores, my mother gives me an allowance.
10. Because the government and several health agencies waged a massive campaign, there is now a heightened awareness about the dangers of smoking.

COMBINING SENTENCES USING SUBORDINATION: ADJECTIVE CLAUSES, PAGE 384

Answers will vary. Sample answers are given.

1. The American writer Alice Walker wrote *The Color Purple,* which was made into a movie.
2. Quito, which is the capital of Ecuador, is a large city that has been damaged by earthquakes several times.
3. Mount Vesuvius, which is the only active volcano on the European continent, was responsible for the burying of Pompeii.
4. The phoenix, which was a mythical bird, rose again from its own ashes after burning.
5. The *Wall Street Journal* is a daily newspaper that contains financial news.
6. Charlotte Brontë, who wrote *Jane Eyre*, was one of three sisters who wrote novels.
7. In 1929 the muralist Diego Rivera married Frieda Kahlo, who was a Mexican painter.

8. Fluoride is a chemical compound that has been effective in preventing tooth decay.

9. One poet who is known for his creative punctuation and lack of ordinary capitalization is E. E. Cummings.

10. Peter, who is a talented athlete and a diligent student, will enlist in the army next year.

COMBINING SENTENCES USING SUBORDINATION: NOUN CLAUSES, PAGE 386

Answers will vary. Sample answers are given.

1. I do not know why the squirrels have been especially active this fall.

2. That my sister made a mess of our bedroom three days after I'd cleaned it upsets me terribly.

3. I do not know where Mykonos is.

4. Give the book to whoever wants to read it next.

5. Please give whoever you met an invitation to the reception.

6. I wonder why snowflakes are in patterns.

7. I don't know who left these notebooks here.

8. I am certain that our class is going to be remembered.

9. I wish that whoever took my lunch money would return it to me.

10. I do not know how my brother charms everyone he meets.

COMBINING SENTENCES USING SUBORDINATION, PAGE 387

Answers will vary. Sample answers are given.

1. When the rain had passed, the clouds parted.

2. Though you were exhausted, you persisted.

3. Maria, who was born in Mexico, is a talented musician and a good friend.

4. Give me some idea of what you want for your birthday.

5. Here is the man to whom I introduced you.

6. Most Americans know that *arrivederci* is an Italian word.

7. When I am lonely, I turn on the radio.
8. The owner of a local nursery is selling plants very inexpensively because she is going out of business.
9. Judge Diaz decided the case, which had been pending for a long time.
10. Stephen Crane, who was an American author, wrote "The Open Boat," which is based on his own experiences after the sinking of the *Commodore.*

PROOFREADING, PAGE 388

Answers will vary. Possible sentence combinations follow.

Alice Walker was born in Georgia, where her parents were poor African American sharecroppers. Graduating at the top of her high school class, Walker won a scholarship to Spelman College in Atlanta, Georgia. Walker attended Spelman for two years; then she transferred to Sarah Lawrence College in New York, where she earned her degree.

After college Walker returned to Mississippi, where she taught writing and African American literature. She also worked to improve welfare rights and to increase voter registration among African Americans in the South.

Walker's first published work, an essay on the Civil Rights movement, was published in 1966. Most of her acclaim as a writer has come from her novels, which reveal the injustice of the racism and sexism faced by African American women. Walker's third novel, *The Color Purple,* which was made into an award-winning movie, won the Pulitzer Prize.

CHAPTER 13 SPELLING AND VOCABULARY

SPELLING RULES, PAGE 401

1. conceive
2. proceed
3. engagement
4. sheriffs
5. brothers-in-law
6. really
7. misspell
8. studying
9. bunches
10. sheep

SPELLING DIFFICULT WORDS, PAGE 406

1. twelfth, unnecessary
2. questionnaire, superintendent
3. persuade, rehearsal, tragedy
4. Division, mathematics, apologetically
5. seize, nutritious, miniature
6. Omitting, acquaintance, embarrassed
7. horizontal, disastrous
8. independent, responsibility
9. procedure, vacuum, commercial
10. calendar, guidance, coming, Wednesday

USING CONTEXT CLUES, PAGE 410

1. complete disorder; definition
2. lacking; example
3. tending to cause sleep; cause and effect
4. decayed; comparison
5. boldness, rashness; contrast
6. very loud; cause and effect
7. threw overboard; general
8. threateningly; contrast
9. proper behavior; comparison
10. false name, pen name; definition, example

ROOTS, PREFIXES, AND SUFFIXES, PAGE 437

Many answers are possible. The following list includes words formed using only the prefixes, roots, and suffixes from the list.

autobiographical, autobiography, autograph, biodegradable, biographical, biography, biped, circumscribe, circumspection, commit, commitment, comport, comportment, concur, concurrent, conductor, congress, congressional, current, cursive, cursor, cursory, deduct, deductible, deduction, degradation, degrade, dejection, deport, deportation, describe, description, ductile, graphic, immortal, immortality, impediment, import, induct, induction, inject, injection, inoperable, inscribe, inscription, inspect, inspection, inspector, interject, interjection, intermittent, missile, mission, mortal, mortality, operable, operation, pedal, portable, portal, precursor, prescribe, prescription, produce, product, production, productive, program, progress, progression, progressive, project, projection, projector, proportion, proportional, proscribe, proscription, prospect, prospective, prospector, recur, recurrent, reduce, reduction, regress, regression, regressive, reject, rejection, remission, remit, report, retrograde, retrogress, retrogression, retrogressive, retrospect, retrospection, retrospective, transcribe, transcription, transgress, transgression, transmission, transmit, transmittable, transmittal, transport, transportable, transportation

Index

establishing conflict in, 463
flashbacks in, 464
ordering time in, 463–464
revealing character in, 460
setting scene in, 460
vivid description in, 461

Nationalities, capitalizing names of, 305

Nauseated, nauseous, 69

Need, knead, 63

Negatives, double, **17–18,** 267
correcting, 267–268

Negative words as adverbs, 118

Newspapers. *See also* Magazines; Periodicals
italics for titles of, 351
in library, 533
locating articles in, 547–548
quotation marks for titles of articles in, 349

Nicknames, quotation marks with, 303

Night, knight, 63

Nominative, predicate, **32**

Nominative absolute, 156

Nominative case, **27**
for personal pronouns, 234, 235, 236

Nonessential clauses, **27–28,** 167–168

Nonessential elements, use of commas to set off, 329–331

Nonfiction books
finding information in, 546–547
locating in library, 541, 542, 545

Nonfiction narratives, 460

Nonrestrictive clauses, 168. *See also* Nonessential clauses

Nonsexist language, 452–453

Note cards, preparing, for research paper, 481

Notes in drafting research paper, 488–489

Note taking
for descriptive writing, 457
for research paper, 481

Noun clauses, **28,** 164, 169–170
in combining sentences, 385–386
diagraming, 291–293

Nouns, **28**
abstract, **4,** 97
of amount and subject-verb agreement, 221–222
collective, **9,** 100, 246–247
common, **10–11,** 99–100
compound, 99
concrete, **13,** 97
definition of, 97
of direct address, diagraming, 277
gerunds, 152
infinitive used as, 153–154
plural, 97
possessive, 98–99
proper, **35,** 99–100, 302
singular, 97
special, and subject-verb agreement, 220–221
and subject-verb agreement, 220

Nowheres, somewheres, anyways, anywheres, everywheres, 48

Number
in pronoun-antecedent agreement, 244–250
in subject-verb agreement, 215

Number, amount, 48

Numbers, **28,** 358–359, 364–366
cardinal
hyphens in spelled-out, 358
spelled-out, 364
ordinal
hyphens in, 358
spelled-out, 364

Numerals, 364–366

Original expressions, quotation marks with, 349
Ought to of, 70
Outlines, 484–487
    capitalization of, 301
      Roman numerals in, 301
Overlook, oversee, 70

P

Paintings, italics for titles of, 351
Pair, pare, pear, 70
Paraphrasing, 481
Parentheses, **29**
    capitalizing first word of sentence in, 298
    with other marks of punctuation, 342–343
    to set off supplemental material, 341–342
Parenthetical documentation, 491–492
Parenthetical expressions, **29**
    brackets with, 343
    commas to set off, 331
Parks, capitalizing names of, 306–307
Participial phrases, **30,** 151
    combining sentences by inserting, 378
    commas to set off introductory, 333
    commas to set off nonessential, 329
    diagraming, 283
Participles, **30,** 150–151
    as adjectives, 112, 150
    commas to set off introductory, 333
    commas to set off nonessential, 329
    diagraming, 283

past, 185–186
    present, 185–186
Parts of speech. *See also* Adjectives; Adverbs; Conjunctions; Interjections; Nouns; Prepositions; Pronouns; Verbs
    in dictionaries, 557
Passed, past, 70
Passive voice, **30,** 206
Past, passed, 70
Past participles, 185–186, 187–190
    as adjectives, 112, 150
Past perfect tense, **30,** 199–200
Past tense, **30,** 196
Pause, paws, 71
Peace, piece, 71
Pear, pair, pare, 70
People, capitalizing names of, 303
Percentages, use of numerals to express amounts of, 365
Periodicals. *See also* Magazines; Newspapers
    in library, 533
    locating articles in, 547–549
Periods, **30–31**
    with abbreviations, 360
    as ellipsis points, 344
    parentheses with, 342
    quotation marks with, 347
    to end declarative sentence, 171, 319
    to end imperative sentence, 171, 319
Persecute, prosecute, 71
Personal, personnel, 71
Personal pronouns, **31,** 102–103, 234–240
    nominative case for, 234, 235, 236
    objective case for, 234, 235
    possessive case for, 234, 235–236
    after *than* and *as,* 239–240
Personal questions, 446

S

semicolons to separate items in, 325

Set, sit, 75–76

Sew, sow, 76

Shall, 196–197

She, it, they, he, 61

Shear, sheer, 76

Shined, shone, shown, 76–77

Ships
capitalizing names of, 307
italics for titles of, 351

Shone, shown, shined, 76–77

Short stories, quotation marks with titles of, 349

Shouldn't ought, had ought, hadn't ought, 60–61

Should of, would of, could of, might of, must of, 56

Shown, shined, shone, 76–77

Sight, site, cite, 53–54

Simple predicates, **38,** 132

Simple sentences, **39,** 172

Simple subjects, **39,** 132

Single quotation marks, 347

Singular noun, 97

Sit, set, 75–76

Site, cite, sight, 53–54

Slang, use of quotation marks to enclose, 349

Slow, slowly, 77

Solutions, proposing, 468–469

Some, somewhat, 77

Somewheres, anyways, anywheres, everywheres, nowheres, 48

Son, sun, 77

Songs, quotation marks with titles of, 349

Sort of, kind of, 63

Sort of a, type of a, kind of a, 63

Sources
citing, 491–497
primary, 480
reading critically, 483–484
secondary, 480

Sow, sew, 76

Spacecraft
capitalizing names of, 307
italics for names of, 351

Span, hyphenating two numerals to indicate, 359

Spatial organization, 458

Special events, capitalizing names of, 307–308

Special nouns and subject-verb agreement, 220–221

Spell checker, 400–401

Spelling
adding prefixes, 392
adding suffixes, 393–396
compound words, 396
difficult words, 401–405
ie and *ei,* 390–391
new words, 400
plurals, 397–399
regular verbs, when adding suffixes, 187
and spell checking on computer, 400–401
unstressed vowels, 391–392
words ending in *cede, ceed,* and *sede,* 391

Sr., capitalizing, 304

States
abbreviations for, 90–91
capitalizing names of, 306–307
use of comma to separate from city, 334, 335

Stationary, stationery, 77

Straight, strait, 77–78

Style guides, 563

Style handbook in dictionary, 561

Subject complements, **39,** 140
diagraming, 280–281

Subject directories, 567

Subjects, **39**
complete, **11,** 133–134
compound, **13,** 134–135, 172
and subject-verb agreement, 218–219
definition of, 131